The Rhetoric of Poetry in the
Renaissance and Seventeenth Century

The Rhetoric of Poetry in the Renaissance and Seventeenth Century

JOHN PORTER HOUSTON

Louisiana State University Press

Baton Rouge and London

Designer: Albert Crochet
Typeface: Linotron Palatino
Typesetter: G&S Typesetters, Inc.
Printer: Thomson-Shore, Inc.
Binder: John H. Dekker & Sons

LIBRARY OF CONGRESS CATALOGING IN PUBLICATION DATA

Houston, John Porter.
  The rhetoric of poetry in the Renaissance and seventeenth century.
  Includes index.
  I. European poetry—Renaissance, 1450–1600—History and criticism.   2. European poetry—17th century—History and criticism.   3. Poetics—History.   4. Rhetoric—1500–1800.   I. Title.
PN1181.H68   1983   808.1'09031   82-17227
ISBN 0-8071-1066-3

Contents

Introduction   1

Chapter 1   Petrarch   5

Chapter 2   Middle-Style Genres: The Evolution of
Sixteenth-Century Lyric   24

Chapter 3   Some Uses of Low Style   54

Chapter 4   Classicizing High Style: Ronsard, Tasso, and
Spenser   86

Chapter 5   Tragic Poetry   115

Chapter 6   Devotional Poetry: A Confluence of Styles   160

Chapter 7   From Baroque to Neoclassicism   202

Chapter 8   Racine and French Neoclassicism   246

Chapter 9   Milton and Epic Style   284

Conclusion   308

Glossary of Technical Terms   311

Index   315

The Rhetoric of Poetry in the
Renaissance and Seventeenth Century

Introduction

This work has grown out of several interests. One was tracing the development in European literature of an equivalent to ancient high style; another was seeing whether, through rhetorical description, one could arrive at a more accurate account of sixteenth- and seventeenth-century poetry than by the usual method of periodization: renaissance style, mannerism, baroque style, and neoclassicism. In regard to this second aim, I have made such abstractions as baroque culture secondary to rhetorical analysis and definition. To continue with the particular example of the baroque, in a work like Jean Rousset's thematically quite coherent *Anthologie de la poésie baroque française* (2 vols.; Paris, 1961) one notices a certain disparity of styles, even though the poems fit nicely into Rousset's conception of baroque subject matter; I have tried to approach the question differently in order to see if, aside from the undeniable existence of baroque culture, there are styles which constitute a more precisely baroque phase of style within the general thematic and cultural context of the baroque period and which coexist with other styles that should be described differently.

In the use of rhetorical concepts I have drawn widely on the ancient rhetoricians known in the renaissance, giving an important place to the ideas of Demetrius and Dionysius of Halicarnassus, for example, alongside the more familiar notions of Aristotle, Cicero, and Quintilian. Renaissance criticism, especially Italian, has provided theoretical contributions. My goal has been to avoid the compartmentalized picture of renaissance poetry one finds in the usual French studies, where only Du Bellay's and Ronsard's statements about poetry are assumed to be of value, or in Rosemond Tuve's *Elizabethan and Metaphysical Imagery* (Chicago, 1947), where excessive reliance on the peculiar strain of English rhetorical works gives a somewhat distorted picture of renaissance theory. The dissemination of rhetorical concepts in the renaissance has been studied in detail in such books as W. T. Baldwin's *William Shakspere's Small Latine and Lesse Greeke* (2 vols.; Urbana, Ill., 1944); I shall not go over again the facts of renaissance education but assume some broader familiarity on the poet's part with the body of rhetorical theory than a purely national approach seems to imply. Furthermore, it is as interesting when a poet recreates some concept of ancient rhetoric as when he learns it as part of his formal education.

I have followed Quintilian's suggestion that there is no virtue in idly multiplying minute distinctions between rhetorical figures and increasing unduly one's vocabulary of Greek terms for them. This is a book about styles, *genera dicendi*, rather than figures, and while I must often refer to the latter, especially the better known ones, I do not bother, for example, to use all the terms for what can generally be described as figures of repetition: adjunctio, anadiplosis, epanalepsis, diacope, epizeuxis, and so forth. I do use a variety of ancient terms for styles, however, but hope that through repetition and translation they will become familiar. An appendix provides a list of technical terms.

Comparative stylistics is one of the methods of this work: I have attempted to explore renaissance and seventeenth-century styles with respect to the structural possibilities of Italian, French, and English. The choice of literatures to study is a fairly obvious one: there is a historical movement of esthetic ideas and stylistic practice from Italy to France and then to England. I have treated Spanish poets only on two occasions, where, for a clearer picture of European literature, it seems absolutely necessary to include them. The development of German poetry does not fit into the major historical pattern so easily, and I have merely alluded to it.

The selectivity necessary in treating such an extensive area of literature has been determined in part by the importance of individual poets and, in part, by what can be learned about the historical development of styles from certain minor poets, whose exemplarity exceeds their strictly esthetic merit. Some omissions need perhaps to be commented upon. I make little reference to the medieval background, beyond brief mention of the troubadours, despite the recent attempts, notably by Peter Droncke (*Poetic Individuality in the Middle Ages, 1000–1150* [Oxford, 1970]), to change our perspective on the character of medieval Latin lyric. In the sixteenth century, Du Bellay is not discussed because Gilbert Gadoffre's book *Du Bellay et le sacré* (Paris, 1978) has convinced me that it is impossible to talk of *Les Antiquités de Rome* or *Les Regrets* without broad reference to the whole of the works, which would not have been convenient. A much greater omission is Shakespeare's *Sonnets*: after some investigation, I felt that the linguistic problems involved in discussing their style would necessitate a treatment out of proportion with the rest of the book, and this feeling has been confirmed by examining the notes to Stephen Bloom's new edition of the *Sonnets* (New Haven, 1977). The origins of genres have been lengthily examined in other books, and I therefore neglect such things as Alamanni's Pindaric odes or the first uses of blank verse in Italy, which have limited stylistic interest. The low-style genres are the least fully dicusssed: elegy is somewhat slighted, and formal satire is entirely omitted, as is verse comedy. Forms which are not significantly involved in the rhetorical tradition, like Elizabethan songs, are also ignored. In the way of general topics, prosody is treated only when it seems quite necessary, and Ramism is not touched on, for I see little in it that actually affects style in comparison with the older tradition of rhetoric..

I do not hold with the distinction, popular with New Criticism some decades ago, between decorative imagery or figures and functional ones. The original document of the antiornamental school of thought, Adolph Loos's *Ornament und Verbrechen* (1908), seems to me by its title, "Ornament and Crime," to indicate sufficiently the moralistic distortions of what one might call the Bauhaus school of poetics. I use the classical concept of *ornatus* quite neutrally and am more interested in the historical understanding of ornament than in pronouncing judgments on it. In any case, there has been a turnabout in recent esthetics, and ornament is no longer a transgression.

Three scholarly works in particular have greatly aided me. O. B. Hardison's *The Enduring Monument: A Study of the Idea of Praise in Renaissance Literary Theory and Practice* (Chapel Hill, 1962) and Bernard

Weinberg's *A History of Literary Criticism in the Italian Renaissance* (2 vols.; Chicago, 1961) help to separate the essentials from the verbiage of renaissance criticism and guide one to the more significant texts. I have avoided burdening my work with extensive quotations from renaissance and ancient rhetoricians because of their leisureliness and complexity of style or because of the capricious-seeming organization of their thought. In respect to the ancient rhetoricians, a word must be said about Heinrich Lausberg's *Handbuch der Literarischen Rhetorik* (2 vols.; Munich, 1960). This summa is in the form of a long outline in which each article contains abundant quotations in Greek or Latin (untranslated) about rhetorical concepts or illustrating their use. The second volume contains Latin, Greek, and French indexes to the whole subject. Some general familiarity with rhetoric is advisable before one attempts to use this *Handbuch*, but its value is inestimable, given how widely scattered all the relevant texts on a topic may be. Good editions of the better known rhetoricians usually contain outlines and word indexes, but with Lausberg's help one may easily compare difference of opinion. For those whose needs are more basic, Richard A. Lanham's *A Handlist of Rhetorical Terms* (Berkeley, 1968) is very usable and goes beyond being simply an alphabetical list of figures. Charles Sears Baldwin's *Ancient Rhetoric and Poetic* (New York, 1924) remains an interesting short introduction to the place of rhetoric in Greek and Roman life and education. References to works on the rhetoric of specific poets will be found in my notes.

The following chapters are organized by types of style but observe, insofar as it is possible, a historical progression. The inclusion of Petrarch is essential for any discussion of later lyric; the chapter on tragic style attempts to treat aspects of Shakespeare's style with as little reference as possible to characterization, which forms the usual way of approaching Shakespeare's diction; and neoclassicism, for reasons which I think will become evident, has been largely confined to the study of three major works. I have tried as much as possible to prevent the history of poetry from appearing to be merely the history of lyric poetry, since such a bias, however common today, would shatter the whole edifice of rhetorical theory.

CHAPTER 1

Petrarch

I

Rhetorical notions are not, in origin or in the better rhetoricians, a matter of pure theory; they are empirical, growing
out of the practice of major writers. Thus it is not surprising that the
same concept should occur in bodies of rhetorical theory between
which it would be difficult to find any direct connection. Such is the
case of the notion of smooth and harsh or austere styles among the
troubadours and in antiquity. Demetrius (first century A.D.) and Dionysius of Halicarnassus (active as a teacher at Rome, 30–8 B.C.),
whose fame was to be great in the renaissance, had formulated the
ideas of smooth and austere, or harsh, diction to account for ancient
traditions of literature, and the troubadours reinvented the same
ideas in the twelfth century.[1] The distinction is a fairly important one
for the earlier centuries of European poetry and is worth exemplify-
ing in its beginnings. The smooth style (γλαφυρός in Greek or *trobar
leu* in Provençal) is perhaps most famously represented in Provençal
by Bertrand de Ventadour:

> Can vei la lauzeta mover
> De joi sas alas contra.l rai,
> Que s'oblid'e.s laissa chazer
> Per la doussor c'al cor li vai,
> Ai, tan grans enveya m'en ve
> De cui qu'eu veya jauzïon,
> Meravilhas ai car desse
> Lo cor de dezirer no.m fon.

1. See Linda M. Paterson, *Troubadours and Eloquence* (Oxford, 1975); W. Rhys Roberts, *Demetrius on Style: The Greek Text of Demetrius' "De Elocutione"* (London, 1902),
181–207; Dionysius of Halicarnassus, *On Literary Composition*, ed. W. Rhys Roberts
(London, 1910), 211–33.

> Ai las, tan cuidava saber
> D'amor, e tan petit en sai!
> Car eu d'amar no.m posc tener
> Celeis don ja pro non aurai.[2]

When I see the lark beating with joy its wings against the ray of the sun until, oblivious, it swoons and drops for the sweetness which enters its heart, ah, such great envy takes me of whatever I see rejoicing, I marvel that on the instant my heart melts not with desire. Alas, I thought to know so much of love, and I know of it so little! For I cannot help loving her from whom good will never come to me.

The smoothness lies in the lyric élan of the opening clause, the soft blend of delight in nature and amorous melancholy, and the linear progression of the thought and syntax. It was what much later would be called simple style, although the rhetorical tradition generally had the wisdom to avoid calling any art simple.

The dark, violent, or rough style (*trobar braus, trobar clus,* or the αὐστηρός, δεινός manner) is to be found broadly in the work of Marcabru, but an especially interesting case is offered by a sestina of Arnaut Daniel's, the troubadour Dante most admired. The sestina, which Daniel invented, takes a series of words and uses them in place of rime in varying codified orders from stanza to stanza. There is a certain humor involved as the poet attempts to make some plausible connected sense out of lines using obligatory and miscellaneous words:

> Pois floris la seca vergua,
> Ni d'En Adam foron nebot ni oncle,
> Tan fin'amors com cela qu'el cor m'intra
> Non cuig qu'anc fos en cors, ni eis en arma;
> On qu'ill estei, fors en plan or dinz cambra,
> Mos cors de lieis no.s part, tan com ten l'ongla.
> ("Lo ferm voler qu'el cor m'intra")

Since there burst into flower the withered rod and from Sir Adam there came nephew and uncle, such pure love as that which in my heart enters I think there never was in body, nor yet in soul. Wherever she be, out in the open or within a bedroom, my heart quits her not by so much as the width of a fingernail.

The problem of making *rod, nail,* and *uncle* fit into a love song produces some cleverly strained sequences of thought. The harshness

---

2. All texts and translations of troubadour poetry are from Alan R. Press (ed. and tr.), *An Anthology of Troubadour Lyric Poetry* (Austin, 1971), 76–77, 190–91.

lies less in sound than in the forced attempt to put miscellaneous things together, and one of the possible aspects of this style is a certain initial crypticness, which goes along with self-consciousness over words and their strange virtualities. Although this kind of art begins in an arbitrary self-imposition of a difficult problem in style, the working out of a sestina, the interest in difficult or contorted diction will become an autonomous motive in composition, and the tone and moods produced will be quite varied.

The ideas of smoothness and harshness recur in the theory and practice of duecento Italian poetry, which was influenced by the troubadour tradition. The most famous lyric poets are those of the *dolce stil novo* group, whose name indicates that its members were committed to the elaboration of smooth effects, the term *dolce* being a new one, in the series beginning with the Greek, γλαφυρός, to describe an effect of pleasantness and continuity. Dante, a *stilnovista* in the *Vita nuova*, theorized about harsh and smooth words in *De vulgari eloquentia*, and the *Commedia* contains abundant examples of both kinds of style. The most interesting document, however, in Dante's elaboration of these ideas is the four late "stony songs," *rime petrose*, in which he addresses a cold, unfeeling woman:

> Così nel mio parlar voglio esser aspro
> com'è ne li atti questa bella petra,
> la quale ognora impetra
> maggior durezza e più natura cruda.[3]

So in my speech I would be harsh as in her acts this beautiful stone is, who more and more achieves greater hardness and crueler nature.

The stony heart is perhaps biblical in origin, but the effects of harsh rime or consonant clusters in treating such a subject completely transforms the not uncommon image into a very strange poem, even by the standards of Dante's other lyrics. One of the most striking images in these songs is the allegory of winter which does not alter the poet's green hope:

> Al poco giorno e al gran cerchio d'ombra
> son giunto, lasso, ed al bianchir de' colli,
> quando si perde lo color ne l'erba:

3. All texts and translations of Dante and Petrarch are from Robert M. Durling (ed. and tr.), *Petrarch's Lyric Poems* (Cambridge, Mass., 1976), 624–25, 616–17. Hereinafter, Petrarch is cited in the text by poem number only.

> e'l mio disio però non cangia il verde,
> sì è barbato ne la dura petra
> che parla e sente come fosse donna.

To the shortened day and to the great circle of shade I have come, alas! and to the whitening of the hills, when the color is lost from the grass: and my desire still does not change its green, it is so rooted in the hard stone that speaks and has sensation as if it were a lady.

This diction with its consonant clusters and the homely image of the beardlike roots antedates the unified, polished, universal poetic diction of Italian, which was later to take shape and spread wide its influence. Generally, the rhetorical tradition does not associate *asprezza* with short lyrics or love poems, and we find that Petrarch, with the exception of a few harsh poems, devoted himself primarily to exploring new ways of creating smooth style, becoming thereby the first great European exponent of this archetypical conception of lyric qualities.

II

One of the most important of Petrarch's innovations was his use of imagery in a structural fashion. At times, the poem is built so that all the conceptual material is translated into images:

> L'oro et le perle e i fior vermigli e i bianchi
> che'l verno devria far languidi et secchi
> son per me acerbi e velenosi stecchi
> ch'io provo per lo petto et per li fianchi.
>
> Però i dì miei fien lagrimosi et manchi,
> chè gran duol rade volte aven che'nvecchi;
> ma più ne colpo i micidiali specchi
> che'n vagheggiar voi stessa avete stanchi.
>
> Questi poser silenzio al signor mio
> che per me vi pregava, ond'ei si tacque
> veggendo in voi finir vostro desio;
>
> questi fuor fabbricati sopra l'acque
> d'abisso et tinti ne l'eterno oblio
> onde'l principio de mia morte nacque.   (46)

The gold and the pearls, and the red and white flowers that the winter should have made languid and dry, are for me sharp and poisonous thorns that I feel along my breast and my sides. Therefore my days will be tearful and cut short, for it is rare that a great sorrow grow old, but most I blame those murderous mirrors which you have tired out with your love of yourself. These imposed silence on my lord, Amor, who was praying to you for me; and he became still, seeing your desire ended in yourself. These mirrors were made beside the waters of hell and tempered in the eternal forgetfulness whence the beginning of my death was born.

We see here some of the famous Petrarchan imagery, the metonymies of gold, pearls, and flowers to describe a woman's head, but used in an unusual fashion, as they metamorphose into a winter landscape. However, the landscape is symbolic—and not of old age but of harshness. With the unexpected introduction of the mirror image, the idea of the lady's face is picked up again: asperity of style is expressed not only by the rimes of the quatrains but also by the abrupt shifts of image. It is characteristic of Petrarch, however, that this bitter theme yields to a tone of quiet desperation and melancholy in the tercets, in which the quality of the sound patterns also changes, as a little study will show. The death he refers to is, as is common in Petrarch, real death and not the daily "deaths" of the subsequent Petrarchist tradition, which made death one of the commonest of figurative words.

More coherently allegorical poems are, if not frequent, an important part of the *Canzoniere*, and the following one shows aspects of Petrarch's imagery which his imitators neglected:

> Almo sol, quella fronde ch'io sola amo
> tu prima amasti, or sola al bel soggiorno
> verdeggia et senza par poi che l'adorno
> suo male et nostro vide in prima Adamo.
>
> Stiamo a mirarla, i' ti pur prego et chiamo,
> o sole; et tu pur fuggi et fai dintorno
> ombrare i poggi et te ne porti il giorno,
> et fuggendo mi tòi quel ch'i' più bramo.
>
> L'ombra che cade da quell'umil colle
> ove favilla il mio soave foco,
> ove'l gran lauro fu picciola verga,
>
> crescendo mentr'io parlo, agli occhi tolle
> la dolce vista del beato loco
> ove'l mio cor con la sua donna alberga.   (188)

Life-giving sun, you first loved that branch which is all I love; now, unique in her sweet dwelling, she flourishes, without an equal since Adam first saw his and our lovely bane. Let us stay to gaze at her, I beg and call on you, O sun, and you still run away and shadow the hillsides all around and carry off the day, and fleeing you take from me what I most desire. The shadow that falls from that low hill where my gentle fire is sparkling, where the great laurel was a little sapling, growing as I speak, takes from my eyes the sweet sight of the blessed place where my heart dwells with his lady.

Hills are always associated with Laura, as is the laurel tree, by one of those word plays, or paronomasias, Petrarch favored in small number and only when they are particularly effective (*Laura, l'aura, lauro, l'oro*). The poet's heart is a flame beside the tree in an interesting variation on Petrarch's more banal imagery of fire, and the setting sun represents death, real death. The sweet melancholy, by contrast with the quatrains of the sonnet quoted previously, brings us closer to the traditional idea of Petrarch's poetry, with its sense of aging and its pleasure in hopelessness.

Even in what is usually thought of as the typical kind of Petrarchan poem, with its prisons, bonds, and alternations of heat and cold, the function of the imagery is to enhance the poem structurally, whether by use of a striking opening or closing image or by sustained imagery. It is important to see this in contrast with the tendencies of previous lyric poetry, where the positioning of imagery is often much more casual. When the troubadours use imagery of any vividness, they are likely to isolate it in one stanza at the beginning of the poem, with a distinct change in tone in the more abstract, often somewhat banal stanzas that follow, or else, as in one of William of Aquitaine's poems ("Ab la dolchor del temps novel"), a striking simile is placed in the midst of a poem where its heightening effect is out of place by the standards of smooth development. Likewise, the poets of the *dolce stil novo* use or do not use imagery according to criteria which have little to do with purely esthetic questions. Guido Guinizelli's "Al cor gentil" uses comparisons as pseudoscientific analogies, while other famous stilnovistic poems, like Guido Cavalcanti's "Perch'io non spero di tornar giammai," scarcely use any imagery at all. Petrarch seems to have been the first European lyric poet with a theoretical, systematic approach to the question of how imagery is to be integrated into the poem.

It is interesting in this respect to see what Petrarch does with Arnaut Daniel's sestina. Whereas Daniel devised the form obviously to create a struggle between continuous sense and the obligatory word repetitions, there is nothing crabbed or odd in Petrarch's sestinas, in which he chooses harmonious terms for the repeated line endings. One of them builds this up to the following voluptuous thought, so different from Daniel's oddly phrased line about his heart not leaving his lady, whether she is in a bedroom or outside walking around:

> Deh, or foss'io col vago de la luna
> adormentato in qua' che verdi boschi,
> et questa ch'anzi vespro a me fa sera
> con essa et con Amor in quella piaggia
> sola venisse a starsi ivi una notte,
> e'l dì si stesse e'l sol sempre ne l'onde!   (237)

Ah, would that with the lover of the moon I had fallen asleep in some green wood, and that she who before vespers gives me evening with the moon and with Amor to that shore might come alone, to stay there one night, and that the day might tarry and the sun, forever under the waves!

This romantic imagery of Endymion and the night is quite unexpected by the usual conceptions of previous Italian poetry, and it makes us think far ahead, beyond the first wave of sixteenth-century Petrarchism, to the more erotic and languorous poetry of the time of Marino. It is easy to see how Petrarch nourished so many kinds of Italian poetry for so long. Comparable sumptuousness occurs in indications of weather or time; the classical chronographia, or imagery of temporal setting, had always tended to be a rather high-flown figure:

> Non vidi mai dopo notturna pioggia
> gir per l'aere sereno stelle erranti
> et fiammeggiar fra la rugiada e'l gielo,
> ch'i' non avesse i begli occhi davanti
> ove la stanca mia vita s'appoggia,
> quali io gli vidi a l'ombra d'un bel velo.   (127)

I never saw after nocturnal rain the wandering stars going through the clear air and flaming between the dew and the frost, that I did not have before me her lovely eyes where leans my weary life, such as I saw them in the shadow of a lovely veil.

The complex of emotion and fairly detailed natural imagery goes well beyond what we find in all but a few Latin lyrics, and its tonal value, its integration into the poem as a whole surpasses the effect of similar imagery in the troubadours. Such passages as this, however, are not the most easily imitated of Petrarch's finer moments, and we must look to certain less magnificently ornamented pieces to find the Petrarch of Petrarchism, the selective and somewhat distorted conception of his poetry that was to have such broad influence on the lyric.

Even in the more frequently imitated poems of Petrarch, we can find a note that is proper to him and separates him from the dominant Petrarchist tradition. His much copied antitheses can be illustrated by lines from the famous sonnet 134, which is constructed entirely of verses embodying contrasts:

> Pace non trovo et non ò da far guerra,
> o temo e spero, et ardo et son un ghiaccio,
> et volo sopra'l cielo et giaccio in terra,
> et nulla stringo et tutto'l mondo abbraccio.
> . . . .
> Veggio senza occhi, et non ò lingua et grido,
> et bramo di perir et cheggio aita,
> et ò in odio me stesso et amo altrui.
>
> Pascomi di dolor, piangendo rido,
> egualmente mi spiace morte et vita.
> In questo stato son, Donna, per vui.

Peace I do not find, and I have no wish to make war; and I fear and hope, and burn and am of ice; and I fly above the heavens and lie on the ground; and I grasp nothing and embrace all the world. I see without eyes, and I have no tongue and yet cry out; and I wish to perish and I ask for help; and I hate myself and love another. I feed on pain, weeping I laugh; equally displeasing to me are death and life. In this state am I, Lady, on account of you.

The question of tone here is all important for the distinction between Petrarch and Petrarchism. Instead of figures of conceit and brilliance, these are pathetic antitheses, and rather than building toward a showy climax, as later poets of the antithesis will do, Petrarch permits a decline of rhetorical intensity with the simple last line. The pervasive melancholy of the *Canzoniere* influences our reading of individual pieces, and the mood here is unquestionably that of lassitude and suffering, with no attempt to make the rhetorical repetitions really ostentatious.

In regard to conceit, the personification is worth looking at. Personified abstractions in Petrarch almost always have the solemnity common to this figure in medieval lyric literature. Although they may seem peculiarly handled, in contrast to the concrete imagery of other poems, I do not think we can think of them in terms of conceit and catachresis, or willfully odd imagery:

> Amor, che nel penser mio vive et regna
> e'l suo seggio maggior nel mio cor tene,
> talor armato ne la fronte vene;
> ivi si loca et ivi pon sua insegna.
>
> Quella ch'amare et sofferir ne'nsegna
> e vol che'l gran desio, l'accesa spene
> ragion, vergogna, et reverenza affrene
> di nostro ardir fra se stessa si sdegna.
>
> Onde Amor paventoso fugge al core,
> lasciando ogni sua impresa, et piange et trema;
> ivi s'asconde et non appar più fore.
>
> Che poss'io far, temendo il mio signore,
> se non star seco infin a l'ora estrema?
> ché bel fin fa chi ben amando more.   (140)

Amor, who lives and reigns in my thought and keeps his principal seat in my heart, sometimes comes forth all in armor upon my brow, stations himself there, and sets up his banner. She who teaches us to love and suffer, and wishes that my great desire, my kindled hope be contained by reason, shame, and reverence, grows angry within herself at our boldness. Whereupon Amor flees in terror to my heart, abandoning his every enterprise, and weeps and trembles. There he hides and shows himself no more. What can *I* do when my lord is afraid, except stay with him till the last hour? For he who dies loving well makes a good end.

This is a rather characteristic medieval personification in that we perceive it as a trifle detailed and mannered, while in the esthetic thinking of the later middle ages, which had no conception of classical sublimity, such a figure seemed quite elevated. The lack of conceit is evident here: a shift in tone occurs at the end, with the prosy, low-style, proverbial-sounding last line. Petrarch dedramatizes his personification of Amor and his flight.

One of the most influential and characteristic devices in Petrarch is the juxtaposition of the concrete not with the abstract as above, but with the figurative. In sonnet 46 we saw a metaphorical landscape yield to the image of real mirrors, for example. This stylistic procedure was to become a great source of conceit in later poets, but it need not have a strained or startling effect:

L'aura serena che fra verdi fronde
mormorando a ferir nel volto viemme
fammi risovenir quand'Amor diemme
le prime piaghe sì dolci profonde,

e'l bel viso veder ch'altri m'asconde,
che sdegno o gelosia celato tiemme,
et le chiome, or avolte in perle e'n gemme,
allora sciolte et sovra or terso bionde,

le quali ella spargea sì dolcemente
et raccogliea con sì leggiadri modi
che ripensando ancor trema la mente.

Torsele il tempo poi in più saldi nodi
et strinse'l cor d'un laccio sì possente
che Morte sola fia ch'indi lo snodi.   (196)

The calm breeze that comes murmuring through the green leaves to strike my brow makes me remember when Love gave me the first deep sweet wounds, and makes me see the lovely face that she hides from me, which jealousy or anger keep hidden from me; and her golden locks now twisted with pearls and gems, then loosened and more blond than polished gold, which she let loose so sweetly and gathered again with such a charming manner that as I think back on it, my mind still trembles. Time wound them afterward into tighter knots and bound my heart with so strong a cord that only Death will be able to untie it.

With marvelous skill Petrarch metamorphoses Laura's hair into bonds. This is precisely the kind of thing the Petrarchists cultivated, but in Petrarch the change from concrete to figurative is not startling; it contributes to the gentle pathos of the poem which characteristically concludes with a reference to real death, rather than to those thousands of deaths which are the typical hyperbolic figure of conceited Petrarchist verse in the sixteenth century.[4]

The antithesis between and the juxtaposition of the concrete and the figurative, or abstract, often do have a hyperbolic character if we take hyperbole in its most strict and logical sense, and pervasive use of this trope marks the *Canzoniere*. But Petrarch's hyperbole is usually of a lyrical rather than ostentatious sort, so that the figure does not have the rhetorical overstatement it was to acquire in certain later poets. It is, in fact, one of Petrarch's great achievements that the tone of his poetry is such as to admit hyperbole as a serious, intense

4. There is one sonnet of Petrarch's (185) that has a truly conceited style: it contrasts noticeably with the other poems.

figure. It is also important to note that the effect of surprise, so essential to the conceit, is generally absent from Petrarch's verse. The *meraviglia* prized in later centuries is limited to a few mythological poems and counters the general tendency to the smoothly pleasing γλαφυρός style.

III

The care for smoothness of structure that we see in Petrarch's handling of imagery is also evident in the logical or thematic elaboration of his poems. The Provençal canso, or major lyric, had generally been very loose in sequence of ideas, owing perhaps to musical considerations. Petrarch's canzoni are somewhat more coherent on the whole, being conceived of in purely verbal terms without any accompaniment.[5] In the case of the sonnet, however, the form seems, from its beginnings in the Sicilian court poetry of the early duecento and by its nature, to encourage quite clear articulation. Furthermore, there was a new need felt for clarity of structure. In the *Vita nuova*, Dante will quote a sonnet and say, "This sonnet is divided into three parts. In the first . . ." This concern for explicit structure was uncommon in Roman literature, where genres like the elegy, epistle, and satire are often quite casually put together: the sense of dispositio (composition) the Romans prized in orations is lacking in their characteristic poetic genres.[6] The sonnet is a perfect expression of the new European regard for design in poetry.

Petrarch takes advantage of the fourfold division of the sonnet to explore all the various elements of parallelism and contrast among its parts. The first quatrain may be parallel with the first tercet; the quatrains and first tercet together (forming perhaps a single sentence, as in 196 quoted earlier) may contrast with the second tercet, and so forth. The combinations are many. Greater or lesser breaks of sense or syntax between lines, as well as a fine sense of liaison and enjambment, contribute to the architecture of the sonnet. Rhetorical figures, most obviously anaphoras, are important tools by which Pe-

5. See Hugo Friedrich, *Epoche della lirica italiana*, tr. Luigi Banfi and Gabriella Bruscaglioni (2 vols.; Milan, 1974), I, 147.
6. See Jean-Paul Boucher, *Études sur Properce* (Paris, 1965), 379, 393, 395, 408.

trarch structures the poem. There is a relatively small number of sonnets in which certain devices pattern the whole piece: we have seen that 134 ("Pace non trovo") consists of antitheses; 160 and 161 are made up of an enumeration of vocatives; 195 is built solely of adynata, or comparisons with the impossible; *if* clauses structure 224; each of the four sections of 299 begins with *Ov'è*, each of the four sections of 300 with *Quanta*. These not very numerous sonnets were to have enormous influence on poets whose taste was for highly stressed articulations in the poem and overtness of rhetorical figures. One interesting device, interesting because of its frequency, is polysyndeton: a series of *and*s may join nouns or sentences. The prototype is "Benedetto sia":

> Benedetto sia'l giorno e'l mese et l'anno
> e la stagione e'l tempo et l'ora e'l punto
> e'l bel paese e'l loco ov'io fui giunto
> da' duo begli occhi che legato m'ànno;
>
> e benedetto il primo dolce affanno.   (61)

Blessed be the day and the month and the year and the season and the time and the hour and the instant and the beautiful countryside and the place where I was struck by the two lovely eyes that have bound me; and blessed be the first sweet trouble.

It is worth noting that such polysyndeton is not borrowed from high classical Latin, but from obscurer sources of perhaps little literary value. In Augustan Latin, polysyndeton, especially involving more than three elements, tends to be somewhat concealed:

> Laudabunt alii claram Rhodon aut Mytilenen
>   aut Ephesum bimarisve Corinthi
> moenia vel Bacco Thebas vel Apolline Delphos
>   insignis aut Thessala Tempe.[7]

Others will praise luminous Rhodes or Mytilene or Ephesus, or the walls of Corinth on the two seas, or Thebes or Delphi that Bacchus and Apollo made famous, or Thessalian Tempe.

Horace's epithets, change of conjunction, and asymmetrical arrangement of words diminish the continuity of the polysyndeton; in contrast, Petrarch uses the figure in a more overt, less varied manner (*cf.* also 134, 118, 292, 100, 12).

7. Horace, *Odes et épodes*, ed. F. Villeneuve (Paris, 1954), 15, my translation.

In Petrarch's work, polysyndeton is a major device in building up elaborate structures, the use of subordinate modifying clauses being comparatively restricted.[8] His tendency toward development appears clearly if we contrast Petrarch's sentence movement with that of the Roman love elegy, the kind of classical verse in which amorous laments are most likely to be found:

> Haec certe deserta loca et taciturna querenti
> et vacuum Zephyri possidet aura nemus.
> Hic licet occultos proferre impune dolores,
> si modo sola queant saxa tenere fidem.
> Unde tuos primum repetam, mea Cynthia, fastus?
> quod mihi das flendi, Cynthia, principium?[9]
> (Propertius, *Elegies*, I, 18)

This is certainly a silent, deserted place suitable for a lamenting poet, and the breath of Zephyr reigns in the empty grove. Here I can safely set forth my sorrow, if indeed rocks do not betray secrets. Where shall I find the first cause of your disdain for me, Cynthia? What is the reason for the tears you make me shed?

In Latin the syntax is highly centripetal; all the words point directly to the verbal complex, without which, because of the flections, they can have no coherent sense. Petrarch's Italian permits a looser accumulation of words, independent in form and value, and his verse form encourages the flowing phrase, whereas the tight syntax of the Latin closed couplet makes elaboration difficult. There is a distinctly discontinuous quality in the Roman elegy, as in the abrupt juxtaposition of the second and third couplets above. The long, sighing sentence is much more felicitously achieved in Petrarch's sonnet style. At the same time, Petrarch's sentence structure is classical in its balance of verbs and adjectives.[10] In word order, he permits himself the usual variations of Italian, as well as the placing of the verb after its object, which is probably a purely literary device, despite the freer word order of older Italian.[11] Some radical displacement of

---

8. See Giulio Herczeg, "La Struttura della frasi nei versi del Petrarca," in *Studi petrarcheschi VII* (Milan, 1961), 73–120.

9. Propertius, *Élégies*, ed. D. Paganelli (Paris, 1947), 27, my translation.

10. For the theory of such a balance, see Josephine Miles, *Eras and Modes in English Poetry* (Berkeley, 1957), 1–19.

11. For the range of word order in earlier Italian, see Gerhard Rohlfs, *Historische Grammatik der Italienischen Sprache* (3 vols.; Bern, 1954), III, 208–23.

words is occasionally found: "questa aspettata al regno delli dei / cosa bella mortal" (248); "quel ch'oggi il Cielo onora / soave sguardo" (343); and there are other examples in 191, 192, and 210. For Petrarch, hyperbaton of an elaborate sort had not yet become the mark of Italian poetic diction it was to be in the sixteenth century. The syntax of the subordinate clause is stylized by the frequent use of *cui* as a dative or *onde* in the sense of "with which," "by which," or other prepositions with a relative pronoun, thus avoiding the less fluid normal romance constructions. In keeping with this, Petrarch tends to choose constructions with only the simplest prepositional complements. Tool words are not prominent.

The general relation of Petrarch's Italian to Latin is of the greatest interest because, as has been observed, Latin was his normal written language, even for notes to himself. Furthermore, Petrarch was rarely in Tuscan-speaking areas, so that his ordinary spoken tongue was apparently, when not Latin, Provençal and northern Italian dialect. As a result, the Tuscan Italian which was his childhood language, before his family removed to Avignon, fulfilled the rôle for him that Latin did so often for others: it was more an esthetic idiom than a practical one.

The relative positions of Italian and Latin, then, were unusual in Petrarch's case, almost the opposite of what they would be for the humanists who chose Latin as their principal language for verse composition, relegating Italian to a lower place. Petrarch was at once concerned with the purity of his Italian (it is less Latinate, in some ways, than Leopardi's or Carducci's), and yet his Italian owes its distinction to Latin, for the superiority of Tuscan over the other dialects lies in its preserving more of Latin phonological structures. Latin is also a guarantee of the semantic authenticity of Italian words: they are rooted in it, resemble it, and sometimes take on the color of Roman literary idiom, as in Petrarch's use of words like *avaro, lento, lieto, cura, securo, acerbo,* and *crudo.* Petrarch often chooses forms as well which are phonetically closer to Latin than the ordinary diphthongized Tuscan forms: *po* for *può, moro* for *muoro,* voto for *vuoto, core* for *cuore.* A few more pronounced Latinisms occur, especially in rime: *eccelso, imago, refulse, folce (fulcit).* Generally we notice in reading Petrarch that he chooses words whose Latin etyma are perfectly clear; only rarely do we encounter such characteristically Italian sounding terms as *ciance, impaccio, intoppo, losco, pispiglio,* or others, which bring no Latin word to mind, whereas in Dante such terms are very numerous. This is again a question of authenticating Italian through the authority of Latin. Occasionally Petrarch will even come closer to Latin for solemnity: "et tutto quel ch'una ruina involve / per te spera saldar ogni suo vizio" ("and all those that this one collapse brings down hope through you to repair their every flaw") (53). This is the kind of diction we find later in Tasso's epic high style.

The general picture of Petrarch's vocabulary is that of a very deftly artificial idiom. He likes building on ordinary roots with prefixes (*s'infingere, impromessa, imperlare, disacerbare*) rather than introducing altogether unfamiliar lexical material, and there is great subtlety in his alternation between parallel forms (*sgombrare, disgombrare; frale, fraile, fragile*). Rare rime is exceptional but does occur: *cibo, bibo, describo, delibo* (193). All of this, of course, is not new with Petrarch, who drew on the language of Dante and the duecento poets, but for subsequent Italian poets, Petrarch's sense of vocabulary, rather than that of his predecessors, was to prove exemplary. Because Petrarch rarely clusters his more unusual words, they gently color his style rather than making it ostentatious or astonishing. The total effect is of a consistent, mild linguistic unfamiliarity, the rising into a superior order of language, which seems not arbitrary but meticulously worked out. Smoothness again dominates, as in the imagistic and logical structure of the poems.

IV

Petrarch's references to his own style seem to suggest that his thinking on it derived from the Roman poets. Following Callimachus, who wrote before the theory of the three styles was fully developed, Virgil (in the *Eclogues*), Horace (in the *Odes*), and Propertius refer to their styles as *deductum carmen* ("thin song") or *parvus* and *mollis* ("small" and "soft") or *tenuis* ("slim") as opposed to *grandis* ("big").[12] They were writing in what were felt to be quite different genres, but the great distinction, which they took from Callimachus, was between the grand traditional epic with its freedom from particular

12. See John Van Sickle, *The Design of Virgil's Bucolics* (Rome, 1978), 103–105.

stylistic doctrines and the shorter, infinitely polished piece of verse. Often this distinction takes the form of contrasting the high theme and style of war with the lower one of love. Petrarch, having written a Latin epic on war, the *Africa*, could hardly be insensitive to such discriminations. In the *Canzoniere*, he refers to the fact that his style is not truly high (314, 309), regrets that his idiom is not rarer (293), and generally terms his style *frale* (187), which is suggestive of Horace's *tenuis*. Of course, rhetorical notions are very flexible, and within the lower domain of lyric poetry, there are distinctions to be observed. In a group of three canzoni (Petrarch often makes significant groupings among his poems), he shows how he conceives of the variations in his own lyrics, the *vario stile* he refers to at the beginning of the *Canzoniere*.

In the first of these canzoni (125), the poet registers discouragement:

> Però ch'Amor mi sforza
> et di saver mi spoglia,
> parlo in rime aspre et di dolcezza ignude;

Since Love forces me and strips me of all skill, I speak in harsh rimes naked of sweetness.

He has sunk into the harsh style after his earlier *dolci rime leggiadre* and wanders disconsolately in the woods. The style is relatively unembellished, and where a simile occurs, it belongs to the humble domain:

> Come fanciul ch'a pena
> volge la lingua et snoda,
> che dir non sa ma'l più tacer gli è noia.

Like a child who can hardly move and untangle his tongue, who is not able to speak but hates to be silent any longer.

The poet concludes with the address to his song:

> O poverella mia, come se' rozza!
> credo che tel conoschi:
> rimanti in questi boschi.

O poor little song, how inelegant you are! I think you know it: stay here in these woods.

Rusticity is traditionally associated with the low style, and Petrarch, with the typical European association of styles and social classes, has made a song not fit for a lady's or society's ears; this is, of course, somewhat figurative, in that the grammar and prosody conform to Petrarch's normal usage. In the next poem, the famous "Chiare fresche et dolci acque," the style is not yet really up to high embellishment, but it is more pastoral than rustic:

> Chiare fresche et dolci acque
> ove le belle membra
> pose colei che sola a me par donna,
>   gentil ramo ove piacque
> (con sospir mi rimembra)
> a lei di fare al bel fianco colonna,
>   erba et fior che la gonna
> leggiadra ricoverse
> co l'angelico seno,
> aere sacro sereno
> ove Amor co' begli occhi il cor m'aperse:
> date udienzia insieme
> a le dolenti mie parole estreme.   (126)

Clear, fresh, sweet waters, where she who alone seems lady to me rested her lovely body, gentle branch where it pleased her (with sighing I remember) to make a column for her lovely side, grass and flowers that her rich garment covered along with her angelic breast, sacred bright air where Love opened my heart with her lovely eyes: listen all together to my sorrowful dying words.

The address to nature is an appropriate figure for simple elegy, and we may perceive it in echoes perhaps of Propertius (I, 18, quoted above), Ovid (*Amores*, II, 16), and perhaps even Tibullus (IV, 13), those few Roman elegies where nature plays a role.[13] The memory of Laura which forms the high point of the poem is just slightly embellished with two of the customary Petrarchan metaphors for describing a lady:

> Da' be' rami scendea
> (dolce ne la memoria)
> una pioggia di fior sovra'l suo grembo,
>   et ella si sedea
> umile in tanta gloria,
> coverta già de l'amoroso nembo;
>   qual fior cadea sul lembo,
> qual su le treccie bionde
> ch'oro forbito et perle
> eran quel dì a vederle,

---

13. See Friedrich, *Epoche della lirica italiana*, I, 50.

> qual si posava in terra et qual su l'onde,
> qual con un vago errore
> girando parea dir: "Qui regna Amore."

From the lovely branches was descending (sweet in memory) a rain of flowers over her bosom and she was sitting humble in such a glory, already covered with the loving cloud; this flower was falling on her skirt, this one on her blond braids, which were burnished gold and pearls to see that day; this one was coming to rest on the ground, this one on the water, this one, with a lovely wandering, turning about seemed to say: "Here reigns Love."

The passage is a very delicate tissue of images bearing different connotations but forming a successful, if vaguely ambiguous complex. There is the obvious echo of Beatrice's descent in a rain of flowers in the *Purgatorio*; *nembo* is another form of *nimbo* "halo," and *gloria* could be either the flowers or heavenly light. But Laura is *umile*, and all the details about the flowers wafting belong to the modest realism of pastoral poetry. The words with high religious associations can be seen conversely as constituting a simple form of nature poetry. The gold and the pearls are somewhat schematic indications, and in the context of Petrarch's poetry, they are not developed enough to have any great heightening value. So we should not be surprised at the poet's concluding address to his song, which he seems to consider as belonging to the slim, *tenue, deductum* genre:

> Se tu avessi ornamenti quant'ài voglia,
> poresti arditamente
> uscir del bosco et gir infra la gente.

If you, song, had as many beauties as you have desire, you could boldly leave the wood and go among people.

This is a step up from the preceding *rozza*, "rough song," which should hide in the woods; Petrarch implies that this canzone has some beginnings of beauty at least, even if it is not elaborately figured. The modern reader may, of course, far prefer this somewhat modest song to a more embellished one: each style is excellent in its own genre, and the idea of a hierarchy of styles should not make us lose sight of the fact that if the proper decorum is fulfilled, a poem cannot be bettered, even though the style is not high.

The third canzone is distinctly ornamented and includes a passage I have quoted earlier ("Non vidi mai dopo notturna pioggia"), but Petrarch rises to an even more elaborate figuration:

Se mai candide rose con vermiglie
in vasel d'oro vider gli occhi miei
allor allor da vergine man colte,
veder pensaro il viso di colei
ch'avanza tutte l'altre meraviglie
con tre belle eccellenzie in lui raccolte:
 le bionde treccie sopra'l collo sciolte
ov'ogni latte perderia sua prova,
e le guancie ch'adorna un dolce foco,
Ma pur che l'ora un poco
fior bianchi et gialli per le piaggie mova,
torna a la mente il loco
e'l primo dì ch'i' vidi a l'aura sparsi
i capei d'oro ond'io sì subito arsi.   (127)

If my eyes ever saw white with crimson roses in a vase of gold, just then gathered by virgin hands, they thought they saw the face of her who excels all other wonders with the three excellences gathered in her: the blond tresses loosened on her neck, where every milk loses by comparison, and the cheeks adorned with a sweet fire. If the breeze but a little moves the white and yellow flowers in the meadows, the place comes back to mind and the first day when I saw freed to the air the golden hair from which I so quickly caught fire.

The elaborate figures work by a somewhat surprising reversal of the normal metaphor-making process. Instead of Laura's head suggesting precious materials (one always compares the commoner thing to the rarer and more valuable, according to Aristotle), the beauties of art and nature metamorphose into Laura. The processes of association and memory replace formal metaphorical structures at the beginning and end of the passage. The *ornatus* is of a very unusual type, suggesting the highest kind of studied writing in the florid middle style. Taken as a whole, Petrarch's three canzoni are a demonstration of stylistic range in love poetry, a practical ars poetica.

Subsequent thinking tended to reinterpret the stylistic levels of Petrarch's lyrics, as we shall see. The revival of classical rhetorical theory in a fuller form in the sixteenth century involved not only a more elaborate description of styles but a certain development which went beyond the ancient rhetoricians' categories. And Petrarch's work, taken as exemplary, played a large role in the newer theorizing about style.

CHAPTER 2

Middle-Style Genres: The Evolution of Sixteenth-Century Lyric

I

For over a century after Petrarch's death Italian lyric poetry was, on the whole, undistinguished. Lorenzo de' Medici's work in lyric genres seems to be that of an unfulfilled talent; other poets' sonnets and short poems are often spoiled by dialectal features which may amuse the philologist but which put them outside the mainstream of Italian poetry. The quattrocento lyric tends also to be structurally ineffective. There is a rich amount of satiric verse and popular poetry, as in other centuries of Italian literature, but those topics are beyond our scope. Toward the end of the quattrocento, three poets acquired some fame, and their names are still met with in footnotes, if more rarely in anthologies: Serafino de' Ciminelli dall'Aquila (1446–1500), Tebaldeo (Marco Antonio Tebaldi, 1463–1537), and Chariteo (Benedetto Gareth, 1450–1515).[1] They are generally said to represent a prebaroque conceitful style, although on examination their work proves not quite to merit this reputation: their conceits are weak, their style generally undistinguished. In some ways, the most remarkable poetry of the quattrocento lies in the work of the neo-Latin poets, who are such a characteristic feature of late fifteenth-century humanism: Politian (Angelo Poliziano, 1454–1494), Giovanni Pontano (1426–1503), Marullus (Michele Marullo Tarcaniota, 1453–1500), Mantuan (Battista Spagnoli, (1447–1516), and Jacopo Sannazaro (1456–1530). They will be a point of reference in discussing the evolution of European low-style genres.

The foundations of a revival in Italian lyric were set by the teach-

---

1. For Serafino, see Mia Cocco, *La Tradizione cortese e il petrarchismo nella poesia di Clément Marot* (Florence, 1978), 104–15.

ings and example of Cardinal Pietro Bembo (1470–1547), one of the most interesting literary theorists of the sixteenth century. Bembo is remembered as a leader of the Ciceronian movement in neo-Latin prose, but his interest in the vernacular was just as great. He argued in his *Prose della volgar lingua* (1524) for the use of Boccaccio as a model for Italian prose and in poetry insisted that diction should be based on Petrarch. Bembo was a learned man, well acquainted with the troubadours and duecento Italian poets, so that his choice of Petrarch as the prototype for modern Italian poetry was informed by an acute historical sense of the development of European poetry. The place which he accorded Petrarch and which he imposed by his authority solved a great problem for Italian poets. Many of them grew up speaking a northern or southern dialect; once the possibility of writing in dialect was rejected, as seemed only wise to those who wished a large audience, the poet had the choice of using a kind of neutral Italian, lacking in any particular savor, or of cultivating Tuscan as it was spoken in his time, a difficult task for one who did not reside in Tuscany. Bembo's solution, the adoption of Petrarch's essentially artificial version of fourteenth-century Tuscan, provided a model easily accessible to all poets.

In his contribution to the *questione della lingua*, Bembo was obviously guided by the analogy with high Roman classicism, which accepted the division between poetic and nonpoetic words,[2] the borrowing of phrases from an earlier model (the echoes of Ennius in the *Aeneid*, the Alexandrian and earlier Greek influence on the lyric poets), and the general principle of imitation by which one steeped oneself in the work of a great predecessor to the extent that one's own style always had a clear but subtle relation with it. Such had been the method of the quattrocento neo-Latin poets as well, in whom the presence of Virgil, Horace, Catullus, and other classical Roman poets can be felt, without there necessarily being a strict verbal borrowing.

Some of the details of Bembo's teachings are interesting to note. Petrarch alone had to occupy the positions such varied poets as Pindar, Catullus, and Horace hold in classical literature. However, there

---

2. See Bertil Alexson, *Unpoetische Wörter* (Lund, 1945).

seems to be little evidence of any real study of Pindar on Bembo's part, so that essentially it is Roman lyric poetry of which Petrarch is the counterpart. Bembo approaches the subject of style by mentioning the three traditional *genera dicendi*, or levels of diction, but low style interests him not in the slightest, save as a way of disparaging Dante. As he proceeds in his exposition, he affirms again and again that Petrarch is the great exemplar of both *piacevolezza* and *gravità*. *Piacevolezza* refers to the quality of charm or *delectatio* ascribed to middle style. Cicero said that the latter was the most delightful style of all, and traditionally it was associated with the lyric, in the strict classical sense of lyric measures like Horace's, excluding eclogue and elegy. *Gravità*, on the other hand, is a key word for describing high style: weightiness and seriousness are regularly attributed to it in the rhetorical treatises, and the high style operates by "moving" its audience, not "delighting" it. In other words, Bembo is elevating Petrarch's lyric style to a position which it apparently did not have for Petrarch himself and which the rhetoricians did not grant shorter lyrics; only the ode or major lyric, such as Pindar's, was considered to belong to high style. This curious way of elevating genres, of equating the *Canzoniere* with Pindar's grand manner, is characteristic of the way renaissance theorists worked on and transformed classical notions of style. Of course, subject matter is not without its importance in this shift of conception: for the Romans, love was a matter for low-style elegy, whereas love poetry like Petrarch's, elevated in feeling and constantly Christian in reference, suggested a much nobler rank in the hierarchy of genres.

Bembo's minute discussion of style in Book III of the *Prose della volgar lingua* bears on small points of grammar and above all on sound combinations. It is too miscellaneous to constitute a coherent theory. Rather, it is in the poetry of Bembo himself and of what one might call his school that we can best find the characteristics of this phase of Petrarchist poetry.

The poets influenced by Bembo are classicists in the sense of using restricted means and striving for refinement of detail. Bembo himself was, in some ways, less gifted than certain of his followers, and as an example of this classicizing cinquecento poetry, I shall take a sonnet by Berardino Rota (1508–1575):

Giaceasi donna languidetta e stanca,
quasi notturno fior tocco dal sole;
e tal era a veder qual parer sole
raggio di sol ch'a poco a poco manca.

Io l'una e l'altra man gelata e bianca
baciava intanto e non avea parole,
fatto già pietra che si move e dole,
sospira, piange, trema, arrossa, imbianca;

e baciando bagnava or questa or quella
col fonte di quest'occhi, e co' sospiri
l'alabastro asciugava intorno intorno.

Partì quest'alma allor per gir con ella
sperando di dar fine a'miei martiri,
poi tornò meco a far tristo soggiorno.[3]

A lady lay languid and tired, like a night flower touched by the sun; and she looked the way the sun usually appears as it gradually fades away. I meanwhile kissed both her cold white hands, and could not speak a word, for I was like a stone which could, however, move, suffer, sigh, weep, tremble, redden, and grow pale. And as I kissed each hand in turn I bathed them with the fountain of my eyes, and dried her alabaster skin all about with my sighs. Then my soul flew off with her, hoping to end my martyrdom, but it came back to sojourn sadly with me.

Several devices, present in Petrarch but especially highly developed in the sixteenth century, give the poet great freedom in the choice and collocation of sounds. Apocopations like *fior* for *fiore* and *veder* for *vedere* permit him to overcome the often too insistently vocalic character of Italian. Abbreviated forms like *tocco* for *toccato*, *a'* for *ai*, and *co'* for *coi* allow for nuances of sound suiting the poet's taste. While the vocabulary is not very interesting with its metaphors like *alabastro* and *fonte*, the art of sound effects, including elaborate and varied repetitions of sounds, is cultivated with great success. But the finest thing about the sonnet is the graceful, easy hyperbaton by which the positions of subject, verb, and object are transposed in lines 1, 3, 4, 5, 6, 11, and 12. Increasingly, poets saw the expressive value of word order. The very effective initial position of the verb *giaceasi*, for example, goes beyond what one usually encounters in Petrarch's inversions. Much of the elegance of this poetry lies in its sentence structure, and we must remember that such syntactic ar-

---

3. Luigi Baldacci (ed.), *Lirici del cinquecento* (Milan, 1975).

rangements are not at all forced in Italian. The ordinary prose of the earlier centuries accepted much dislocation of word order, and even today, in highly formal prose, inversions are to be found which have no equivalent in English or French.

The most famous follower of Bembo was Giovanni della Casa (1503–1555), whose verse was noted for its expressive use of enjambment:

> O dolce selva solitaria, amica
> de' miei pensieri sbigottiti e stanchi,
> mentre Borea ne' dí torbidi e manchi
> d'orrido giel l'aere e la terra implica;
>
> e la tua verde chioma ombrosa, antica,
> come la mia, par d'ogn'intorno imbianchi,
> or, che'nvece di fior vermigli e blanchi,
> ha neve e ghiaccio ogni tua piaggia aprica;
>
> a questa breve e nubilosa luce
> vo ripensando, che m'avanza, e ghiaccio
> gli spirti anch'io sento e le membra farsi:
>
> ma più di te dentro e d'intorno agghiaccio,
> ché più crudo Euro a me mio verno adduce,
> più lunga notte e dí piu freddi e scarsi.[4]

O sweet solitary wood, the friend of my dismayed and weary thoughts, while the North Wind, in these turbid, truncated days, enfolds the air and earth in horrid ice. And your ancient shady green foliage, like my hair, seems to grow white all over, now that your sunny stretches have snow and ice instead of red and white flowers. I think of this short cloudy light, which is all that is left to me, and I feel my vital spirits and limbs turn to ice. But I am, inside and out, more icy than you, for the East Wind brings to me the crueler winter of old age, a longer night, and colder, more abbreviated days.

The sonnet is again written in the universal Italian poetic idiom derived from Petrarch. At a glance, one immediately picks up key terms of this style, which technically are Latinisms but have become so much a part of Italian poetic language that one scarcely thinks of them as Latinisms in the same way one does when encountering *oppugnancy* in English verse or *emolumentz* in French. Terms of this halfway language between Italian and Latin include *aere, chioma, aprico, nubiloso, crudo* (in the sense of "cruel"); *implica* here provokes a slightly stronger impression of Latin, since one must refer to the

---

4. *Ibid.*

concrete sense of the roots. This word belongs to the category of what might be called extraordinary Latinism, permitted in moderate amounts in the Petrarchist style. Finally, the characteristic cinquecento hyperbaton is coupled with enjambment to produce an exceptionally supple sentence structure, one we can scarcely imagine being adapted to postmedieval French or English. We also observe that love is not the only subject matter of the cinquecento sonneteers; here the cause of melancholy is age, but elsewhere religious themes play a strong role. This is, of course, authentically Petrarchan, since the *Canzoniere* does not just dwell on Laura. In any case, the Petrarchan technique of relating the inner and outer worlds is observed and forms the matter of the sonnet. Unfortunately the superior technique of the Bembist poets is little known or appreciated, although its historical importance, for Milton notably, is unquestionable. The only poet close to this first phase of Petrarchism whose reputation endures is the Spaniard Garcilaso de la Vega.

The Italian lyric poet of the sixteenth century who does continue to attract attention, outside Italy as well as within, is Michelangelo, whose strange, uneven work is marked by a fitfully strong individuality of style and conception. Michelangelo often made use of Petrarchist elements in his poetry, but his language is erratic in its deviations from literary forms; its abrupt, often unfinished character; and the way in which, when his thought is not banal, it can be very contorted. This curious love sonnet was addressed to his friend Tomaso de' Cavalieri:

> D'altrui pietoso e sol di sé spietato
> Nasce un vil bruto, che con pena e doglia
> L'altrui man veste, e la sua scorza spoglia,
> E sol per morte si può dir ben nato.
>
> Così volesse al mio signor mio fato
> Vestir sua viva di mia morta spoglia,
> Che, come serpe al sasso si discoglia,
> Pur per morte potria cangiar mio stato.
>
> O fussi sol la mia l'irsuta pelle,
> Che, del suo pél contesta, fa tal gonna,
> Che con ventura stringe si bel seno,
>
> Ch'i' l'are' pure il giorno; o le pianelle
> Che fanno a quel di lor base e colonna,
> Ch'i' pur ne porterei due nevi almeno.[5]

5. *Ibid.*

Tender toward others and harsh to itself, the low silk worm is born, who with effort and pain dresses another's hand by stripping off its outer skin, and only by its metamorphosis through death can it be said to be noble. Thus my fate would have me clothe my lord's living body with my dead one, which, as a serpent rubs off its skin against a rock, could, in death, change my state. O could my hairy skin make a garment of its woven hairs that would have the good fortune to bind so beautiful a breast, so that I would be with him all day long, or if I were turned into slippers, which are the base of the body's column, I could bear his weight for at least two years.

The images are an odd mixture of the elevated and the low, the concrete and the periphrastic; the erotic thought is combined with a reminiscence of the flaying of Saint Bartholomew, whom Michelangelo portrayed in the Sistine Chapel holding his own skin in his hands. The syntax is a trifle inelegant, with its repetition of *che* at the beginning of so many lines and becomes somewhat obscure toward the end. Michelangelo is not an easy poet to read, and ambiguities of his language are matched often by one's uncertainty of the degree to which his poems can be said to be finished in the manner of a poet writing for the normal literary audience. Roughness is associated with his work, but one hesitates to call it the calculated asperity of the rhetorician.

II

When we turn to Maurice Scève, the first poet in French to write a long series of poems dedicated to one woman, the question of Petrarchism becomes more problematic than it is with the generality of cinquecento Italian poets. Scève borrowed some key words, figures, and a few types of poems from Petrarch and the Petrarchists, but he did not imitate them in the renaissance sense: there is no relation between the basic conceptions of style in Petrarch and in Scève. Scève also wrote in Middle French, unlike Ronsard and his followers, with all that that implies in the way of the special stylistic tradition, elaborated both in prose and in verse, of the *rhétoriqueur* poets of the late fifteenth and early sixteenth centuries, who enjoyed fame and court favor.

Here is the first numbered poem of the *Délie*:

L'Oeil trop ardent en mes jeunes erreurs
Girouettoit, mal cault, à l'impourueue:
Voicy—ô paour d'agreables terreurs!—
Mon Basilisque avec sa poingnant' veue
Perçant Corps, Coeur, et Raison despourueue,
Vint penetrer en l'Ame de mon Ame.
　　Grand fut le coup, qui sans tranchante lame
Fait que, viuant le corps, l'Esprit desuie,
Piteuse hostie au conspect de toy, Dame,
Constituée Idole de ma vie.[6]

My eye, too hot in my youthful wanderings, turned like a weathervane, uncautious and imprudent. Behold—O fear of delightful terrors—my Basilisk, who, with her piercing glance, boring through body, heart, and helpless reason, penetrated into my soul of souls. The blow was great, for without a sharp blade, it made my vital spirits die, while my body lived, and I was a pitiful victim in your eyes, Lady, who are now made the idol of my life.

The eye and sight are emphasized as in Petrarch, but the peculiar tone of the poem, with its basilisk, the lizard whose glance kills, and the references to a sacrificial victim (*hostie*) and to an idol, suggests that we are far from Petrarch's essentially Christian *Canzoniere*. Indeed, Scève is a neoplatonist and refers abundantly to widely diffused ideas of the theorists of love from Marsilio Ficino on.

The vocabulary mixes very French, if unusual words like *girouetter* and *cault* with striking Latinisms that stand out against the romance texture: the *conspect* of the last two lines brings out the classical character of *hostie, constituée,* and *idole.* All this is held together in a syntax where nouns, participles, and prepositional phrases play the principal role. The lines have no flowing quality; as is often the case in Middle French prose, the complexity of the grammar makes for many pauses.

The list of bodily, psychological, and spiritual faculties in the dizain which I have just quoted belongs very much to the late medieval French tradition; only a few poems of Petrarch employ this kind of semiabstract language, with its reminiscences of science and philosophy, in any abundance. In the following dizain, there is not only a division between the soul, body, and self, but the soul has an eye as well as the body:

6. All quotations of Scève's *Délie* are from I. D. McFarlane (ed.), *The "Délie" of Maurice Scève* (Cambridge, 1966), and are hereinafter cited in the text by poem number.

> Le iour passé de ta doulce presence
> Fust vn serain en hyuer tenebreux,
> Qui faict prouuer la nuict de ton absence
> A l'oeil de l'ame estre vn temps plus vmbreux,
> Que n'est au Corps ce mien viure encombreux,
> Qui maintenant me fait de soy refus.
>   Car dès le poinct, que partie tu fus,
> Comme le Lieure accroppy en son giste,
> Ie tendz l'oreille, oyant vn bruyt confus,
> Tout esperdu aux tenebres d'Egypte.   (CXXIX)

Your sweet presence yesterday was a cloudless day in dark winter, which makes my soul's eye feel the night of your absence to be a more shadowy, wearisome time than my cumbersome life is now to my body, my life which is withdrawing from me. For from the moment you left, like the hare in its warren, I pricked up my ear, hearing a muffled sound, lost and frantic in Egyptian darkness.

The first sentence has four subordinate clauses attached to one another—a striking number for lyric poetry—including the ponderous infinitive clause to which Middle French writers were much given. The somewhat tortuous movement of Scève's verse can often be attributed to its grammar.

In the concluding section, typically set off with a causative conjunction like the tercets of a sonnet, Scève introduces imagery which, like the basilisk of the preceding poem, draws on tradition. The hare is customarily an emblem of timidity, and the darkness over Egypt is one of the plagues in Exodus. The important thing, however, about much of Scève's imagery is that no matter how much you explain it by traditional lore, no other lyric poet used it with such remarkable concision and brilliance. Old commonplaces become entirely new and surprising in Scève's stylistic technique. There is little in the Petrarchist tradition comparable to the startling effects Scève creates. At the same time, the feeling of surprise is not accompanied by the recognition of cleverness and wittiness, as it is in the poetry of conceits; Scève's tone is too serious and solemn.

Petrarch's evident theory of the image as a valuable structural element was carried further by Scève, who developed the technique of using a contrastive concluding image of great originality of diction after an abstract exposition:

> Tout iugement de celle infinité,
> Où tout concept se trouue superflus,

Et tout aigu de perspicuité
Ne pourroyent ioindre au sommet de son plus.
 Car seulement l'apparent du surplus,
Premiere neige en son blanc souueraine,
Au pur des mains delicatement saine,
Ahontiroyt le nud de Bersabée,
Et le flagrant de sa suaue alaine
Apouriroyt l'odorante Sabée. (CLXVI)

Any judgment made of her infinitude, where all intellectual apprehension is superfluous, and any attempt at piercing insight could not add to the height of her perfection. For even merely the appearance of her outer being, her skin, like the first snow, sovereign in whiteness, delicately wholesome in the purity of her hands, would put naked Bathsheba to shame, and the fragrance of her soft breath would make perfumed Arabia smell rotten.

The language at first represents a kind of mystic neoplatonism. The abstract terms, in the still-groping philosophical idiom of Middle French, have a certain archaic charm, which is quickly changed, by the hinge word *surplus*, abstract in form but concrete in meaning, to a comparison which, though traditional in its use of archetypes of beauty and scent, is made unusually vivid by Scève's curious use of compound verbs, the second one in a rare causative sense.

Much of the feeling of a somewhat alien idiom in this poem, as elsewhere in Scève, comes from the use of adjectives as nouns, in ways unfamiliar to modern French. Such constructions, like substantivized infinitives and other unusual features of his vocabulary, are not limited to Scève's diction but have a certain general currency in the sixteenth century. The impression Scève so often gives readers of absolute uniqueness is belied by careful philological investigation.[7] Nevertheless, as in the case of imagery handed down through the ages, Scève had such a strong feeling for creating an individual style that analogous examples from other writers never seem to produce the effect proper to the *Délie*.

Antitheses and paradoxes, the stuff of which so many later poets made conceits, frequently possess as little wittiness as they do in Petrarch. The subject announced at the beginning of the *Délie*, "les mortz, qu'en moi tu renouvelles," is present in "L'Oeil trop ardent"

7. *Ibid.*, 48–59. Also on Scève's language, see Henri Weber, *Le Langage poétique de Maurice Scève dans la "Délie"* (Florence, 1948).

and "Le iour passé" but without any pointed play on the idea of life and death. Even when Scève employs antitheses overtly, the serious tone eliminates any suggestion of the purely delightful handling of words. In VII, Scève says that Délie

> tellement tient mes espritz rauiz,
> En admirant sa mirable merveille,
> Que, presque mort, sa Deité m'esueille,
> En la clarté de mes desirs funebres,
> Où plus m'allume, et plus, dont m'esmerueille,
> Elle m'abysme en profondes tenebres.

She holds my vital spirits so in ecstasy, as I wonder at her wondrous wonder, that, when I am almost dead, her deity awakens me into the brightness of my funereal desires, wherein the more she illuminates me, the more—a thing which I marvel at—she plunges me into deep darkness.

The play of alliteration and polyptoton in the second line is a persistent medieval device Scève occasionally carries to great lengths; it expresses solemnity here and the celebration of rare beauty in a difficult figure. Words like *deité*, *abysme*, and *funebres* stress the neoplatonic-mystical content of the antithesis; the religious connotations of the paradox of life and death, analogous to that of Christianity, are finally made clear in the admirable series of dizains on immortality near the end of the *Délie*. Despite a number of light poems, Scève's is a work informed by the new theology of love, and perhaps the most poetically serious and convincing such work of the sixteenth century.

Scève's middle style is highly ornamented in individual words, tropes, and sound figures, but while not discontinuous or asyndetic in any way, it does not conform to the classical idea of the smooth lyric style, which Petrarch had cultivated. Scève lived at the moment when Middle French, which is a matter both of grammar and style, was yielding to the more modern form of the language we find in Du Bellay and Ronsard, but perhaps a certain conservatism in him inclined Scève to adhere to the older stylistic practices of blatant Latinism, omission of articles and pronouns and augmentation of the role of the noun through multiple prepositional phrases, appositions, and substantivized infinitives and adjectives. The sentence structure at times even recalls that of Latinizing French prose, more involuted than the syntax of late medieval verse. Its sentence patterns are distinguished by an emphasis on logical connection as well as hypotaxis, and we observe that the argument of Scève's poems is as carefully articulated as is that of Petrarch's sonnets. Despite the care for sequence and overall order in his dizains, however, Scève's own term for them is not without validity; in the liminary poem of the *Délie*, he refers to his "durs Epygrammes." *Dur* is not solely a comment on the experiences embodied in the poems, but a characterization of his dense, slow-moving style, with its sometimes puzzling vocabulary, frequent pauses, and general avoidance of enjambment. We shall also see that the word *hard* has interesting relations with the tendencies of French poetry at the end of the sixteenth century.

Scève's major poetic gift was for the middle-style lyric devoted to love. However, he also made an important contribution to the establishment of classical rhetorical theory in Europe. With the *Délie*, his eclogues *Arion* (1536) and *La Saulsaye* (1547), and the didactic epic *Le Microcosme* (1564), which begins with the creation and Eden, Scève's work constitutes a "wheel of Virgil." He wrote in the low pastoral style, the middle style, and finally in high epic style, in accordance with the circular medieval diagram showing Virgil's achievement. What is especially interesting is that Scève actually made real distinctions of style among the three levels; *Le Microcosme* and the eclogues could not easily be confused with the manner of the *Délie*. Although these other works are poetically less successful, the fact that Scève had clearly present to his mind the necessary distinctions among the three levels of style makes him one of the earliest vernacular poets to realize the classical rhetorical system in theory and in practice.

III

With Scéve's *Délie*, the existence of a genuine French mode in the short lyric of the sixteenth century is evident, no matter how many Italian sources may be found for individual lines or poems.[8] The the-

---

8. See Stephen Minta, *Love Poetry in Sixteenth-Century France: A Study in Themes and Traditions* (Manchester, 1977); Dorothy Gabe Coleman, *The Gallo-Roman Muse: Aspects of Roman Literary Tradition in Sixteenth-Century France* (Cambridge, 1979).

oretical affirmation of the independence of the French lyric appears most clearly in Du Bellay's *Deffense et illustration de la langue françoise* (1549), presumably inspired to a great extent by Ronsard, and in Ronsard's own later *Abrégé de l'art poétique françois* (1565). The Du Bellay work is not an ars poetica or a rhetorical essay in the traditional fashion but unites a defense of the vernacular, derived somewhat from arguments advanced in the Italian *questione della lingua*, with very specific recommendations about genres and diction.

The ideas on diction in the *Deffense* and in Ronsard's *Abrégé* interest us most here for the contrast they form with Bembo's theory of Italian classicism. Du Bellay and Ronsard advocate neologisms, archaisms, dialectal words, and terms borrowed from the technical vocabularies of the various metiers.[9] The absence of any praise of Latinisms like those the Italian cinquecento poets use so successfully is conspicuous. It is clear that whereas Bembo's theory of style derives from Augustan Roman practice, with its carefully worked out opposition between poetic and prosaic vocabulary, the French poets' conception of style is modeled on older Greek poetry, Homer and Pindar most specifically. The distinction between the high and poetic, on the one hand, and the low and prosaic, on the other, had not yet occurred in so early a period, and dialectal mixture is also one of the striking characteristics of Homer and Pindar's Greek. Their large body of rare words inspired both neologism and archaism in imitation. So obsessed was Ronsard with the peculiarities of early Greek poetic style that he even recommended and practiced the use of metaplasm, or alteration of customary sounds in words, the typical example in his work being the use of *chouse* alongside *chose* and analogous changes from *o* to *ou*. Ronsard specifically refers to the Greek doublet οὔνομα and ὄνομα to justify this extraordinary aspect of his vocabulary.

Something we observe particularly in Du Bellay's *Deffense* is that his lexical proposals do not constitute an integrated theory of style, as do the traditional distinctions between high, middle, and low systems of diction. His ideas lie more in the direction of Erasmus' doctrine of *copia*, of abundance and variety in words and hence thought. It has been noted that the principle of *copia* (Du Bellay's *copie*) does

9. See Louis Terreaux, *Ronsard correcteur de ses oeuvres* (Geneva, 1968), 250, 256–57.

away with the traditional structure of rhetorical doctrine in the sense that invention, or the summoning up of one's matter, and elocution, or style, are assimilated in the search for variety of expression.[10] Ronsard, in his *Abrégé*, keeps the traditional distinctions of invention, disposition (that is, composition), and elocution, but he has very little to say about the first two. His extraordinarily intense feeling for individual words greatly surpasses his interest in general rhetorical theory. Obviously we are dealing here with ideas on style so remote from those of Italian contemporaries as to constitute an independent tradition, for all the shared Petrarchan background. Italian had a modest form of *copia* and metaplasm in the various doublets derived from Petrarch's example (*frale/fragile; move/muove*), but these are limited in number. Theoretically French poetic diction was open to the most wide-ranging linguistic vagaries, and the necessity of purity of language, a traditional commonplace of the rhetorical treatises, was abandoned. Latinity, which was the guardian of purity in Italian style, has no equivalent in these French conceptions of poetic vocabulary.

IV

In his actual poetic practice, Ronsard's vocabulary is much less startling, on the whole, than the aggressively put theories of the *Deffense* might suggest. However, his use of certain rhetorical devices, unmentioned by Du Bellay, is very prominent and may be illustrated beginning with the first poem in the *Amours* of 1552.[11]

> Qui voudra voyr comme un Dieu me surmonte,
> Comme il m'assault, comme il se fait vainqueur
> Comme il r'enflamme, & r'englace mon cuoeur,
> Comme il reçoit un honneur de ma honte,
>
> Qui voudra voir une jeunesse prompte
> A suyvre en vain l'object de son malheur,
> Me vienne voir: il voirra ma douleur,
> Et la rigueur de l'Archer qui me donte.[12]

10. See Terence C. Cave, *The Cornucopian Text: Problems of Writing in the French Renaissance* (Oxford, 1979), 3–77.

11. See Alex L. Gordon, *Ronsard et la rhétorique* (Geneva, 1970).

12. All texts of Ronsard are the unrevised versions of the first editions reproduced in Pierre de Ronsard, *Oeuvres complètes*, ed. Paul Laummonier (19 vols.; Paris, 1931–75), hereinafter cited in the text by poem number.

> Whoever wishes to see how a god overcomes me, how he attacks me, how he conquers me, how he rekindles and freezes again my heart, how he gains honor from my shame; whoever wishes to see a young man quick to follow in vain the object of his wretchedness, let him come look at me: he will see my sorrow and the rigor of the Archer who tames me.

The anaphoric repetitions of *qui voudra voir* and *comme il*, the alliteration of the unusual *r'enflamme* and *r'englace*, and the polyptoton of *voir: il voirra* make a ringing, insistent sound pattern that all but drowns out the rimes themselves. It is an interesting poem to compare in its display with the openings of Petrarch's and Scève's *canzonieri*, where Petrarch expresses shame at being a conspicuous lover and Scève, the most private-seeming of poets, merely addresses Délie herself. Ronsard's language is an invitation to admire the verbal pyrotechnics which follow.

Figures of sound are prominent in the *Amours*: XIX is filled with repetitions of *tu* and its possessives, *ta, ton,* and *tes*; XX uses anaphora to mark each section of the sonnet, as does XLIV. Ronsard also continues, on occasion, the medieval play of repetition, alliteration, and polyptoton, as in LXIII, a sonnet in *m*; or in LXI, in part based on forms of *voler*; and most of all, in the *doulx* sonnet, number XXXVIII:

> Doulx fut le traict, qu'Amour hors de sa trousse,
> Pour me tuer me tira doulcement,
> Quand je fuz pris au doulx commencement
> D'une doulceur si doulcettement doulce.

Sweet was the arrow that Love, to kill me, drew for me from his quiver, when I was caught at the sweet beginning of a so sweetly sweet sweetness.

This kind of rhetoric could not be more opposed to the classicizing notions of moderation in effect, of avoidance of excessive repetition, and of giving each word a full enough value that it would not risk seeming a purely idle repetition of a preceding one. Ronsard's allegiance, however, is to abundance of figures, and forcefulness, as much as elegance, guides his choice in diction.

Other patterns are on the borderline between figures of sound and figures of thought: XII is a sonnet in antitheses; CXVII is made all of questions. *Si* clauses structure XXIX, and *vers rapportés* form a part of XVII. But the most frequent figure is unquestionably enumeration, sometimes with anaphora (CXLV and XLVI have a string of vocatives preceded by *O*; in CXLIII and XCV, nouns in a series are each introduced by the negative *ny*), sometimes without anaphora:

> Ce beau coral, ce marbre qui souspire,
> et cest ébénne ornement d'un sourci,
> Et cest albastre en vouste racourci,
> Et ces zaphirs, ce jaspe, & ce porphyre,
>
> Ces diaments, ces rubis qu'un zephyre
> Tient animez d'un souspir adouci,
> Et ces oeilletz, & ces roses aussi,
> Et ce fin or, où l'or mesme se mire . . .   (XXIII)

This beautiful coral, this sighing marble, and this ebony ornamenting an eyebrow, and this alabaster rounded in a vault, and these sapphires, this jasper, and this porphyry, these diamonds, these rubies that a zephyr keeps animated with a soft sigh, and these carnations, and these roses also, and this fine gold, in which gold itself is reflected . . .

The first eight lines start off as the metonymic description of a lady's face common in Ronsard and the Petrarchists. But Ronsard goes much beyond the roses and lilies we find even in Virgil; he is not satisfied with marble for skin but adds alabaster as well, and the number of words designating something red or pink is positively bewildering. This enumerative profusion brings out two potential characteristics of the device; we lose track of the exact value of the metonymies, or one-word metaphors, and become aware of the loose, disjunctive quality of the syntax. The latter effect is even stronger when Ronsard uses an enumeration of infinitives, as in LXXIV. Ronsard's handling of these devices definitely anticipates the grammar of many later French poets.

The rest of the sonnet illustrates another typical procedure in Ronsard's composition. After the enumeration in the quatrains, we find that each tercet has a distinctive figure:

> Me sont au cuoeur en si profond esmoy,
> Qu'un autre object ne se presente à moy,
> Si non le beau de leur beau que j'adore,
>
> Et le plaisir qui ne se peult passer
> De les songer, penser, & repenser,
> Songer, penser, & repenser encore.

These cause such a deep emotion in my heart that no other object presents itself to my thought save their beauteous beauty which I worship, and the unending pleasure of dreaming of them, thinking of them, and thinking of them again, dreaming of them, thinking of them, and thinking of them yet again.

Le beau de leur beau is a kind of odd hyperbole much admired by sixteenth-century poets, and the repetition of the last tercet rounds off the poem with a figure of some weight. We find, then, in this sonnet a form of unitary composition by which the quatrains together and each tercet have rhetorical figures peculiar to them. Unitary composition plays a large role in the *Amours*, and it has two notable effects. The units can be juxtaposed in an abrupt, asyndetic fashion, as in XX, where the four wishes are somewhat disconnected, or there may be an imbalance in brilliance of style between sections, as in LI, where the second quatrain seems merely a perfunctory filler between the striking images of the first quatrain and those of the tercets.

All this insistence on rhetorical units goes much beyond whatever of the sort we find in Petrarch and the Italian Petrarchists, both in intensity and frequency. A special case of unitary design involves the comparison sonnet, where a lengthy simile can constitute half or more of the poem. This use of the high-style epic simile in lyric is not fully realized by Petrarch, whose comparisons tend to be shorter. Here is an example of the kind of comparison sonnet which was to become widespread, with the quatrains grouped in opposition to the tercets:

> Quand le grand oeil dans les Jumeaux arrive,
> Un jour plus doulx seréne l'Univers,
> D'espicz crestez ondoyent les champz verdz,
> Et de couleurs se peinture la rive.
>
> Mais quand sa fuite obliquement tardive,
> Par le sentier qui roulle de travers,
> Atteint l'Archer, un changement divers
> De jour, d'espicz, & de couleurs les prive.
>
> Ainsi quand l'oeil de ma deesse luit,
> Dedans mon cuoeur, dans mon cuoeur se produit
> Un beau printempz qui me donne asseurance:
>
> Mais aussi tost que son rayon s'enfuit,
> De mon printempz il avorte le fruit,
> Et à myherbe il tond mon esperance.   (CLXIV)

When the great eye of the sun reaches Gemini, a gentler light makes the universe serene; the green fields undulate, crested with ears of grain, and the river bank is colorfully painted. But when the sun, in its late, oblique flight, by the elliptical path of the Zodiac, reaches Sagittarius, a varying change robs the fields of light, grain, and color. Thus when my goddess' eye shines into my heart, in my heart there arises a beautiful springtime, which reassures me. But as soon as the beam of her eye turns elsewhere, the fruit of my spring is blasted, and my hope mowed down when it is only half-grown.

The diction here is sustained, and Ronsard achieves his ideal of a strong final line through the splendid use of the unusual, concise *à myherbe*. The sonnet is unitary to a second degree in that the first and second quatrains and tercets contrast by use of *mais*. In the quatrains Ronsard vivifies his imagery by the metonymic *oeil* for sun and the unusual *serener*; the general manner is that of the classical *chronographia*, or periphrastic description of a time of the day or year. The word *oeil* then becomes literal in line nine, but everything that follows it is metaphoric, a reversal of the relations of the concrete and the figurative in the quatrains. This sense relation from quatrains to tercets might be called a conceit, and we should pause for a moment over the notion of the conceit in imagery.

Unlike anaphora, genitive metaphor (A is the B of C), or other rhetorical figures, the conceit cannot be objectively defined. It lies in the way we look at a particular figure, in the degree to which we find it clever or strange. Most conceits are simply standard tropes (more rarely figures of sound) to which we attach an evaluation which is partly subjective, partly based on the poem's historical context or the general tendencies of the poet. The superabundant enumeration in XXIII, quoted earlier, might be called a conceit because of the exaggerated and puzzling number of its metonymies. A very common kind of conceit derives, as in the poem just quoted, from the juxtaposition of words with concrete, literal meanings to ones which have a purely figurative value. This occurs especially when they are in the same sentence or in juxtaposed sentences. In the tercets *oeil* is literal, but *luit / Dedans mon cuoeur, printempz, rayon*, and *fruit* are all metaphoric. Another relation that often seems conceitful is the mythological comparison. Long similes or sustained comparisons are structuring devices, but analogies can be either logical or decorative, as Aristotle pointed out. Many mythological comparisons are utterly decorative, raising the tone of the poem, but analogies can also provide the pseudologic of conceit, a comparison which seems to have some obscure fittingness because of its protraction. Such is the case of the *métaphore filée* or continuous metaphor in the following sonnet:

> Pour estre en vain tes beaulx soleilz aymant,
> Non pour ravir leur divine estincelle,
> Contre le roc de ta rigueur cruelle
> Amour m'atache à mille cloux d'aymant.
>
> En lieu d'un Aigle, un soing horriblement
> Claquant du bec, & siflant de son aille,
> Ronge goulu ma poictrine immortelle,
> Par un desir qui naist journellement.
>
> Mais de cent maulx, & de cent que j'endure,
> Fiché, cloué, dessus ta rigueur dure,
> Le plus cruel me seroit le plus doulx,
>
> Si j'esperoys, apres un long espace,
> Venir vers moy l'Hercule de ta grace,
> Pour delacer le moindre de mes nouds.   (XIII)

Because I love in vain the beautiful suns of your eyes, and not because I attempted to steal their divine spark, Love has fixed me with a thousand adamantine nails against the rock of your cruel rigor. In place of an eagle, an anxiety, horribly snapping its beak, and with whistling wings, gnaws avidly at my immortal breast, through a desire that is reborn each day. But of the hundreds of pains I endure, fastened, nailed, to your harsh rigor, the cruelest one would be the sweetest to me, if I hoped, after much time, that the Hercules of your pardon would come to me and untie the least of my knots.

There is not only a sustained mythological comparison here but also a particular form of metaphor, the concrete of abstract (*roc de ta rigueur*, for example), which differs somewhat in effect from the yoking of literal and figurative. Abstractions are personified (*soing*) or turned into objects. We actually have three ontological levels in the sonnet: the real man represented by *je*, the abstract emotions, and the story of Prometheus and Hercules. The significance of a poem like this one, however, goes well beyond any merit or interest it may have in itself. The use of abstractions in somewhat metaphorical, non-Petrarchist contexts becomes a major device of French poetry as it evolves in the sixteenth and seventeenth centuries.

Conceits often terminate poems, and the variations or means used toward that end are of considerable interest. Here a single word, *nails*, with its unpoetic, practical connotations, greatly intensifies the figurative language:

> Heureux, cent foys heureux, si le destin
> N'eust emmuré d'un fort diamantin,
> Si chaste cuoeur dessoubz si belle face:
>
> Et plus heureux si je n'eusse arraché
> Mon cuoeur de moy, pour l'avoyr attaché
> De cloudz de feu sur le froid de sa glace.   (V)

I would be happy, a hundred times happy, if destiny had not walled up, in a diamond fortress, so chaste a heart beneath so beautiful a face. And I would be happy, if I had not torn my heart out of myself, to fix it with nails of fire against the chill of her ice.

Ronsard greatly rejuvenates the commonplace of the hard heart (*diamantin* is one of his typical neologistic adjectives) and the conflict of fire and ice, *ardo e gelo*. Elsewhere the surprise and wit associated with the conceit is brought about by a bold neologism:

> Et de là [her mouth] sort le charme d'une voix,
> Qui touts raviz fait sauteler les boys,
> Planer les montz, & montaigner les plaines.   (CX)

And from her mouth comes the charm of a voice which makes the ravished woods leap, mountains spread into plains, and plains rise up in mountains.

The figure is the hyperbole of the impossible, a frequent basis for conceit, and a truly odd neologism like *montaigner* fulfills, in its form, meaning, and antithetical function, the goal of delightful amazement (the θαυμαστόν of Aristotle and the *admiratio* of Roman rhetoricians) proper to the conceit.

The very first poem in the *Amours* of 1552 ("Qui voudra voir . . . me vienne voir") signals the beginning of a lengthy verbal display demanding *admiratio* and admiration. Cassandre, the poet's lady, is virtually absent from the collection in a way Laura and Délie are not absent from their *canzonieri*. There is scarcely that suggestion of a plot which we find in Laura's death or in Scève's speaking of his rivals, his reconciliations, and his coming immortality. Cassandre's marriage is indeed alluded to, but obscurely, and it hardly seems to change the tone of the work. Instead, we are diverted by an intense consciousness of rhetorical means. Of these perhaps the unusual words are, in general, the least important. Ronsard most often merely changes a word from one grammatical category to another, much in the fashion of Shakespearean English: *diamantin, ivoirin, montaigner, cheveux jaunement longs*. More striking is the use of enumeration and unitary composition, devices which tend to produce a feeling of abruptness and disjunction contrary to the ideal of the smooth middle-style lyric. Accompanying this is an intermittent stridency or violence of tone. Two of Ronsard's recent critics have been led to speak in this connection of *cruauté* and *âpreté*, and we find in the *Amours* most un-Petrarchan terms, such as *garrot* and *bransle*, in the sense of "copulation."[13] There is nothing in the theoretical writings of Du Bellay or Ronsard to suggest any acquaintance with the idea of rough or harsh style, but a version of it is not altogether absent from the *Amours*, nor are the great color and richness of effects of Ronsard's sonnets completely separable from such a tone.

V

In the French love poetry of the last fifty years of the sixteenth century, there are two particularly interesting strains: syntactic ingenuity and somberness of imagery. Of the numerous ways of word patterning that emerged, one of Jodelle's sonnets gives a fine example; it is in the form of the distributory sonnet or *vers rapportés*:[14]

> Des astres, des forests, et d'Acheron l'honneur,
> Diane, au Monde hault, moyen et bas preside,
> Et ses chevaulx, ses chiens, ses Eumenides guide,
> Pour esclairer, chasser, donner mort et horreur.
>
> Tel est le lustre grand, la chasse, et la frayeur
> Qu'on sent sous ta beauté claire, promte, homicide,
> Que le haut Jupiter, Phebus, et Pluton cuide,
> Son foudre moins pouvoir, son arc, et sa terreur.

13. See Michel Dassonville, *Ronsard: Étude historique et littéraire* (3 vols.; Geneva, 1968–76), III, 32–40; André Gendre, *Ronsard poète de la conquête amoureuse* (Neuchâtel, 1970), 167–248.
14. See Dámaso Alonso, *Pluralità e correlazione in poesia* (Bari, 1971).

Ta beauté par ses rais, par son rets, par la craincte
Rend l'ame esprise, prise, et au martyre estreinte:
Luy moi, pren moy, tien moy, mais hélas ne me pers.

Des flambans forts et griefs, feux, filez, et encombres,
Lune, Diane, Hecate, aux cieux, terre, et enfers
Ornant, questant, genant, nos Dieux, nous, et nos ombres.[15]

Diana is the honor of the stars, the forests, and the Acheron, presiding over the high, middle, and low worlds; she leads her horses, dogs, and Furies to brighten the way, hunt, give death and horror. Such is the great luster, the skill at hunting, and the terror that we feel connected with your bright, quick, homicidal beauty, that high Jupiter, Phoebus, and Pluto think your powers greater than those of their thunderbolt, bow, and terror. Your beauty, through its beams, nets, and fear, enamors the soul, traps it, and torments it: shine on me, catch me, hold me, but, alas, do not destroy me. Strong flames and grievances, fires, nets, and torments, Moon, Diana, Hecate, in the sky, the earth, and hell, embellishing, hunting, and torturing our gods, ourselves, and our shades.

Nouns, verbs, and adjectives, are arranged in triplets, with or without asyndeton, and in an intensification of the word patterning, the sentence form vanishes in the last tercet, a rather unusual grammatical feature in the sixteenth century. The multiplicity of elements tends to militate against any effect of smooth style, since grammatical continuity is constantly interrupted by the expansion of one component of the sentence. Diana is invoked in her three forms, a complex of imagery found first in Scève, since Délie (born of Delos) is also Diana, and later in Desportes and in d'Aubigné. Other poets invoke the myth of Actaeon (the poet-lover) and Diana, with a similar sense of fatality and destruction.

The altar of Diana is the subject of poems by both Desportes and d'Aubigné. In the Desportes piece we see the beginnings of a new form of metaphor:

Solitaire et pensif, dans un bois écarté,
Bien loin du populaire et de la tourbe espesse,
Je veux bastir un temple à ma fiere deesse,
Pour appendre mes voeux à sa divinité.

Là, de jour et de nuict, par moy sera chanté
Le pouvoir de ses yeux, sa gloire et sa hautesse;
Et, devôt, son beau nom j'invoqueray sans cesse,
Quand je seray pressé de quelque adversité.

15. Marcel Raymond (ed.), *La Poésie française et le maniérisme* (Geneva, 1971).

> Mon oeil sera la lampe, ardant continuelle
> Devant l'image saint d'une dame si belle,
> Mon corps sera l'autel, et mes souspirs les voeux.
>
> Par mille et mille vers je chanteray l'office,
> Puis, espanchant mes pleurs, et coupant mes cheveux,
> J'y feray tous les jours de mon coeur sacrifice.[16]

Solitary and thoughtful, in an out-of-the-way wood, far from the masses and the dense crowd, I want to build a temple to my proud goddess, to affix my ex-votos in honor of her divinity. There, day and night, I shall sing the power of her eyes, her glory, and her high rank, and devoutly I shall invoke endlessly her beautiful name, when some misfortune menaces me. My eye will be the lamp burning continually before the holy image of so beautiful a lady; my body will be the altar, and my sighs the vows. In thousands of verses I shall sing her liturgy; then, pouring out my tears and cutting off my hair, I shall daily make sacrifice of my heart.

"I am the altar" is the unstated formula, and in the later sixteenth century, we encounter copulative expressions like "Je suis cet Actéon de ses chiens déchirés" (Sponde). This dramatic ellipsis for *I am like* is a significant gain in concision and vividness of expression. It is one of those seemingly small shifts of phraseology which actually contribute to the identification of a new phase of style. In d'Aubigné, the equivalence is stated more overtly than in Desportes:

> Ouy, je suis proprement à ton nom immortel
> Le temple consacré, tel qu'en Tauroscytie
> Fust celuy où le sang appaisoit ton envie,
> Mon esthomac pourpré est un pareil autel.[17]

Yes, I am indeed the temple consecrated to your immortal name, like the temple in Tauroscythia, where blood calmed your desires: my red-stained stomach is such an altar.

D'Aubigné's imagery is richer in connotations than Desportes'. Diana (Artemis) had a temple in what for the ancients was the most barbarous of all countries, Scythia, now Russia. It forms the setting of Euripides' *Iphigenia Among the Taurians*, which provides a classic idea of the bloody worship of Diana in "Tauroscythia." This curious byway of humanistic learning is reinforced in a related poem by de-

---

16. Phillippe Desportes, "Les Amours de Diane," XLIII, *ibid*.
17. Agrippa d'Aubigné, *Le Printemps: L'Hécatombe à Diane et les Stances*, ed. Henri Weber (Paris, 1960), sonnet XCVII, hereinafter cited in the text by poem number.

tailed reference to the Greco-Roman methods of prediction by study
of the sacrificial victim's organs:

> J'ouvre mon estommac, une tumbe sanglante
> De maux enseveliz: pour Dieu, tourne tes yeux,
> Diane, et voy au fond mon cueur party en deux
> Et mes poumons gravez d'une ardeur viollente,
>
> Voy mon sang escumeux tout noircy par la flamme,
> Mes os secz de langeurs en pitoiable point
> Mais considere aussi ce que tu ne vois point,
> Le reste des malheurs qui sacagent mon ame.
>
> Tu me brusle et au four de ma flame meurtriere
> Tu chauffes ta froideur: tes delicates mains
> Atizent mon brazier et tes yeux inhumains
> Pleurent, non de pitié, mais flambantz de cholere.
>
> A ce feu devorant de ton yre alumée
> Ton oeil enflé gemist, tu pleures à ma mort,
> Mais ce n'est pas mon mal qui te deplaist si fort,
> Rien n'attendrit tes yeux que mon aigre fumée.
>
> Au moins après ma fin que ton ame apaisée
> Bruslant le cueur, le cors, hostie à ton courroux,
> Prenne sur mon esprit un suplice plus doux,
> Estant d'yre en ma vie en un coup espuisée.   (*Stances*, VI)

I open my stomach: a bloody tomb of buried ills. For the sake of God,
turn your eyes, Diana, and see in my body the heart divided in two and
my lungs marked by a violent burning. See my foaming blood blackened
by the flame, my bones pitifully dry from languor. But think also of what
you do not see: the rest of the misfortunes that ravage my soul. You burn
me and heat your coldness by the murderous flames of the hearth. Your
delicate hands stir up my coals, and your inhuman eyes weep, not for
pity but flaming with anger. In this consuming fire of your kindled wrath,
your swollen eye moans, you weep at my death. But it is not my death
which is so disagreeable to you: only the bitter smoke from it moistens
your eyes. I hope that after my death your satisfied soul, having burned
my heart and body as a sacrifice to your anger, will torment my ghost
less, since you will have exhausted your fury along with my life.

In this striking poem, as elsewhere, d'Aubigné deliberately changes
the *heart* of the Petrarchist tradition to the *stomach*, which has no figurative, poetic meaning. The tension between the necessarily metaphoric sense of his opening himself and the concrete, literal terms of
the imagery is greatly heightened. However, the whole process of
vivisection is not merely a private, morbid invention but has behind

it all the sacrifices in Homer and Virgil: the references to the state of the lungs, blood, and bone and the allusion to the quality of the smoke fit into the ancient framework of ritual examination of the victim. This peculiar use of erudition adds a certain solemnity to what at first seems an extremely unpleasant conceit.

In another poem d'Aubigné uses the imagery of the contemporary wars of religion; here the *I am* type of metaphor recurs:

> Ouy, mais ainsi qu'on voit en la guerre civile
> Les debats des plus grands, du foible et du vainqueur
> De leur doubteux combat laisser tout le malheur
> Au corps mort du païs, aux cendres d'une ville,
>
> Je suis le champ sanglant ou la fureur hostile
> Vomit le meurtre rouge, et la scytique horreur
> Qui saccage le sang, richesse de mon coeur,
> Et en se debattant font leur terre sterile.   (Sonnet VIII)

Yes, but as one sees in civil war the debates of the great, the weak, and the victor leave all the misfortune of their uncertain battles in the dead body of the countryside and in the ashes of cities; I am the bloody field whereon hostile fury vomits red murder, and the Scythian horror ravaging my blood, the wealth of my heart, leaves me a sterile land after the struggle.

Civil war is not an accidental catastrophe of the moment for d'Aubigné, as becomes clear in *Les Tragiques,* but a disturbance of the universe of theological proportions; the reference to sterile lands conjures up a long history of wars from biblical to Roman times. This permanent danger is reflected in the individual, the microcosm of renaissance thought, and so it takes the place among the inner conflicts of renaissance love poetry like the hostilities of fire and ice. In his poems to Diane Salviati, d'Aubigné distorts or abandons the Petrarchist basis of sixteenth-century love poetry in a more consistent way than previous poets. He maintains, nevertheless, the structural peculiarity of Petrarchist metaphor in his transformations of it and substitutions for it: this is the relation between the outer and the inner, the world or lady and the poet's heart, the concrete and the figurative. The violence of late sixteenth-century French poetry sharpens this metaphorical principle to a far greater degree than do the more elegant figures dominant in cinquecento Italian lyric. Furthermore, the construction of metaphors of this type will remain a major device in poetry for some time to come.

VI

The movement in French poetry we have been examining represents a turning away from the conception of the smooth, γλαφυρός lyric. Lyrics of the latter type were written, of course: much of the love poetry of Du Bellay and other members of the Pléiade falls into this category, and Desportes, whose style varies considerably, often wrote sonnets in the "pleasing" manner, whose limited vocabulary and traditional commonplaces can be attributed to the close imitation of Italian poetry, for which he is well known. In England the ornamental style arrived late, but what is especially striking about the form it took is that we find that whole new aspect of lyric which C. S. Lewis called "golden verse." Golden verse is not necessarily great poetry or even a sustained manner; we find it occurring in the work of undistinguished poets such as the anonymous author of the sonnet cycle *Licia* (1593).

> Seven are the lights that wander in the skies,
> And at these seven I wonder in my love:
> So see the moon, how pale she doth arise,
> Standing amazed as though she durst not move;
> So is my sweet much paler than the snow,
> Constant her looks, those looks that cannot change.[18]

Typical of the golden manner are the elegant sound patterns, the small but significant syntactic turn in the sixth line, and the way in which the moon is evoked with some care—we pass from the moon to the lady of the sonnet cycle in a subtle, nicely imagistic fashion. This is a very different kind of style from the allegorical or semi-abstract images that characterize minor Petrarchism; in these lines the moon has a concrete vividness unlike the largely symbolic sun in countless sonnets. Best of all, we might compare this very real moon with the boat or ship which symbolically but not very vividly ploughs the deep in a favorite Petrarchist allegory. A certain reality

18. Sidney Lee (ed.), *Elizabethan Sonnets* (2 vols.; New York, 1964), II, poem XXV.

of the terms of comparison sets off this English poetry from the common Italian or French sonnet manner.

Golden style may consist only of an occasional juxtaposition of words, as in these lines on vain effort: "Unto remorse who goes about to move her / Pursues the wingèd winds and tills the shore." These winds and shore have, thanks to the beauty of the diction, no purely abstract existence. In a poem by Robert Greene we find what might seem impossible; fresh diction is used in a poem on Amor, though the *topos* is commonplace: "Cupid abroad was latèd in the night, / His wings were wet with ranging in the rain." It would be easy, of course, to exemplify golden style from Shakespeare's *Sonnets* or even from those of a lesser but distinguished craftsman like Samuel Daniel (*Delia*, 1594). What must be emphasized, however, is that there appears to be a genuine period style which characterizes sonnets, some poetic drama, certain narrative poems, and lyrics or songs from plays. In regard to plays, it is noteworthy that one of the most famous golden lyrics was written by a man who is known more for his prose than for his poems; the following lines are from a song in Thomas Nashe's *Summer's Last Will and Testament* (1600):

> Beauty is but a flower
> Which wrinkles will devour:
> Brightness falls from the air,
> Queens have died young and fair,
> Dust hath closed Helen's eye.
> I am sick, I must die.
>   Lord, have mercy on us![19]

The way in which *wrinkles* is juxtaposed to *flower* rather than to *beauty*, the term *brightness*, which seems to come from some duecento Italian poem rather than from Petrarchist language, and the final syntactic connection of *dust* and *eye*—all these details show at once an acquaintance with the major dictional conventions and a certain independence from them.

The notion of *piacevolezza* in diction, of middle-style beauty as a

19. William Percy, "Coelia," I, *ibid.*; Robert Greene, "Orpharion," in J. Churton Collins (ed.), *The Plays and Poems of Robert Greene* (Freeport, N.Y., 1970), II; Thomas Nashe, "In Plague Time," in E. K. Chambers (ed.), *The Oxford Book of Sixteenth Century Verse* (London, 1932).

conspicuous esthetic end, thus received a remarkable reinforcement and new direction in England, when such an idea was largely spent in sixteenth-century France and Italy. We await at present a detailed account of just how English lyric style in its formation obviated the stale phraseology of so much continental poetry. A study of the structural along with the esthetic history of English—a kind of examination almost unknown in the English-speaking world—should provide some kind of answer.

The technical range of the English sonneteers is close to that of French poets in the sense that they can be said to have evolved a rhetoric more in accordance with the possibilities of their own language than with those of the classicizing Italian lyric, with its heavy reliance on hyperbaton for elegant effect. However, at the time when the Elizabethan sonnet was just coming into being, French poets had been divising figures and effects incompatible with the smooth style: lexical adventuresomeness, a cultivation of sound effects of the more extreme sort, enumeration, various types of unusual word distribution and repetition, the simile reduced to the copula with a noun, and finally, an especially intense exploitation of the contrast between the concrete and the figurative or abstract.[20] Furthermore, the theory of the suitable style for the sonnet was a subject of disagreement in the second half of the sixteenth century. While Italian critics, adhering to more classical ideas, considered it a middle-style genre, Ronsard referred to his style in the *Amours* as Pindarization, thus ascribing to it a kind of diction not traditionally associated with short lyrics. There is, of course, nothing Pindaric about the *Amours* in any exact sense, but Ronsard's willingness to elevate in theory the style of the sonnet is significant; Du Bellay, not long before, had said that the sonnet and the high-style ode differed only through the former's rules of versification. In Italy, Tasso was much concerned with the range of the sonnet, since it occupied so enormous a place

20. Petrarch's enumerations are mostly polysyndetic and therefore conjunctive in effect; there are only two prominent examples of disjunctive enumeration in the *Canzoniere*: the famous line "Fior, frondi, erbe, ombre, antri, onde, aure soavi" (303) and the first quatrain of the sonnet "Non Tesin, Po, Vari, Arno, Adige, et Tebro" (148). As is often the case, Petrarch seems to have invented something without extensively exploiting it.

in contemporary literature, and concluded that its style might be pitched at any level.[21]

It is obvious, in any case, that from Ronsard to d'Aubigné we find a style which fits neither the notions of a smooth middle style nor of a stately, grandiose high style. We must have recourse to the rhetorical theories parallel to the usual three-style division, as did many of the more sophisticated critics of the late renaissance. Demetrius had distinguished a fourth style, the δεινός, which is found in works of great power, as well as the μεγαλοπρεπής manner, or style of high decorum. The δεινός "character," to use the old Greek term for style, was rough in sound or thought, forceful even to the point of violence, hyperbolic, asyndetic, ironic, and abrupt. Dionysius of Halicarnassus was concerned with stylistic extremes: the smooth lyric style of Sappho, on the one hand, and, on the other, the rough, harsh, αὐστηρός manner exemplified by Pindar and Aeschylus. We see that his rough-style poets belong, according to the common classification, in the high-style group. For Homer, Dionysius distinguished a mixed style, combining extremes, which reflects other rhetoricians' habit of pointing out various levels of style in the great epics. Hermogenes, for his part, found that the grand style reflected a variety of effects, from gravity and splendor to asperity and vehemence.[22] Quintilian, who was more interested in detail than in generally characterizing styles, found there was a bold or *audacior ornatus* differing from the pleasing middle-style ornament. And finally, Aristotle, before the systems of style were thought of, often used ξενός and ξενικός in his *Rhetoric* to characterize an extreme of poetic diction: the meaning ranges from "unfamiliar" to "strange," and some of his examples certainly suit the notion of strangeness. Therefore we have ample evidence and precedent for seeing the harsh, more contrastive, more daring elements of style as efforts to rise above middle style, while not aiming at the stately magniloquence usually associated with the idea of high style. An instinctive drift toward this kind of style can be discerned in Scève and Michelan-

---

21. See Bernard Weinberg, *A History of Literary Criticism in the Italian Renaissance* (2 vols.; Chicago, 1974), I, 213.

22. See Annabel M. Patterson, *Hermogenes and the Renaissance: Seven Ideas of Style* (Princeton, 1970).

gelo, with their peculiar images which are completely devoid of conceitful wit in the middle-style fashion. The ostentatiousness of their figures reflects pure intensity, rather than the self-consciousness of delightful, *piacevole* verse. Later in the century, when ancient rhetoric had been more fully explored, there was perhaps more awareness on the part of d'Aubigné of the stylistic prototypes, largely Greek, of contorted and vehement style.

The term mannerism, one of the more recent borrowings from the critical vocabulary of the fine arts, presents many problems when applied to poetry, but it is not an unclear notion if we contrast the peculiar developments of the French lyric with Italian classicism in the Bembist fashion. Usually mannerism is taken to refer to a strained, contorted, often morbid style, as opposed to the more epideictic, expansive baroque style, with its delight in phenomena. Discussions of mannerism, like those of the baroque, tend to be thematic or to mingle primarily thematic considerations with some stylistic ones. On the whole the notion of mannerism seems to me of greater practical than theoretical value and inferior, in any case, to a close rhetorical description. I shall occasionally speak of mannerism, but with a certain diffidence.

CHAPTER 3

Some Uses of Low Style

I

The term *low style* unfortunately tends to conjure up the idea of low characters, base emotions, and coarse speech. The more usual Latin terms for this style have no such pejorative connotations; it is called the *genus subtile, tenue,* or *extenuatum.* The customary Greek word, ἰσχνός which is translated by "plain style," is fairly neutral, except for the fact that it suggests a total absence of ornamentation, an inaccurate description for all low styles. Elegance, indeed, was felt to be a possibility in low style. As for the Christian *sermo humilis,* for which "low style" is a more accurate rendering, we shall not treat it here.

There is perhaps no term in rhetorical tradition that covers more ideas than *low style,* and it is for each one to judge whether the expression is strained or not by being applied to a complex of varied modes of discourse. Hermogenes evidently thought so, and what we call low style is divided up into several categories in his treatise *On the Ideas* [of style]. To begin with, narration, being factual and often direct, usually belongs to low style. Argumentation, or proving, is another use of low style, suggesting a relatively cool, logical presentation rather than a heated attempt at persuasion. Proverbs and common wisdom are also covered by low style, as, of course, is satire, provided it is not too grand in its verbal means. There is, in addition, a group of low-style genres—epistle, epigram, formal satire, eclogue, and elegy—and with regard to the latter two especially, we shall see that the range of effects included in low style is distinctly more varied than the adjectives *low* or *plain* suggest. We shall begin with the question of narration.

Ariosto's *Orlando Furioso* is among the most insistently narrative of poems that tell a story, as the traditional comparison with Tasso's high-style *Gerusalemme Liberata* reveals.[1] Ariosto is a master of what Hermogenes calls the rapid style, which in the *Orlando* is swift but not jerky; the narrative movement is nimble and elegant. The ironic tone fits the low-style category, and Ariosto even occasionally uses a somewhat popular-sounding expression, as in the well known sixth line of the following octaves:[2]

> Bagna talor ne la chiara onda e fresca
> l'asciutte labra, e con le man diguazza,
> acciò che de le vene il calore esca
> che gli ha acceso il portar de la corazza.
> Né maraviglia è già ch'ella gl'incresca;
> che non è stato un far vedersi in piazza:
> ma senza mai posar, d'arme guernito,
> tremila miglia ognor correndo era ito.
>
> Quivi stando, il destrier ch'avea lasciato
> tra le più dense frasche alla fresca ombra,
> per fuggir si rivolta, spaventato
> di non so che, che dentro al bosco adombra:
> e fa crollar sì il mirto ove è legato,
> che de le frondi intorno il piè gli ingombra:
> crollar fa il mirto e fa cader la foglia;
> né succede però che se ne scioglia.[3]   (VI, 25–26)

At times he wets his dry lips in the clear fresh stream and stirs it with his hands, that the heat kindled in him by the wearing of his corselet might leave his veins. No wonder it annoyed him, for this has not been a showing-off in the public square, but without ever stopping, clad in armor, he has been rushing on three thousand miles every hour. While he was there, the steed, that he had left among the densest bushes in the pleasant shade, turned to flee, terror-stricken by I know not what that hides in the grove; he makes the myrtle to which he is fastened so shake that he litters the leaves around its feet; he makes the myrtle shake and makes its leaves fall, but he does not by that succeed in getting loose.

We observe that the style is highly clausal; that is, finite verbs are especially frequent, moving the action onward. We might note, by

---

1. On the narrative quality, see C. P. Brand, *Ludovico Ariosto: A Preface to the "Orlando Furioso"* (Edinburgh, 1947), 144.
2. See Dieter Kremers, *Der "Rasende Roland" des Ludovico Ariosto* (Stuttgart, 1973), 198.
3. Ludovico Ariosto, *Orlando Furioso*, ed. Lanfranco Caretti (Milan, 1963), VI, 25–26, hereinafter cited in the text. Translations are from Ludovico Ariosto, *Orlando Furioso: An English Translation with Introduction, Notes, and Index*, tr. Allan Gilbert (2 vols.; New York, 1954).

contrast, that Hermogenes very specifically speaks of the dominance of the noun in high style, and something of the sort seems implied in other rhetoricians as well. The word order is worth noting. The verbs often come at the end of the clause, sometimes because the clause is short and has no object, an effect of rapidity, and sometimes because verbs make handy rimes. Ariosto uses little hyperbaton except for transposed prepositional phrases, again a convenience of versification; inversions of the verbal complexes like *stato sono*, which seem to have roots in early Italian speech;[4] and placing verbs at the end of the clause after an object. Many of his subject-verb inversions are so common as hardly to be called hyperbaton. In other words, the syntax is close to speech, with the exception of a few devices to aid prosodic construction. In this way, Ariosto's poetic syntax is more like that of French than that of the elaborately hyperbatic, classicizing Italian style of the cinquecento lyric.

In respect to the question of hyperbaton, the history of the text of the *Orlando* is significant. The first, shorter edition of the poem was published in 1516, and its language bears strong traces of Emilian dialect. In the successive editions (1521 and 1532), the influence of Bembo's doctrine is felt to the extent that the language is largely Tuscanized or made to conform to that of Petrarch. However, this applies to morphology and vocabulary: the sentence structure of the poem never assumed the typical Bembist configurations, which are middle-style and distinctly hyperbatic. Thus Ariosto maintained a certain low-style syntactic color, while accepting the general idea of Bembist purity of language.

The use of the octave in narration, which goes back to Boccaccio, curiously parallels the rise of the sonnet as a major form. But the final couplet of the octave, which is not found in the Italian sonnet, tends to give a sense of ending and definition to the stanza, which is sometimes sharpened to the point of epigram. Opposed to this is the grave movement of high style, with its lengthier sentences and greater continuity.

Pure low style, however, is not customary among major works of the sixteenth century. The sense of rhetorical experimentation was

4. See Gerhard Rohlfs, *Historische Grammatik der Italienischen Sprache* (3 vols.; Bern, 1954), III, 208–23.

too great, and although the basis of the *Orlando Furioso* is low style, Ariosto embellishes his poem with long similes, geographical periphrases, echoes of Virgil (as in that last line of the poem, where Rodomonte's shade flees like Turnus' in the *Aeneid*), and set pieces like the epideictic genealogy of the house of Este in Canto III. We should note, however, a varying and sometimes indefinable quality of irony in the high-style touches. Certainly the Homeric simile (II, 5) in which knights are compared to fighting dogs is of ambiguous elevation. Shifts of style are generally condoned by the rhetoricians, especially in long works, but Ariosto's sometimes have a questionable purity. A good example of his ambiguity lies in the famous rose passage in the first canto:

> La verginella è simile alla rosa,
> ch'in bel giardin su la nativa spina
> mentre sola e sicura si riposa,
> né gregge né pastor se le avicina;
> l'aura soave e l'alba rugiadosa,
> l'acqua, la terra al suo favor s'inchina:
> gioveni vaghi e donne inamorate
> amano averne e seni e tempie ornate.
>
> Ma non sì tosto dal materno stelo
> rimossa viene e dal suo ceppo verde,
> che quanto avea dagli uomini e dal cielo
> favor, grazia e bellezza, tutto perde.
> La vergine che'l fior, di che più zelo
> che de' begli occhi e de la vita aver de',
> lascia altrui côrre, il pregio ch'avea inanti
> perde nel cor di tutti gli altri amanti.   (I, 42–43)

The young virgin is like the rose that neither flock nor shepherd draws near to while it rests alone and secure in a beautiful garden on its native thorn. The soft breeze and the dewy dawn, the water, the earth bend to favor her; gracious youths and enamored women love to have their breasts and foreheads decked with her. But no sooner is she taken from the maternal stalk and the green bush than she loses all the favor, grace, and beauty, however much, that she had from men and from heaven. The virgin who lets anyone pluck that flower for which she ought to have more fervor than for her beautiful eyes and for her life, loses the worth she had before in the hearts of all her other lovers.

One of the knights then picks up the theme:

> Corrò la fresca e matutina rosa,
> che, tardando, stagion perder potria.
> So ben ch'a donna non si può far cosa

che più soave e più piacevol sia,
ancor che se ne mostri disdegnosa,
e talor mesta e flebil se ne stia:
non starò per repulsa o finto sdegno,
ch'io non adombri e incarni il mio desegno.   (I, 58)

I shall pluck the fresh and morning rose, for, if I delay, I may lose my chance. I know well that a thing cannot be done to a woman that will be sweeter and pleasanter, even though she may show herself indignant and sometimes be sad and tearful at it. Because of repulse or pretended wrath I shall not keep from forming and carrying out my plan.

Some of Ariosto's commentators, evidently starved for conventional poeticness, exclaim over the exquisite lyricism and immortal beauty of the first rose passage, whereas its imitativeness and the general context of the poem suggest the unserious, low-style quality of the octaves, to say nothing of the later use the theme is put to. We shall see other examples of this kind of lyricism which belies the notion of unrelieved plainness in low style, for which *genus tenue,* or "slight style," would be the more suggestive term. Of course, there is an amusing paradox about Ariosto's use of low style. Aside from modern commentators' sentimentality over the rose, cinquecento commentators allegorized the whole of the *Orlando Furioso* into an endless series of platitudes about the various virtues and their triumph. The desire to elevate material above the traditional connotations of its stylistic level was, as we have seen, a prevailing characteristic of sixteenth-century thinking about literature; in this case, it has generally seemed to modern readers bizarre, foolish, or unwarranted by the author's whole literary orientation, but we cannot be sure that Ariosto would have found this urge toward loftiness of interpretation altogether reprehensible. It is harmless in that it does not damage the text for anyone who disagrees with it, and the paradoxical quality that reading virtues into the *Orlando Furioso* might seem to have is not out of keeping with the union of wit and hidden profundity that a sixteenth-century writer such as Rabelais makes so much of.

II

No effort was ever made, so far as I know, to allegorize Ronsard's very explicit use of low style. After the *Amours,* still in the decade of his greatest stylistic inventiveness, the 1550s, Ronsard announced and demonstrated, in the *Continuation des amours* (1555), his determination to write in a "beau stille bas." It is usually said that he did so because his courtly audience disliked his erudite poetry; nevertheless the *Amours* had been a successful, widely read book, and it seems evident to me that Ronsard's change in style came about because he had simply exhausted his earlier sonnet manner. Ronsard was a serious, tireless investigator of styles and not merely an entertainer.

Low style was imposed by tradition for the subject of the *Continuation des amours*—the beauty of the peasant girl Marie and Ronsard's involvement with her. The social level of subject matter determined style, implicitly in classical literature and quite explicitly from the time the medieval scheme known as the wheel of Virgil demonstrated that each of Virgil's three works represented a rise in social level along with style, beginning at the bottom with shepherds and low style.

Many commentators, unfamiliar with the theory of rhetoric, have been confused as to how a *stille bas* can be *beau* and have been disturbed at finding a certain amount of Petrarchan or other ornamentation in the *Continuation des amours*. We can nicely demonstrate the differences between the *beau stille bas* and middle-style lyric by comparing a sonnet to Marie with a famous Horatian ode to Cassandre. Here is Marie's poem:

> Je vous envoye un bouquet de ma main
> Que j'ai ourdy de ces fleurs epanies:
> Qui ne les eust à ce vespre cueillies,
> Flaques à terre elles cherroient demain.
>
> Cela vous soit un exemple certain
> Que voz beautés, bien qu'elles soient fleuries,
> En peu de tems cherront toutes flétries,
> Et periront, comme ces fleurs, soudain.[5]

I am sending you a bouquet I have made, weaving it of these fully opened flowers. If they had not been gathered this evening, they would lie limp on the ground tomorrow. Let that be a reliable example to you, for your beauties, although they now are in full flower, shortly will wither and fall and die suddenly like these flowers.

---

5. Pierre de Ronsard, *Oeuvres complètes*, ed. Paul Laummonier (19 vols.; Paris, 1931–75), XXXV.

The quatrains are phrased in the manner of a demonstration, which the word *example* underscores. The slightly schematic proof does not preclude, however, a certain elegance, which the fourth line, with its expressive word order, shows especially. The idea of the comparison is consonant with middle-style lyric, though its elaboration is somewhat different. A conclusion follows in the tercets:

> Le tems s'en va, le tems s'en va, ma Dame:
> Las! le tems non, mais nous nous en allons,
> Et tost serons estendus sous la lame:
>
> Et des amours desquelles nous parlons,
> Quand serons morts n'en sera plus nouvelle:
> Pour-ce aimés moi, ce pendant qu'estes belle.

> Time is vanishing, time is vanishing, my lady. Alas, not time, but we, rather, are going to vanish, and soon will lie under death's stroke. And when we are dead, there will be no more question of the love we talk about: therefore love me while you are beautiful.

There is a certain colloquial familiarity in the initial repetition; *ma Dame* is a less high-flown address than what we find elsewhere but a trifle ironic since Ronsard is addressing a peasant girl. the penultimate line has the air, if not of a proverb, at least of popular wisdom, which is part of the low manner.

"Mignonne, allons voir si la rose" ("Ode à Cassandre" in *Amours*, 1553 edition) is too well known to need quotation in entirety; the first stanza will demonstrate the differences from the Marie poem:

> Mignonne, allons voir si la rose
> Qui ce matin avoit desclose
> Sa robe de pourpre au Soleil,
> A point perdu ceste vesprée
> Les plis de sa robe pourprée,
> Et son teint au vostre pareil.

> Dear one, let us go see whether the rose, which this morning opened its purple robe in the sun, has by this evening lost the folds of its purple robe and its color soft like that of your cheeks.

The image of the rose clad in a *royal* garment is worked out in a sentence spanning six lines. The insistence on color and the lady's complexion is far more evocative than the vague "beauties" of the other poem. This is a middle-style poem classified as an ode by the fact that Horace's brief lyrics, just as Pindar's high-style poems, were called odes; and the care for decorative, descriptive effect is characteristic of the middle manner.[6] If we go back to the rose passage in Ariosto, we find that, although Ariosto's style is at first decorative and epithetical, he concludes with a (doubtless ironic) show of stern moralism, which is not at all in keeping with the lyric devoted to beauty but is rather a low-style intrusion.

In the long, discursive "À son livre" concluding the *Nouvelle continuation des amours* (1556), Ronsard mentions Catullus, Ovid, and Tibullus as his models, thereby specifically identifying his *beau stille bas* as that of the elegy. The curious thing about the elegy in the early and middle sixteenth century is that its stylistic range was more clearly conceived of than the actual structure and content of the genre.[7] The *genus subtile floridius*, the somewhat ornamented low style, by no means devoid of figures but free of sustained sequences of tropes, is reasonably well reproduced in the vernacular and written in couplets in France or terza rima in Italy. The neo-Latin poets of the quattrocento had especially favored the elegiac couplet but had not limited it to the subject of love, as the Romans mostly did; *poésie des ruines*, death laments or epicedia, epistles, and familiar discursive pieces, all received treatment in the classical couplet. In the vernacular, elegy came then to mean a medium-length poem often but not exclusively dealing with love. The title *elegy* was taken from and given to poems in a rather capricious fashion as they were republished; the history of Ronsard's elegies is exemplary in this respect.

Since Ronsard was known as the *prince des élégies*, his work in this genre can exemplify the general idea of the elegy in the sixteenth century. He had moved further than his predecessor Marot in the direction of ornamenting the elegy and making it into a smoothly articulated poem. The small group of later pieces addressed to "Genevre," about whom we know little, is especially interesting:

> Sur la fin de Juillet que le chaut violent
> Rendoit de toutes pars le ciel estincelant,
> Un soir, à mon malheur, je me baignoy dans Seine,
> Où je te vy danser sur la rive prochaine,

6. Ronsard was one of the first, certainly the first in France, to imitate Horace' lyrics.

7. For a synthesis of the subject, see John E. Clark, *Élégie: The Fortune of a Classical Genre in Sixteenth-Century France* (The Hague, 1975).

> Foulant du pied le sable, & remplissant d'amour
> Et de ta douce voix tous les bords d'alentour.
> Tout nud je me vins mettre avecq' ta compaignie,
> Où dansant je brulay d'une ardeur infinie,
> Voyant sous la clarté brunette du croissant
> Ton oeil brun, à l'envy de l'autre apparoissant.
> Là je baisay ta main pour premiere acointance,
> Car autrement de toy je n'avois cognoissance:
> Puis d'un agile bond je resautay dans l'eau,
> Pensant qu'elle esteindroit mon premier feu nouveau.
> Il advint autrement, car au milieu des ondes
> Je me senty lié de tes deux tresses blondes,
> Et le feu de tes yeux qui les eaux penetra
> Maugré la froide humeur dedans mon coeur entra.   (XII, 257)

Toward the end of July when the violent heat made the sky glitter all over, one evening, for my misfortune, I went swimming in the Seine, where I saw you dancing on the nearby bank. You were dancing on the sand and filling all the shore with love and your sweet voice. Stripped, I came to join you and your friends and danced with infinite ardor, observing, in the quarter moon's dark light, your dark eye which resembled it. Then I kissed your hand in greeting, for I did not know at all who you were. Then with a light jump I leaped back into the water, thinking that it would put out my new flame. Things happened otherwise, for in the middle of the waves, I felt myself bound by your two blond tresses, and the fire of your eyes, penetrating the water, despite the coldness of the element, entered my heart.

This piece is close to some of the best Roman elegies in that it sketches a scene, a realistic and therefore low-style one, but Ronsard terminates the passage on his meeting Genevre with Petrarchist word plays on the figurative and concrete: the imagery elevates and idealizes the episode rather beyond the customary range of Roman elegy. We might contrast the tone and style of Ronsard's poem with one of Propertius' finest elegies, in which he finds Cynthia sleeping:

> Qualis Thesea iacuit cedente carina
>   languida desertis Gnosia litoribus;
> qualis et accubuit primo Cepheia somno
>   libera iam duris cotibus Andromede . . .[8]

She lay like Ariadne, the daughter of Cnossus, languid on the desert shore of Naxos, while Theseus' ship receded into the distance; like Andromeda, the daughter of Cepheus, as she first fell asleep after being freed from the hard cliff . . .

---

8. Propertius, *Élégies*, ed. D. Paganelli (Paris, 1947), I, 3.

The mythological comparisons are developed further. Then the heroic manner breaks off, and we learn that the poet is drunk and has forced his way into Cynthia's house:

> ebria cum multo traherem uestigia Baccho
>   et quaterent sera nocte facem pueri.
> Hanc ego, nondum etiam sensus deperditus omnis,
>   molliter impresso conor adire toro;
> et, quamuis duplici correptum ardore iuberent
>   hac Amor hac Liber, durus uterque deus,
> subiecto leuiter positam temptare lacerto
>   osculaque admota sumere et arma manu,
> non tamen ausus eram dominae turbare quietem,
>   expertae metuens iurgia saeuitiae . . .

So she appeared, as I staggered on my feet, drunk with much wine, and my slaves waved their torches in the late night. Softly, for I had not lost all my senses, I tried to approach her and sat down on the bed. And, although Love and Bacchus, both imperious gods, as I burned with urges from both of them, ordered me to attack with kisses, lightly slipping my arm under her, and to disarm her, I did not dare disturb my mistress' sleep, fearing the outbursts of her all too familiar fury . . .

The military metaphor of Roman elegy occurs, and as usual, it forms a tacit stylistic commentary. The elegist, as he states openly in various poems, is not up to writing epic, the celebration of real battles; rather, he makes conquests in bed, and this is a witty way of admitting the lowness of his subject matter and the essential inferiority of his way of life to the old Roman martial virtues. A striking image occurs:

> donec diuersas praecurrens luna fenestras,
>   luna moraturis sedula luminibus,
> compositos leuibus radiis patefecit ocellos.
>   Sic ait in molli fixa toro cubitum:
> "tandem te nostro referens iniuria lecto
>   alterius clausis expulit e foribus?"

Meanwhile, as the moon gleamed through the windows opposite, the moon attentive with its lingering light, Cynthia opened her closed eyes at its gentle beams and said, leaning on her elbow in the soft bed, "So a refusal has brought you back to my bed; someone else threw you out the door?"

Cynthia's words are harsh and weary, and we see again the contrast between the traditional poetic material (the moon and its light) and the sour realities of the poet's situation. Ovid, too, though less bitter and basically less serious in the *Amores*, likes the mock-heroic effect created by mythological reference and military metaphor in scenes that are essentially low and commonplace.

It is clear that the whole spirit of Roman elegy was foreign to the French and Italian lyric poets of the sixteenth century, steeped as they were in idealizing, courtly traditions. Only at the end of the century, with Donne's *Elegies*, do we find a major poet recapturing some of the bluntness, realism, and wit in imagery that the Roman elegists had at their best. The cultivation of the low-style elegy, however, was not a negligible factor in Ronsard's poetic development. The elegies mark a trend away from rare vocabulary and anticipate the very French taste for subdued rhetoric that was to culminate in the neoclassical movement.[9] It is notable that in the *Sonnets pour Hélène* (1578), where the conceits of love poetry reappear, the hyperbole lacks the strong color of the *Amours*; the conceit is enfeebled. We also observe that Hélène de Surgères is represented in many familiar ways, walking, talking, or gazing out the window. Such situations never occur in the sonnets for Cassandre. Finally, the most famous of all the *Sonnets pour Hélène*, "Quand vous serez bien vieille," opens with a distinctly low-style description of an old woman laboring at her household tasks.

III

The eclogue or pastoral was in many ways an easier genre to establish in European literature than the love elegy, which is intimately connected with the mores of ancient Rome. The pastoral does not really have to take place in any specific geographical location; it is stylized and derives from a very few Greek and Latin texts: the *Idylls* of Theocritus, Virgil's *Eclogues*, the remains of Bion and Moschus' work, and some minor Roman pieces. There was a vast production of pastorals, much of it in neo-Latin, and a general tendency to adopt situations, characters, and even passages from the Greco-Roman models.[10] There tend to be two strains in the genre: the rustic and mildly comic and the pastoral celebrating a death, a variant de-

9. See Louis Terreaux, *Ronsard correcteur de ses oeuvres* (Geneva, 1968).
10. See W. Leonard Grant, *Neo-Latin Literature and the Pastoral* (Chapel Hill, 1965).

rived from the old Greek death elegy. In Europe, Mantuan created the archetype of the somewhat buffoonish pastoral, devising for it a curious kind of rustic neo-Latin, which is a delight to read. The more elegant death pastoral is represented by some of the finest pieces of Pontano and Sannazaro. Of the vernacular eclogues, there are skillful and entertaining ones, such as Ronsard's few attempts at the genre, and in most of these, as often in the neo-Latin pastorals, the work becomes either an allegory or a transposition of real people into a pastoral setting and convention. This double level of the pastoral accords with certain interpretations of Virgil's work and gives resonance and immediacy to what otherwise is an extremely remote low-style convention. Very little of this vast pastoral literature had more than a contemporary interest. However, Spenser's "Aeglogues" are, in part, an important source of later English style.[11] Most of *The Shepheardes Calender* is Mantuan-rustic, and a good deal of religious polemic is brought in, after the custom of making modern allusions in poems removed in other respects from any particular English reality. A notable feature is the use of archaism and dialect, which gives a more pronounced countrified savor to the poems than the somewhat neutral language of Ronsard, for example. Spenser's "November" and "December" eclogues, however, are less conspicuously rustic and contain the earliest examples of the poetic diction associated with English nature poetry, which is such a large part of English poetry itself. An unknown lady's death is lamented in "November":

> But nowe sike happy cheere is turned to heauie chaunce,
> Such pleasaunce now displast by dolors dint:
> All Musick sleepes, where death doth leade the daunce,
> And shepherds wonted solace is extinct.
> The blew in black, the greene in gray is tinct,
>   the gaudie girlonds deck her graue,
>   The faded flowres her corse embraue.
>   O heauie herse,
> Morne nowe my Muse, now morne with the teares besprint.
>   O carefull verse.
>   . . . .
> Ay me that dreerie death should strike so mortall stroke,

11. See Arthur Sherbo, *English Poetic Diction from Chaucer to Wordsworth* (East Lansing, Mich., 1975).

> That can vndoe Dame natures kindly course:
> The faded lockes fall from the loftie oke,
> the flouds do gaspe, for dryed is theyr source,
> And flouds of teares flowe in theyr stead perforse.
>   The mantled medowes mourne,
>   Theyr sondry colours tourne.
>   O heauie herse,
> The heauens doe melt in teares without remorse.
>   O carefull verse.[12]

We recognize some of the most characteristic terms of English poetry here: *pleasaunce, dolor, wonted, tinct, gaudy, besprint, dreary, kindly, lofty, flood,* and *mantled.* Elsewhere, the adjectives ending in *y,* so familiar in later periods of poetry, play a large role: *dainty, pretty, fiery, weary, bushy, mazy, craggy, hoary, grisly, ghastly, weedy,* and so forth. Other Spenserian terms, such as *baleful, barren, sere, blasted* (of flowers), *eke, yclad, welkin, wight,* were also to persist in the poetic tradition. The importance of "November" and "December" is all the clearer when we realize that they are imitations of Marot's attempts at the eclogue. In Marot's work the eclogues stand out as some exotic thing, filled with borrowings at first or second hand from the ancient pastorals. They are recognizably very different from the rest of his poetry and had no particular influence on the major currents of French poetry after him. Aside from the use of words necessary to translate borrowed commonplaces, they show nothing which could be called a distinctive, thought-out style. Their major interest lies in the way they show the low-style pastoral aiming at lofty matters, for royal figures are their subject. Pastoral thus contradicts the theory of low-style content by its allegorical method. Spenser's eclogues, on the other hand, show no such interesting use of transposition but, rather, derive their importance from their linguistic medium. One strain of English poetry continued to draw on Spenser's pastoral language through the eighteenth-century, and it is not an insignificant strain if we remember that "Lycidas" is part of it. The framework and much of the diction of Spenser's eclogues are recognizably intended as low style, but seen from the perspective of later English poetry, Spenser's low style in "November" and "December" acquires that relative elevation which was to characterize some distinguished

12. Edmund Spenser, *The Shepherd's Calendar,* ed. W. L. Renwick (London, 1930).

examples of pastoral in the following century. Again, the principles of classical rhetoric were undergoing a modification in keeping with their purely empirical origin and flexible character.

IV

The pre-Petrarchist native strain of English lyric in the sixteenth century has been the object of some study, deriving from a remarkable essay by Yvor Winters. Far from characterizing all the poetry before Sidney and Spenser as "drab style," to use C. S. Lewis' term, Winters distinguished, within a narrow technical range, poems of "restrained and refined subtleties," whose virtues are classicizing in nature.[13] This lyric is commonly aphoristic and not unrelated in its ironies to satire. One of Winters' examples suggests the stylistic ambit of this verse:

> The common speech is, spend and God will send;
> But what sends he? a bottle and a bag,
> A staff, a wallet, and a woeful end,
> For such as list in bravery to brag.
> Then if thou covet coin enough to spend,
> Learn first to spend thy budget at the brink,
> So shall the bottom be the faster bound:
> But he that list with lavish hand to link
> In like expense, a penny with a pound,
> May chance at last to sit aside and shrink
> His hare-brained head without Dame Dainty's Door.[14]

This is a clausal, nonepithetical style, relying on nimble movement and careful choice of nouns. The proverbial-sounding "Dame Dainty" has that purely English quality which is one of the charms of this verse, as is its sententious wit, for which didacticism would be too strong and pompous a word. There is no reason to call such verse medieval, as has been done, because it is not Petrarchist. The renais-

13. Yvor Winters, "The Sixteenth-Century Lyric in England: A Critical and Historical Reinterpretation," in Paul J. Alpers (ed.), *Elizabethan Poetry: Modern Essays in Criticism* (New York, 1967), 93–125; Clive Staples Lewis, *English Literature in the Sixteenth Century* (Oxford, 1962). See also Wesley Trimpi, *Ben Jonson's Poems: A Study of the Plain Style* (Stanford, 1962), 119; and Douglas L. Petersen, *English Lyric from Wyatt to Donne* (Princeton, 1967).
14. George Gascoigne, untitled poem from the collection *Flowers*, quoted in Winters, "The Sixteenth-Century Lyric," 98.

sance taste for aphorism is reflected frequently in the sixteenth-century theorists of poetry. George Gascoigne (1542–1577), according to Winters, is the master of this school, and certainly one may prefer this verse to the none-too-graceful Petrarchism of Wyatt.[15]

This preference for English poetry before the great wave of "sugared" Petrarchism reflects the modern taste for the unadorned and colloquial and is just the reverse of the popular feeling about the capacities of English which began to prevail after 1575 or so.[16] There was a *questione della lingua* in England, as in Italy and France, but the terms of it were slightly different in accordance with the nature or supposed nature of the language. Italian poets had adopted an archaic and stylized form of Italian which, with greater or lesser subtlety, reflected the Latin origins of the language better than could any spoken form of sixteenth-century Italian. Faced with the overwhelmingly superior grammatical suppleness of Latin, French defenders of their language, like Ronsard or the philologist Henri Estienne, found a fanciful similarity between French and Greek. (The existence of a definite article in both was one of their key arguments.) The analogy with Greek was ennobling and suggested a wealth of lexical innovations. English had been generally considered rough and indocile before the great vogue of writing Petrarchist sonnets and other lyrics established the language as being comparable in literary terms with Italian and French. However, attitudes toward language do not change all at once, and the recurrence of a colloquial element in English verse with Sidney's later sonnets and with Donne suggests that for them a certain bluntness or roughness was the authentic mark of English and that the Petrarchist manner was foreign and artificial.

These feelings about language are, of course, a bit mythic and mysterious, like notions of national character. It is in a sense erroneous to compare an Italian poetic idiom remote from the *Umgangssprache* of any part of Italy with English low-style colloquialism. Presumably there could have been a more colloquial kind of Italian lyric; however, there was not, except in dialect, and so the identifica-

15. *Cf.* "the laborious difficulty of Wyatt": W. L. Renwick, *Edmund Spenser: An Essay on Renaissance Poetry* (London, 1925), 70.
16. See Richard Foster Jones, *The Triumph of the English Language* (Stanford, 1953).

tion of plain style or colloquialism with the properly English style of poetry persisted and has had much adherence in the twentieth century. It is sometimes said that the poetry of the Romance languages is more rhetorical than that of English, but this idea reflects a simplistic conception of rhetoric, which embraces all kinds of styles. As we shall see, English poets in many cases developed a rhetoric peculiar to them, but it is a rhetoric all the same; indeed, to exploit the supposed roughness or familiarity of English, rather than trying to suppress it, constitutes quite a brilliant rhetorical idea.

In *Astrophel and Stella*, Sidney makes abundant ironic allusions to the tropes he is himself so generous with elsewhere:

> Let dainty wits cry on the sisters nine,
> That, bravely masked, their fancies may be told;
> Or Pindar's apes flaunt they in phrases fine,
> Enam'ling with pied flowers their thoughts of gold;
>
> Or else let them in statelier glory shine,
> Ennobling new found tropes with problems old;
> Or with strange similes enrich each line,
> Of herbs or beasts which Ind or Afric hold.[17]

This is not the gross anti-Petrarchism of the sixteenth-century parodies but a more serious objection to high-flown ornament. Sidney regularly punctuates his conceitful sonnets with critical introspection about the value of imagery and even writing itself:

> Come, let me write. And to what end? To ease
> A burthened heart. How can words ease, which are
> The glasses of thy daily vexing care?
> Oft cruel fights well pictured forth do please.
> . . . .
> What idler thing than speak and not be heard?
> What harder thing than smart and not to speak?
> Peace, foolish wit! with wit my wit is marred.
>
> Thus write I, while I doubt to write . . .[18]

Sidney's simultaneous delight in and mistrust of poetic idiom is a juxtaposition of the plain-style attitude, critical and even satiric, with techniques of the middle-style lyric.[19] It is unquestionably the

17. Philip Sidney, *Astrophel and Stella*, poem 3, in Robert M. Bender (ed.), *Five Courtier Poets of the English Renaissance* (New York, 1967).
18. *Ibid.*, poem 34.
19. See Neil L. Rudenstine, *Sidney's Poetic Development* (Cambridge, Mass., 1967).

feeling that the ornaments of the contemporary sonnet are borrowed, foreign, and put-on that leads Sidney to his bemused tone. He can do neither with nor entirely without this exotic plumage.

In Sidney, however, we have little more than a hint of what could be done with low style by itself or in confrontation with middle-style ornaments. Donne's extremely varied lyric production shows the range of effects that could be obtained from subtle combinations of styles.

Donne's low-style techniques take several forms, but one of the most important of these is the translation of characteristic middle-style material into a new mode. "A Feaver" is a good example to begin with: the initial thought is that with the death of a beloved lady, the world will be, if not destroyed, at least bereft of nobility:

> Oh doe not die, for I shall hate
>   All women so, when thou art gone,
> That thee I shall not celebrate,
>   When I remember, thou wast one.
>
> But yet thou canst not die, I know;
>   To leave this world behinde, is death,
> But when thou from this world wilt goe,
>   The whole world vapors with thy breath.
>
> Or if, when thou, the worlds soule, goest,
>   It stay, 'tis but thy carkasse then,
> The fairest woman, but thy ghost,
>   But corrupt wormes, the worthyest men.

Helen Gardner refers the reader to Petrarch for the prototype of this idea.[20] The subject is Laura's death:

> Ahi orbo mondo, ingrato,
> gran cagion ài di dover pianger meco,
> che quel bel ch'era in te perduto ài seco.
>
>   Caduta è la tua gloria
>   . . . .
> Nel tuo partir partì del mondo Amore
> e Cortesia, e'l sol cadde del cielo.[21]

Rubel notes the absence of archaisms in Sidney and the fact that, aside from compound words, his usage is close to prose. See Veré L. Rubel, *Poetic Diction in the English Renaissance: From Skelton Through Spenser* (New York, 1941), 203.

20. See John Donne, *The Elegies and the Songs and Sonnets*, ed. Helen Gardner (Oxford, 1965), 187. All quotations from the *Songs and Sonnets* are taken from this edition.

21. Robert M. Durling (ed. and tr.), *Petrarch's Lyric Poems* (Cambridge, Mass., 1976), 268, 352.

> Ah bereaved, ungrateful world! you have great reason to weep with me, for with her you have lost all the good that was in you. Your glory is fallen. With your [Laura's] departure Love left the world and Courtesy, and the sun fell from the sky.

We observe immediately that Donne has converted an elevated, hyperbatic rhetoric containing general terms—*quel bel, gloria, Cortesia,* the Latinate *orbo,* and *sol,* the essential attribute of life—into a physical matter of *vapor, carkasse,* and *wormes,* the latter reminiscent of the low-style sermon. Furthermore, Donne is not speaking of some absolute unanalyzable death (Petrarch does not mention that Laura died of the plague) but the possible consequences of a fever, and the poet's first reaction is not to deplore lost glory but to complain cleverly about how he will turn misogynist. When he rises to a rather grand apostrophe, the conclusion is again in terms of the particular and local:

> O wrangling schooles, that search what fire
>   Shall burne this world, had none the wit
> Unto this knowledge to aspire,
>   That this her feaver might be it?

Petrarch's rhetoric is moral and symbolic rather than literal: the sun which fell does not constitute a cosmological event; but Donne transforms the idealized, metaphoric Italian thoughts into a quite concrete English. Taking middle-style, idealized imagery at its face value is one of his principal means of ironic conversion into low style, which deals with the factual and the scientific.

It is very important that we know not simply the ideas, abstractly stated, that Donne drew on in his verse but the tone of the philosophers of love he had studied and alludes to. A scanty footnote does not convey the character of Donne's references. For example, "The Good-morrow" begins in Donne's colloquial, local, dramatic fashion (so unlike philosophical generality) and mentions a dream, which seems to be a rather caustic comment on the inferiority of his mistress to what he has just seen in his sleep:

> I wonder by my troth, what thou, and I
>   Did, till we lov'd? were we not wean'd till then?
> But suck'd on countrey pleasures, childishly?
>   Or snorted we i' the seaven sleepers den?
> 'Twas so; But this, all pleasures fancies bee.

> If ever any beauty I did see,
> Which I desir'd, and got, 'twas but a dreame of thee.

However, *dream* is an important term in the dialectics of Italian philosophy of love, as is suggested by this passage from Castiglione's *Il Cortegiano*:

> E vede in se stessa un raggio di quel lume che è la vera imagine della bellezza angelica a lei communicata, della quale essa poi communica al corpo una debil'ombra; però, divenuta cieca alle cose terrene, si fa oculatissima alle celesti; e talor quando le virtù motive del corpo si trovano dalla assidua contemplazione astratte, ovvero dal sonno legate, non essendo da quelle impedita, sente un certo odor nascoso della vera bellezza angelica, e rapita dal splendor di quella luce comincia ad infiammarsi, e tanto avidamente la segue, che quasi diviene ebria e for di se stessa, per desiderio d'unirsi con quella, parendole aver trovato l'orma di Dio nella contemplazione del quale, come nel suo beato fine, cerca di riposarsi, e però, ardendo in questa felicissima fiamma, si leva alla sua più nobil parte, che è l'intelletto, e quivi, non più adumbrata dalla oscura notte delle cose terrene, vede la bellezza divina.[22]

> And the soul sees in herself a beam of that light which is the true image of the angelic beauty communicated to her and of which she then communicates to the body a feeble shadow; thus, having become blind to earthly things, the soul has a clear vision of heavenly ones; and sometimes when the forces of the body are abstracted by assiduous contemplation or else bound by sleep, and the soul is no longer impeded by them, she smells a certain hidden odor of true angelic beauty, and ravished by the splendor of that light, she begins to catch fire, and she follows that light so avidly, that she almost becomes intoxicated and in an ecstasy, through the desire to unite with it, for it seems to the soul that she has found the trace of God, in whose contemplation, as in her blessed end, she seeks to rest, and thus, burning in this most happy flame, she rises to her most noble part, which is the intellectual one, and hence, no longer shadowed by the dark night of earthly things, she sees divine beauty.

It may be succinctly stated that physical beauty is inferior to the dreamlike perception of absolute beauty, but such a summary says nothing of the enraptured tone of the Italian prose, running on and on, adding superlative image to image. Donne constantly makes comparatively dry and sometimes ironic-seeming references to the endlessly amplificatory and magniloquently phrased theory of neoplatonic love.

22. Baldassare Castiglione, *Il Cortegiano*, IV, 68, in Carlo Cordié (ed.), *Opere di Baldassare Castiglione, Giovanni della Casa, Benvenuto Cellini* (Milan, 1960).

The references to the microcosm, the little world of man, in the second stanza of "The Good-morrow" follow the same process of conversion. Here is Castiglione on this common renaissance analogy:

> Il ciel rotondo, ornato di tanti divini lumi, e nel centro la terra circundata dagli elementi, e dal suo peso istesso sostenuta; il sole che girando illumina il tutto, e nel verno s'accosta al più basso segno, poi a poco a poco ascende all'altra parte; la luna che da quello piglia la sua luce, secondo che se la appropinqua o se le allontana, e l'altre cinque stelle che diversamente fan quel medesimo corso. Queste cose tra sé han tanta forza per la connession d'un ordine composto così necessariamente, che mutandole per un punto, non poriano star insieme, e ruinarebbe il mondo; hanno ancora tanta bellezza e grazia, che non posson gl'ingegni umani imaginar cosa più bella. Pensate or della figura dell'omo, che si po dir piccol mondo; nel quale vedesi ogni parte del corpo esser composta necessariamente per arte e non a caso, e poi tutta la forma insieme esser bellissima.[23]

> The round sky, adorned with so many divine lights, and in the center the earth surrounded by the elements, and held up by its own weight; the sun which, as it goes around, illuminates everything, and in the winter approaches the lowest sign, then gradually rises on the other side; the moon which takes its light from the sun, as it draws near to it or moves away from it, and the other five planets which variously follow the same course. These things in themselves have such strength because their order is composed and connected in such a necessary fashion, that if you changed one in the slightest, they could not hold together, and the world would be ruined; they have such beauty and grace that human imagination cannot conceive of a more beautiful thing. Think now of the figure of man, who can be called a little world; in whom you see each part of the body put together by necessity and not chance, so that then the total form is most beautiful.

Castiglione's speaker cannot talk of man as microcosm without first surveying the sun and stars and God's great design; his prose is the equivalent of some rambling, ecstatic canzone, full of decorative but general terms. Donne, on the other hand, speaks first of an ordinary little room:

> And now good morrow to our waking soules,
>   Which watch not one another out of feare;
> For love, all love of other sights controules,
>   And makes one little roome, an every where.
> Let sea-discoverers to new worlds have gone,
> Let Maps to others, worlds on worlds have showne,
> Let us possesse one world, each hath one, and is one.

23. *Ibid.*, IV, 58.

Sea-discoverers heads us in the direction of expansive, evocative imagery, but Donne immediately reduces the great adventures of the sixteenth century to maps, practical indications of what Magellan or Vasco da Gama did, and then concludes with an abstract line made all the more prosaic by its pauses and its explanatory final clauses. Donne has moved in the opposite direction from poetic amplification; he begins with more emotive terms and ends with plain, denotative language, which is, however, a condensed reference to the kind of cosmic vision Castiglione offers his reader. Donne speaks of the microcosm as if it were a practical rather than a speculative matter, but we cannot appreciate his dry tone unless we have Italian *piacevolezza* in our memories, the highly rhetorical tradition of the philosophy of love and beauty with Petrarch at its base and the neoplatonists as elaborators.

There are other ways of creating a low-style lyric as well: the argument and proof belong to low style. Actually, there had been a certain amount of theorizing among cinquecento critics about how the lyric involved a proof, and the enthymeme, or literary syllogism, is to be found classified among poetic ornaments.[24] However, the Italians must have had a far more embellished and idealized diction in mind than what we find in Donne's "Love's Infiniteness," which is formal and overt in its argumentative structure; logical articulations like *if yet*, and *if then* shape it:

> If yet I have not all thy love,
> Deare, I shall never have it all;
> I cannot breath one other sigh, to move,
>   Nor can intreat one other teare to fall.
> All my treasure, which should purchase thee,
>   Sighs, teares, and oathes, and letters I have spent,
> Yet no more can be due to mee,
>   Then at the bargaine made was ment.
> If then thy gift of love were partiall,
> That some to mee, some should to others fall,
>   Deare, I shall never have Thee All.

The low-style, that is, technical and practical, aspect of the diction is evident in the legal and financial terminology, as well as in the pat-

---

24. See, for example, Bernard Weinberg, *A History of Literary Criticism in the Italian Renaissance* (2 vols.; Chicago, 1974), II, 643. A check of Weinberg's index reveals much more interesting material pertaining to the poem as logical structure.

tern of hypothesis and conclusion. The second stanza explains why the poet feels he does not have all the lady's love by putting the bargain into a temporal perspective. Donne's presentation of the reasoning process is thus dramatic as well as logical, in that essential information is held back at first:

> Or if then thou gav'st mee all,
>   All was but All, which thou hadst then,
> But if in thy heart, since, there be or shall,
>   New love created bee, by other men,
> Which have their stocks intire, and can in teares,
>   In sighs, in oathes, and letters outbid mee,
> This new love may beget new feares,
>   For, this love was not vowed by thee.
> And yet it was, thy gift being generall,
> The ground, thy heart is mine, what ever shall
>   Grow there, deare, I should have it all.

Here the argument turns on a technicality, a legal term: her gift was general, and therefore any further love that has accrued belongs to him also.

In the third stanza, the thought of a rival is dismissed, and the paradox of infinity is introduced:

> Yet I would not have all yet,
>   He that hath all can have no more,
> And since my love doth every day admit
>   New growth, thou shouldst have new rewards in store;
> Thou canst not every day give me thy heart,
>   If thou canst give it, then thou never gav'st it:
> Loves riddles are, that though thy heart depart,
>   It stayes at home, and thou with losing sav'st it:

One can speak of giving all, but that is an impossibility because all is infinite. The word *all* has been echoing throughout the poem in such a way that, although each use of the term is explainable and even a cliché—"you are my all"—we experience a certain ill ease, as if some logical trick were being played on us. The poet feels dissatisfaction as well with his previous reasoning and concludes with a correction, a different meaning of *all*, and an allusion to another order of ideas:

> But wee will have a way more liberall,
> Then changing hearts, to joyne them, so wee shall
>   Be one, and one anothers All.

Donne has up to this point been exploring the commonplace of gallantry by which men and women exchange hearts like valentines. From this courtly cliché he turns to the higher truth of Italian philosophy of love. "We shall be one" is a characteristic statement of Donne's. The use of the copula recalls syllogistic formulas, as well as the dramatic concision of the metaphors we have seen formed with the verb *to be* in sixteenth-century French poetry. The proposition itself is an allusion to neoplatonism: when the right man and woman come together, they re-form the androgyn they originally constituted, according to Plato in the *Symposium*. "We are one" is simply an elliptical, shorthand way of expressing the idea, but its brevity gives it a conceitful effect. It then follows quite simply that if two are one, each is the other's all, and thus the problem of the word *all* running through the poem is solved.

The conceit in Donne has various bases, but the treatment of high-flown ideas in so literal, so terse a fashion as to be surprising and at first glance rather cryptic is a major source of understated wit. Sometimes the conceit derives from hyperbole as in "A Feaver," where the lady's high temperature risks setting the world on fire, but elsewhere Donne's conceits can work rather differently from the customary overstatement that creates them. The startling, clever quality of extreme brevity, of referring to the subjects of Italian rhetoric, with its artificial idiom, in laconic, commonplace English, forms a low-style conceit, whereas what we usually think of as conceit is an elaborate middle-style effect in the handling of figures.

The *Songs and Sonnets* show quite a variation in style and structure. Whereas "Love's Infiniteness" is ordered like an argument, "The Canonization" is more dramatic in construction and shows shifts of style between the first three stanzas. After the technical connotations of the title, the poem opens with an example of Donne's famous colloquialism, in a seeming address to an outsider:

> For Godsake hold your tongue, and let me love,
>   Or chide my palsie, or my gout,
> My five gray haires, or ruin'd fortune flout,
> With wealth your state, your minde with Arts improve,
>   Take you a course, get you a place,
>   Observe his honour, or his grace,

> And the Kings reall, or his stamped face
> Contemplate; what you will, approve,
> So you will let me love.

The example of Donne has contributed to that admiration for the conversational in poetry which is all but an obsession with certain critics and is scarcely to be met with outside the English-speaking world. The use of the colloquial in French or Italian nonsatiric verse tends toward the politely familiar, with none of Donne's abusiveness. Certainly Donne's violence is justified by the strategy of shifting tone in the second stanza, with its "Alas, alas," which belongs to pathetic expression in the technical rhetorical sense:

> Alas, alas, who's injur'd by my love?
> What merchants ships have my sighs drown'd?
> Who saies my teares have overflow'd his ground?
> When did my colds a forward spring remove?
> When did the heats which my veines fill
> Adde one man to the plaguie Bill?
> Soldiers find warres, and Lawyers finde out still
> Litigious men, which quarrels move,
> Though she and I do love.

There is a version here of one of Donne's elliptic propositions. In "A Valediction: Of Weeping," the poet fears that the individual, the microcosm, will, by his analogy, influence the macrocosm. To his weeping mistress he says,

> O more then Moone,
> Draw not up seas to drowne me in thy spheare,
>   . . . forbeare
> To teach the sea, what it may doe too soone;

for he is about to make a voyage. In "The Canonization," however, the poet denies that the perturbations of his little world will cause meteorological catastrophes in the macrocosm. Analogy as a logical category, well grounded in the classical tradition, underlies these lines, as well as the philosopher's assumption that what is logical in a logical world may well come about. As before, commonplaces of thought take on the character of conceit in Donne through the concision with which he formulates them and the dramatic way he introduces them.

In the third stanza, there is more elliptical allusion: "Call us what you will, wee'are made such by love; / Call her one, mee another flye." The image of the fly (that is, moth) flying into a candle at night and dying is a not uncommon way of representing the lover and his lady from duecento Italian poetry on. Donne gives us just a part of the simile but, by association, moves immediately to another image involving candles, which die by living, that is, burning: "We'are Tapers too, and at our owne cost die." We rarely encounter such tight associationism in renaissance poetry, dramatically reinforced by the use of the copula instead of a standard simile construction. Donne is, in a sense, rushing through the commonplace poetic ornaments that a middle-style renaissance poet would typically amplify. The reference to the phoenix, which is found next, usually appears with images of fire and the sun, but Donne reduces it to a familiar "riddle," needing no gorgeous trappings. The reconciliation of opposites prepares us for the assertion that we are one:

> And wee in us find the' Eagle and the Dove;
>   The Phoenix ridle hath more wit
>   By us, we two being one, are it,
> So, to one neutrall thing both sexes fit.
>   Wee dye and rise the same, and prove
>   Mysterious by this love.

The absolute participial expression "we two being one" is a nice example of the typical syntax of expository prose used in verse—a device comparable to the logical articulations elsewhere in Donne. The point of this stanza is not, however, the allusion to the androgyn but lies in the word *dye*, to which the moths, candles, and phoenix have been leading us. Here, of course, *dye* has its sexual meaning, but it is immediately complemented by the theological *rise*, so that a double pun is created. The sexual sense of *die* occurs in sixteenth-century French poetry, but the conceit is rarely so surprising as when Donne joins it with the notion of resurrection, finally bringing us to the idea of the title, "The Canonization," which occupies the subsequent stanzas.

Many things contribute to the effect of low style in Donne. Instead of elaborate mythology we have images that are well worn, like the moth and the phoenix, or references to the commonplace, as in the case of the famous compasses of "A Valediction: Forbidding Mourning." The unusual words are not those commonly thought of as poetic but rather prosaic technical terms, as in "A Valediction: Of the Book":

> Study our manuscripts, those Myriades
>   Of letters, which have past twixt thee and mee,
>   Thence write our Annals, and in them will be,
> To all whom loves subliming fire invades,
>   Rule and example found;
>   There, the faith of any ground
>   No schismatique will dare to wound
> That sees, how Love this grace to us affords,
> To make, to keep, to use, to be these his Records.

The use of prose language, which is, of course, altogether different from the colloquial in the sixteenth century, belongs to low style in the sense that discourse primarily designed to convey information, and the vocabulary proper to it, is another facet of the unelevated and commonplace. The poem suggests, as Helen Gardner says, the antiquarian scholarship of the Elizabethan age,[25] and this enthusiastic cross of learning and pedantry counters, in its low tone, the idealization of love underlying all this reference to books and the contents of technical books.

The relations of philosophy, low style, and irony are delicate points in the study of Donne's lyrics. There are many flippant, cynical lyrics which we have not alluded to; there is also, perhaps, behind the obvious ironies of the poems drawing on philosophy, some sense of playful speculation, rather than real conviction. We perceive this especially well when Donne reverses his arguments in "Loves Alchymie" and "A Nocturnall upon S. Lucies Day Being the Shortest Day." The latter has always seemed to me one of Donne's most original and haunting poems, in which we perceive the peculiar mixture of low, unidealized, curious images so characteristic of Donne, yet used in a much darker ironical mode than elsewhere:

> 'Tis the yeares midnight, and it is the dayes,
> *Lucies*, who scarce seaven houres herself unmaskes,
>   The Sunne is spent, and now his flasks

25. See Donne, *The Elegies*, 193.

> Send forth light squibs, no constant rayes;
> The world's whole sap is sunke:
> The generall balme th'hydroptique earth hath drunk,
> Whither, as to the beds-feet, life is shrunke,
> Dead and enterr'd; yet all these seeme to laugh,
> Compar'd with mee, who am their Epitaph.

The sun's flasks are powder flasks, the comparison being with a musket. *Balme* seems to refer to winter rains and suggests the idea of *embalming* as well. *Beds-feet* deftly gives the picture of corpses, as one might see them by approaching the end of the bed. The imagery is perhaps hyperbolic but tempered with an irony and mild delight in the grotesque for which it is difficult to find true analogues in other contemporary poets of death, whose tone, like d'Aubigné's, for example, is more strident. There is a long enough Christian tradition of mortuary images, but it tends to be used as a violent contrast to worldly ambition and glory; it is shrilly didactic. Donne's vision of the world's death is more mysterious and avoids the usual ideas of worms and rot.

The alchemy of nothingness is a brilliant inversion of the more ordinary search for essences, in this case the divine essence of love; the idea of such an alchemy is developed in this somber, almost sardonic elegy:

> Study me then, you who shall lovers bee
> At the next world, that is, at the next Spring:
>   For I am every dead thing,
>   In whom love wrought new Alchimie.
>   For his art did expresse
> A quintessence even from nothingnesse,
> From dull privations, and leane emptinesse:
> He ruin'd mee, and I am re-begot
> Of absence, darknesse, death; things which are not.
> . . . .
> But I am by her death, (which word wrongs her)
> Of the first nothing, the Elixer grown;

We know that Donne actually did not believe in the original chaos before creation, but the conception suited the mood of his poem.[26] Matching the negative alchemy is a view of goatish vitality:

---

26. *Ibid.*, 218.

> But I am None; nor will my Sunne renew.
> You lovers, for whose sake, the lesser Sunne
>   At this time to the Goat is runne
>   To fetch new lust, and give it you,
>   Enjoy your summer all;
> Since shee enjoyes her long nights festivall,
> Let mee prepare towards her, and let mee call
> This houre her Vigill, and her Eve, since this
> Both the yeares, and the dayes deep midnight is.

The eclipse of life represented in the last lines is utterly at variance with the imagery of superlunary permanence found elsewhere in Donne. Obviously philosophy is a generator of mood for Donne, who saw with the rhetorician's skill the arguments for and against all the propositions about love. But the nihilistic conceits—conceits in the sense that science has brought about the impossible—of the "Nocturnall" suggest the hardness and despair of some mannerist poetry. Donne moves from low style into a kind of forceful, harsh $\alpha\dot{v}\sigma\tau\eta\rho\dot{o}\varsigma$ manner. The goatish population served by the sun's visit to Capricorn and the conception of the first nothing suggest the darkest side of the poetry that grew out of the high renaissance. Although Donne does not observe the characteristic syntactic tendencies of mannerist poetry, his prosody is notable for the irregular relations of line and sentence structure; asymmetries abound in the elaborate song forms. But this mannerism, if we wish to call it such, has no analogies in the Romance languages, despite occasional attempts at comparison. Donne's general freedom from poetic diction, his plain language alluding to an elevated body of thought, his idiosyncrasy in choice of images make his style a peculiar exploitation of English and Donne the master of the minor English tradition of a tone and vocabulary very difficult to conceive of in the other major renaissance literatures. Erudition, an elaborate sense of rhetoric as a philosophical as well as literary instrument, and a profoundly bemused study of the poetic philosophy of the renaissance in its florid Italianate form contributed to the elaboration of so distinctive a style, which, however high it rises on occasion, is based in the low-style manner Donne first learned writing his *Elegies* and *Satires*.

There has been some controversy over whether Donne had a subsequent "school" working with his idiom. I think it a more profitable question to ask to what extent Donne's contemporaries shared his stylistic usage. At first, Donne seems so brilliant and idiosyncratic as to stand alone, but when we consider some of the materials of his and his coevals' poetry, we realize there are more bonds between them than one might think. A key lexical field for the tracing of low style or low-style influence in English is figures pertaining to money, for these are scarcely to be found in the Italian or French lyric. In those of Shakespeare's sonnets addressed to his young patron, we find abundant references to thrift, use of wealth, lending, legacies, audits, and usury. That these expressions may also have a medical-sexual aspect (the "expense of spirit" of sonnet 129 is a "waste of semen" among other things) confirms their low-style character, for they belong to a long tradition of scientific folklore with its technical pretensions.

Beyond Shakespeare's work, however, we find other significant intrusions of financial vocabulary into the ostensibly middle-style sonnet. Daniel's early cycle *Delia*, for example, begins with images of the "Ocean of thy beauty" receiving "tribute of my duty," only to become more ledgerlike when the poet proceeds to the "casting," or addition of accounts, of care, sums of sighs, and expenses of youth, as recorded by a "charged soul." All this metaphoric dimension is managed without grotesqueness, whereas Michael Drayton, in the final revised form of *Idea* (1619), stresses the dissonant character of love and money matters:

> And thus dividing of my fatal hours,
> The payments of my love, I read, and cross,
> Subtracting, set my sweets unto my sorrows . . .[27]

But Drayton brings to his love sonnets an even more pronounced low-style, half-satirical note:

> How many paltry, foolish, painted things,
> That now in Coaches trouble ev'ry street,
> Shall be forgotten, whom no Poet sings,
> Ere they be well wrap'd in their winding sheets?   (*Idea*, 6)

The shift in tone which Donne cultivated is remarkable also in this

27. Michael Drayton, *Idea*, 3, in Sidney Lee (ed.), *Elizabethan Sonnets* (2 vols.; New York, 1964), II, hereinafter cited in the text.

sonnet, for in the second quatrain Drayton passes to a lyrical, middle-style theme and manner:

> Where I to thee Eternity shall give,
> When nothing else remaineth of these days,
> And Queens hereafter shall be glad to live
> Upon the alms of thy superfluous Praise.

These alms, being employed in an act of charity, are not quite the same as other financial references. Drayton experimented with low-style devices such as a sonnet in proverbs (*Idea*, 54) or comparisons from vulgar or daily life; one of the latter, for example, is based on the popular belief that if a murderer is confronted with his victim's body, the body will begin to bleed (*Idea*, 46).

Although Donne is by far the greater poet, a glance at Drayton's work shows that he as well knew how to make use of low style in poetry and that this low style is not simply the old blunt pre-Petrarchist English manner, for lines like the second quatrain of *Idea*, 6, quoted above, presuppose a considerable lyric gift. Moreover, if we use argumentative figures taken from finance as an experimental index, we can begin to plot the dissemination of low style in Elizabethan verse, where it can be seen to have a distinctive place.

V

The poetry we have been looking at is based on various facets of low style (narration, modest elegiac embellishment, satire, argument), but it is often impure in the sense that the ornaments and ironies of Donne or Ariosto go somewhat beyond the normal limits of low style. Another conception of low style is the specifically plain one, and Ben Jonson made himself the principal exponent of it.[28] Again, however, we must not take this further type of English low style as merely a continuation of an earlier unadorned diction, for it has a distinct esthetic of its own. Jonson, who lived on through the heart of the baroque period, formed his own idea of authentic English, which seems, like the fundamental notion of French neoclassicism, to consist of a somewhat idealized, stylized version of educated

28. Sources, classical and late renaissance, for the theory of plain style are put forth in detail in Trimpi, *Ben Jonson's Poems*, 3–91.

speech. Roman models were very much in his mind, and he attempted to recreate in English an equivalent of the Latin epigram, satire, epistle, and elegy. Jonson was a teacher, if an informal one, of younger poets, and it is not surprising that he wrote a grammar. His influence is significant in that it represents a form of native English neoclassicism.

While Jonson's poetry can be better appreciated when read in some quantity, an epigram on the death of his son will demonstrate some of his qualities:

> Farewell, thou child of my right hand, and joy;
>   My sin was too much hope of thee, loved boy.
> Seven years thou wert lent to me, and I thee pay,
>   Exacted by thy fate, on the just day.
> Oh, could I lose all father now! For why
>   Will man lament the state he should envy?
> To have so soon 'scaped world's and flesh's rage,
>   And if no other misery, yet age!
> Rest in soft peace, and asked, say, Here doth lie
>   Ben Jonson his best piece of poetry.
> For whose sake henceforth all his vows be such
>   As what he loves may never like too much.[29]

For all Jonson's importance, however, there is a limitation to his theory and practice of the plain style: his poems are mostly in the classical low-style genre which excludes much of what the ancients thought truly fine in literature. Nonetheless, everyone cannot write epics or odes, and his association between neoclassicism and plain style was an idea of far-reaching significance, fully appreciable perhaps only from the vantage point of the later seventeenth century.

The importance of English poetry in our examination of low style presents two aspects: whether English culture was belated in absorbing renaissance modes of thought is not my concern here, but it is obvious that the high rhetorical culture of the renaissance arrived late in England, so that till near the end of the sixteenth century, the closest analogy with English poetry is perhaps to be found in Marot's sense of rhetoric. The second stage of low style, involving Sidney's later poetry somewhat but especially Donne, must not be

29. Ben Jonson, "On My First Son," William B. Hunter, Jr. (ed.), *The Complete Poetry of Ben Jonson* (New York, 1963).

thought of, in Donne's case, as a mere reaction to or rejection of foreign poetic rhetoric. Donne's absorption of the Italianate tradition is obvious, but he was also living at a time when the complex of Petrarchism, neoplatonism, and Bembism had grown old, and a new culture, very evident in French poetry of the late sixteenth century, was replacing it. In its search for a new mode of expression, Donne's verse is comparable to some of the more eccentric French mannerist verse though infinitely more successful, sustained as it was by greater intellect, greater poetic talent, and greater freedom from the habit of basing newer poetic figures on the old Petrarchist analogies and techniques.

Jonson's roughly parallel attempt to create a new poetic style represents, on the other hand, a conscious effort to start afresh with Roman low-style genres as models; the Petrarchist manner is rejected as irrelevant to the creation of a new version of classical style. This idea is not unlike Ronsard's attempt to base the ode on the models of Pindar and Horace or later determinations to see ancient poetry as the major source of literary art, from which recent modern work is a deviation. In this sense, Jonson's conception of how to go about writing poetry is, in many ways, more important than his poetry itself: it constitutes a major esthetic idea.

I have withheld speaking of attempts at high-style poetry because of the lateness and greater difficulty of them. They have increasing importance, however, in the late renaissance and especially in the seventeenth century, and we shall consider them next.

CHAPTER 4

Classicizing High Style: Ronsard, Tasso, and Spenser

I

The modern reader may find the verbal art of the lyrics of Petrarch, Ronsard, and Donne sufficiently elevated, but for the rhetorically minded poets and theorists of the sixteenth century, there was an all-important further domain of poetry, that of high style. Consciousness of the classical system of styles increased in the course of the century, and thus, while Bembo considered Petrarch's *gravità* the highest poetic mode, Minturno, in the middle of the century, felt Petrarch's subject matter was not truly suitable to high style and proposed Pindar as a model of the most elevated lyric art.[1] This is a significant change in theory, for Pindar's work constitutes the authentic classical ideal of the long, boldly ornamented ode with its asperities, digressions, and strikingly unusual words. At the same time, Ronsard arrived at a conception of the high ode by studying Pindar himself apparently more than the critical tradition. The other prominent aspect of high style, epic diction, which was, of course, of equal importance to the odic manner, was the object of a careful theoretical examination by Tasso before he undertook to write his own great epic. There was a clarification of what high style actually meant, rather than a loose assimilation to it of anything one admired in the vernacular lyric, and the practical results were of long-reaching consequence.

At the same time, the syncretic side of renaissance thinking tended to come into play, modifying pure ancient doctrine. Dante's *De vulgari eloquentia*, published for the first time in the sixteenth century, proposed a complementary view of what he calls "tragic style,"

---

1. See Clay Hunt, *"Lycidas" and the Italian Critics* (New Haven, 1979), 84.

meaning the *genus grande*. He maintained that the canzone treating arms, love, and virtue fulfilled the demands of the highest level of poetic art. Aside from the fact that some of his own canzoni could plausibly be seen as representing the rougher version of high style, Dante's theories helped to modify the notion of the ode or epic in the direction of exalted love poetry, something more suited to the European temperament than Pindar's celebrations of athletes or the minute epic preoccupation with battles. He effected a theoretical synthesis of classical heroics and European courtly ideals. The long stanzas of the canzone were, furthermore, seen as corresponding to Pindar's triadic arrangement of strophe, antistrophe, and epode.

Consciousness of the odic nature of biblical poetry, as well as that of the traditional long European lyrics, contributed further toward a syncretic view of the ode. The problem that the poet faced, however, was not simply one of calling any long poem an ode, as was fairly freely done, but of assuring himself that there was an authentic high style distinguishing the major lyric. As we have seen, poets and theorists were very quick simply to affirm that the sonnet was a high-style genre without ever analyzing what the *genus grande* meant in the way of diction and effect on its audience.

The first half of the sixteenth century is marked by several attempts to write major lyrics under the name of ode, *cantique*, or canzone, these terms being taken as synonyms. Marot's small amount of work in this genre is especially interesting for its early conception of elevated style and form. His "Cantique I" addressed to Marguerite de Navarre to ask for aid for Renée de France and himself, persecuted in Ferrara, is written in a short but curiously effective stanza:

> Plaigne les mortz qui plaindre les vouldra;
> Tant que vivray, mon cueur se resouldra
> A plaindre ceulx que douleur assauldra
> En ceste vye.
>
> O fleur que j'ay la premiere servie;
> Tu metz chascun hors de peine asservie
> Et toy, tu as peine non desservie;
> Bien je le sçay.[2]

Let him who will pity the dead; as long as I live, my heart is determined to pity those who are assaulted by sorrow in this life. O flower whom first

2. Clément Marot, *Oeuvres lyriques*, ed. C. A. Mayer (London, 1964).

I served, you withdraw everyone from the suffering imposed on them; yet you suffer and are not relieved, I know it well.

The first stanza constitutes a model exordium, a general idea relevant to the rest of the poem but detached from it somewhat. The first word of the apostrophe plays on the name Marguerite, or "daisy," and intermittent comparisons alternate with the easy figures of address, question, and anaphora. Here he apostrophizes Francis I, attempting to move him at the thought of the hostility of Renée de France's husband toward her:

> O Roy Françoys, elle porte tes armes,
> Voire, et à toy s'adressent telz alarmes,
> Dont le plus doulx ne pourroit pas sans larmes
> Estre desduict;
>
> Et ne peult l'aultre à raison estre induit
> Par cil honneur où France l'a conduit,
> Ne par enfans que tant beaulx luy produit
> Par maincte année.
>
> Ne la bonté de la noble Renée,
> Ne la doulceur qui avec elle est née,
> Ne les vertus qui l'ont environnée
> N'y ont povoir.
>
> J'auroys plustot entrepris d'esmouvoir,
> Comme Orpheus, en l'infernal manoir
> Caron le dur, voire Pluton le noir
> Et chien Cerbere.[3]

O King Francis, she bears your arms, and even addresses to you such cries for help that the mildest one of them could not be told of without tears. And her husband cannot be brought to reason by the honor France has bestowed on him, nor by his beautiful children, which she brings forth many a year. Neither the goodness of noble Renée, nor the sweetness that was born with her, nor the virtues that surround her have any power over him. I could just as easily have undertaken, like Orpheus in the infernal dwelling, to move hardhearted Charon or even black Pluto and the dog Cerberus.

Rhetorically speaking, the poem has much that is medieval about it; one can scarcely call it high style as the term was to be understood shortly afterward. Elevation and formality obtain through simple devices and through the thought of the piece, rather than by means

3. *Ibid.*

of any special figures other than the simile that we could identify as belonging primarily to high style. The poem is particularly interesting in Marot's work because the middle-style lyric is almost totally lacking, and one finds, besides an abundance of low-style genres, a few attempts at elevated style.

The defenders of the plain style in the sixteenth-century English lyric should certainly approve of Marot's "Cantique," but they might be less in sympathy with another approach to high style, this one also related to English poetic practice. The *grands rhétoriqueurs*, the dominant court poets of the late fifteenth and early sixteenth centuries, carried out fully the program of Latinization and use of complex sound figures which is to be encountered here and there, under the name of aureation, in the works of a few English and Scottish poets. We must not think of the *rhétoriqueurs* as belonging entirely to the age before Marot; although they died well before he did, their work, especially that of Guillaume Cretin, continued to be admired right into the mid-century, when Ronsard was publishing his first odes. There is variation in the genres and styles of the *rhétoriqueurs*, but a notable attempt at high style is to be found in a series of *chants royaux* which Cretin wrote on the subject of Adam, Eve, the fall, and redemption. Here, in a strophe that by its length suggests high style, is the establishment of Christ's role in the divine order:

> L'altitonant supreme plasmateur,
> Monarque et chef en l'art d'architecture,
> Avant qu'il fut des siecles formateur
> Fist ung pourtraict de nouvelle structure,
> Pour repparer l'offense et forfaicture
> Du pere Adam. Et lors la Trinité,
> Du grant conseil d'immense eternité
> Preordonna ça bas ung ediffice,
> Ou decreta le Filz en Deité
> Y desdier en sa solempnité
> Temple construit par divin artifice.[4]

The high-thundering supreme maker, the monarch and first of all architects, before he formed the world, made a new kind of image to redeem the offense and crime of father Adam. And then the Trinity, in its eternal counsel, ordained there to be on earth an edifice in which the Son of God, it was decreed, would solemnly make a temple built by divine skill.

4. Guillaume Cretin, "Chant royal," *Oeuvres poétiques*, ed. Kathleen Chesney (Paris, 1932).

Cretin's Latinizing principle of style seems misguided today, but that may only be because he was not a major poet; Scève's Latinity has survived perfectly well, by contrast. From the point of view of the sixteenth century, there was no absolute reason why such a style should not be valid; Italian poets Latinized, and Shakespeare and Milton were, in many passages, to demonstrate the great beauty obtainable from the formal, polysyllabic, noun-heavy grand manner reinforced with classical terms.

We might contrast Cretin's odic style with Ronsard's by observing that whereas the former brought Latin words into French, Ronsard, using purely French words, adopted Greek idiom in his *Odes*:

> Comme un qui prend une coupe,
> Seul honneur de son tresor,
> Et donne à boire à la troupe
> Du vin qui rit dedans l'or:
> Ainsi versant la rousée,
> Dont ma langue est arousée
> Sus la race de VALOIS,
> En mon dous Nectar j'abreuve
> Le plus grand Roi qui se treuve,
> Soit en armes ou en lois.[5]

Like one who takes a goblet, the most precious thing he owns, and to the multitude gives wine sparkling in the golden cup: thus, pouring the dew, with which my tongue is moist, onto the race of the Valois, I drench in my sweet Nectar the greatest king there is, both in arms and laws.

This is the opening of Ronsard's first book of odes, and quite consciously presents, in dense fashion, major characteristics of his Pindaric manner. The first lines are swift, surprising, and indirect; the metaphoric language is rather strange (the poet showers the king with the contents of his mouth), and the metaplasms *rousée* and *arousée* represent a somewhat strained effort to suggest the dialectal mixture of Greek. Ronsard succeeds admirably in creating a supple syntactic movement for ten lines.

It is customary to deplore Ronsard's lack of understanding of Pindar's design and purpose. I think it is relevant to make a brief comparison, for poetic method, with a passage of Pindar. Here is the

---

5. Pierre de Ronsard, "Au Roi," *Oeuvres completes,* ed. Paul Laummonier (19 vols.; Paris, 1931–75), I, hereinafter cited in the text.

opening of the "First Olympian Ode," in antiquity the most admired of Pindar's poems and therefore placed at the beginning of collections of his odes. (In the sixteenth century the ode would have been printed all in short lines, whence Ronsard's heptasyllabic lines in imitation.)

> Ἄριστον μὲν ὕδωρ, ὁ δὲ χρυσὸς αἰθόμενον πῦρ
> ἅτε διαπρέπει νυκτὶ μεγάνορος ἔξοχα πλούτου·
> εἰ δ᾽ ἄεθλα γαρύεν
> ἔλδεαι, φίλον ἦτορ,
> μηκέτ᾽ ἀελίου σκόπει
> ἄλλο θαλπνότερον ἐν ἀμέρᾳ φαεννὸν ἄστρον ἐρήμας δι᾽
>   αἰθέρος,
> μηδ᾽ Ὀλυμπίας ἀγῶνα φέρτερον αὐδάσομεν·[6]

Water is most noble, but gold, like a burning fire standing out at night, is more excellent than lordly wealth. Dear heart, if you wish to speak of athletic prizes, do not look for any star shining more warmly in the day, in the lonely sky, than the sun, nor shall we tell of a competition greater than that of Olympia.

We perceive that Ronsard has imitated Pindar's abrupt style of opening an ode; however, Pindar is far more indirect in his method. The initial noun, *water*, never comes up again. The two parallel comparisons, one with fire at night, the other with the sun in the day, seem momentarily odd, because of the usual opposition of night and day, and furthermore, they are separated by the poet's address to himself and by the *if* clause. We see why the sudden shifts and discontinuity of the rough version of the high style were attributed to Pindar. The four elements of the metaphors, fire, wealth, the sun, and the Olympic games, are more juxtaposed than explicitly related.

Ronsard, on the other hand, cultivated a much more carefully articulated sentence structure, for he aims more at the stately high style than the rough, at the μεγαλοπρεπής, or style of high decorum, rather than at the αὐστηρός. The total shape of his odes is more immediately apparent than that of Pindar's. Ronsard tended to develop his royal odes along the lines of the topics of praise laid down by the late antique rhetorician Aphthonius and much studied in the renaissance: the personage's antecedents, birth, education,

6. John Sandys (ed.), *The Odes of Pindar* (London, 1968).

and feats are set forth in orderly fashion.[7] When Ronsard presents a myth in imitation of Pindar, the connection is perfectly clear, again unlike his model. Ronsard tended to adapt isolated details of the Greek used by Pindar rather than its larger movement.[8] The result can hardly be called a misunderstanding of Pindar, for Ronsard took what he found most valuable and imbedded it in the kind of clearly articulated work toward which renaissance poets strove by and large.

Ronsard's odes in high style are not all Pindaric in the sense of using the strophic triad and Greek idiom. However, classical influence in general is quite evident. The following ode is a Horatian imitation of the best sort. It does not follow any poem of Horace's closely, but the overall effect recalls the Roman ode in its more grandiose form:

> Qui par gloyre, & par mauvaistié,
> Et par nonchallante paresse,
> Aura tranché de l'amitié
> Le noud qui doulcement nous presse:
> A celuy de rigueur expresse
> Je deffen qu'en nulle saison,
> Ne s'eberge dans ma maison:
> Et qu'avec moy sur le rivage,
> Compagnon d'un mesme voyage,
> Pollu, ne couppe le lien
> Qui tient l'hosteliere navire:
> Car Juppiter le Philien
> Quelque fois avecque le pire
> Punist le juste, & peu souvent
> Souffre la vengeresse Peine
> D'une jambe boiteuse et vaine
> Le mechant galloper devant.   (*Odes*, V, 10)

He who through vainglory and wickedness and indifferent laziness cuts off the knot of friendship, which binds us so gently, I forbid that he ever lodge in my house or, by me at the coast, intending to travel on the same ship, cut the rope which ties the hospitable ship to the shore, for he is impure, and Jupiter the god of hospitality sometimes will punish the just along with the wicked, and rarely allows an evil man to gallop ahead of his avenging penalty on his lame, foolish leg.

---

7. See O. B. Hardison, *The Enduring Monument: A Study of the Idea of Praise in Renaissance Literary Theory and Practice* (Chapel Hill, 1962), 195–97.
8. For the details, see Isidore Silver, *The Pindaric Odes of Ronsard* (Paris, 1937).

Ronsard starts with a highly developed general statement for his exordium: three long clauses (*Qui . . . je deffen . . . car*) are smoothly joined. The style has a stately leisure: the three *par* phrases; the full, explicit development of the image of cutting the knot; the parallel images of sharing a shelter and a ship; the second cutting image echoing the first; and the *quelquefois* and *peu souvent* all produce balancing, equilibrated movement within the triad of clauses. The expert syntactic movement is heightened by the isolated *pollu*, an effective detachment of the adjective learned from Latin. The epithets *jambe boiteuse et vaine* are a means, later much imitated, of elevating the rather commonplace *galloper*. *Vengeresse Peine* is in the solid, evocative style of Roman personifications, for the Romans erected so many temples to moral concepts that their use of such words was more than a mere shadowy figure of rhetoric. Their syncretic religious world recognized a diversity of unseen forces.

Ronsard continues the indirect approach to his subject in the second stanza, which again is of a general order and is cast, this time, in the form of a rhetorical question and comparison:

> Que sert á l'homme de piller
> Tous les printemps de l'Arabie,
> Et de ses moissons despouiller
> Soit la Sicile, ou la Lybie,
> Ou desrober l'Inde annoblye
> Aux tresors de son bord gemmé;
> S'il n'ayme & s'il n'est point aymé?
> Si tout le monde le dedaigne,
> Si nul second ne l'accompaigne
> Solliciteux de son amy:
> Comme un Patrocle pitoyable
> Suyvoit Achille, fut parmy
> La nuë la plus effroyable
> Des Lyciens, lors qu'odieux
> Contre Priam soufloit son ire,
> Ou quand, paisible, sus la lyre,
> Chantoit les hommes & les Dieux.

What profit has a man in pillaging the fruits of the Arabian spring or despoiling Sicily or Libya, or robbing noble India of the treasures of its jeweled coast, if he does not love and is not loved?—if everyone disdains him, if no one helpfully accompanies him, concerned for his friend: as pitiful Patroclus followed Achilles, even through the most horrible cloud of Lycian warriors, when full of hate, Achilles breathed his wrath against Priam or when, at peace, he sang on his lyre of men and the gods.

The comparison or example was recognized as a major means of heightening (*amplificatio* in the proper classical sense) one's argument. We see the fitness of the device here, for the tension is increased by so long a development preceding the central statement in the following stanza. In his *amplificatio* Ronsard pursues the Horatian pattern of enumerating many things briefly, with emphasis on geography, on events of Greek and Roman history, and finally, on heroic myth: the allusion to Patroclus and Achilles condenses several episodes of the *Iliad*, quickly juxtaposed in very fluent syntax.

Finally, after a periphrasis, Ronsard arrives at the specific theme of the poem:

> Le temps qui a commandement
> Sur ces grands Masses sourcilleuses,
> Qui devallent leur fondement
> Jusques aux ondes sommeilleuses,
> Ne les menaces orgueilleuses
> Des fiers Tyrans, ne sçauroyent pas
> Esgrouller, ne ruer en bas
> La ferme amour que je te porte . . .

Neither time, which controls the eyebrowlike masses of mountains whose base descends to the slumbering waves, nor the proud threats of haughty tyrants can shake or cast down the firm love I bear you.

The expansive, enumeratory argument, with its epithetic imagistic development of the idea of time and its almost gratuitously hypothetical threats of tyrants, suddenly emerges into a clear, concise statement. We find here a double, antithetical, and complementary means of emphasis: expansion and brevity, which heighten each other.

The structure of the opening of this ode demonstrates both Pindaric indirection and the influence of the classical oration on elevated poetry. It was one of the recurrent ideas of sixteenth-century theorists to find elements of the oration in verse because the oration was the only sort of nontheatrical writing in antiquity that had a fixed form, if a flexible one.[9] In this ode, the exordium is followed by a kind of argument, which concludes with a peroration. As a poem, the ode demonstrates a large-scale planning proper to the idea of continuity associated with high style: the first two stanzas hold the

9. See Bernard Weinberg, *A History of Literary Criticism in the Italian Renaissance* (2 vols.; Chicago, 1974), I, 197.

reader in suspension, as it were, before the specific occasion of the ode is introduced. In terms of style, it represents the majestically sustained, tranquil phase of high style more than the rough, brilliant manner.

Ronsard was not absolutely the first to write Pindaric or other odes in the vernacular, nor are all of his odes in high style.[10] He took advantage of the ambiguity of the term to introduce the lighter sort of Horatian ode into his collection and, not satisfied with this tacit distinction, later devised the term *odelette* for truly slight poems. Although the significance of his odes, especially the elevated ones, was recognized in his time, modern taste has tended to ignore them somewhat in favor of the middle-style lyrics and sonnets. In our century, taste has followed the opposite direction from the evolution of renaissance feeling for style. Modern interest in middle and low styles is marked, whereas in the sixteenth and seventeenth centuries, poets and readers pursued ever higher, more grandiose conceptions of writing.

Ronsard is the first renaissance poet in whom we see the complicated interplay of a minute study of much of the major poetry of antiquity, an imaginative grasp of how such styles could be recreated in the vernacular, and at the same time, certain tastes and prejudices of his own time which modified his neoclassicism and led him to hold opinions and write poems which were not altogether in accordance with his humanist culture. Most authentic humanist poets had written in Latin, but Ronsard, after some early attempts, abandoned that solution. Because he was both a humanist and a poet of superior gifts, we find that he could, near the same period when he was writing his unprecedentedly classicizing odes, call the *Amours* a work of Pindarization or transpose the Roman love elegy into a courtly mode. In general, his work after the first books of odes becomes less exactly classical, and his hymns are a relevant example. The hymn, referring in this case to the Homeric hymns or Callimachus' hymns and not to biblical poetry, was felt to belong to essentially the same category as the Pindaric ode, and still in his great decade of experimentation, Ronsard turned to it after the *Amours*.

The idea of the hymn is a somewhat general one, like that of the

---

10. See Carol Maddison, *Apollo and the Nine: A History of the Ode* (Baltimore, 1960).

ode. In Ronsard it takes the form of either a discursive poem or a mythological narrative. Ronsard's great innovation here is the working out of a narrative style in alexandrine couplets, the form which was to become so characteristic of French poetry. The diction of the hymns becomes much more purely French, with little suggestion of the classical languages:

> Des le commencement (S'il faut le croire ainsi)
> Les Estoilles n'avoient noz destins en soucy,
> Et n'avoient point encor de tout ce Monde large,
> Comme ell' ont aujourd'huy, ny le soing ny la charge.
> ("Hymne des astres")

> From the beginning, if we are to believe it, the stars were not concerned with our destinies and did not have, as they do today, the care and burden of the whole wide world.

This is almost the idiom of La Fontaine or some other neoclassical narrative poet. Ronsard's myth of why Jupiter ultimately fixed the stars in their place takes on the air of a fable. To be sure, Ronsard periodically introduces similes which reflect his earlier theories of diction:

> Lors des Astres divins (pour leur peine d'avoir
> Envers Sa Majesté si bien faict leur devoir)
> Aresta la carriere, & tous en telle place
> Qu'ils avoient de fortune, & en pareille espace,
> D'un lien aimantin leurs plantes attacha,
> Et comme de grans cloux dans le Ciel les ficha,
> Ainsi qu'un mareschal qui hors de la fornaise
> Tire des cloux ardans, tous rayonnez de braise,
> Qu'à grandz coups de marteaux il congne durement
> A-lentour d'une roüe arengez proprement.

> Then Jupiter stopped the movement of the divine stars (because they had taken the trouble to do so well their duty to His Majesty) and attached their feet with an adamantine bond in the place they happened to be and in that space, and stuck them like great nails into the sky, like a blacksmith, who, from the forge, draws burning nails, covered with embers, which he then pounds hard with great strokes of the hammer around a wheel in proper arrangement.

Here we find the comparison drawn from a métier which Ronsard felt was an important source of variety in poetic effect. As for the general movement of the verse, Ronsard's sentences are frequently spread over two or more couplets, and modest enjambment is used.

There is no question but that Ronsard perfected the prosody of alexandrine narration at the same time as he invented it, but one may wonder whether the *Hymnes* are truly in high style, as theory would have them. The use of the alexandrine (*vers heroïques* is Ronsard's term) doubtless seemed to have an imposing breadth, but in retrospect we note the absence of typical high-style characteristics: the idiom is too fluent and devoid of impressive words, for the alexandrine, as Ronsard noted in his *Abrégé de l'art poétique françois*, risks becoming prosaic if the diction is not quite special. The couplet rimes, furthermore, constantly ring with their neat symmetry, and symmetry is more often a middle-style effect. One is reminded of the decorative Ovidian narrative rather than true epic style, and in this respect, Ronsard's *Hymnes* anticipate a fairly widespread renaissance and seventeenth-century genre, from Marlowe's *Hero and Leander* to La Fontaine's *Adonis*. They do not point toward a high epic style.

II

We see that Ronsard's aspirations toward high style dwindled, and when he came to write an epic, *La Franciade* (1572), he chose for it a style which he thought Homeric in its relative plainness, but here the idea of imitation failed him. Homeric plainness recreated in French decasyllabic lines turns into words of little weight, compared with the more massive Greek ones, joined to a comparatively nervous meter.

The question of means in the vernacular, as much as any abstract equivalence with the classical languages, preoccupied Tasso in the long period he spent theorizing about Italian poetry and preparing to write the *Gerusalemme liberata* (1575). We can find the results of his thinking in the *Discorsi del poema epico* (1594) and in other works. Tasso's epic is a touchstone for the understanding of Italian poetic tradition and realizes to an extraordinary degree the ideal of classical high style. Since the writing is very consistent, the various textures could be illustrated from many parts of the poem. Godfrey of Bouillon's opening address will serve to show a medium complexity in the speech style Tasso evolved:

> già non lasciammo i dolci pegni e'l nido
> nativo noi (se'l creder mio non erra),
> né la vita esponemmo al mare infido
> ed a i perigli di lontana guerra,
> per acquistar di breve suono un grido
> vulgare e posseder barbara terra,
> ché proposto ci avremmo angusto e scarso
> premio, e in danno de l'alme il sangue sparso.[11]

We have not left our dear bonds and our native nest (unless I am mistaken), nor have we exposed our lives to the treacherous sea and to the dangers of a distant war in order to acquire brief fame among the populace and to acquire foreign land, for in that case we would have taken as our aim a narrow, slight reward and shed our blood to the danger of our souls.

The general structure of the speech is binary, the sign of the stately manner, with the two preterite verbs, each with a double complement; the two infinitives after *per*; and the double adjective in the penultimate line. However, within this formal and elevated manner, the discourse is haughty and scornful. The enhancing metonymies of *dolci pegni* and *nido* for wives, children, and homes are followed by an ironic parenthesis (how should the leader of the army not know their goal?); the central phrases are grandiose with the poetic, Latinate-sounding *mare infido*, the *vanitas* expressed by *grido vulgare* (and not *volgare*, a more "vulgar" form), and the magnificently disdainful *barbara terra*, an expression of revulsion borrowed from the Greeks. But all this would be nothing without Tasso's study of expressive sound in Italian. Double consonants, as in the preterites, suggest grandeur in his opinion, and his opinion seems sound in this case. The penultimate line demonstrates the harsh, contemptuous style, with its consonant clusters in the choice phrase *angusto e scarso*. In general, the epithets and the development of the phrases, which are full without being markedly periphrastic, belong very much to high style.

The αὐστηρός, the harsh side of high style, greatly concerned Tasso, and he felt that ellipsis, hyperbaton, and enjambment, as well as sounds, could contribute to it. Somewhat later in the same speech, there is a superb example of an elliptical figure expressive of scorn:

11. Torquato Tasso, *Gerusalemme liberata*, ed. Marziano Guglielminetti (2 vols.; Milan, 1974), 1, 22, hereinafter cited in the text.

Dunque il fatto sin ora al rischio è molto,
più che molto al travaglio, a l'onor poco,
nulla al disegno, ove o si fermi o vòlto
sia l'impeto de l'armi in altro loco.
Che gioverà l'aver d'Europa accolto
sì grande sforzo, e posto in Asia il foco,
quando sia poi di sì gran moti il fine
non fabriche di regni, ma ruine?

Thus what we have done up to now is a great deal in respect to the danger we encountered; it is more than a great deal if you take our effort into consideration, but it is not much in regard to honor acquired and nothing at all compared with our goal, whether we stop here or turn our military force in another direction. What is the value of having brought such a great armed force from Europe and set Asia on fire, if the purpose of such a great undertaking was not to create kingdoms but ruins?

Tasso uses all the figures of speech but with an appropriateness that prevents his style from seeming idly ornate. Here the octave begins with an unusual construction, a kind of positive, then negative *incrementum*, moving from *più che molto* to *nulla*, as the words expressing the intended worth of their action rise in value, so that there is antithesis and negative climax, as well as grammatical ellipsis. No personal pronoun is used in the octave, to heighten the objective contempt of the speaker, and the stately use of binary constructions continues as an ironic note. The question of the last four lines shows a fine sense of grammar and sound: the *Che gioverà l'aver d'Europa* elegantly repeats *e*, *r*, and *a*, while from *accolto* to *foco* there is an accumulation of consonant clusters or the harsh sound *k*. The penultimate line has no distinctive phonetic character, for it is used to separate two very strong lines. After the expansively periphrastic *Che gioverà*, with its elegant mingling of abstract (*sforzo*) and concrete (*foco*), the final line is brutally concise like the opening of the octave: *fabriche* is a high-style metonymy, using the shorter verbal derivate instead of the infinitive *di fabbricare*, and *regni* and *ruine* demonstrate the high-style play on words which has no humor about it. Enormous scorn is compressed into the verbless brevity of the final line.

It is hardly necessary to demonstrate after this that Tasso was a master of all the ordinary figures of speech, though not often, by high-style standards, a mannered user of them. However, I must comment on some further general stylistic principles. There is a ten-

dency for high style to place the emphasis on nouns, their modifiers, and participles, and Tasso's somewhat circuitous diction, which
is also a feature of high style, depends to a large extent on this:

> Era la notte, e non prendean ristoro
> co'l sonno ancor le faticose genti:
> ma qui vegghiando nel fabril lavoro
> stavano i Franchi a la custodia intenti,
> e là i pagani le difese loro
> gian rinforzando tremule e cadenti
> e reintegrando le già rotte mura,
> e de' feriti era comun la cura.   (12, 1)

It was night, and the weary people were not taking rest with sleep; but
the French were staying up at their forges keeping careful watch, and
elsewhere the pagans were going about strengthening their trembling,
crumbling defenses and repairing the broken walls. And both sides were
occupied with their wounded.

Prendean, stavano, gian, and *era* are characteristic uses of weak and
common finite verbs in a context thick with other parts of speech.
However, there is something to be noted here as elsewhere about
the Italian verb and its use in high style. The literary language pos-
sesses a large number of verbs of some length and weight, and even
though Tasso has a strong tendency to use past participles forming
passives, gerunds, verbal adjectives, and substantivized infinitives,
these verbal derivates, by their bulky form, constitute an important
part of the vocabulary: *reintegrando, rinforzando,* and *vegghiando* fill
the other high-style requirement of words impressive in size and
sound. Even though the finite verbs are often insignificant, the com-
pensating nonfinite forms are so prominent as to give a sense of care
and imagination in verb usage. In the following passage, the verbal
adjective *espugnatrice,* replacing a relative clause, is just the first
word showing the underlying richness of the verb roots:

> Ma cadde a pena in cenere l'immensa
> machina espugnatrice de le mura,
> che'n sè novi argomenti Ismen ripensa
> perchè più resti la città secura;
> onde a i Franchi impedir ciò che dispensa
> lor di materia il bosco egli procura,
> onde contra Sion battuta e scossa
> torre nova rifarsi indi non possa.   (13, 1)

Hardly had the immense war machine for taking the walls fallen, than Ismeno went over in his mind new plans for keeping the city safe; he tried to think of a way to prevent the French from getting lumber from the forest, so that they could not build a new attack tower to use against Jerusalem, which had been so beaten and shaken.

The condensed expression *egli procura onde*, meaning "he tries to think how he might," and *a i Franchi impedir*, in the sense of "preventing the French from getting," are remarkable examples of the tightness of expression verbs can provide which steadily counters the circuitous tendency of the style, represented here by the locution *ciò che dispensa*. Actually, Italian tends to be richer in the number of verbal forms used than French, and part of the success of the *Gerusalemme* lies in the variety they provide, in such expressions as "già fornita / de l'opere notturne era qualcuna" (12, 2), where the verb is precise, while *opere* is a most general term. Here are some other examples: "D'alto rinchiusa oprai l'arme lontane" (12, 3): in this case, the verb is both unusual and strong in sense; "In sé raggira / un non so che d'insolito e d'audace / la mia mente inquieta" (12, 5): the prefix here gives weight and a greater imagistic value to the verb; "Oh se sperar ciò lice, altera sorte!" (12, 99): the Latinate impersonal verb shows the extent to which Italian can adopt concise classical verbs; "Ma già venirne qui lor non si toglie" (13, 11): here the reflexive passive makes a substantial verbal unit; "Marte co'l sol fia ch'ad unir si vada" (13, 13): the verbal periphrasis obviates the dominance of nouns in the line. As French moved toward its neoclassical form, it lost verbal richness to an extent which is even somewhat perceptible in Ronsard's odes, and narrative poetry became noticeably weaker than other genres. But actually, the difference is not only a stylistic one but a question of lexical range, morphology, and basic idomatic tendencies. Italian has a gerund differentiated from the verbal adjective, and a substantivized use of the infinitive which is far more verbal in feeling than many French verbal nouns. The free use of compound forms from Latin like *precorrere, addurre, infingere, contessere*, and *dilungare*, for example, provides a rich array of imposing verbs. Furthermore, the alternative forms of ordinary verbs can offer the choice of smooth or harsh style: *vedo* or *veggio*, *devo* or *deggio*. The Italian lyric has less occasion to display the verb in all its richness (just as its subject matter confines its nouns and adjectives) than does Tasso's epic; but high-style narrative, which demanded all the resources of language within the classicizing range, shows Italian to possess features that would not be seen again until Milton set about creating his high epic manner.[12]

Finally, it should be stressed that, as the necessary complement to enjambment, as an aid to expansive diction, or for purposes of density, Tasso constantly uses his favorite trope, hyperbaton, which is inseparable for him from high style and variety in epic narration. The scope of his hyperbaton tends also to be greater than that found in the cinquecento sonnet. Hyperbaton, by introducing an element of irregularity, of unpredictability in word order counters the natural drift of formal style toward doublings and parallelisms:

> Te, la cui nobiltà tutt'altre agguaglia,
> gloria e merito d'opre a me prepone,
> né sdegnerebbe in pregio di battaglia
> minor chiamarsi anco il maggior Buglione.
> Te dunque in duce bramo, ove non caglia
> a te di questa sira esser campione,
> né già cred'io che quell' onor tu curi
> che da' fatti verrà notturni e scuri;   (5, 10)

The glory and merits of your works put you ahead of others in my eyes, and your nobility equals any other. Nor would the elder Bouillon be disdainful of being called lesser than you in military valor. You, therefore, are the one I wish as leader, although you have no desire to be the champion of this Syrian woman, nor, I believe, are you interested in the honor that could come from inglorious, nighttime exploits.

None of the sentence elements fall into their more normal position here, and the pronoun constructions are mostly what might be called emphatic or Latinate, except that here they are so regular a part of Tasso's idiom that they seem merely elevated and literary. The parallelisms are not completely disguised by any means, but they seem much less a mechanical dominant of style when word order is elaborately varied. Here again we see a contrast with Ronsard's and later French high style, where only the most modest hyperbaton is allowed and rarely with striking effect. Doublings constitute much more of a danger in French high style than Italian,

12. See F. T. Prince, *The Italian Element in Milton's Verse* (Oxford, 1954), and in general, Fredi Chiappelli, *Studi sul linguaggio del Tasso epico* (Florence, 1957).

for without varied word order, their repetition can lead more to monotony than grandeur.

The *Gerusalemme* is often referred to as mannerist or baroque because of its erotic and religious themes, but in style the epic is as pure an attempt at classicism as one could find. The descriptive passages show no trace of the conceitful manner associated with the baroque. When, in Canto 18, Rinaldo walks up the Mount of Olives as part of his penance, the episode opens with a *chronographia* of traditional character:

> Era la stagion ch'anco non cede
> libero ogni confin la notte al giorno,
> ma l'oriente rosseggiar si vede
> ed anco è il ciel d'alcuna stella adorno;
> quando ei drizzò ver l'Oliveto il piede,
> con gli occhi alzati contemplando intorno
> quinci notturne e quindi mattutine
> bellezze incorrottibili e divine.   (18, 12)

It was the time when night has not yet abandoned the edges of the scene to day, but the east is growing red, and there is still a star or two adorning the sky, when Rinaldo directed his steps up the Mount of Olives, gazing upward at the surrounding beauties, here nocturnal, there sunlit, all imperishable and divine.

Cedere libero ogni confin represents the characteristic kind of idiom devised by Tasso which is unusual, expressive, full but not markedly periphrastic or excessive in the number of words for what must be said, considering that we are in the high decorum of ample phrasing. The last three lines illustrate the polysyllabic tendency of high style, for which Tasso used words relatively uncommon in poetry. The description itself is not profuse in detail:

> Così pregava, e gli sorgeva a fronte
> fatta già d'auro la vermiglia aurora
> che l'elmo e l'arme e intorno a lui del monte
> le verdi cime illuminando indora;
> e ventilar nel petto e ne la fronte
> sentia gli spirti di piacevol òra,
> che sovra il capo suo scotea dal grembo
> de la bell'alba un rugiadoso nembo.   (18, 15)

Thus he prayed, and the red dawn, become golden, rose opposite him and with its light gilded his helmet and arms and the green peaks of the mountain around him; and he felt gusts of pleasant air blow over his chest and forehead, gusts cast over his head from the mist of a dewy cloud in the beautiful dawn.

The classical manner is selective of detail and eschews the lengthy enumerations we find a few decades later in Marino's *Adone*. Just enough is said to make the scene vivid, and then comparisons follow, which bring out the spiritual character of the action, for it is the purification of Rinaldo's soul:

> La rugiada del ciel su le sue spoglie
> cade, che parean cenere al colore,
> e sì l'asperge che'l pallor ne toglie
> e induce in esse un lucido candore;
> tal rabbellische le smarrite foglie
> a i matutini geli arido fiore,
> e tal di vaga gioventù ritorna
> lieto il serpente e di novo or s'adorna.   (18, 16)

The dew from heaven falls on his armor, which had an ashen color, and so polished it that its dull cast was removed and a shining whiteness was revealed. Thus a dry flower's dying petals are brought back to beauty by the morning frost, and thus the molting snake turns over happy in its lovely new youth and is covered again with golden skin.

The artistic sensibility involved here doubtless belongs to the counterreformation, but in style the passage is eminently classical and even Virgilian.

The Latinity evidenced by the very title of Tasso's epic, which in standard Italian idiom would be *La Liberazione di Gerusalemme*, informs the language down to the characteristic omission of articles. All this is in keeping with the poetic tradition since Petrarch, but Latinity is brought to new heights for purposes of the high style. The element of harsh style is also an inseparable facet of Tasso's classicism, deriving from both ancient practice and theory. These two factors, along with systematic hyperbaton and a carefully worked-out esthetic of sound combinations, distinguish Tasso's high style from Ronsard's, which, in comparison, seems closer to pastiche, though brilliant pastiche, of Pindar or Horace. There is a further difference, however, between the two poets. Tasso represents the culmination of Italian neoclassicism, high style, and epic writing. The perfection of his manner is such that only Milton, working in another language, could profitably adapt some of his techniques. The next major Italian movement in style—that associated with Marino—drops down to a smooth middle style and competes in no way with Tasso's often harsh grandeur. With Ronsard the situation is different; he stands at the beginning of French neoclassicism, and while much of his manner, such as the pastiche effects, was to be discarded, his odes basically set the precedent for using largely the same vocabulary in high verse as in normal prose, actually limiting linguistic resources while in theory encouraging all experiments. His work in this respect is polymorphous and ambiguous, looking forward and backward, while Tasso, like Racine and Milton, represents the definitive form of high neoclassicism in his language. However, we should not forget in respect to his relation to Milton that Tasso did indulge in the late experiment of blank verse in *Le Sette Giornate del Mondo* which, while of no more than historical importance in Italian, points like a number of other works toward English epic blank verse.

III

It has often been observed that, while *Orlando Furioso* was Spenser's principal poetic source book for *The Faerie Queene*, Tasso's epic comes closer to his esthetic ideals, although its late publication precluded extensive influence. Spenser created the first sustained version of high-style narrative in English that has more than a purely historical interest.

The question of authenticity of language arose for Spenser, as it had to at a time when great linguistic changes had been taking place. Archaism, in the form of a limited but substantial number of words, was his solution, and Chaucer was his source.[13] We see the parallel with cinquecento Italian style and Petrarch; a further and more significant parallel lies in the analogy between Ennius and Chaucer, on the one hand, and Virgil and Spenser, on the other. The archaisms of Virgil's epic language are comparable in number and

13. See Veré L. Rubel, *Poetic Diction in the English Renaissance: From Skelton Through Spenser* (New York, 1941), and A. C. Partridge, *The Language of Renaissance Poetry: Spenser, Shakespeare, Donne, Milton* (London, 1971). For the various styles in Chaucer, see A. J. Gilbert, *Literary Language from Chaucer to Johnson* (New York, 1979).

nature to Spenser's, and Spenser must have been aware of the pro-
totypical place occupied by Ennius in Roman epic.[14] Spenser's archaisms and neologisms, for the latter tend to resemble the former, play
a much more prominent role in his style than do old words and neologisms in Ronsard and his French imitators, despite all their theoretical endorsement of them. The problem of blending unusual
terms with contemporary language constituted, therefore, a greater
problem in the elaboration of *The Faerie Queene*.

Spenser's means of naturalizing archaisms and neologisms in his
style lie in the use of sound figures, rime, alliteration, assonance,
and meter. The peculiarity of all four sound patterns in verse is that
they tend to make whatever fits them seem motivated and necessary. In the following examples the odd word is blended in phonetically with its surroundings: "In which they measure mickle weary
way" (V, ii, 29); "Her glorious glitterand light doth all mens eyes
amaze" (I, iv, 16); "That in the same did wonne some living wight"
(III, vii, 5); "And furious fits at earst quite weren quaild" (II, iv, 14);
"Perdy me lever were to weeten that" (III, v, 7). It is principally
meter which serves to naturalize the forms in which a final *e* or *ed*
must be pronounced, as well as verb forms with the prefix *y*. In the
domain of rime, there are various combinations which assimilate the
archaic or unusual to the familiar: *sate, amate, aggrate* (II, ix, 34); *sex,
wex, vex, flex* (III, i, 47); *brame, flame, became* (III, ii, 52); *strond, fond,
withstond* (III, ii, 52); *shape, awhape, gape, rape* (IV, vii, 5); *adaw, aw,
withdraw* (III, vii, 13).[15]

An aspect of English which greatly facilitates the blending in of
archaisms is the general character of its spelling. Spenser must have
been acutely aware that when we see English on a page, we are looking at a very different kind of spelling system from that of Latin or
Italian, in which spelling is by and large both phonetic and a mere
convenience. English words on the page have all sorts of idiosyncra-
sies—silent *es*, varying spellings of the same vowel sound, and capricious consonant groups—which remind us of the history of the

---

14. For Virgil's archaisms, see André Cordier, *Études sur le vocabulaire épique dans
l'"Éneide"* (Paris, 1939), 35–48.
15. Edmund Spenser, *The Works of Edmund Spenser: A Variorum Edition* (9 vols.; Baltimore, 1932–49), hereinafter cited in the text.

language and of the people speaking it. Although modern English was not very old in Spenser's time, the spelling had the antique air of a system in which there are numerous obsolete and purely ornamental parts. The language had, and has, a strong visual interest and suggestion of national tradition, unlike the artificial idiom of cinquecento Italian poetry, which did not really belong to any specific ethnic or political unit of the peninsula. The very idea of using peculiar archaisms is connected with Spenser's idea of the national epic, so dissimilar from the cosmopolitan material of the *Orlando Furioso* or *Gerusalemme liberata.*

Into the varied aspect of English words there is little difficulty inserting such alternate spellings as *sprite/spright* or *hand/hond.* We observe *fond* ("found") and *found* (I, x, 66, 67) and *mercy* and *mercie* (I, iii, 37) used in conjunction, and the variation of the latter is an aid toward rendering plausible and acceptable the less frequent forms like *lond* or the old words like *essoyne.* It is the general leveling character of imperfectly phonetic spelling that allows the mingling of archaism and neologism, Romance and Germanic forms, dialectal terms like *glitterand,* Chaucerian words, and purely sixteenth-century ones.[16] Thanks to the vagaries of spelling, Spenser's language does not look heteroclite, and it is only with the help of modern dictionaries that we become aware of what an odd lot of words he used.

English presents a special problem to the writer of epic in that high style, according to the rhetoricians, favors massive words, especially nouns. A reader of Virgil and Tasso, when he considers the possibilities of English epic diction, cannot but be struck by the enormous role of monosyllabic words in English, as opposed to the polysyllabism of Latin and Italian. Leaving Latin, with its elaborate, lengthening flections, aside, one observes that, whereas about half of Tasso's or Ariosto's words are monosyllabic, the proportion of them is much higher in *The Faerie Queene.* Here Archimago is following the Redcross knight:

> Still as he went, he craftie stales did lay,
> With cunning traines him to entrap vnwares,
> And priuie spials plast in all his way,

16. For the range of Spenser's vocabulary, see Rubel, *Poetic Diction in the English Renaissance.*

To weete what course he takes, and how he fares;
To ketch him at a vantage in his snares.
But now so wise and warie was the knight
By triall of his former harmes and cares,
That he descride, and shonned still his slight:
The fish that once was caught, new bait will hardly bite.

(II, i, 4)

Of seventy-odd words only twelve have two or more syllables. While other stanzas may contain a somewhat higher proportion, the mono-syllable nevertheless predominates. In addition, the monosyllable cannot be contracted very readily as in *è'n, nel, che'l*, which obtain the maximum meaning from a minimum of sounds. On the other hand, when it comes to verbs, nouns, and adjectives, English mono-syllabism offers a splendid semantic density, such as we see, for ex-ample, in Shakespeare's sonnets. However, such effects tend to be metaphorical and imagistic, to belong, in short, to middle-style lyric. Epic high style eschews inspissation of metaphor and aims at *gravitas*, which is a matter of both thematic seriousness and words weighty in form.

The archaisms or other rare words in Spenser often contribute to weightiness: "Eftsoones her steps she thereunto applyde" (III, vii, 5). *Thereunto* belongs to a class of heavy-seeming alternate forms that have by and large become infrequent in English, save for a few, such as *thereby, therefore,* or *whereupon. Eftsoones* is of note because, while only two syllables long, it contains a remarkable number of consonants; *otherwhiles* is similar in this respect. Some words are striking for being longer than the usual forms (*sithence, withouten*), while still others like *whylome* or *nathemore* derive their imposing effect solely from rarity. The relative *the which* is also an example of an alternate term with an extra syllable ("But thou thy treasons fruit, I hope, shalt taste / Right sowre, and feele the law, the which thou has defast" [II, vii, 31]); *the which* is especially interesting in that Spenser drops many articles where they would ordinarily be used. *For to* before an infinitive or *from to* ("Or who shall let [prevent] me now / On this vile body from to wreake my wrong," [II, viii, 28]) are fine examples of tool expressions more massive than are ordinarily needed; they therefore have not survived but suited Spenser's pur-pose excellently.

Epic *gravitas* can be aided by other devices as well. The compound sentence is a help and, even more so, the long sentence covering as much as a stanza:

> So forth she comes, and to her coche does clyme
> Adorned all with gold, and girlonds gay,
> That seemed as fresh as *Flora* in her prime,
> And stroue to match, in royall rich array,
> Great *Iunoes* golden chaire, the which they say
> The Gods stand gazing on, when she does ride
> To *Ioues* high house through heauens bras-paued way
> Drawne of faire Pecocks, that excell in pride,
> And full of *Argus* eyes their tailes dispredden wide.   (I, iv, 17)

This is a fine example of developed verse syntax which, written out as prose, would be difficult to follow; syntax, verse line, and caesura are subtly combined so that the subordinate clauses are perfectly clear. In this stanza we observe the additional weighting devices of the doublet (*gold and girlonds*), the epithet, and notably, the compound epithet (*bras-paued*). This precious Greek syntactic resource never fully established itself in Latin or in French, despite Ronsard's intermittent use of it. The variety of ways the compound epithet is formed in English and in Greek makes it a highly flexible poetic device.

Hyperbaton in English verse usually takes the form of placing the verb at the end of the clause, often making of it a rime word. It has a certain suggestion of formality in English ("With this ring I thee wed") which is, on the whole, lacking in the French use of end-position verbs; in French they are a more neutral than elegant sign of poetic language. Of course, there is no possibility in English of such varied hyperbaton as in Italian, but Spenser manages at times to create the impression of density proper to the figure by slightly unusual displacements of various parts of speech ("Alone he wandering thee too long doth want" [I, v, 13]).

The principle complementary to weight in epic style is continuity. The notion of an epic written in stanzas would seem to contradict this stylistic aim, but Spenser makes considerable use of connectives joining sentences both within and between stanzas: "Who all this while with charms and hidden artes" (I, i, 45); "Whom such whenas the wicked hag did vew" (III, vii, 11); "Who thereat wondrous wroth"

(I, ii, 19); "Whereto whenas they now approached neare" (I, xi, 1); "From whence when him she spyde" (I, iii, 26); "Therewith the knight thence marched forth in hast" (I, vi, 40). A number of these connectives also fulfill the criterion of weightiness by their phonetic and syntactic density; this offsets somewhat the suggestion of prose, especially Latin prose, they may have.

In regard to the general movement of Spenser's verse sentence, it has been at times maintained that his stanza with its leisurely alexandrine at the end, is inappropriate to narration, because it creates such a strong stop. I feel, on the contrary, that the reposeful effect of the alexandrine nicely varies the distribution of weight in the stanza, something Homer or Virgil could more easily attain by lexical means. The continuity advocated for epic style does not preclude pauses, and as we have seen, the alexandrine is not always a complete syntactic halting point, for the stanza connectives like *who when* lie somewhere between actual syntactic closure and the continuity associated with a single sentence.

It is appropriate now to examine the total articulations of a narrative stanza from *The Faerie Queene*:

> So wept *Duessa* vntill euentide,
> That shyning lampes in Ioues high house were light:
> Then forth she rose, ne lenger would abide,
> But comes vnto the place, where the'Hethen knight
> In slombring swownd nigh voyd of vitall spright,
> Lay couer'd with inchaunted cloud all day:
> Whom when she found, as she him left in plight,
> To wayle his woefull case she would not stay,
> But to the easterne coast of heauen makes speedy way.
>
> (I, v, 19)

So connects the stanza with the preceding one, and subsequent main verbs have adverbs making their relationships explicit: *then, ne, but* and the *but* of the last line. There are three sentences, Spenser's average, and the third is joined to the second by a *whom when* all the more prominent in that the antecedent is at some distance. The end-position verbs, in their natural place with *were light* and *would abide* but placed after their complements in the cases of *would not stay* and *left in plight*, clarify and punctuate the clausal structure. Finally, we observe that in the sixth line there is no article in the prepositional phrase; Spenser thus economizes on one empty mono-syllable. Likewise he does not use pronouns before verbs when they can be dispensed with, as in certain cases here, and even in many passages where their omission is singular. Spenser had a system of compensation by which much use of *yet* or *but* or of forms as osten-tatious as *the which* is counterbalanced by the dropping of many monosyllables he judged superfluous. This immensely refined and elaborate grammatical system was erected with the principle of epic high style in mind and the possibility of creating an equivalent to it in a language whose syntactic and lexical resources differ so greatly from those of Spenser's models in Latin and Italian.[17]

I have dwelt at length on technical matters which are often ne-glected but are vital to the conception of epic high style. A much more famous aspect of Spenser's art is his descriptions, and here cer-tain discriminations must be made. Description tends to be thought of as a middle-style figure, and it occurs in high classical epic either in compartmentalized fashion (the description of Achilles' shield in the *Iliad*) or mingled with narration in such a way as not to consti-tute units unduly halting the forward pace of the action. The other descriptive tradition, the detailed *ut pictura poesis* manner of describ-ing an object for itself is distinctly middle-style and is represented in the renaissance by Remy Belleau, with his poems on the oyster, the firefly, the cherry, the snail, and so forth. All of these uses of de-scription are based on the idea of imitation of nature and are irrele-vant to Spenser's achievement because the latter's descriptions are allegorical. Usually, however, allegorical poets had been dry and schematic in their visual indications, since these were, after all, merely signs of moral ideas.

The same rather summary approach to visual representation can also be seen in allegory in the fine arts: Botticelli's *La Calunnia* is a highly rationalized work of little sensuous appeal. On the other hand, *La Primavera* is sufficiently rich in color and detail that its alle-gory is readily neglected in favor of enjoying its purely painterly as-pects, and it is the use of this kind of elaborate technique that makes

17. See Herbert W. Sugden, *The Grammar of Spenser's "Faerie Queene"* (Philadelphia, 1936.

Spenser's descriptions rather different from the general tradition of self-conscious allegory. The "dream pictures" can be read as sheer pictorial units:

> His yron coate all ouergrowne with rust,
> Was vnderneath enueloped with gold,
> Whose glistring glosse darkned with filthy dust,
> Well yet appeared, to haue beene of old
> A worke of rich entayle, and curious mould,
> Wouen with antickes and wild Imagery:
> And in his lap a masse of coyne he told,
> And turned vpsidowne, to feede his eye
> And couetous desire with his huge threasury.   (II, 7, 4)

Modern students of Spenser have become much concerned with the allegorical significance of his detail, but Spenser must have been conscious of the possibility of reading his work at various levels. In fact, the little interpretive jingles placed at the head of each canto underscore the difference between summary idea and visual realization. The relation, much more complex than the obvious moral allegories attached to the *Orlando Furioso*, is a genuine stylistic problem in that the pictorial writing is denser for the aware reader than it is in the *ut pictura poesis* tradition of *imitatio*. There is an element of mystery in Spenser's diction, that is, a sustained form of the old rhetorical figure of enigma, which we find Aristotle discussing (*Rhetoric* 1412a) well before the idea of allegory had been worked out. And the context in Aristotle suggests that enigma is another facet of the "strange" quality of high poetry.

Aside from the fact that it is unfinished, *The Faerie Queene* in many ways offers a somewhat imperfect, labored version of high style in its heavy, if ingenious syntax, but the quality of depth in its language is comparable to the audacious or forceful effects aimed at in high style and makes it an even more rewarding example of high style in many places than the more perfect *Gerusalemme liberata*. The great English poets of the renaissance had far greater-seeming difficulties in their medium than Italian ones, but they overcame them in uniquely bold manners. It is striking that in English at the end of the sixteenth century there were such different solutions to the problem of creating a poetic idiom; Spenser, Shakespeare, Donne, and Jonson—to pass completely over the horde of Petrarchist poets—working with a language that had generally been judged recalcitrant to poetic expression, each devised a highly consistent style based on his own appraisal of the nature of English. However, if we look at their work in terms of rhetorical theory, it becomes evident that questions of level of style and genre were of the greatest aid in the choices they made. The differences among them reflect how the rhetorical tradition, always flexible and always undergoing modifications, served each in its way as the catalyst of inspiration.

IV

Genuine high style is not easily achieved. Virgil's epic and Horace's Roman odes are the major Augustan examples of it in Latin, which was the classical language most poets were more familiar with. There are two versions of epic style, according to Ronsard's prefaces to *La Franciade*: the plain Homeric one and the more ornate Virgilian manner. The difficulties of imitating Homer are immense, and so, paradoxically, the complicated style served as an easier model than did the plain one. We should also remember in this connection that, although Longinus' *On the Sublime* had been published in the sixteenth century, it scarcely seems to have been read with any serious interest at this early date, and so the idea of the simple sublime style did not enter into most theoretical considerations.

Although the idea of some necessary harshness in epic style was to be found in well-known treatises, Tasso alone seems to have been particularly concerned with it, and Tasso's harshness is a relatively mild thing, when we compare it to the developments in the French lyric of the sixteenth century. Actually, two means of creating harshness are at work: in Tasso the strain of constant hyperbaton, as well as sound combinations, supplies it, whereas in the French lyric of the later sixteenth century harshness comes from the disjunctivity of enumeration and sentence asyndeton. There is actually one long poem of the period, Du Bartas' *La Semaine ou la création du monde* (1578), a didactic and hence middle-style work, in which the practice of asyndeton and enumeration informs not only the detail of the style but the larger elements of composition. The seventh day of *La Semaine* is constructed almost entirely by enumeratory juxtapositions of subject matter, within which sentence asyndeton and word enumeration abound. The vocabulary derives appropriately from Ronsard's early experiments. However, as we reach the end of the sixteenth century, we find that the idea of asperity is developed in even further ways, all in keeping, nonetheless, with the theories of Demetrius, Dionysius of Halicarnassus, and Hermogenes.

CHAPTER 5

Tragic Poetry

I

Agrippa d'Aubigné's *Les Tragiques* presents a number of problems when one attempts to situate it in the history of styles and rhetorical theory. The use of the word *epic* to describe this long, plotless polemic against the Roman Catholic church is less singular than it seems at first since, recalling *The Faerie Queene*, we see that an epic could be conceived of in thematic terms, rather than according to Aristotelian ideas of plot. To those who read Homer and Virgil allegorically, theme was what counted in the epic, not the incidental element of story.[1] Furthermore, the idea of an invective epic dealing with very recent history had been realized in Lucan's *Pharsalia* or *De Bello Civili*, a work to which d'Aubigné alludes and about which we shall have more to say in connection with the rhetoric of *Les Tragiques*.

The title of d'Aubigné's poem would seem to be a translation of *tragica*, "things tragical," and tragedy refers to a grave subject but not necessarily one ending in catastrophe: thus Milton called Revelation a "high tragedy."[2] Other theorists followed Aristotle's remark that tragedy needs no performance or actors; Tasso, for example, says in the dialogue *La Cavalletta* (1587) that tragedy can be epic or lyric. Of course, the Aristotelian parallel between epic and tragedy made the line between the two rather slight for those judging the spirit of a work, not its outward form.

In the foreword to *Les Tragiques*, d'Aubigné has some fascinating

---

1. See O. B. Hardison, *The Enduring Monument: A Study of the Idea of Praise in Renaissance Literary Theory and Practice* (Chapel Hill, 1962), 84.
2. *Ibid.*, 96.

theoretical remarks about his work. His assertion that "Misères," the first book, is written in a "style bas et tragique" completely upsets the traditional agreement between style and genre. *Style bas* probably refers not to the few low words in the work, but rather to the peasants and townspeople whose lot during the late sixteenth-century wars of religion forms part of the subject of the book. This use of *low style* to designate the social level of characters is in the tradition that assigned low, middle, and high styles to Virgil's work according to the subject of each of his three books—shepherds, farmers, or military leaders.

There is another sense, however, in which *low* and *tragic* can go together: one of the uses of low style is reproof and satire, and following the theory that all poetry is either praise or blame, the renaissance recognized the existence of invective tragedy (like *Coriolanus*) alongside laudatory tragedy.[3] Thus the low style and tragedy concur in blaming and assigning guilt.

The diction of "Misères" is rhetorically elaborate:

> Puis qu'il faut s'attaquer aux legions de Rome,
> Aux monstres d'Italie, il faudra faire comme
> Hannibal, qui par feux d'aigre humeur arrosez
> Se fendit un passage aux Alpes embrasez.
> Mon courage de feu, mon humeur aigre et forte
> Au travers des sept monts faict breche au lieu de porte.
> Je brise les rochers et le respect d'erreur
> Qui fit douter Cesar d'une vaine terreur.
> Il vid Rome tremblante, affreuze, eschevelee,
> Qui en pleurs, en sanglots, mi-morte, desolee,
> Tordant ses doigts, fermoit, defendoit de ses mains
> A Cesar le chemin au sang de ses germains.[4]

Since I must attack the Roman legions, the Italian monsters, I must do as did Hannibal, who split a passageway through the burning Alps drenched in vinegar fire. My fiery courage, my acid, strong temperament makes a breach rather than a gate through the seven hills. I am breaking rocks and the respect for error which frightened Caesar with its empty terror. He saw Rome trembling, dreadful, disheveled, who in tears, in sobs, half-dead, sorrowful, twisting her fingers, clenched her hands, defended with her hands the path to his brothers' blood that Caesar was attempting to take.

3. *Ibid.*, 52–53.
4. Agrippa d'Aubigné, "Misères," in d'Aubigné, *Les Tragiques*, ed. Jacques Bailbé (Paris, 1968), ll. 1–12, hereinafter cited in the text.

D'Aubigné uses a kind of typological symbolism in which references to ancient Rome apply to the Catholic church. The legend first alluded to is that Hannibal melted the alpine rock with hot vinegar. The *sept monts* are the seven hills of Rome. This matter is presented in language dense with figures: for example, with the opening comparison, we note that d'Aubigné is very fond of juxtaposing two terms in asyndeton which may or may not be synonymous (*aux legions de Rome /aux monstres d'Italie*). This device is quite rare in earlier French poets or in a classical style like Virgil's; it produces momentary ambiguity and tends to have an asymmetrical effect (unlike *les legions de Rome et les monstres d'Italie*), especially when combined with the epic enjambment d'Aubigné practices. Line 6 contains a similar construction. *Breche au lieu de porte* is a kind of *correctio*, an increasingly favored figure in the later sixteenth century, and *les rochers et le respect* constitutes a case of zeugma, a particular form of that joining of the abstract or figurative with the concrete that d'Aubigné indulges in abundantly. Line 9 contains the first of many personifications, and this one is modified by a triplet and a quadruplet of adjectival expressions and is finally complemented by a triplet of verbs, all these multiple constructions being in asyndeton, which is in the new taste of the late sixteenth century. D'Aubigné does not use extensive enumerations like Ronsard or du Bartas, but his presentation of his subject often has an enumeratory movement, and he frequently groups two to four parallel words or constructions. The enumeratory tendency is marked, even if he does not make great accumulations of nouns and adjectives.

The Roman reference changes from the Punic Wars to the civil war started by Caesar when he crossed the Rubicon, the subject of Lucan's poem:

> Mes desirs sont des-ja volez outre la rive
> Du Rubicon troublé: que mon reste les suive
> Par un chemin tout neuf, car je ne trouve pas
> Qu'autre homme l'ait jamais escorché de ses pas.
> Pour Mercures croisez, au lieu de Pyramides,
> J'ai de jour le pilier, de nuict les feux pour guides.
> Astres, secourez-moi: ces chemins enlacez
> Sont par l'antiquité des siecles effacez,
> Si bien que l'herbe verde en ses sentiers acreuë
> En fait une prairie espaisse, haute et druë:

> Là où estoyent les feux des prophetes plus vieux,
> Je tends comme je puis le cordeau de mes yeux,
> Puis je cours au matin; de ma jambe arrosee,
> J'esparpille à costé la premiere rosee,
> Ne laissant apres moi trace à mes successeurs
> Que les reins tous ployez des inutiles fleurs,
> Fleurs qui tombent si tost qu'un vrai soleil les touche,
> Ou que Dieu fenera par le vent de sa bouche.   (17–34)

My wishes have already flown beyond the bank of the turbid Rubicon: may the rest of me follow on a completely new path, for I do not think that any other man has ever skinned its surface. For sign posts, rather than Pyramids, I have Moses' column of smoke in the day, the pillar of fire at night. Stars, help me: these twisting roads have been worn away by the length of the centuries, so that green grass growing in the path has made of the roads a thick, high, densely covered meadow. In the direction the old prophets' fire took, I stretch the measuring rod of my eye; then I run forth in the morning; with my damp leg, I scatter the first dew, leaving behind me, as tracks for my followers, only branches bent low with useless flowers, flowers that fall as soon as the true sun touches them or that God shall wilt with the wind of his mouth.

D'Aubigné here follows the custom of inserting in one's poem a comment on its genre and style: the *chemin tout neuf* is his way of writing, and it recalls the ancient lost paths of the prophets with their invective style. The lines on flowers are a reference to d'Aubigné's profane love poems, which he leaves behind him. In this passage we find the metaphors *écorcher un chemin* and *le cordeau de mes yeux*: there are a number of brief metaphors in d'Aubigné's work which suggest the imagery of Shakespeare more than that of any previous French poet in that the figure is striking, yet used in passing and not developed.

The epic invocation comes not at the very beginning of the poem but at line 35:

> Tout-Puissant, tout-voyant, qui du haut des hauts cieux
> Fends les coeurs plus serrez par l'esclair de tes yeux,
> Qui fis tout, et conneus tout ce que tu fis estre;
> Tout parfaict en ouvrant, tout parfaict en connoistre,
> De qui l'oeil tout courant, et tout voyant aussi,
> De qui le soin sans soin prend de tout le souci,
> De qui la main forma exemplaires et causes,
> Qui préveux les effects dès le naistre des choses;
> Dieu, qui d'un style vif, comme il te plaist, escris
> Le secret plus obscur en l'obscur des esprits:
> Puisque de ton amour mon ame est eschauffee,
> Jalouze de ton nom, ma poictrine embrazee

De ton feu, repurge aussi de mesmes feux
Le vice naturel de mon coeur vicieux;
De ce zele tres sainct rebrusle-moi encore,
Si que (tout consommé au feu qui me devore,
N'estant, serf de ton ire, en ire transporté,
Sans passion) je sois propre à ta vérité.   (35–52)

Omnipotent, all-seeing one, who from the height of high heaven split the tightest hearts with the thunderbolt of your eyes, who made all, and knew all you made to be; all perfect in works, all perfect in knowledge, whose eye running everywhere and seeing everything also, whose careless care concerns itself with everything, whose hand formed archetypes and causes, who foresaw the consequences as soon as things were created; God, as it pleases you, write with a sharp point the darkest secret in the darkest part of men's minds; since my soul is heated by your love and jealous of your name, since my breast is ablaze with your fire, purge me with the same fire of the natural vice of my vicious heart; burn me again with your holy zeal, so that (consumed in the fire devouring me, being never brought to wrath without passion, as I am the servant of your wrath) I be fit for your truth.

The sound figures abound here: repeated words (*haut, tout, obscur, feu, ire, soin*), anaphora (*de qui*), polyptoton (*vice, vicieux*). The passage is at once enumeratory and amplificatory: the concluding lines restate the fire image in different ways.

In the preface to *Les Tragiques*, d'Aubigné asserts that "Misères" only slightly departs from the "laws of narration," a somewhat surprising expression if we do not consult the theorists of the sixteenth century. Minturno will provide us with some idea of these laws: in *L'Arte poetica* (1564) he states that narration consists of a story, into which one may insert episodes and laudatory or invective digressions.[5] The poet, furthermore, may speak in his own voice in epic. Actually, d'Aubigné departs more than a little from the laws of narration in that there is no basic narrative at all but a continuous series of embellishing units. There are the prosopopoeias of Melpomene, the earth, and the Pope-Nero; apostrophe regularly occurs, and one long specific episode about cannibalism is worked into the book. Long comparisons, developed to allegorical length, describe France as a mother, a dying giant, a ship full of mutineers, and an old man. "Misères" exhibits a constant procession of the most showy and extended figures. The uninterrupted use of vehement rhetoric creates

5. Antonio Sebastiano Minturno, *L'Arte poetica* (Fac. ed.; Munich, 1971), 18.

an oppressive atmosphere of turbulent emotion. Such figurative density belongs to the decadent Latin manner, as does the enormous accumulation of descriptive detail. Interestingly enough, however, for all his endless developments, d'Aubigné never falls into cliché, into the familiar poetic language of the time.

We have seen the kind of emphasis that comes from the contrast of lengthily developed phrases and short direct ones. An exaggerated form of this can be seen in the postclassical epic of Lucan and in d'Aubigné, where the variations seem more abrupt and obey less clear principles of design. There is a noticeable oscillation in "Misères" between patches of short, asyndetic, paratactic sentences and long hypotactic constructions. Nor is the clipped style reserved for narration as one might expect: reflections and recounting can occur in either syntactic mode. It is important to understand that such mannerist peculiarities of the style of d'Aubigné and other late sixteenth-century French poets were encouraged by their study of silver-age Latin. Lucan, whom Ronsard, with his classicizing taste in epic, disliked, provides innumerable examples of the juxtaposition of long sentences and short ones, illustrating the two forms of emphasis:

> At nunc semirutis pendent quod moenia tectis
> Urbibus Italiae lapsisque ingentia muris
> Saxa iacent nulloque domus custode tenetur
> Rarus et antiquis habitator in urbibus errat,
> Horrida quod dumis multosque inarata per annos
> Hesperia est desuntque manus poscentibus arvis,
> Non tu, Pyrrhe ferox, nec tantis cladibus auctor
> Poenus erit; nulli penitus descendere ferro
> Contigit; alta sedent civilis volnera dextrae.[6]

If the walls have caved in under the half-demolished roofs in Italian cities and huge stones are what remains of collapsed houses and no dwellings are guarded and only an occasional inhabitant wanders through the ancient cities; if Italy is covered with thorny thickets and lies unploughed for many years and there are no hands to work the fields which cry out for them, it is not you, ferocious Pyrrhus, who are the creator of such a disaster nor the Carthaginian; no other sword has been able to pierce so mortally: the wounds from a hand in civil war are deep.

Here we recognize both d'Aubigné's theme of the desolation of civil war and the abundant descriptive detail that separates his and Lu-

6. Lucan, *The Civil War (Pharsalia)* (London, 1962), I, 24–33, hereinafter cited in the text.

can's styles from the high classical manner. The apostrophic, interventional, and sententious manner differs markedly from the largely impersonal tone of Virgil, where the poet speaks in his own voice but rarely and for special effect. The Lucanian version of epic seems rather like a long meditation with outbursts of fury. The violence of short sentences characterizes these lines on the last phase of Sulla's revolt, as reported in Brutus' long account of civil wars in Rome:

> Periere nocentes,
> Sed cum iam soli possent superesse nocentes.
> Tunc data libertas odiis, resolutaque legum
> Frenis ira ruit. Non uni cuncta dabantur,
> Sed fecit sibi quisque nefas; semel omnia victor
> Iusserat. Infandum domini per viscera ferrum
> Exegit famulus; nati maduere paterno
> Sanguine; certatum est, cui cervix caesa parentis
> Cederet; in fratrum ceciderunt praemia frates.   (II, 43–51)

The guilty die, but only the guilty have been able to survive. Freedom was given to personal hatreds, and wrath, free of the restraints of law bursts forth. The deeds done were not committed in the name of one man, but each one executed his crimes for himself. The conqueror had once and for all ordered all crimes committed. The servant pierced his master's belly with his accursed sword; sons dripped with their fathers' blood; there was a struggle to see who could behead a parent; brothers fell as the battle prizes of their brothers.

This jerky, asymmetrical style was developed as an extreme reaction against the cult of continuity in high classical Latin. It is associated with stoicism and with emphasis on the grisly. The fact that it occurs in a speech pages long indicates Lucan's unbalanced conception of narrative structure, which is like d'Aubigné's in its digressions and amplificatory units. It is interesting, when one has finished the fourth book of the *Pharsalia*, to compare the amount of strictly narrative material encompassed with what one finds in the first four books of the *Aeneid*; it becomes apparent that very little has actually happened in Lucan's epic, but the reader has been through the most intense and strident embellishments on a few episodes and above all on the general thematic matter of the poem. D'Aubigné went one step further and made the narrative almost implicit, while the commentary and rhetorical elaborations swell to fill almost entire books. The sections following "Misères" are different in some ways but concur in scantiness of actual events in sequence.

The later books of *Les Tragiques* are also described in the preface. "Princes" and "La Chambre doree" are characterized as belonging to a "style satirique moyen," which is the ornamented satiric style not recognized by most rhetorical treatises but exemplified in antiquity by some of Juvenal's work. The enumeratory aspect of d'Aubigné's writing shows up particularly in "La Chambre doree," where we see a parade of personified abstractions such as Ire, Hypocrisy, Stupidity, and Hatred. The book on martyrs which follows, "Feux," is again enumeratory and cast in a "style tragique moyen." The explanation for the *moyen* would seem to lie in the fact that the martyrs are on earth, whereas in the last two books, "Fers" and "Jugement," whose style is tragic and "elevated," we see images of heaven and the Last Judgment. In other words, only the eschatalogical belongs to the high tragic style. The stylistic terminology does not describe any very readily perceptible change in diction but rather the nature of the subject matter.

It is interesting that d'Aubigné, who was a very learned man, found the three-style system adequate to describe his poem, once he had modified some of its customary associations of genre and style. One would have thought that the style theory and terminology of Demetrius, Dionysius of Halicarnassus, or Hermogenes would have better suited his purposes, since they give a prominent place to such qualities as harshness, violence, invective, and terrible grandeur. When we analyze the style of tragedy, ancient or modern, in the form of a play or of a long poem like *Les Tragiques*, these theorists, who focused less on the oration and more on what we would call imaginative literature, seem to have a greater relevance than the more conventional exponents of the three styles.

II

The writing of formal tragedy in the renaissance was accompanied, as one might expect, by theorizing on the language it should have. The ancient tradition, including Seneca, offered no unambiguous solution to the question since between Aeschylus and Euripides, for example, the differences are such that one cannot speak of any one Greek conception of tragic style. The two basic theoretical answers to the question are that (1) tragedy is in high style, concerned with kings and queens, and therefore employs the most elevated language, and (2) even kings and queens, under the stress of misfortune, forget their grandeur and speak simply. Of course, the mixed solution is to vary the style with the parts of the tragedy. On the whole, the view that uniformly grand language best became the genre was accepted.[7]

In practice, the more or less elevated style suited the purposes of Giraldi Cinthio and Robert Garnier, the best-known tragic poets of Italy and France, because their plays were built largely of set speeches with relatively little interaction among characters. Giraldi Cinthio's *Orbecche*, his most famous play, is written in the Bembist-Petrarchan manner, as an epilogue tells us, though the work admittedly includes a few words Petrarch never used. The syntax is less hyperbatic than that of the lyric; the expected ornaments are present in the form of similes, sententiae, and imagistic choruses, and the blank verse is competent. The play is Senecan—for Seneca was felt to be a more elevated poet than Euripides, the most accessible of the Greeks—and contains suitable horrors. Accepting the limits of cinquecento classicism, we find it consistent, but the language is very restricted in its capacities. Robert Garnier, who wrote the same kind of tragedy with long set speeches, is more varied in language, since he followed the Pléiade notions of style with their greater elasticity. There is a kind of relation, however, between the static character of the play's structure and the style. The speeches are often amplified to excess because there is little to interrupt them in the way of conflict.

Something of the limits of earlier tragedy remains in Marlowe, especially in *Tamburlaine*, despite superior poetic powers, and it is only with Shakespeare that we find a playwright who, like Spenser and later Donne, made a careful analysis of the possibilities of English as a poetic language and developed it to the point of an entirely new and viable conception of style.

Perhaps the most general question that arises in regard to Shakespeare's poetry, though this of course varies somewhat with each

7. See Wolfgang Clemen, *English Tragedy Before Shakespeare: The Development of Dramatic Speech*, tr. T. S. Dorsch (London, 1961), 25–29.

play and the parts of the play, is that of idiomaticness. *Idiomaticness* might be described as the feeling that for each noun only a certain number of verbs and adjectives are appropriate, for each verb only a limited number of complements, and so forth, the whole being dictated by custom. The most extreme affirmation of the importance of idiomatic language was made by Dominique Bouhours, one of the most distinguished, if often overly peremptory, theorists of French neoclassicism, who stated that actually only a few combinations of verb and noun, noun and adjective were possible. There is little to distinguish this notion from a theory of cliché, but Bouhours, for purposes of argument, overstated the neoclassical case.

Be that as it may, the range of idiomatic divergences is probably at its narrowest in French neoclassical literature, because the small audience envisaged for a work of art would tend toward homogeneity of *Sprachgefühl*. In contrast, nineteenth-century prose in English, spread over two hemispheres not yet united by easy communication, was extremely varied in idiom. Sociological and geographical factors, therefore, influence the diversity of a language, and in Shakespeare's case the range and origins of the audience certainly had some effect on variety of discourse. The pure courtier poet often tended to be limited in this respect in the sixteenth century, and some of the most original styles were created by writers like Scève, Spenser, and d'Aubigné who did not reside at a court, with its daily molding of the sense of what choice and necessary usage should be. However, even more important than the question of audience, doubtless, was the yearly increase in the number of words used in English in the later years of the sixteenth century.[8] Such increases break down the imperatives of idiomaticness, for those receptive to the new words at least, by presenting problems in choice of word combinations that had never arisen before. The sense of idiom is modified as the vocabulary available to poetry ceases to be in any way homogeneous.

When we look at the theoretical background of idiomatic variation, we find that with a characteristic dialectical subtlety, rhetorical doctrine held that a case of unidiomaticness, or *soloecismus*, a vice of

8. See Richard Foster Jones, *The Triumph of the English Language* (Stanford, 1953), 207.

language, could actually constitute a new figure and thus rise to the stylistic virtue of *ornatus*: the offensive expression becomes a beautiful *trouvaille*.[9] And so we have ancient authority for that indeterminacy of idiom which characterizes much of Shakespeare's most striking diction, especially on the more elevated level. When the feeling for idiom is willingly suspended, there is a gain in invention and the feeling of surprise (θαυμαστόν) which Aristotle praised and prized in language.[10] (*Rhetoric* 1404b). The poet of course can only impose a suspension of idiomatic expectations by the brilliance of his devisings. Otherwise, the result is the "frigidity" of language Aristotle also spoke of and warned against which comes when invention dominates but art fails. We may see Shakespeare's creativity at work in the details of word formation and in simple combinations like the doublet before approaching his rhetoric on the level of passages embodying tropes.

Often Shakespeare's inventiveness consists of taking some fairly standard element of English and employing it in an unusual but correct fashion. Thus Henry IV speaks of his fear of God's punishment for his "mistreadings" (*HIV PI*, III, ii, 11).[11] The word is an acceptable synonym for misstep, meaning mistake, but putting the verb in the plural gerund gives it an entirely fresh quality. Shakespeare is especially fond of negative formations like *-less* ("aidless," *Cor* II, ii, 116), *un-* (the glowworm dims "his uneffectual fire," *Ham* I, v, 90), and *dis-* (you must "disquantify your train," Lear is told, I, iv, 254). These negative formations have a curious vividness created in no small part by their rarity. The verb-stem nouns are another matter, having totally dropped from the language (*amiss, compare, attest*), and curiously, they go against the taste for new words of more than one syllable, so necessary to weighting style. In a similar vein are adjectives used as nouns: *fair, content*. The switching of a word from one part of speech to another without the addition of prefixes or suf-

9. Quintilian, *Institutio oratoria* (4 vols.; London, 1933), I, 5, 152, XI, 3, 1–2.

10. Aristotle. *Rhétorique*, ed. Médéric Dufour (3 vols.; Paris, 1932, 1960, 1973), 1404b, hereinafter cited in the text.

11. All quotations are from William Shakespeare, *The Complete Works*, ed. G. B. Harrison (New York, 1948), cited hereinafter in the text using the following abbreviations: *AC (Antony and Cleopatra), Cor (Coriolanus), Ham (Hamlet), HIV PI (Henry IV, Part I), KJ (King John), Lear (King Lear), Mac (Macbeth), Oth (Othello), RII (Richard II), RJ (Romeo and Juliet)*, and *Tro (Troilus and Cressida)*.

fixes is a recognized peculiarity of English, but Shakespeare extends it beyond normal expectations. The truly fine case of changing a part of speech is found in the use of nouns as verbs: "he words me" (*AC* V, ii, 192); "he pageants us" (*Tro* I, iii, 151); and

> I shall see
> Some squeaking Cleopatra boy my greatness
> I' the posture of a whore.   (*AC* V, ii, 223–25)

These constructions provide figurativeness and, especially if they are monosyllabic, the semantic density so characteristic of English. Idiom is disturbed in a way that realizes the remarkable potential of a uniquely English lexicosyntactic feature. The other changes, from adjective to noun and from infinitive to noun, are comparable to sixteenth-century French and Italian constructions, but "boy my greatness" is impossible in the structure of other western European languages.

We have seen that doublets play a significant role in high classicizing style, but it must be observed that their stately effect is often due more to the pure syntactic form than to any truly unusual semantic interest. Shakespeare, on the other hand, made of this widespread device, so common and so dull in many minor poets, a figure that can be fascinating quite beyond its rhythmically elevating function; he demonstrates with it a number of features of his aesthetic of diction. In "the dull and factious nobles of the Greeks" (*Tro* II, ii, 209), we see the German-Latin contrast, which in Shakespeare manages to be exciting rather than heteroclite. The common and rare adjective join in "our just and lineal entrance to our own" (*KJ* II, i, 85), a reference to King John's claim of legitimate rule. In "before the eye and prospect of your town" (*KJ* II, i, 208), there is compression: we have the idea both of those looking onto the town and out from it. A striking periphrasis for war occurs in "your industrious scenes and acts of death" (*KJ* II, i, 376), while the semantic density possible in a heavily monosyllabic language is demonstrated by "And we were better parch in Afric Sun / Than in the pride and salt scorn of his eyes" (*Tro* I, iii, 370), where, furthermore, we hardly know whether salt is a hypallage referring to the implied African desert or an elliptic allusion to putting salt into figurative wounds inflicted by Achilles' eye. The abstract and the concrete are juxtaposed in "his ponderous and marble jaws" (*Ham* I, iv, 50), applied to a tomb. Positioning of the adjectives is striking in "my youth / Hath faulty wandered and irregular" (*HIV PI*, III, ii, 27), as is the turning of *wander* into a copulative verb. Finally, many of the asymmetries that make Shakespeare's doublets so memorable are brought together in an expression describing an attack, "by interims and conveying gusts" (*Cor* I, vi, 5). The monosyllabic and polysyllabic are contrasted; only one noun has a modifier; Germanic, Old French, and Latin forms are present; and most striking of all, the two nouns are not semantically parallel; they seem unlikely ever to find themselves together.

Shakespeare's tropes are so numerous that we scarcely perceive many of them as such, having merely the general impression of a rich and strange texture.[12] The simplest trope is the metonymy, a single word substituted for another, usually more common one. It may be seen as a one word metaphor or simply as a means of variation in expressing some basic idea, as when Hotspur and his allies, dividing the map of Britain among them, speak of changing the course of a river and "gelding the opposed continent" (*HIV PI*, III, i, 110). There is no metaphoric context, merely this isolated figurative way of saying "cut off a piece of." The word can be unusual and not so easily synonymous with a customary term, as when Coriolanus speaks of the plebeians "feebling such as stand not in their liking / Below their cobbled shoes" (*Cor* I, i, 198–99). *Feebling* is so different from the common idiom *crushing* that there seems to be some ellipsis in thought here: they are crushed until all strength has left them. When two metonymies occur in the same sentence, their effect will vary according to the reader:

> Can it be
> That so degenerate a strain as this,
> Should once set footing in your generous bosoms?
> (*Tro* II, ii, 153–55)

I would not take this as a mixed metaphor or catachresis, but merely as two quite independent substitutions for *thought* and *enter* which need not be seen as being in conflict. Shakespeare's true mixed metaphors are intentional and more vivid.

---

12. For a complete enumeration, see Sister Miriam Joseph, *Shakespeare's Use of the Arts of Language* (New York, 1966).

When more than one term is used in the making of a figure, we have metaphor in the stricter sense. It may be very elliptical as here, where a metaphoric term is motivated by a concrete one: "Their armors, that marched hence so silver-bright, / Hither return all gilt with Frenchmen's blood" (*KJ* II, i, 315–16). The standard complete form of metaphor has four terms and a rather formal air:

> And like bright metal on a sullen ground,
> My reformation, glittering o'er my fault,
> Shall show more goodly and attract more eyes
> Than that which hath no foil to set it off.
> (*HIV PI*, I, ii, 236–39)

But perhaps more often, Shakespeare has an odd way of introducing some other expression into a basically simple metaphor which gives it complexity and brilliance: "A slave, whose gall coins slanders like a mint, / To match us in comparisons with dirt" (*Tro* I, iii, 193–94). The *gall*, a kind of metonymy for the slave's mind, and the *dirt*, so vividly contrasting with the implied idea of gold, makes the equation of *coins* to *makes* and of *like a mint* to *abundantly* much more involved-seeming.

Sometimes Shakespeare's use of Latin roots introduces very peculiar effects into a context. His Latinate words are not always formed on particularly sound or logical linguistic principles, but their odd ring has something artistically impressive about it:

> [They are nought else]
> But the protractive trials of great Jove
> To find persistive constancy in men.   (*Tro* I, iii, 20–21)

Here, of course, *protracted* and *persistent*, which correspond to the proper Latin forms, would have introduced an unpleasant repetition of consonants within each line. But there is more than a matter of sound in the choice of *-ive* endings. Historians of English have observed that the *-ive* ending was one of the favorite suffixes for the formation of new words in Shakespeare's day. Such words are often pseudo Latin, for they correspond to no standard Latin form; thus "protractive," "persistive," and elsewhere "plausive" represent the purely hypothetical *protractivus*, *persistivus*, and *plausivus*. Doubtless, semantic flexibility contributed to the favor *-ive* enjoyed, for we note in our examples a passive form (protracted), an active form (persistent), and a gerundive (to be applauded). These impressive formations with *-ive* bear witness to a special esthetic of language independent of true Latin usage but drawing on elements of it; indeed, the single case of *-ivus/-ive* gives us an insight into the whole peculiar savor the Latinate often has in Shakespeare, where we find that learned Elizabethan English has a philological existence of its own, unlimited by classical or vernacular usage.

Yet further peculiarities are to be found in Shakespeare's deployment of Latin-based words. Their meaning can be virtually invented; the populace is described as being tired of seeing Richard II

> with such eyes
> As, sick and blunted with community,
> Afford no extraordinary gaze.   (*HIV PI*, III, ii, 74–76)

Community makes an elegant sound contrast with *blunted* (itself a metonymy), even though the word in Latin does not seem quite to bear the meaning Shakespeare would give it. Instead of "community" or "fellowship," he seems to convey something like "commonly seeing Richard" or "the commonness of the sight of him." By using *community* in a rather unorthodox fashion, Shakespeare has packed a great deal more meaning into it than any single standard word could bear. Often Shakespeare's Latin words seem to exist in some sort of halfway world of language between English and Latin. One gets odd resonances, for example, from the following lines in which the root *ped* occurs in two words: "you foresee not what impediments / Drag back our expedition" (*HIV PI*, IV, iii, 18–19). The lines are enriched if we see the image of feet in them because of the word *drag*; yet one cannot read the words too literally without rather strange conflicts of sense. An "impediment" would have to stand in the way of an "expedition" but could scarcely drag it.

With commoner words from Latin, Shakespeare tends to alter idiom, so that abstract forms sometimes assume concrete implications. When, after a discussion of Helen in *Troilus and Cressida*, it is proposed "to deliver her possession up" (*Tro* II, ii, 152), the abstract word means the thing possessed, Helen herself. Similarly, when Henry IV makes a hypothesis about the turn of events that would have occurred if "opinion . . . / Had still kept loyal to possession" (*HIV PI*, III, ii, 43), *opinion* means people holding opinions, and *pos-*

session is Richard II's possession of the throne. Shakespeare's use of *opinion* is not surprising, it being a figure that has entered common idiom, but *possession*, following much the same model, is an oddity. With this and like usages of verbal nouns and other abstractions Shakespeare was cultivating a fairly new, extensive use of abstracts used metonymically. Latin affords only certain limited examples of this phenomenon, but French poetic diction, beginning with Malherbe, was to make of it a major feature of the high French neoclassical manner.

An extreme case of converting a discussion of polity into abstractions occurs in *Coriolanus*:

> This double worship,
> Where one part does disdain with cause, the other
> Insult without all reason; where gentry, title, wisdom
> Cannot conclude but by the yea and no
> Of general ignorance—it must omit
> Real necessities, and give way the while
> To unstable slightness. Purpose so barred, it follows
> Nothing is done to purpose.   (*Cor* III, i, 142–49)

English-speakers, in accordance with commonly disseminated notions of English style, tend to think of abstract terms as less sharp, less biting than concrete ones, but Shakespeare demonstrates here that they can have a kind of elevated vehemence. Actually, if we go back far enough in literature to a point when languages tended to employ fewer abstract forms, we find that Sophocles, for example, was admired for the grandiose effect of the abstract nouns he introduced into poetic diction.[13]

As for the general relation of abstraction and concreteness, the poetic tradition since Petrarch had juxtaposed the categories of the abstract, the concrete, and the figurative, but within on the whole a rather narrow thematic and stylistic ambit. Shakespeare transfers this interplay to greater areas of poetry and from the middle-style lyric to a high, often rough and vehement eloquence. It is particularly revealing for the contrast with Shakespeare to see how these categories work together without any clash in Tasso's style, particularly in the magniloquent passages with their loftiness of thought:

13. See A. A. Long, *Language and Thought in Sophocles* (London, 1968).

—Guerrier di Dio, ch'a ristorar i danni
de la sua fede il Re del Cielo elesse,
e securi fra l'arme e fra gl'inganni
de la terra e del mar vi scòrse e resse,
si ch'abbiam tante e tante in sì pochi anni
ribellanti provincie a lui sommesse,
e fra le genti debellate e dome
stese l'insegne sue vittrici e'l nome.[14]

Warriors of God, whom the King of Heaven chose in order to restore the
defeat of his faith and has guided and directed safely through arms and
deceptions, so that, in so few years, we have put under his sway so many
rebellious provinces and stretched forth his victorious standards and his
name among conquered and tamed peoples.

This is a tissue of words of different types: *danni* is as concrete as
injury, damage, or defeat, but its broad usage makes it fit nicely with
the abstract *fede*. English *arms* and *deceptions* are phonetically less of
a piece than *fra l'arme e fra gl'inganni*, and the presentation of the latter as a series of obstacles through which God guides the army uni-
fies them further. The literary forms *debellate e dome* (rather than
domate) are less sharp than *defeated* or *sconfitti*; they are more ideas
than images. The parallel of *standards* and *name* is justified by the
metaphysical reality of the latter. Tasso manages to form a semantic
continuum of words differing in level of frequency, degree of literary
tone, and concreteness of reference; the common Latin origin of the
terms and their phonetic homogeneity permits him a unified yet
quite varied diction. Shakespeare is almost assured, on the other
hand, of a certain amount of contrast—of asperity in Dionysius'
sense—which is one of the peculiar virtues of his mixed vocabulary.
The intermittent disparities of concreteness and of etymology in his
language provide an undercurrent of forcefulness and, so to speak,
linguistic willfulness.

At the same time the many degrees of similarity and heterogeneity in Shakespeare's vocabulary permit him to exploit ambiguities in
terms like the word *shape*, a favorite of his, with its shadowy suggestion of the concrete: "Our project's life this shape of sense assumes, /
Ajax employed, plucks down Achilles' plumes" (*Tro* I, iii, 385–86).
The whole first line has an elusively figurative quality, with *project*,

14. Torquato Tasso, *Gerusalemme liberata*, ed. Marziano Guglielminetti (2 vols.;
Milan, 1974), 1, 21.

life, shape, and *sense* giving the Greek leaders' plot a kind of vital emanation of will. The parallel construction of abstract and concrete terms, reminiscent of the figure of zeugma, is not infrequent:

> Where they did spend a sad and bloody hour,
> As by discharge of their artillery,
> And shape of likelihood, the news was told.
>   (HIV Pl, I, i, 56–58)

Here again the word *shape* mediates between the factual artillery discharge and the supposition of a great battle. This mediating function contributes here to a smooth shift between opposing types of words.

Another distinctive problem arises with abstract nouns in that they may be personified or represented as concrete things:

> What Custom wills, in all things should we do't,
> The dust on antique time would lie unswept,
> And mountainous error be too highly heaped,
> For Truth to o'er-peep.   (Cor II, iii, 125–28)

There is a kind of clash between abstract and concrete here; the imagery is deliberately grotesque, suiting Coriolanus' polemical attitude. A certain incoherence qualifies the passage as a catachresis, in keeping with the harshness of the tone. It is important to note, in regard to this passage and to all our other examples of possible or real mixed metaphors and of catachretic forcing of words, that in antiquity catachresis was associated with the spontaneity and inventiveness of speech, either in actual conversation or in the orator's attempt to put across his meaning at the expense or in the lack of a *verbum proprium.* Thus a clear and defensible motivation was seen for any deviation from coherent metaphor or normal idiom. Our next example is especially relevant.

In a famous passage from *Hamlet,* we begin with a standard four-term metaphor, only to drift into uncertainty as to the exact status of the following expressions:

> Thus conscience does make cowards of us all,
> And thus the native hue of resolution
> Is sicklied o'er with the pale cast of thought,
> And enterprises of great pitch and moment
> With this regard their currents turn awry
> And lose the name of action.   (Ham III, i, 84–89)

The *regard*, neither quite concrete nor abstract, seems to come from the sickly face, and instead of just influencing enterprises, which are exteriorized although they are actually in the mind behind the regard, it turns the enterprises into some vague suggestion of a river. Externalization, when we deal with abstractions pertaining to psychology, adds a spatial and therefore concrete element to the texture. Such verbal situations occur in love poetry from Petrarch on, but Shakespeare's terms here are couched in a much more subtle, ambiguous fashion than the *amor* and *heart* which so often move about in the Petrarchist tradition.

There is a much more formal, full type of personification enriched with many concrete terms:

> So shaken as we are, so wan with care,
> Find we a time for frighted peace to pant
> And breathe short-winded accents of new broils
> To be commenced in stronds afar remote.
> No more the thirsty entrance of this soil
> Shall daub her lips with her own children's blood.
> No more shall trenching war channel her friends,
> No bruise her flowerets with the armèd hoofs
> of hostile paces.   (*HIV PI*, I, i, 1–9)

This is the opening of a play, and therefore, as often, great ceremony is evidenced in the language. Unlike those of the passage from *Hamlet*, the personifications here are quite clearly distinguishable in respect to the main abstract words and their concrete attributes. There is an amplitude here not present in the personifications of time, error, and truth in *Coriolanus*. This abundantly pictorial form of the figure realizes the high classical conception of it we find in Virgil's *Fama* or "Rumor." Shakespeare practiced many degrees of personification, reflecting different styles and tones, as he did with other figures. Coriolanus' words are biting; Henry IV's, solemn. Ulysses' personification of time in *Troilus and Cressida* is also in the solemn vein but uses more abstract attributes:

> Time hath, my Lord, a wallet at his back
> Wherein he puts alms for oblivion,
> A great-sized monster of ingratitudes.
> Those scraps are good deeds past, which are devoured
> As fast as they are made, forgot as soon
> As done. (*Tro* III, iii, 145–50)

This constant shifting between the concrete and the abstract is especially characteristic of Shakespeare, as are the lines which follow the picture of time. Ulysses moves from one imagistic aphorism to another, and that movement in figurative terms brings us to the question of mixed metaphor.

In the mildest degree of mixed metaphor we find figurative terms brought together in an unusual fashion, but like *bond* and *knit* here, they are strictly speaking within the possible realm of consistency:

> Your speeches: which were such
> As Agamemnon and the hand of Greece
> Should hold up high in brass: and such again
> As venerable Nestor, hatched in silver,
> Should with a bond of air, strong as the axletree
> On which heaven rides, knit all the Greekish ears
> To his experienced tongue   (*Tro*, I, iii, 62–68)

As often in Shakespeare's metaphors, a half-abstract word like *bond* makes the question of metaphoric coherence somewhat moot and dependent on rather subjective appreciations. What is not uncertain, however, is the addition of the axletree simile in the midst of the metaphor. This very Shakespearean touch precludes simple analysis of the passage in traditional rhetorical terms, for two different figures have been woven together. The fact that all terms bear on words, sound, and air—intangibles—makes these lines quite clear, however, despite the intricate linguistic mechanism. The quick, caustic mixed metaphor, the one to which the rhetorical term catachresis is most appropriately applied, can often be analyzed as an ellipsis:

> So shall my lungs
> Coin words till they decay, against those measles
> Which we disdain should tetter us, yet sought
> The very way to catch them.   (*Cor* III, i, 77–80)

Coriolanus speaks against a disorder of society which is compared to measles. Very often, as here, the mixed metaphor seems to arise from metonymy (*coin* for "form," *measles* for "disease of the body politic"), but the metonymies take on more visual qualities in juxtaposition. Catachresis is especially appropriate to vehement scorn, the discordant image being a form of linguistic violence and aggressivity. But there is a larger metaphorical context as well: on the fringes of perception, we are aware of the simultaneous presence of *lungs* and *measles*, so that the passage seems half consciously related to one of those typical sixteenth-century images of the body and its warring parts. The healthy lungs want none of the attacks from the outside which would mar the skin.

The improvisational effect of the mixed metaphor is evident in a passage from Hamlet:

> So oft it chances in particular men,
> That for some vicious mole of nature in them,
> As in their birth—wherein they are not guilty,
> Since nature cannot choose his origin—
> By the overgrowth of some complexion,
> Oft breaking down the pales and forts of reason,
> Or by some habit that too much o'erleavens
> The form of plausive manners, that these men—
> Carrying, I say, the stamp of one defect,
> Being Nature's livery, or Fortune's star—
> Their virtues else—be they as pure as grace,
> As infinite as man may undergo—
> Shall in the general censure take corruption
> From that particular fault.   (*Ham* I, iv, 23–36)

We can see the mixed metaphor in part as a series of metonymic variations made up in the heat of speaking: *mole, complexion, stamp, livery,* and (influence of a) *star*. The series begins with the adjective *vicious*, from *vitium*, "defect," and ends with the closely related *fault*, so that we are brought back to essentially the same abstract idea. It is interesting to compare the form of this wavering, repetitive, spontaneous attempt at oratorical fullness with the calculated neat syntax of the accomplished, prepared orator like Ulysses speaking of time or with the solemn introductory speeches of *Henry IV, Part I* or of *Measure for Measure*.

The distinction between mixed metaphor and a dense series of metaphors might theoretically be made in terms of grammar: metaphors in different main clauses constitute a series, rather than a mixture. However, such a separation is weak in practice, since independent clauses or main verbs can be joined by conjunctions. Here we would seem to have a series:

> He was a thing of blood, whose every motion
> Was timed with dying cries. Alone he entered
> The mortal gate of the city, which he painted

> With shunless destiny; aidless came off,
> And with a sudden reinforcement struck
> Corioli like a planet.   (*Cor* II, ii, 113–18)

As usual, Shakespeare introduces complications; the city is concrete; the painting, figurative; and destiny, an abstract metonymy for death. Nonetheless, we have a strong sequential impression in this passage, as well as in the following one:

> In that day's feats,
> When he might act the woman in the scene,
> He proved the best man i' the field, and for his meed
> Was brow-bound with the oak. His pupil age
> Man-entered thus, he waxèd like a sea,
> And in the brunt of seventeen battles since,
> He lurched all swords of the garland.   (*Cor* II, ii, 99–105)

The compound epithet stands in an absolute construction and is therefore in a sense independent. The epithet has greater ellipsis, is more sentencelike than the type *man-made* or *heaven-sent*, for the noun is not an agent but the equivalent of *like a man*. This extraordinary compression, of which the English compound epithet alone is capable, helps set off the absolute clause from the sea image. Interestingly, the *brunt*, part of the sea metaphor, and *battles*, anticipating the gaming metaphor *lurched*, are tightly joined grammatically; yet they serve as a clear transition, so that the sea and the battle figures appear not mixed but sequential.

There is even more syntactic interweaving in the following images, of which those of one word are perhaps too vivid in the context of imagery to be taken as simple metonymies:

> The hearts
> That spanieled me at heels to whom I gave
> Their wishes, do discandy, melt their sweets
> On blossoming Caesar, and this pine is barked
> That overtopped them all.   (*AC* IV, xii, 34–38)

Here, and in the passages from *Coriolanus* above, we have that effect of surprise and movement which characterizes metaphors in a series rather than mixed metaphors.

Circumlocution and amplification, which tend to be classed with the vices of renaissance writing, deserve some special notice, although they are, of course, part of many preceding examples. A common small unit of circumlocution consists of using a grammatically expanded form in place of one word, as in "If you have hitherto concealed this sight, / Let it be tenable in your silence still" (*Ham* I, ii, 247–48). *Let it be tenable*, the third-person pseudopassive imperative, is substituted, with a Latinizing touch, for the simple second-person active imperative *hold it*. The purpose here is manifestly to create a line which, set off by pauses, will have two points of weight, *tenable* and *silence*, for the sake of equilibrium. In "you are too much of late i' the frown" (*Lear* I, iv, 208), the substitution, very common in Shakespeare, of a verb and noun for a simple verb, is emphatic and demonstrates that while monosyllables like the verb *frown* have semantic density, the counterprinciple of emphasis through length is still valid. Indeed, one of the most extraordinary and highly perceptible features of Shakespeare's style is his working out of the opposed advantages of pregnant English monosyllables and lengthy classicizing expressions.

A longer passage more fully shows the manner in which amplification and concision can be joined despite their theoretical opposition. One of the officers in the first act of *Hamlet* makes an inquiry about military preparations; it is probably the high-style nature of war which gives a minor character so embellished a speech:

> Good now, sit down and tell me, he that knows,
> Why this same strict and most observant watch
> So nightly toils the subject of the land;
> And why such daily cast of brazen cannon
> And foreign mart for implements of war;
> Why such impress of shipwrights, whose sore task
> Does not divide the Sunday from the week;
> What might be toward, that this sweaty haste
> Doth make the night joint laborer with the day?
> (Ham I, i, 70–78)

The parallelism of the questions is a typical sign of amplification, but when we look at the detail of the lines, we notice the omission of verbs and articles at a number of points, which provides tightness, and furthermore, if we attempt to paraphrase the passage, we find that the figures—ranging from singular for plural (*the subject*), noun for participle (*foreign mart* means "buying in foreign countries"), and hypallage (*sweaty*), to personification (*night joint laborer*)—are actu-

ally very condensed ways of expressing a good deal of detailed action. These lines demonstrate in the fullest the positive values of
rhetoric in dealing with relatively ordinary and concrete matters.

I have gone to such lengths in examining some figures because it
is not enough to know that Shakespeare uses rhetoric—like every
other poet of his period. There are special features in Shakespeare's
rhetoric, such as frequent ellipsis in meaning and the multiple uses
of abstract terms, that we do not encounter everywhere. The figures
are not something Shakespeare merely used. He elaborated them,
altered them, and created a texture in which they are so interwoven
that one finds new aspects of them the more one looks. There are,
finally, further exploitations of figures as they color individual plays
in different ways.

III

Shakespeare's early conception of tragic style is in keeping with renaissance theory and practice in that he envisaged more a high stage
language than a medium in which individual characters would be
sharply distinguished by their diction. Seeing the play more in terms
of a plot rendered with sufficient pomp, he made considerable use
of rhetorical units larger than the single figure: these are outstand-
ing substructures in the texture of the whole. Richard III's opening
speech is just such a unit and suggests much about the composition
of later scenes. An elegant metaphor with the ritualistic ambiguity
sun/son opens the monologue, and a series of more or less parallel
phrases follow, picked up occasionally with anaphora:

> Now is the winter of our discontent
> Made glorious summer by this sun of York,
> And all the clouds that lowered upon our house
> In the deep bosom of the ocean buried.
> Now are our brows bound with victorious wreaths,
> Our bruisèd arms hung up for monuments,
> Our stern alarums changed to merry meetings,
> Our dreadful marches to delightful measures. (*RIII* I, i, 1–8)

The lines tend to have a marked bipartite structure, with or without
antithesis. The imposing individual line is of great concern to Shakespeare at this period especially, and parallel nouns, parallel adjec-

tives, and alliteration are employed to create it. This symmetry shows up again in the division of the speech into two large parts. The sun of York is contrasted with Richard:

> But I, that am not shaped for sportive tricks,
> Nor made to court an amorous looking-glass;
> I, that am rude stamped, and want love's majesty
> To strut before a wanton ambling nymph;
> I, that am curtailed of this fair proportion,
> Cheated of feature by dissembling nature,
> Deformed, unfinished, sent before my time
> Into this breathing world, scarce half made up . . .   (14–21)

The sentence with suspended syntax (*I, that* . . .) is many lines long and constitutes a very formal grammatical device, lengthened again with parallelisms. "And therefore," Richard concludes, "I am determinèd to prove a villain." The passage is easily analyzed into the parts of an oration: exordium, narrative, argument, summary, and peroration, but the most significant thing about it is the reflection of the renaissance taste for highly structured, usually symmetrical or bipartite poetic units. Many sixteenth-century sonnets, in which theorists found tiny orations, have much the same kind of rhetorical art on a small scale.

Epitheton and enumeration, as in late renaissance French poetry, are regularly observable; here the vicissitudes of Elizabeth, Edward IV's queen, are described:

> These both put by, a poor petitioner,
> A care-crazed mother of a many children,
> A beauty-waning and distressèd widow,
> Even in the afternoon of her best days,
> Made prize and purchase of his lustful eye,
> Seduced the pitch and height of all his thoughts
> To base declension and loathed bigamy.   (*RIII* III, vii, 183–89)

Here we have a rapid sequence of figures which might be seen as a dazzling mixture of metaphors. The lines demonstrate the theory of high style as noun dominated, with the resultant concern for sonorous, balanced single lines. This kind of line construction could be said to constitute a sound figure, but figures which are more usually grouped in that category are also abundant, and a number of scenes are built around them. Richard's dialogue with Anne in act I, scene ii, is made up of repetitions and antitheses. The group scene in act II, scene iii, is again patterned to a mannerist degree, as this short excerpt shows:

> QUEEN ELIZABETH: Oh, for my husband, for my dear lord
> Edward!
> CHILDREN: Oh, for our father, for our dear lord Clarence!
> DUCHESS: Alas for both, both mine, Edward and Clarence!
> QUEEN ELIZABETH: What stay had I but Edward? And he's
> gone.
> CHILDREN: What stay had we but Clarence? And he's gone.
> DUCHESS: What stays had I but they? And they are gone.
> QUEEN ELIZABETH: Was never widow had so dear a loss.
> CHILDREN: Were never orphans had so dear a loss.
> DUCHESS: Was never mother had so dear a loss.
> Alas, I am the mother of these moans!
> (*RIII* II, ii, 71–80)

There is a strong analogy again with the patterned French poetry which began with Ronsard. The smaller ornaments of the play include such characteristic devices as an enumeratory apposition made of periphrases:

> [Calamity is full of words:]
> Windy attorneys to their clients woes,
> Airy succeeders of intestate joys,
> Poor breathing orators of miseries!
> Let them have scope. (*RIII* IV, iv, 127–30)

This is but part of another heavily patterned scene.

A formal stage language is found again in *Richard II*, and there we encounter a superb example of the lengthy simile. Richard II compares himself to the sun in contrast with Bolingbroke:

> Discomfortable Cousin! Know'st thou not
> That when the searching eye of Heaven is hid
> Behind the globe that lights the lower world,
> Then thieves and robbers range abroad unseen
> In murders and in outrage, boldly here;
> But when from under this terrestrial ball
> He fires the proud tops of the eastern pines
> And darts his light through every guilty hole,
> Then murders, treasons, and detested sins,
> The cloak of night being plucked from off their backs,
> Stand bare and naked, trembling at themselves?
> So when this thief, this traitor, Bolingbroke,
> Who all this while hath reveled in the night

> Whilst we were wandering with the Antipodes,
> Shall see us rising in our throne, the east,
> His treasons will sit blushing in his face,
> Not able to endure the sight of day,
> But self-affrighted tremble at his sin.
> (*RII* III, ii, 36–53)

The ceremonious simile like this one has an important function in rhetoric in that, while the figure may be sometimes purely decorative, the simile is a figure of logic as well, and here the universal correspondences are attested to prove that Richard is king, like the sun or God. Aristotle dwelt on the simile as *parabole*, or argument by analogy, as opposed to the simile as icon, or embellishment.[15] The antithesis likewise has a pleasant suggestion of logical argument for Aristotle (*Rhetoric* 1410a), and we must be careful not to see ornament or merely pathetic figures where logical ones are being used. Even the repetitions of the patterned scenes in *Richard III* demonstrate moral relations among the characters. The heaviness of this rhetoric does not represent simply the esthetic of high *gravitas* but has a thematic function as well.

The idea of an unvaryingly grand stage language is excellently illustrated in *Richard II* by the conversation of the gardeners sympathetic to Richard and his queen who make an allegory in act III, scene iv, of the state of England and the well-tended garden:

> Oh, what pity is it
> That he had not so trimmed and dressed his land
> As we this garden! We at time of year
> Do wound the bark, the skin of our fruit trees,
> Lest, being overproud in sap and blood,
> With too much riches it confound itself.
> Had he done so to great and growing men,
> They might have lived to bear and he to taste
> Their fruits of duty. Superfluous branches
> We lop away, that bearing boughs may live.
> Had he done so, himself had borne the crown.
> (*RII* III, iv, 55–65)

Again the logic of universal correspondences is at work. What is striking from the stylistic point of view is that there is no distinction

---

15. See March H. McCall, Jr., *Ancient Rhetorical Theories of Simile and Comparison* (Cambridge, Mass., 1969), 32–53.

of level made between the language of gardeners and that of royalty. Everyone speaks in the same high-style manner.

If we do not immediately insist on comparing these early plays with *Lear* or *Macbeth*, they appear for what they are: extraordinary culminations of the renaissance theory of tragic style, including the particular obsession with highly overt verbal patterns that had emerged in nondramatic poetry. The development of the drama, if seen too exclusively in terms of Aristotelian plot theory, does not make any sense as poetry or take its proper place in the history of high style. Likewise, an excessive concern with the depiction of character will blind us to the significance of such plays as *Richard III* or *Richard II*. Even worse, perhaps, is to look for middle-style lyric qualities in this grand oscillation between vehement, harsh language and mannered pathos. Once we accept the stylistic terms in which such plays are conceived, then we may allow ourselves to appreciate character traits like the nuance of vanity in Richard II's comparison of himself with the sun or the Longinian simplicity of "For God's sake, let us sit upon the ground / And tell sad stories of the death of kings" (*RII* III, ii, 155–56). These nice touches are perhaps what most attracts us to the play, but they will not help us understand the esthetic in which Shakespeare was working.

IV

Another very interesting play in its connections with renaissance poetry is *Romeo and Juliet*, which stands apart from Shakespeare's major line of development in some ways. The end-stopped line, which dominates in the early plays, here is combined with that tendency to asyndeton and parataxis which we have remarked on in French poetry of the later sixteenth century:

> But soft! What light through yonder window breaks?
> It is the East, and Juliet is the Sun!
> Arise, fair Sun, and kill the envious moon,
> Who is already sick and pale with grief
> That thou her maid art far more fair than she.
> Be not her maid since she is envious.
> Her vestal livery is but sick and green,
> And none but fools do wear it. Cast it off.

> It is my lady, oh it is my love!
> Oh, that she knew she were!
> She speaks, yet she says nothing. What of that?
> Her eye discourses, I will answer it.
> I am too bold, 'tis not to me she speaks.   (*RJ* II, ii, 1–13)

In high moments of the play the short, tense sentences often recur. In act I, scene i, Romeo's speeches average less than two lines per sentence; the same is true of Juliet's speeches in act II, scene ii, of the lovers' speeches together in act III, scene v, and of Romeo's last speech in act V, scene iii. Editors sometimes punctuate speeches so as to improve continuity, but the spirit of the style in such passages, which is often aided by questions and imperatives, is discontinuous.

The combination of such syntax with conceit suggests an excited lyric style quite different from the usual high-style continuity. We have here something d'Aubigné's term *style tragique moyen* might apply to, and indeed, with its strongly domestic character, represented not only by the nurse but by the parents, the situation could be characterized as belonging more to the middle style than to that of the later, grander tragedies.

Of course, of all the stylistic elements, it is the conceit that brings the play closest to lyric. The star image of act II, scene ii, is an especially appropriate example, being complicated, considerably developed, and probably not much to anyone's taste at the present moment:

> Two of the fairest stars in all the heaven,
> Having some business, do intreat her eyes
> To twinkle in their spheres till they return.
> What if her eyes were there, they in her head?
> The brightness of her cheek would shame those stars,
> As daylight doth a lamp; her eyes in heaven
> Would through the airy region stream so bright
> That birds would sing and think it were not night.   (15–22)

This is an appropriate place to ask whether Shakespeare normally uses conceits in tragedy, since the term is employed so indiscriminately in discussions of Shakespeare and other poets of his period. If we look at the origins of the word *concetto* in a literary sense, we find that cleverness and wit are implied. Italian poetry from the late sixteenth century through the seventeenth confirms this. The notion of the concetto was devised to characterize a certain brilliant, middle-style poetic tone, which is not at all that of Shakespeare's tragedies in general. The most extraordinary embodiment of the conceit in Shakespeare is doubtless that passage in the middle-style, Ovidian *Venus and Adonis* where the boar, intending to kiss Adonis, inadvertently gores him. Any strange or farfetched idea is not necessarily a conceit in the proper historical meaning of the word or in the context of rhetorical theory generally. In high style there are many bold thoughts which might seem absurd in another context:

> Forthwith a power of English shall we levy,
> Whose arms were molded in their mothers' womb
> To chase these pagans in those holy fields
> Over whose acres walked those blessed feet.
>   (*HIV PI*, I, i, 22–25)

Such fantastic teleology is comparable to saying we have noses to facilitate the wearing of glasses, but tone is everything in such matters, and Henry IV goes on eloquently to describe the Holy Land and his intended crusade. The role of bold and striking thought in poetry is noticeable in the examples ancient rhetoricians quote from Aristotle on, and any witty intent is absent from them. They belong to the general category of the *sententia*, much discussed by renaissance critics, which means not simply a maxim but any remarkable thought, however specific the reference of it. Such sententiae, if unusual enough, fall under Quintilian's general notion of *audacior ornatus*, the bold, high-style ornament which moves rather than delights like a middle-style conceit. Rare ideas not uncommonly have some physical improbability, like that of Lear's great lines:

> Thou art a soul in bliss, but I am bound
> Upon a wheel of fire that mine own tears
> Do scald like molten lead.   (*Lear* IV, vii, 46–48)

Here we find a hyperbole, often the source of conceit, used with perfect gravity and fittingness. Much the same might be said of Macbeth's hand, which will "the multitudinous seas incarnadine" (*Mac* II, ii, 62). However, when middle-style situations and passages occur in tragedy, the conceit may be perfectly appropriate. In *Othello*, Cassio comments on Desdemona's safe arrival in Cyprus with a conceit which is a courtly compliment to her almost supernatural charm:

> Tempests themselves, high seas, and howling winds,
> The guttered rocks, and congregated sands,
> Traitors ensteeped to clog the guiltless keel,
> As having sense of beauty, do omit
> Their mortal natures, letting go safely by
> The divine Desdemona.   (*Oth* II, ii, 68–73)

This is a conceit based on personification, rhetorically alike to the star conceit in *Romeo and Juliet*. But since it is not especially Petrarchist, it seems more the expression of elegant manners than an entry in a sonnet competition.

The mixed metaphor, which, with no sense of the origin and connotations of the term *concetto*, is not uncommonly called a conceit, is frequently just the opposite in tone; it often represents agitation, improvisation, anger, and polemic. The term *catachresis*, being neutral, is appropriate whether the mixed metaphor be a bold thought like taking "arms against a sea of troubles" (*Ham* III, i, 59); an expression of terror like Macbeth's fear that cherubim "shall blow the horrid deed in every eye, / That tears shall drown the wind" (*Mac* I, vii, 24–25); or one of Coriolanus' scornful comments on the plebeians. The degree to which people visualize such matters varies enormously, as was proved long ago, but we know from the study of emblem books that many renaissance readers had a keen taste for visual renderings of mixed metaphors or paradoxical expressions.[16] There appears thus to be more behind the formation of catachreses than simply freedom from idiomatic restraints. If at all costs one must relate mixed metaphors with concetti, rhetorical distinctions would be appropriate among the low-style paradox or joke, the middle-style witty concetto, and the rough, forceful, δεινός catachresis.

V

With the major phase of Shakespeare's work, we encounter the use of more than one style in each play as well as stylistic variations among the plays.[17] There are Greek antecedents for shifts of style

16. See Ivor Armstrong Richards, *Practical Criticism: A Study of Literary Judgment* (New York, 1939), 235–36; Leonard Forster, *The Icy Fire* (Cambridge, 1969), ix–xii, 52–54.

17. See B. Ifor Evans, *The Language of Shakespeare's Plays* (London, 1952); F. E. Halliday, *The Poetry of Shakespeare's Plays* (London, 1954).

within a play, but Shakespeare's treatment of this technique is very much his own. The obvious example is the use of comic prose scenes alternating with serious verse scenes as in *Henry IV, Part I*, but combining styles came to be much more subtle than that. The loosening of Shakespeare's prosody and syntax (see, for example, the broken grammar of "O that this too too solid flesh . . ." in *Ham* I, ii, 129 *et seq.*) makes the passage between verse and prose easier. The clash of *Henry IV, Part I* is not always present, although there are some new clashes of style, for styles may either be blended with transitions, stand unrelated to each other, or contrast violently. All style variations within one work are countenanced by Ciceronian theory, as well as Greek examples, and it is only in a rather tendentious interpretation of Horace's *Ars Poetica* that we find strict unity of style defended.

The esthetics of mixed style are quite diverse. *Hamlet*, for example, has a remarkable number of variations between prose and verse, both among the characters and between a character's various appearances. It might be maintained that the stylistic resources of this long play are, in fact, somewhat heteroclite, the parts standing out too much from the whole. In *Othello*, on the other hand, the combination of styles has perhaps met with more favor among subtler critics, although the complexity of means involved is so great as to seem theoretically unworkable. We find a certain amount of pleasant, relatively low-key diction in the roles of Desdemona and Cassio, but the most surprising thing in some ways is the kinds of base expression the play contains. Iago and Rodrigo's exchanges tend to be low in matter, especially in prose, like many such passages on sex in Shakespeare, but Othello's use of a violent low style is of great originality. Othello's style as he broods or rages in morbid jealousy is not the ordinary low style except perhaps when he uses prose in act IV, scene i, before falling into his "trance." Otherwise there is a certain decorum observed in the use of verse and literary metaphor, a decorum which abruptly yields to degrading imagery, so often that of animals:

> But there where I have garnered up my heart,
> Where either I must live or bear no life,
> The fountain from the which my current runs

> Or else dries up—to be discarded thence!
> Or keep it as a cistern for foul toads
> To knot and gender in!   (*Oth* IV, ii, 57–62)

The shift from fountain to cistern is a remarkable clash of the conventional poetic word and the highly visualizable, everyday household adjunct. Shakespeare has created in this play a new version of the rough, forcible, δεινός style. In theory, this style can rank on a plane with high style for its serious intent, but its means may be grotesque metaphors, heavy ironies, and vituperation. It is the negative side of magnificent style, used by high speakers in the grips of intense unpleasant emotion. However, classical thinking did not anticipate sexual jealousy as the major element in a serious piece of heroic writing. The violence and recourse to crude images we find in the accusations and insults hurled about in the first scene of *Richard II* more closely represent the kind of situation and theme for which ancient theorists would have found the δεινός style appropriate. Shakespeare has modified the category of style, making it much lower by classical standards of subject matter. It should be remembered, of course, that jealousy on the part of a woman such as Medea or Phaedra, found in Seneca as well as the Greeks, had a place in classical literature. It was an entirely different matter, however, to lend this kind of jealousy to a hero, with his necessarily freer language. To do so was to introduce a new form of the violent style, whose ambiguous nature, at once high in seriousness and low in means, was open to the coarser color Shakespeare gave it by a careful adjustment of expression.

However, if Othello had only the δεινός manner at his disposal, the play might have been the "bloody farce" Thomas Rymer objected to. Shakespeare carefully provides Othello with other types of style, at intervals. Othello is relatively plain spoken in the first act, rises to a mysterious eloquence in describing the origins of the handkerchief (III, iv, 54–75), speaks with great nobility of thought and expression as he approaches the sleeping Desdemona (V, ii, 1–22), rages somewhat with remorse on learning of Desdemona's innocence (V, ii, 259–82), and then begins his final speech (V, ii, 338). This last speech, the culmination of Othello's other style, is one of remarkable invention. It begins quietly, with short, largely para-

tactic sentences, after Lodovico's curt, peremptory words summariz-
ing the legal situation:

> Soft you, a word or two before you go.
> I have done the state some service, and they know't.
> No more of that, I pray you, in your letters,
> When you shall these unlucky deeds relate.
> Speak of me as I am, nothing extenuate.
> Nor set down aught in malice.   (338–43)

Then the syntax expands, as the style moves from the practical, factual plain language of the first sentences to an *allegoria*, which in
Latin terminology means a short passage describing an action in figurative terms:

> Then must you speak
> Of one that loved not wisely but too well,
> Of one not easily jealous, but, being wrought,
> Perplexed in the extreme, of one whose hand,
> Like the base Indian, threw a pearl away
> Richer than all his tribe—of one whose subdued eyes,
> Albeit unusèd to the melting mood,
> Drop tears as fast as the Arabian trees
> The medicinal gum.   (343–51)

The third person, substituted for the first, serves like the imagery to
distance the action described, to idealize it and put a noble, honor-
able interpretation on the whole ugly intermixture of base prose and
violent low outbursts which had preceded. We shift to a more conventional tragic point of view, although the language is far from the
old conventions. The asymmetry of the relations of verse line and
syntax in Shakespeare's later style more easily permits the passage
from one style to another than would have been possible with the
stricter, more formalized sentence and line movement of the early
plays. The exotic imagery identified with Othello in the description
of the handkerchief and elsewhere prepares us for the geographical references of the concluding lines, which are introduced indi-
rectly, almost as an afterthought, rather than announced with an
ear-catching opening phrase, as in the traditional practice of
rhetoric:

> Set you down this,
> And say besides that in Aleppo once,
> Where a malignant and a turbaned Turk
> Beat a Venetian and traduced the state,

> I took by the throat the circumcisèd dog,
> And smote him thus.   (V, ii, 351–57)

Two bipartite lines with *and*s and alliteration, as in Shakespeare's old grand manner, heighten the style, as do the polysyllables *Aleppo, malignant, turbaned Turk* (taken together as an expression), and *circumcisèd*, but the last line of four words consists of dense English monosyllables, providing that stunning change of pace Shakespeare so liked. The coincidence between the verbal development—the play as poem—and Othello's stabbing himself—the play as action—produces that spectacular interplay between rhetoric and deeds which poetic theater before Shakespeare had generally lacked.

This fascinating use of contrasting styles within Othello's role, as well as within the play, is a considerable advance over the classical theory of shifting styles, which applied primarily to the various decorums of exordium, narration, argument, praise, and so forth, and anticipates modernist uses of double or multiple styles. In *Othello*, however, we are not dealing so much with a clash of styles (as in *Henry IV, Part I*) as with a sudden shift of perspective brought about by level of diction.

VI

With *King Lear* we encounter another problem in multiple styles. Here we may distinguish three main levels: the carefully written but comparatively colorless language of Edmund, the daughters, and their husbands, whether it be polite, practical, or vituperative; the prose and the rimed language of Lear, the Fool, and Edgar; and Lear's major outbursts, particularly the one on the heath in act III, scene ii, to which we may add Gloucester's wrought-up language, with its parallel relation to Lear's in the double plot of the play.

The thematic material of *Lear*, aside from the constant references to nature, tends to be concentrated in the nonsense language of the prose with its dark *allegoriae*, and I shall not treat it here. What is more remarkable in the verse style is the rant which Lear indulges in:

> Blow, winds, and crack your cheeks! Rage! Blow!
> You cataracts and hurricanoes, spout
> Till you have drenched our steeples, drowned the cocks!

> You sulphurous and thought-executing fires,
> Vaunt-couriers to oak-cleaving thunderbolts,
> Singe my white head! And thou, all-shaking thunder,
> Smite flat the thick rotundity o' the world!
> Crack nature's molds, all germens spill at once
> That make ingrateful man!   (III, ii, 1–9)

Invocation, imperatives, and hyperbole often characterize rant, as does personification of great forces:

> Rumble thy bellyful! Spit, fire! Spout, rain!
> No rain, wind, thunder, fire, are my daughters.
> I tax not you, you elements, with unkindness.
> I never gave you kingdom, called you children,
> You owe me no subscription.   (14–18)

Rant might be defined as a violent style so exaggerated that it tends to pass beyond high forceful style into absurdity if it is not carefully prepared by situation and character, which are very much parts of Aristotle's philosophical approach to rhetoric. Attitudes toward rant have varied. This scene in *Lear* has been much admired in the past, and the widespread character of rant in the sixteenth and seventeenth centuries suggests that for many it appeared as genuine high style, without any qualifications. Lear's rant is exceptionally well written, we must observe. The nouns and epithets of the first eight lines are varied, imaginative, and follow the classical principle of creating grandeur through dominance of nouns and their modifiers, especially weighty ones. Perhaps less could be said of Hamlet's monologue when he is preparing himself to see Gertrude:

> 'Tis now the very witching time of night,
> When churchyards yawn and Hell itself breathes out
> Contagion to this world. Now could I drink hot blood,
> And do such bitter business as the day
> Would quake to look on.   (*Ham* III, ii, 406–10)

The language is perfunctory rant, yet might be justified on the ground's of Hamlet's attempt, even with clichés, to work himself up into a fury. Iago's private language tends also toward rant, though generally well phrased, but there we are dealing with a character convention justified by the working out of the whole play, and the fact that Iago has a double language, public and private, gives interest to his monologues.

The problem of rant is different in an unsuccessful play or in another genre like d'Aubigné's *Les Tragiques,* where we find a good share of it. Rant is a disorder of high forceful style, resulting in what Aristotle called frigidity of effect, and would seem, in the history of renaissance style, to be an almost unavoidable aspect of the attempt to raise style higher and higher which can be observed in the course of the sixteenth century. The corresponding phase of Roman style came after the high classical manner and is observable in Seneca, of course, but best of all in Lucan, who was the more gifted poet. In the *Pharsalia,* Caesar's apostrophes when he attempts to sail alone at night and in the stormy winter from Greece to Italy, as was never done, constitute a great model of a whole scene of rant.

But rant, however uncomfortable it tends to make one, has a theoretical justification in extreme psychological states like that of Lear or at times that of Macbeth, and Shakespeare, on the whole, salvages this peculiar form of violent style. It might be said to lie at the opposite end of the spectrum of the δεινός from Othello's jealous ravings, which are the lowest level of forcible, terrible style imaginable in a tragedy of some grandeur; rant, on the other hand, tends to exceed the top pitch of violent tragic intensity.

VII

Although one of those moralizing critics who are so attracted to Shakespeare has doubtless claimed the opposite, we may take *Antony and Cleopatra* as an example of laudatory tragedy, to use the renaissance distinction, whereas there is a large measure of guilt and harsh invective in *Hamlet, Lear, Othello,* and *Macbeth.* We shall find an appropriate difference in style and may take, as the index of it, the handling of the figure of hyperbole. Hyperbole is not simply one figure among many but occupies a special place in ornament.[18] It presents particular problems in treatment because of its violation of normal canons of belief and yet is not sheer fantasy but must be grounded somehow in reality. These extreme and paradoxical aspects of hyperbole make it difficult to handle in a serious style, for it may take on comic or ironic tones when they are least wanted.

Curiously enough, the first expression in *Antony and Cleopatra* that

18. Quintilian, *Institutio oratoria,* VIII, 67, 68.

one could plausibly call a hyperbole is the very scornful antithesis used by Philo in the initial scene, where he calls Antony "The triple pillar of the world transformed / Into a strumpet's fool" (I, i, 12–13). There are curious associations here. *Triple pillar* is an odd way of saying "one of the triumvirate," which is what Philo means. The expression suggests Atlas and mythological dimensions, both because of *pillar* and because of the double meaning of *world*, which is either the Roman Empire and its fringes in classical terms or the globe, the earth, as it was for Shakespeare's audience. In a sense, the movement of the play will consist in persuading the reader, by linguistic means, that Antony was indeed the pillar of the world in a greater sense than Philo intends.

Philo's words suggest the hyperboles common in speech, the need for exaggeration when one speaks with emotion. Likewise, the first hyperbole Antony uses is based on the colloquial model of extreme expression used in mild annoyance:

> Let Rome in Tiber melt, and the wide arch
> Of the ranged empire fall! Here is my space.
> Kingdoms are clay. Our dungy earth alike
> Feeds beast as man. The nobleness of life
> is to do thus, when such a mutual pair
> And such a twain can do't . . .   (I, i, 33–38)

Shakespeare builds a very grand, expansive idea on what is first an emphatic equivalent of cursing. Cleopatra immediately answers Antony with the wry "Excellent falsehood!"

There are two processes at work in *Antony and Cleopatra* which produce a much more complicated texture than that of most plays. Antony and Cleopatra change moods very rapidly, and their language moves correspondingly, sometimes within the same speech, from a colloquial model to a high level of expression suitable to noble and laudatory feelings. There are several examples of this in the first act, establishing it as a characteristic stylistic mode. Cleopatra dismisses Antony with the same type of hyperbole Antony had used in our last example; they are the world's archetype:

> Eternity was in our lips and eyes,
> Bliss in our brows' bent, none our parts so poor
> But was a race of Heaven. They are so still,
> Or thou, the greatest soldier of the world,
> Art turned the greatest liar.   (I, iii, 35–39)

The ironic last remark has the characteristic effect of holding in ambiguous suspension one's notion of the pair, just as they seem to view themselves ambiguously. The rhetorical form of this is the laudatory hyperbole and the belittling remark, or meiosis.

Here is a further example. Antony and Cleopatra have been bantering in taking leave of one another, and Cleopatra uses a hyperbole, half serious in tone, to which Antony replies lightly (*idleness* probably means "frivolousness"):

> CLEOPATRA: Oh, my oblivion is a very Antony,
>   And I am all forgotten.
> ANTONY: But that your royalty
>   Holds idleness your subject, I should take you
>   For idleness itself.
> CLEOPATRA: 'Tis sweating labor
>   To bear such idleness so near the heart
>   As Cleopatra this.

In Cleopatra's reply the rhetoric of paradox suddenly becomes serious as the meiotic *sweating labor* introduces the thought of the unpleasant features of their situation.

A final instance of these changes of tone occurs after Antony has left and Cleopatra imagines him on horseback: "O happy horse, to bear the weight of Antony" (I, v, 21). The idea of Antony's size and heaviness has at first sexual connotations, but by the process of word ambiguity it leads into the imagery of Antony as universal figure:

> Do bravely horse! For wot'st thou whom thou movest?
> The demi-Atlas of this earth, the arm
> And burgonet of men.   (22–24)

Of course, the literal reference is again to Antony's role in the triumvirate; he along with Caesar supports the world. But the hyperbolic image is much stronger in our minds than the precise expression it represents, just as "triple pillar of the world" has an imagistic quality that far outstrips in vividness our recollection of the exact political arrangement. This existence of diverse, if not discordant, levels of visual and theoretical-practical meaning gives the image, typically a bit hyperbolic, an unusually distinctive role in this play. At the end of her speech, Cleopatra matches her picture of Antony with a distancing description of herself:

> Think on me,
> That am with Phoebus' amorous pinches black
> And wrinkled deep in time? Broad-fronted Caesar
> When thou was here above the ground, I was
> A morsel for a monarch. And great Pompey
> Would stand and make his eyes grow in my brow.
> There would he anchor his aspect and die
> With looking on his life.   (I, v, 27–34)

The movement in the course of her entire speech from the joke about the horse to a mythical vision of herself is accomplished through serious hyperbole. In the context, *wrinkled deep in time* seems to mean that she is interwoven with the events of history like a figure of fate.

Act II demonstrates in sober and literal fashion that Antony is indeed half the world, in the political sense of controlling half the Roman Empire. In addition, the play of perspectives, of what one character says about another, invests Cleopatra with archetypal qualities in Enobarbus' speech and elsewhere. The interplay of levity and serious hyperbole in Antony and Cleopatra's speeches is reinforced by the varying comments on them; from Philo's opening scorn through Caesar's retrospective description of Antony, the mingling of hyperbole and meiosis is just the same as in the pair's own speeches. An interesting combination of distancing and hyperbole occurs again in the Roman scenes when Caesar hears that Antony, back in Egypt, calls himself king of kings and Cleopatra takes herself for Isis. Here we perceive their hyperbolic views of themselves through Caesar's disgusted account: hyperbole is subjected to a meiotic view.

Rapid changes in mood mark Antony's behavior after the battle of Actium, as he reproaches and forgives Cleopatra for her actions (III, ix, 51–71) and, much more significantly because it is put into images, when he makes these two remarks in the space of less than thirty lines:

> Alack, our terrene moon
> Is now eclipsed, and it portends alone
> The fall of Antony . . .   (III, xiii, 153–55)

and

> Let's have one other gaudy night. Call to me
> All my sad captains, fill our bowls once more.
> Let's mock the midnight bell.   (183–85)

The significance of all the reverses in Antony and Cleopatra's attitudes is again to create a suspension of judgment through ambiguity. Enobarbus' actions in this part of the play, with his own shifting view of Antony, serves to reinforce the main psychological action.

After Antony's death come the great hyperboles applied to him, always in the form of images:

> The crown o' the earth doth melt. My Lord!
> Oh, withered is the garland of the war,
> The soldier's pole is fall'n.   (IV, xv, 63–65)

The definitive hyperbolic passage consists of Cleopatra's recounting her dream of Antony:

> His face was as the heavens, and therein stuck
> A sun and moon, which kept their course and lighted
> The little O, the earth. . . .
> His legs bestrid the ocean. His rearèd arm
> Crested the world. His voice was propertied
> As all the tunèd spheres, and that to friends.
> But when he meant to quail and shake the orb,
> He was as rattling thunder. For his bounty,
> There was no winter in 't, an autumn 'twas
> That grew the more by reaping. His delights
> Were dolphinlike, they showed his back above
> The element they lived in. In his livery
> Walked crowns and crownets, realms and islands were
> As plates dropped from his pocket.   (V, ii, 79–92)

This is the climax of the world imagery, which is much more significant than the repeated imagery so often studied in Shakespeare's other plays.

We may now define the rhetorical mechanisms of the play more closely: the hyperboles of the earlier parts of the play are hypothetical and often qualified by meiosis. Since it is very difficult to say exactly how Antony is great, there is a tendency for the hyperboles to be metaphoric: "the triple pillar of the world." The shifts from colloquial, often meiotic language to high style and the figurative reflect this basic ambiguity about the stature of Antony. Antony and Cleopatra themselves, in their changing moods, are not always certain that "the nobleness of life is to do thus, when such a mutual pair and such a twain can do't." After Antony's death, however, there are no actions to belie epideictic expression, no obstacles to pure praise. Praise, however, does not in the least resemble that of the classical funeral oration. No precise virtues other than generosity are mentioned, and that idea is immediately converted into an image of expansion. Indeed, the telling of Cleopatra's dream, which replaces any formal eulogy, is a web of comparisons of Antony to the universe. The nature of his greatness can only be expressed in high-style imagery, in poetry rather than in rational prose. Thus there is a final ambiguity about the play: it starts with a moralistic comment on Antony, but by the end, after all the real and historical action, instead of there being refutation and countermoralizing, Antony is transformed into poetic myth which is immune to criticism except of poetry itself. The basic analogy of the world as man, unlike the commonplace comparison of man to a world, belongs, furthermore, to the obscurer realms of myth.

It is quite clear now, I think, how a laudatory hyperbole may work in high style, as opposed to the witty hyperboles of middle-style lyric and narrative. Again, we find that a comparison from which a conceit could perfectly well be made imposes itself as an absolute, if momentary truth to the reader of tragedy, ode, and epic. The difference lies in the basic rhetorical distinction that middle style "delights," whereas high style "moves" one to identification, belief, and total oblivion of the notions of exaggeration or excess. Shakespeare set himself an extraordinary task in style by using a historical subject which consistently introduces levity or meiosis as a lower level of language. The transitions or juxtapositions necessary are a remarkable part of his art.

VIII

Shakespeare's first fully realized conception of tragic style—which we find perhaps best exemplified in *Richard II* and in *King John* with its admirably dense, heavy rhetoric—in many ways embodies the theories of Du Bellay and Ronsard better than their own work. Totally disregarding any questions of influence and humanistic learning, we can see that Aristotle's few remarks on figurative style and Ronsard's interpretation of early Greek poetic idiom provide the background for Shakespeare's style. The emphasis is on *copia*, metaphor, and general linguistic inventiveness, although Shakespeare differs from this body of theory in avoiding archaism.[19] The idiomatic aspects of English are put aside if they prove to be a hindrance to these goals. It is very instructive to see how different the basis of Shakespeare's tragic language is from Spenser's pseudo Virgilianism, with its archaism worked into a generally not too unidiomatic texture, and from Jonson's version of classicism. These three esthetics of language are all derived from humanist studies, and each emphasizes a different aspect of Greco-Roman tradition.

The ancient theories generally most relevant to Shakespeare's tragic styles (*Antony and Cleopatra* is an exception) are those of Demetrius, Dionysius of Halicarnassus, and Hermogenes, whose frame of reference was Greek rather than Roman and who attempted to account for the complex styles of Aeschylus and Pindar, as well as the invective of the Greek orators. The notion that there was a harsh, rough version of high style, in sounds, vocabulary, and idiom, gives a proper basis to tragic vehemence and vituperation. This δεινός quality, which ranges in sense from the forceful to the terrible, is much less concerned than later theories with a hierarchy of vocabulary, ranging from low to high; it is therefore possible to find in the forceful or violent style what seems by later, more Roman classical standards to be a mingling of the base and the noble, the colloquial and the rare word. This is the interpretation given to early Greek poetic style, although, of course, in the absence of fuller documentation on ordinary early Greek, such an interpretation remains somewhat speculative.[20] Modern terms like *dark comedy, tragic satire* (used in the title of a book on Webster[21]), or d'Aubigné's *low tragic style* and *middle tragic style* are attempts to characterize works for which the idea of a high Augustan serious style is obviously inadequate.

What Shakespeare does in practice with tragic style, however, tends to go beyond the classical examples associated with the theory of the δεινός. Heterogeneity of materials is essential to his effects, many of which might be criticized according to certain precepts of the rhetorical tradition. We find dissonance and even discongruity

---

19. See G. L. Brook, *The Language of Shakespeare* (London, 1967).

20. See William Bedell Stanford, *Aeschylus in His Style: A Study in Language and Personality* (Dublin, 1942).

21. See Travis Bogard, *The Tragic Satire of John Webster* (Berkeley, 1955).

in Shakespeare's divergence from normal idiom, contrasting of double epithets, swift changes of metaphor, unusual metonymies, and juxtapositions of prose and verse. Still other related devices are contrasts between Germanic and Romance terms, between Latinate and ordinary words, or between monosyllabic and polysyllabic terms. The juxtaposition of abstract and concrete words, the use of catachresis, and the constrast of irony and serious hyperbole as in *Antony and Cleopatra* create further possible clashes of style. Incongruence in local effects is reflected in larger oppositions of style such as those in Othello's speeches.

From the relatively unvaried grand manner of *Richard II*, Shakespeare moved to an esthetic of language in which discordance plays a major role and whose unity is to be sought in a higher imaginative order than the ordinary rhetorical principles usually point to. If we adopt the point of view of Italian or French readers, accustomed to greater homogeneity of linguistic means, Shakespeare's dissonant compositional devices become yet more striking, although even comparison with the tragedies of Chapman, Marston, or Webster would bring out the peculiar intensity with which Shakespeare exploits heterogeneity of stylistic elements. I prefer to emphasize the effects of clash and discongruity in Shakespeare's style—using such terms as neutral descriptive designations—because they constitute a principal line of development from Shakespeare's earlier tragic plays or scenes to the high tragic period running from *Hamlet* (*ca.* 1600) to *Coriolanus* (*ca.* 1608). It would be difficult to find another aspect of diction so widely applicable to the plays Shakespeare wrote in the opening years of the seventeenth century.

Looking somewhat broadly at Shakespeare's position in late renaissance poetry, we observe that the notion of mannerism could be invoked to connect his tragic poetry with a more general movement in style. The peculiarities of Shakespeare's rhetoric do impart to some of the tragedies and histories the harsh effect toward which we see certain French poets striving in the later sixteenth century, an effect which is related to much of Donne's lyric work and of which examples are to be found, to some extent, in Tasso and Michelangelo. Some of the syntactically peculiar penitential poetry we shall look at in the next chapter is also related in expression to the rough or mordant style. Provided that one realizes that there are variations of level and genre in all these versions of Demetrius' and Dionysius' harsh style, there is no reason why it cannot be identified as mannerism, using the term to cut broadly across rhetorical categories so that it includes Donne's low-style-based work as well as high tragic poetry. The mannerist possibilities seem especially great in English, although it is essential to remember that more or less contemporaneously with Shakespeare's work in tragedies, poets like Spenser, Jonson, and the Petrarchists were striving to circumscribe the lexical plethora of Elizabethan and Jacobean English. Despite his greatness, we must not take Shakespeare as the only or the primary representative of English esthetics of style at the end of the sixteenth century. Modern interest in Ben Jonson and plain style has been especially salutary in this respect and corrective of romantic prejudices.

CHAPTER 6

Devotional Poetry: A Confluence of Styles

I

As a preface to devotional poetry, we can take the literature of *vanitas*. It overlaps historically with more strictly devotional work but can be distinguished from it by its negative character.[1] At the same time, it is extremely difficult to say where the stoicism of the late sixteenth century is divided from Christian *contemptus mundi*. In one of the most characteristic French poets of *vanitas*, we find the two strains of thought completely intermingled, although here and there a particular poem exhibits one trait or the other. Chassignet's sonnet XLIV develops an explicitly Senecan paradox:

> Nous n'entrons point d'un pas plus avant en la vie
> Que nous n'entrions d'un pas plus avant en la mort,
> Nostre vivre n'est rien qu'une eternelle mort,
> Et plus croissent nos jours, plus decroit nostre vie:
>
> Quiconque aura vescu la moitié de sa vie,
> Aura pareillement la moitié de sa mort,
> Comme non usitée on deteste la mort
> Et la mort est commune autant comme la vie:
>
> Le tems passé est mort et le futur n'est pas,
> Le present vit et chet de la vie au trespas
> Et le futur aura une fin tout semblable.
>
> Le tems passé n'est plus, l'autre encore n'est pas,
> Et le present languit entre vie et trespas,
> Bref la mort et la vie en tout tems est semblable.[2]

---

1. See Terence C. Cave, *Devotional Poetry in France, c. 1570–1613* (Cambridge, 1969).
2. Jean-Baptiste Chassignet, *Le Mespris de la vie et consolation contre la mort*, ed. Hans-Joachim Lope (Geneva, 1967), hereinafter cited in the text.

As soon as we have taken a step further in life, we have taken a step further into death: our life is nothing but an eternal death; and the greater the number of our days, the shorter our life. Whoever has lived half of his life, has likewise lived half of his death. We hate death as unknown, and death is as common as life. Time past is dead, and the future does not yet exist. The present lives and falls from life into death. And the future will end the same way. Time past no longer exists; the other doesn't exist yet, and the present languishes between life and death. In short, death and life are at all times alike.

Chassignet developed a rhetoric of the sonnet which exemplifies the further experiments in French word-patterning after its beginnings in Ronsard and Jodelle. There is often an extraordinarily large number of sentences or independent clauses for a sonnet. Here they total twelve; elsewhere they add up to as many as thirteen or sixteen. Parataxis is usual; both linkage and asyndeton of sentences are present. Chassignet's favorite pronouns are *quiconque, celui qui*, and *nous*, as is fitting to such sententious verse, and the repetition of the first-person plural ending of the verbs can be part of the constant, dense play of sounds. Words and sounds are repeated within lines and sometimes are identical with the line endings. Alliteration, assonance, polyptoton, and anaphora are frequent. These devices, so abundant in certain sonnets, would be fatiguing to list in detail. The general rhetorical formulation might be said to be an enumeration of *sententiae*, the stoic rhetorical pattern which we see in the duke's speech in the third act of *Measure for Measure* or Ulysses' speech on time in *Troilus and Cressida*. The relationship of this kind of verse to prose imitated from Seneca is evident. Montaigne's early essays contain patches of asyndetic general statements.

The other side of Chassignet's inspiration—which I am separating here somewhat artificially since the division is not always apparent—lies in Old Testament poetry with its parallel, enumeratory, sententious character and its many images of life failing:

> L'enfance n'est sinon qu'une sterile fleur,
> La jeunesse qu'ardeur d'une fumiere vaine,
> Virilité qu'ennuy, que labeur, et que peine,
> Viellesse que chagrin, repentance, et douleur,
>
> Nos jeus que desplaisirs, nos bon-heurs que mal-heur,
> Nos thresors et nos biens que tourment et que geine,

> Nos libertez que laqs, que prisons, et que chaine,
> Nostre aise que mal-aise et nostre ris que pleur.
>
> Passer d'un age à l'autre, est s'en aller au change
> D'un bien plus petit mal, en un mal plus estrange
> Qui nous pousse en un lieu d'où personne ne sort.
>
> Nostre vie est semblable à la mer vagabonde,
> Où le flot suit le flot et l'onde pousse l'onde,
> Surgissant à la fin au havre de la mort.   (LIII)

Childhood is only a sterile flower, youth only the ardor of empty smoke, manhood only weariness, labor, and trouble, old age only sorrow, repentence, and pain. Our games are displeasures, our happiness only unhappiness, our treasures and our possessions only torment and hindrance, our freedom only bonds, prison, and chains, our ease only discomfort and our laughter only tears. Going from one age to another is changing a lesser evil for a less well known one, which pushes us toward a place from which no one returns. Our life is like the wandering sea, where wave follows wave, and current pushes current, until we reach in the end the port of death.

The formula *être* plus noun in place of a regular comparison is brought to full use here. The images, water flowing, withering flowers, and vanishing smoke, belong to the kind of natural comparisons that Job, Isaiah, and the Psalms are rich in. Of course, the identity, in translation, of Hebraic poetic syntax and Senecan sentence structure is one of the strange coincidences that gives this poetry its ambiguous pessimism which could be that of the nonbeliever as well as of the Christian.

Chassignet tends repeatedly to exploit the same devices, but they are not peculiar to him. The enumeration sonnet on *vanitas* belongs to an international stylistic movement. In Barnabe Barnes's *Divine Century of Spiritual Sonnets*, we can find an analogous phenomenon:

> A blast of wind, a momentary breath,
> A wat'ry bubble symbolized with air,
> A sun-blown rose, but for a season fair,
> A ghostly glance, a skeleton of death;
>
> A morning dew, pearling the grass beneath,
> Whose moisture sun's appearance doth impair;
> A lightning glimpse, a muse of thought and care,
> A planet's shot, a shade which followeth,
>
> A voice which vanisheth so soon as heard,
> The thriftless heir of time, a rolling wave,
> A show, no more in action than regard,

> A mass of dust, world's momentary slave,—
> Is man, in state of our old Adam made,
> Soon born to die, soon flourishing to fade.[3]

But French and English literature are far from the richest in religious sonnets on this general syntactic model. The literature of enumeratory sonnets on *vanitas* or devotional themes has long been familiar to readers to German poetry. Those poets customarily called baroque, Daniel von Reigersfeld Czepko, Paul Fleming, Andreas Gryphius, Catharina Regina von Greiffenberg, Martin Hanke, and Quirinus Kuhlmann, all used syntax of this sort, as did Christian Hofman von Hofmannswaldau in the domain of secular baroque poetry. Indeed no other seventeenth-century lyric poetry seems quite so characterized by enumeratory patterns as German.

II

The attitudes of *contemptus mundi* and praise of creation are interwoven in seventeenth-century piety, and they both shade off into secular forms of thought: stoicism, on the one hand, and delight in worldly things, on the other. The sources of laudatory attitudes are also sacred in many cases. Psalms and hymns, just like the Old Testament texts concerning the vanity of life, provide a basis of elaboration. The rhetorical form, enumerative parallelism, is often the same. Father Martial de Brives, in the prefatory material to his *Les Oeuvres poetiques et sainctes* speaks of *agrémens*, and his sacred paraphrases or amplifications are not dissimilar in tone from worldly baroque poetry. The following is an enlargement of a liturgical text taken from Daniel: "Benedicite rores et pruinas, Domino" (Daniel 3:68). From the word *ros* (plural: *rores*), Martial de Brives extracts:

> Grains de Crystal, pures Rosées
> Dont la Marjoleine & le Thin
> Pendant leur feste du matin
> Ont leurs Couronnes composées:
> Liquides Perles d'Orient,
> Pleurs du Ciel qui rendez riant
> L'esmail mourant de nos Prairies;
> Benissez Dieu qui par les Pleurs

3. E. K. Chambers (ed.), *The Oxford Book of Sixteenth Century Verse* (London, 1932).

> Redonne à nos Ames fletries
> De leur éclat perdu les premieres couleurs.[4]

Grains of crystal, pure dews of which the crowns of the marjoram and thyme are made, during their morning rejoicing; liquid oriental pearls, tears from heaven which enliven the dying green of our meadows; bless God, who by flowers gives our withered souls their lost colors and brilliance.

The apostrophe becomes a series of periphrases. The process is the same one at work as in the Litany of Our Lady except that here the figures do not all have a symbolic meaning; the element of decorative exuberance is noticeable. We find this characteristic even more pronounced in a paraphrase of Psalm 148, where the simple phrase asking the moon to praise God becomes:

> Lune qui dans les Nuicts plus sombres
> Entretenez un petit Jour,
> Attendant que par son retour
> Le Soleil dissipe les ombres:
> Reyne de la moitié de l'An,
> De qui le superbe Ocean
> Suit le carosse comme un Page;
> Loués le Seigneur obligeant,
> Qui pour avoir cét équipage
> Par les mains du Soleil vous preste de l'Argent.

Moon who in the darkest nights maintain a little light, until with his return the Sun dissipates the shadows, queen of half the year, whose carriage the haughty ocean follows like a page, praise the obliging Lord, who, so you could have this equipage, has the sun lend you silver money.

The carriage of the queen moon, paid for, in a pun, by the Lord, would seem to belong very much to the worldly baroque manner with its fancifulness, although the Jesuits, who encouraged the worldly decorative style, could have perhaps pointed to an edifying moral beneath the conceit. Of course, there is a fundamental ambiguity here, which we must take account of in reading certain devotional poets. Delight in the physical world, which is, after all, God's creation, is as orthodox an attitude as Pascalian *contemptus mundi*. Christianity has always embraced these antithetical attitudes, each of which, carried too far, has its own deviation into heresy: igno-

4. Martial de Brives, *Les Oeuvres poetiques et sainctes* (Lyon, 1655).

rance of original sin or the hatred of God in his works, including the self. However, we need not worry about the orthodoxy of Martial de Brives; his fondness for enumerative structures, notably in his development on the dew is characteristic of the florid piety of his day.

This descriptive enumeration, which can be opposed to Chassignet's more often sententious type, reveals, nevertheless, the same traits. The individual elements stand out in the absence of much logical or progressive organization. We have here the coincidence of a tendency marked in French secular poetry since the middle of the sixteenth century with a type of structure we encounter everywhere in sacred texts—scriptures, liturgy, or hymns like the "Te Deum laudamus." It would be a vast oversimplification to attribute so broad a movement in poetic grammar to any one source or even to assume that the poets were all conscious of tending in the same stylistic direction. The background for such enumerative tendencies lies in universal rhetorical studies and in various postclassical Latin examples, as well as in the liturgical forms which entered the poet's consciousness through the intense religious education of the day and through the constant presence of the church in postreformation life.

If we characterize Martial de Brive's work in secular rhetorical terms, as is not entirely unfitting, it obviously belongs to the flowery middle style, but it is marked by a new tendency to let image follow densely on image, usually with the verse line as dividing point. There is a type of sonnet evolved by another devotional poet, the Protestant pastor Drelincourt, which carries this tendency even further:

> Vaste Elément, Ciel des Oiseaus;
> Corps leger, subtile Peinture;
> Maison, dont la fine structure
> Comprend trois Etages si beaus:
>
> Riche Tente, dont les rideaus,
> Par le Maître de la Nature,
> Sont étendus, pour Couverture,
> Et sur la Terre, & sur les Eaus:
>
> Ministre du grand Luminaire;
> Hôte fidéle, & nécessaire;
> Cause, qui produis tant d'Efets:

> Messager de Calme & d'Orage:
> Je voy, dans ton Sein, le Passage
> Qui méne à l'éternelle Paix.[5]

Vast element, heaven of the birds, light body, subtle painting; house whose delicate structure includes three such beautiful floors; rich tent, whose curtains are spread out by the Master of Nature as a cover, over both earth and the waters; minister of the great luminary, faithful host and necessary; cause producing so many effects, messenger of calm and of storms, I see, in your depths, the passageway leading to eternal Peace.

The rhetorical form of the first twelve lines is, strictly speaking, a series of apostrophes, but the effect is not that of the apostrophe at all. Baroque vocatives in series tend to be figurative and to resemble the appositional cascades of images that Hopkins and Laforgue use. Moreover, the periphrases do not follow one another in a logical order: surprise is rather the effect aimed at. Without the title, this would almost be an enigma poem. The disjunctive quality of the periphrases and the enumeration is such that all feeling of syntax vanishes until the last two lines rather weakly pull the whole together. This is an extreme development from a type of syntax we saw earlier in Ronsard in which a quatrain could consist entirely of nouns. The heteroclite quality of Drelincourt's images, along with the touches of scientific description we find here and there in baroque poetry, make his enumeration more capricious than a sixteenth-century one. The exuberant delight of the poem expressed by its syntax and images is, again, a quality that joins the secular and some strains of the devotional spirit. The actual theological content of the poem is so slight and conventional compared with the rest that we risk ignoring that Drelincourt's thought on eternal peace, forming the conclusion, is very important in the "economy" of the poem as the Greek rhetoricians called its structure.

It is not surprising that one of the earliest of the modern poets to use a rather broken, enumeratory syntax was Hopkins, whose poetry is so much given over to devotional praise of the world. The litanic movement is also not rare in the early French modernists like Corbière or certain minor symbolists. We may, in the latter case, see

---

5. Laurent Drelincourt, "Sur l'air," in Drelincourt, *Sonnets chrétiens* (Paris, 1948), hereinafter cited in the text.

such phenomena as a reaction against overrationalized syntax, with its pretensions to completeness and logical connection, but the baroque motivation for such grammar is undoubtedly more positive and aims to give a direct apprehension of the world and its spiritual qualities.

III

The poems we have looked at so far involve no interpretive problem as regards their religious thought. A somber tone, associated with mannerist poetry, predominates in Chassignet, while Martial de Brives and Drelincourt are full of a baroque delight in the world. With Richard Crashaw, however, the problems of poetic form are greater, and the theology informing his poetry has, at times, that *outré* quality which is as old as Tertullian's affirmation that he believed in Christianity because it was absurd. First we observe a problem in form; the following stanza is from "Saint Mary Magdalene; or, The Weeper," the most famous of seventeenth-century lachrymal celebrations:

> 'Twas his well-pointed dart
> That digg'd these walls, and drest this Vine;
> And taught the wounded *Heart*
> The way into these weeping Eyn.
> Vain loves avaunt! bold hands forbear!
> The lamb hath dipt his white foot here.[6]

The synthesis of Petrarchism, the Song of Songs, and general Christian imagery is characteristic of Crashaw, as is the movement of the images. This is a kind of spiritual narration which breaks up into an enumeratory, sententious series of affirmations. Since the sense is not secular and literal, the catachretic effect of the whole is not important. On the spiritual plane the sense is perfectly coherent as Crashaw leaps from one aspect of the Magdalene's conversion to another.

The stanza which follows, containing Crashaw's most famous lines, is more narrative in the ordinary sense, as it opens:

6. Richard Crashaw, *The Verse in English of Richard Crashaw* (New York, 1949).

> And now where'er he strays,
> Among the Galilean mountains,
> Or more unwelcome ways,
>   He's follow'd by two faithful fountains;
> Two walking baths; two weeping motions;
> Portable, and compendious oceans.

The lines on the Magdalene's tears form a series of figurative appositions, a typical seventeenth-century trope. The physical improbability of these portable oceans, like the heart entering the eyes in the previous stanza, reflects doubtless the love of emblems, like the weeping fire and the locked up heart, which illustrate catachreses in a rather surrealistic way. These emblematic notions, being paradoxical, do not lend themselves to development or continuity so much as to pure juxtaposition.

However, the role of the emblem books is secondary to the verbal mechanism of such poetry, which is the moral or sacred epigram with some sort of curious play on ideas: "Here, where our Lord once laid his Head, / Now the Grave lies buried." This epigram "Upon the Sepulcher of Our Lord" is one of many Crashaw wrote and shows the basic unit of his imagination. We are all so familiar with the common word play of Christianity, like dying to be reborn or like Saint Peter's being the rock on which the church is built, that we risk ignoring the vast number of physically paradoxical thoughts that accumulated in Christian literature after the scriptural canon was closed, but which show some of the same spirit. For example, in one of La Ceppède's sonnets, we read that the wounds in Christ's hands are windows through which to gaze on heavenly secrets. The shallow kind of criticism which is merely confused by seventeenth-century rhetoric would call this a conceit and find it witty or, more likely, horrid. But La Ceppède makes his own commentary, following it up with an authoritative reference:

> The Church Fathers consider in their meditations that these openings of the wounds which remained on Jesus Christ are so many windows . . . through which we look and see the most secret and profound mysteries of God's love and wisdom. Here, on this subject, are the rest of the aforementioned words of Saint Bernard: "Who knows God by his senses," he says, "or who takes counsel with him? But the nail has become for me a key to an opening so that I see the will of God. Why should I not see through the hole? The nail cries out, the wound cries out, the secret of

the heart is visible through the holes in the body. The great sacrament of faith stands revealed: the viscera of God's mercy are revealed, through which he visited us coming from on high."[7]

There is not a trace of wit in the modern or the seventeenth-century sense here. Saint Bernard's Latin sermon is based completely on acceptance that physical phenomena in sacred texts or history have a spiritual meaning and that sometimes words by their form illustrate this, for he plays on the terms *clavis*, "key," and *clavus*, "nail." It may seem grotesque to us to peer through the wounds on Christ's hands, but that is irrelevant to the interpretation of devotional imagery.

This problem in reading is analogous to the one we encountered with middle-style conceits and bold *sententiae* in secular literature. It is very important to understand the variations of tone and genre behind figures of speech. In Martial de Brives' notion that the sun lends silver to the moon through God, the intermediary, we find something like a secular conceit. The tone of the paraphrase is exuberant, and dealing only with God's works, the world, and not sacred history, the piece resembles middle-style description in which wit is not out of place. But Crashaw's poems, like La Ceppède's, deal with sacred events, and he takes it upon himself to elaborate images in the age-old Christian manner. Sometimes an ecclesiastical text can be found to authorize this or that paradoxical image, but authority is not so important as the mechanism of assembling images which are coherent in the spiritual sense, if catachretic on a worldly plane. Crashaw's song "Upon the Bleeding Crucifix," so characteristic of high devotional poetry in its subject matter, is one of his finest poems and illustrates a certain degree of artistic continuity in the imagery which the more famous poem on the Magdalene sometimes seems to lack:

> Jesu, no more! It is full tide.
> From thy head and from thy feet,
> From thy hands and from thy side
> All the purple Rivers meet.
>
> What need thy fair head bear a part
> In show'rs, as if thine eyes had none?

7. Jean de La Ceppède, *Les Théorèmes sur le sacré mystère de notre rédemption* (Geneva, 1966), II, 294, hereinafter cited in the text.

> What need Thy help to drown thy heart,
> That strives in torrents of its own?
>
> Thy restless feet now cannot go
> For us and our eternal good,
> As they were ever wont. What though?
> They swim. Alas, in their own blood.

Correctio, an ever more favored device of amplification in the baroque period, is here used to intensify the picture. The main figure is a sustained, seemingly hyperbolic comparison of blood to flowing bodies of water. Development of the shifting analogy is countered by abrupt figurative statements ("It is full tide" and "They swim") in which we see Crashaw's art of concision used admirably to punctuate amplification. The picture itself forms of one those visualized meditations that were practised with greater or lesser strictness of method by the devout and whose principle of focusing on details was imitated by poets.[8] Crashaw's representation of Christ as totally bathed in blood is not normally encountered in the Italianate iconographic tradition, but it recurs with some frequency in devotional poetry.

Correctio continues to dominate the poem, as the meditation completes the circle by representing the blood as one river, as at the beginning of the poem:

> But o thy side, thy deep-digg'd side!
> That hath a double Nilus going.
> Nor ever was the Pharian tide
> Half so fruitful, half so flowing.
>
> No hair so small, but pays his river
> To this red sea of thy blood,
> Their little channels can deliver
> Something to the General Flood.
>
> But while I speak, whither are run
> All the rivers nam'd before?
> I counted wrong. There is but one;
> But o that one is one all o'er.

A key to Crashaw's tonal treatment of Christ's "fruitful" wounds is suggested by a phrase near the end of the poem, "A deluge of Deliverance," which constitutes the moral of the meditation. It is part of

---

8. See Louis Martz, *The Poetry of Meditation* (New Haven, 1954).

the ambiguity of Christian thought that the passion is both a sad and a happy event; the same paradox as is illustrated by the expression "fortunate fall." The perfectly valid possibility of seeing something cheering in all sacred history tends to determine Crashaw's curious exuberance, which is tempered only slightly by expressions of sadness, when detailing the stream of Christ's blood or the tears of the Magdalene. The rhetorical tones and patterns of his own day, so often used to express interest, marvel, and delight, have a curious appropriateness to Crashaw's theology. At the same time, the images of the poem are not merely hyperboles. The river evokes the idea of being washed in Christ's blood as John the Baptist immersed Christ in the Jordan. The reference to the flood also constitutes a soteriological allusion. Indeed, Crashaw's imagery is perhaps more symbolic than hyperbolic, a distinction which is important if we are to develop a sense of the idiom of devotional poetry. It is baroque with a difference, a difference that a reader properly prepared, as presumably some of Crashaw's audience was, should recognize.

Crashaw's poetic methods are less successful from an artistic point of view in his longer, rather uneven poems, for which perhaps *enumeratory* is not so exact a term as *additive*. There seems to be no strong design governing the relation of the parts and the length. At his least successful, the pungent, epigrammatic ideas are interspersed with rambling developments. The esthetic problem is much like that found in d'Aubigné or Lucan, whose taste for extreme concision is countered by wordy developments.

We have examined some of the historical background of the use of odd or catachretic figures in devotional verse, and now a minor French poet, Father Zacharie de Vitré, will allow us to see a bit more closely how a seventeenth-century poet looked at his *Essays de meditations poetiques sur la passion, mort, et resurrection de Nostre Seigneur Iesus Christ* (1660). Vitré prefaces his poems with a long, somewhat devious account of how he wrote them. Amid endless conventional apologies for his lack of art, he manages to suggest that embroidering a little on sacred history is acceptable, that his manner is new, and that he hopes his readers will find "quelque pointe dans les pensées." *Pointe* is usually taken as a synonym of concetto, although its etymology relates it to the idea of the *acutum* in classical rhetoric.

However, the *acutum* designates a certain intellectual sharpness included in the original meaning of *concetto*, and therefore it belongs to the same semantic area as does wit in earlier English. Nevertheless, there are distinctions to be made. *Pointe de pensée* is a fuller expression than *pointe* and was probably used to avoid the connotations of précieux cleverness with its little jokes. Actually, Vitré's poems contain more of what we could call images than thoughts, but this distinction was not regularly made. Father Dominique Bouhours, somewhat later in the century, speaks of "new thoughts" (obviously a translation of sententiae) when he discusses baroque literature, and by that he designates a complex of intellectual and figurative qualities.[9] Given the middle-style, secular connotations of *pointe* and *concetto*, Bouhours' translation of sententia, *pensée neuve*, seems to me as valuable as the use of the Latin term to distinguish the bold thought of secular high or harsh style from the middle-style conceit. If we think of seventeenth-century writers as striving for a style which has intellectual acumen and includes the choice of images as part of the process of intellection, we arrive at a view of seventeenth-century literature which is not dominated by the essentially secondary features of witty conceits and puns. In the twentieth century, critics have gone about the analysis of seventeenth-century style backwards, stressing conceits and puns, and are therefore obliged to invent paradoxes like "serious conceit" and "serious pun" to explain why poems on Christ's wounds or the crown of thorns are not funny, even though they contain verbal mechanisms which can be used for wit. Bouhours' *pensée neuve* is a term indicating the general ideal of seventeenth-century literature of baroque tendencies: précieux, florid, devotional, dramatic; low, middle, or high. It is not out of place whether one speaks of gravity or *delectatio* in poetry.

Vitré in his poems shows the same kind of relish in the details of the Passion as Crashaw; he elaborates hyperbolically or symbolically, as the case may be:

> Verges qui fendés l'air? Instrument d'un Carnage,
> Scorpions venimeux! petits Dragons sifflans,
> Coutres multipliés? qui seillonnans ces Flancs,
> Arosez un Terroir qui fait nostre heritage.

9. See Dominique Bouhours, *La Manière de bien penser dans les ouvrages d'esprit* (1715; rpr. Brighton, 1971).

Cometes rougissans? la cause & le presage
D'un meurtre executé, par des bras insolents,
Rude, & sanglante gresle? où mille brins volans
Font sur ce Champ d'Amour leur horrible ravage.

Serpenteaux acharnés? dessus un Corps si blanc,
Dipsades? altérés de son illustre Sang
Qui ressautés en l'Air du mal que vous luy faites.

Rasoirs à cent tranchans? qui donnés mille Morts,
Balay de nos pechez? Sanglantes Espoussettes?
Nettoyez en mon coeur, sans déchirer son Corps.[10]

Scourges which fend the air? The instruments of a carnage, venimous
scorpions! Little whistling dragons, multiplied plough colters? Which fur-
row those sides, water a land which is our heritage. Red comets? The
cause and the anticipation of a murder executed by insolent arms. Rough
and bloody hail? In which many flying stones make a terrible wreck of
this Field of Love. Serpents eager to bite? On so white a body, thirst-
giving snakes?—craving his illustrious blood, snakes who leap into the
air from the pain you cause him. Razors with a hundred edges? Which
give a thousand deaths. Broom to sweep away our sins? Bloody feather-
dusters? Clean in my heart, without tearing his body.

Here we find another example of an extreme patterning and enumeration of nouns in the baroque period. The questions in the sonnet seem to be a form of *correctio* in which each succeeding periphrasis is stronger or presents a different aspect of the whips from
the preceding one. A certain taste for surprising miscellany seems,
at least superficially, to govern the choice of the periphrases, which,
as we have now become aware, are a major resource of baroque art.
Although a number of the nouns are biblical and the others may
have some patristic or other authority, their juxtaposition is more
striking than any nuance of symbolism.

The right of the poet to invent *pensées neuves* along the lines of the
church fathers' curious images seems fairly certainly the implication
of Vitré's hope that his readers will find "quelque pointe dans les
pensées." Not all devotional poets, by any means, availed themselves of this privilege. There is a good deal of routine imagery used,
but it is interesting that an essentially minor figure like Vitré should
have come up with such an unusual assortment of images and that

10. Zacharie de Vitré, "Aux Verges dont Jesus fut foüetté," in Vitré, *Essays de meditations poetiques sur la passion, mort, et resurrection de Nostre Seigneur Iesus Christ* (Lyon,
1660).

there should be some association in rhetoric between the *acutum,* the *pointe de pensée,* and enumeration.[11] In one of his sonnets on the crown of thorns Vitré moves easily and naturally from what seem to be images of his own invention to a scriptural expression:

> Parasol? dont le Port rend un mortel ombrage,
> Oreiller espineux? propre au Lit de la Croix,
> Tortis? entrelassez de Viperaux de bois,
> Herissons vegetans? animés de la rage.
> . . . .
> Tes esguillons pointus ne sont plus redoutez:
> Depuis que mon Jesus les a dessus sa Teste,
> Contre une telle Pierre ils se sont épointez.[12]

A parasol? Which to hold casts a deadly shadow. Thorny pillow? Right for the bed of the Cross. Wreath? Laced with wooden vipers. Vegetable hedgehogs? Quivering with hydrophobia. Your pointed goads are no longer feared, since my Jesus has them on his head; against such a rock they are blunted.

In one of those notes we find sometimes in baroque poets, the author reminds us that Christ is called a rock in 1 Corinthians 10. Vitré passes quite normally from baroque elaboration to Christian double meaning.

As we have seen, the notion of the *pensée neuve* covers the secular and devotional and permits the use of figures like catachresis, periphrasis, apposition, and enumeration to find an appropriate place in both domains of poetry. We need, however, to emphasize the interpenetration of secular and religious life in the seventeenth century which created an audience for both types of poetry, an audience that did not mistake grave brilliance for levity and had a strong taste both for sermons on the vanity of the world and for court ceremonies. While there was a great and well-known range of piety and forms of piety, perhaps the most striking general feature of religious life was the ease with which lay persons passed without any break in continuity from frivolous to spiritual preoccupations. Poems like Martial de Brives' or Drelincourt's show the mingling of secular middle-style *delectatio* and religious culture. At a further point toward devotional seriousness, one finds meditations like Vitré's, but they offer a dis-

11. See Heinrich Lausberg, *Handbuch der literarischen Rhetorik* (2 vols.; Munich, 1960), I, 278.
12. Vitré, *Essays de meditations.*

tinctly rhetorical and hence intellectual interest along with spiritual nourishment. The same intellectualizing spirit in the public found theological questions and disputes an attractive side of religion and considered rhetoric as pertinent to devotion as to the theater. The literary public's hierarchical conception of life and literature made it easy to distinguish between the tone and character of a *pointe de pensée* in a religious meditation and the *pointes* of the household verse written around the Marquise de Rambouillet.

IV

It is evident that with poets like Crashaw or Vitré the traditional levels of style are not entirely applicable. If ornamented poetry represents a sacred meditation, while there is some end of attraction and delight in ornament as in secular poetry, this end is subordinated to a spiritual aim. Of course, one could say that there is a spiritual goal in Petrarch's and Scève's poetry as well, and that the European version of middle style had, from an early point on, been partly oriented toward some ulterior end unforeseen in classical theory. This shift in rhetorical function corresponds to the general rule of progressive heightening of genre and style which we observe in European poetry. In any case, the secular work to which the devotional verse we have been examining has the greatest resemblance is middle-style lyric. Its forms, especially the sonnet, its rhetorical figures, and its disjunctive movement have their principal counterpart in the poetry of *delectatio*. The most profound difference lies in the opposition of the figurative conceit to spiritual meanings; both have their point of departure in concrete language, but their history, the way they are handled, and their place in culture differs.

With Father Pierre Le Moyne's "L'Amour divin: Hymne second," we encounter a quite different strain of devotional verse. Its thought is mystic, and its broad continual movement bears some relation to the high-style ode. Le Moyne's subject is "ce beau Centre des beaux feux," which is divine love seen as a sun, and he describes the metaphysical structure of the world in which everything is turned toward or reflects the central spiritual fire. Here, after descriptions of angels, is the Milky Way:

> Ainsi ces lumineuses glaces,
> Ces grands et mobiles miroirs,
> Qui nous éclairent tous les soirs
> Au soleil decouvrent leur faces;
> Ils se remplissent tout le jour
> Des nobles feux de son amour,
> Ils se parent de sa lumiere;
> Et de nuit, quand il est des ombres effacé,
> Ils demeurent épars le long de sa carriere,
> Comme les grands éclats d'un grand miroir cassé.[13]

Thus these luminous glasses, these great moving mirrors, who light us every evening, uncover their faces to the sun. All day long they fill themselves with the noble fire of his love; they take on his light. And at night, when he is obscured by shadow, they remain scattered along his course, like great splinters of a great broken mirror.

This imagery is less pretty than grand, as one can see by comparing the conceit about the moon's borrowing light from the sun in Martial de Brives. The diction tends toward the generality of the noble style, a fact which stands out as the Passion is next alluded to in more metaphysical than concrete terms:

> Et sur les os d'Adam tirez de leur tombeau,
> Par un dessein qui fut, en son effet, étrange,
> D'un Dieu mis sur un bois, il se fit un flambeau.

And over Adam's bones, taken from their tomb, by a truly strange plan, he made a torch of a God affixed to wood.

All receives its significance from its relation to fire, and the imagery consists of accumulating synonyms like *étincelle, flambeau, flamme, feu, allumer, brûler*:

> Mille brillantes étincelles,
> Qui volerent de ce flambeau,
> Soit sur la terre, soit sur l'eau,
> Firent mille flames nouvelles.
> Tous les coeurs touchez de ces feux
> Se releverent avec eux,
> Et sous la Croix se rassemblerent;
> Et pour s'en allumer se pressant alentour,
> Firent par la chaleur de laquelle ils brûlerent,
> D'un Calvaire de mort, un Vesuve d'amour.

13. Jean Rousset (ed.), *Anthologie de la poésie baroque française* (2 vols.; Paris, 1961), II.

A thousand burning sparks which flew from this torch, onto earth or the waters, made a thousand new flames. All hearts touched by this fire rose in it and gathered under the cross. And to kindle themselves, they pressed close about and made, by means of their burning heat, a volcano of love from a hill of death.

The last line is one of the few touches of typical baroque metaphorics, for the vision is largely different in style. This is the point of view of mystic poetry, even if the poem does not describe a personal mystic experience like those of Saint John of the Cross, Jeanne Guyon, or, seemingly, Claude Hopil.

Fire tends to be the key symbol of godhead, and subsidiary ideas are related to it. Instead of a dark night of the soul, purification is put in terms of suffering through fire, which may be a reference to purgatory, except that on such a highly symbolic plane one cannot always be sure whether words are periphrases for a more common idea:

> Sur ce beau theâtre de flames,
> Ou l'Amour a son element,
> Il se consume à tout moment
> Des troupes d'innocentes ames;
> Plus elles souffrent de chaleur,
> Et plus rare est le bonheur
> Dont leur belle cendre est suivie;
> Le seul feu qui les blesse, a de quoy les guerir;
> Il leur donne la mort, pour leur donner la vie;
> Et s'il ne les brûloit, il leur faudroit perir.

In this beautiful amphitheater of flames, where Love has his element, new crowds of innocent souls are constantly burnt up. The more they suffer from the heat, the rarer their happiness is, which rises from their beautiful ashes. Only the fire which wounds them can cure them. It kills them to give them life, and if it did not burn them, they would have to perish.

Here again we observe the tendency of images to be rather general; the picture derives both scope and a certain unspecific character from the word *theâtre*. Such abstraction befits a philosophical or theological conception, and to its sustained quality we might contrast the rapidly changing imagery of Crashaw's verse on the Magdalene. Here the language seems to obey more of the principles of secular high style.

The customary notion of receiving life through death is next translated into the phoenix symbol, just before the poem concludes:

> Ainsi sur un lit de canelle
> L'oiseau sans sexe et sans pareil
> Se brûle aux rayons du soleil,
> Et par sa mort se renouvelle;
> De ce beau planete amoureux,
> Luy-mesme il provoque ses feux,
> Et donne aux astres de l'envie;
> Du mesme bois il fait son nid et son tombeau;
> Et le soleil à peine a consumé sa vie,
> Que l'Amour la rallume avecque son flambeau.

Thus on a bed of cinnamon, the sexless unique bird burns himself up in the sun's rays and by his death renews himself. He himself draws down the fire from the beautiful love-filled heavenly body and makes stars wish to do the same. From the same wood he makes his nest and his tomb. And scarcely has the sun consumed his life, than Love rekindles it with his torch.

The phoenix expresses the essential Christian paradox better than anything except the Passion itself, and in this symbolic mode the phoenix appropriately receives more lines than the crucifixion, since the latter has too many accessory, concrete associations.

The final stanza brings the poem to an address and exhortation:

> Que ces feux causent de delices!
> Qu'il est doux de s'en approcher!
> Et qu'il s'en fait un beau bûcher,
> Pour nos amoureux sacrifices!
> Sens la vive ardeur de ce bois;
> Voy ces ronces et cette Croix,
> Qui brillent de flames divines.
> Arreste icy, mon coeur, ta vie est en ce lieu;
> Sois un bouton de feu sur ces belles épines,
> Tu seras un rubis sur le thrône de Dieu.

What delights these fires cause! How sweet it is to draw near them! What a beautiful pyre they make for our love sacrifices! Feel the intense heat of this wood; see these brambles and this Cross, which burn with divine flames. Stop here, my heart, your life lies here. Be a fire bud on these beautiful thorns; you will be a ruby on God's throne.

The conclusion mingles references to the phoenix and to Christ. The allusion to *épines* almost certainly concerns the crown of thorns, which especially attracted the baroque imagination. Le Moyne has made such an ample use of his fire imagery that it would seem difficult to find a strong ending for the poem; yet he does so, having saved the images of the fire flower and the gem for this crucial point, and the word *throne* focuses the imagery in a more conventional way. We are not left entirely with images of the intangible.

Although Le Moyne's mystique of fire has its origin in Saint John's equation of love and light and God, we find little else of the customary, often erudite, devotional Christian language here, such as the detailed meditation on events of sacred history. In the dominance of nouns, the sustained images like that of the mirror for the Milky way, the circuitous but not always periphrastic language, the general sweep and continuity of the verse, there is an analogy with high style or that special form of it recognized in the Psalms, which are often formulated in general and lofty terms. This is not the true high style of the period, which is secular and which we shall examine later, but it is unlike the usual devotional genre, with its middle-style analogies, in rhetoric and form. It can be plausibly argued that there exists no true high-style baroque poetry, that the baroque always reflected middle-style *ornatus*, and that an exception like Le Moyne's hymn is a curiosity but not sufficient in itself to warrant modifying our conception of the baroque to include in it a version of high style.

V

Jean de La Ceppède, was the kind of poet for whom even the devout seventeenth-century reader needed footnotes, and he supplied them in the form of a magnificent detailed commentary on the two parts of *Les Théorèmes sur le sacré mystère de notre rédemption* (1613 and 1622). There exists no modern edition of the work, but a reproduction of the original edition has been published (Geneva, 1966). This very readable means of studying La Ceppède with his own notes, as he must be studied, has helped make his name familiar, but his poetry has not as yet been so widely explored as it deserves to be.

La Ceppède undertook to recount the life of Christ from his leaving Jerusalem for the Mount of Olives through his appearances to the disciples after his death, concluding with an account of the descent of the Holy Ghost among men. The work consists of a total of 513 sonnets, a number which may dismay the prospective reader unwilling to believe that enough of poetic value can be contained in so many sonnets by such a relatively little known figure. The fact is, however, that La Ceppède with the help of his notes is the most readable of devotional poets, at least through Part I (three hundred sonnets).

La Ceppède used several styles, separately or in combination, and the sonnets fall into a number of types. There are, for example, narrative sonnets, scenes, meditations of a visual or intellectual nature, symbolic and literal poems. A vast religious culture along with contemporary humanist learning informs the work. Subjects are treated variously, as in the case of the sweat of blood in the garden of Gethsemane, which is handled first in a doctrinal sonnet with a long commentary on the debated sense of this phenomenon, then in a more poetic description of the event, and finally, in a superb sonnet on the symbolism of the hematidrosis.

On the plainest stylistic level, that of necessary narrative usually, La Ceppède tends to be concise and free of clichés, if not poetically very rich. He uses a good many second-person pronouns and questions to enliven this side of his work, following well-established rhetorical principles. The first level of ornament in *Les Théorèmes* is Ronsardian in a highly individual way. La Ceppède accepted the theory of *copia* in vocabulary, so that we find such classical touches as the use of *Olympe* for heaven, *haut-tonnant* applied to God, and expressions like *Minervé combat*. There are other neologistic adjectives, such as *ta venteuse constance*, as well as low words (*peloter, picoter*), archaisms (*greigneur, emmi, onc, cil*), and oddities like *bellesse* (from *bellezza*) or *ratiociner*, a fine word but singular in poetry. A complete list of everything unusual in La Ceppède's vocabulary would be very long indeed. The properly Christian levels of style vary from low realism (in, for example, a startlingly naturalistic description of the nailing of Christ to the cross) to a symbolic, figural language drawn from all parts of the Bible, its commentators, the church fathers, and sermon writers. Rather than the characteristic baroque type of periphrasis like his *ergoté trompette* (cock), La Ceppède's more distinctive form of expression lies in the use of sacred *figurae*.[14]

A sacred *figura* is nicely illustrated by lines on the sweat of blood:

> Cette rouge sueur goutte à goutte roulante
> Du corps de cet Athlete en ce rude combat,
> Peut estre comparée à cette eau douce & lente,
> Qui la sainte montagne en silence rebat.
>
> L'aveugle-nay (qui mit tous les siens en debat
> Pour ses yeux) fut lavé de cette eau doux-coulante,
> Et dans le chaud lavoir de cette onde sanglante
> Toute l'aveugle race en liberté s'esbat.   (I, 1, 39)

This red sweat rolling drop by drop from the body of this athlete in this hard struggle can be compared to that sweet and slow water that flows down the holy mountain in silence. The man blind from birth (whose family debated the cause of his blindness) was washed in this sweet soft flowing water, and in the warm bath of this bloody wave, the whole blind race frolicks in deliverance.

A literal episode about the waters of Siloam at the foot of Mount Zion (John 9) is the second term of a figural comparison; then the image of the blind man is extended allegorically to the human race in general, and the first term of the comparison returns. There is scriptural and patristic authority for the *figurae*, which, of course, should really not be called comparisons at all since they represent the metaphysical identity of the details of the Old and New Testaments. The stylistic method of juxtaposing three sentences, each of a different order of meaning, is biblical, but whereas biblical poetry is often given to long developments where connections are not obvious, La Ceppède's tight form focuses the utmost attention on the detail and working out of the images.

At times a whole piece is based on the *figurae* of biblical interpretation: every thing or event in the Old Testament corresponds to an aspect of Christ's life:

> L'Autel des vieux parfums dans Solyme encensé,
> Fait or' d'une voirie un Temple venerable,
> Où du Verbe incarné l'Hypostase adorable
> S'offre tres-odorante à son Pere offensé.

---

14. See Erich Auerbach, *Scenes from the Drama of European Literature* (New York, 1959), 11–76.

> Le vieux Pal sur lequel jadis fut ageancé
> En Edom le Serpent aux mordus secourable,
> Esleve ores celuy qui piteux a pensé
> Du vieux Serpent d'Edem la morsure incurable.
>
> Le pressoir de la Vigne en Calvaire est dressé,
> Où ce fameux raisin ce pressoir a pressé,
> Pour noyer dans son vin nos lethales Viperes.　(I, 3, 23)

The altar in Jerusalem lit with old incense now makes a dungheap into a venerable temple, where the worshipful incarnation of the Word offers himself, richly scented, to his angry Father. The ancient pole, on which once Moses fixed the brass serpent which cured the serpent-bitten in Edom, now bears him who piteously thought of the incurable bite of the old serpent in Eden. The winepress of the vine is set up in Calvary, where the press has pressed the famous bunch of grapes, to drown in its wine our lethal vipers.

The altar is a *figura* of Christ; the serpent on the pole (Numbers 21:8–9) represents the crucifixion, and the grapevine and winepress came from Isaiah to put it succinctly, for La Ceppède also cites many supporting references. We cannot speak here of metaphorics in the rhetorical sense, any more than we can speak of correspondences like the sun and king, for the linguistic configuration represents a view of history which has its own logic within theologized thinking and is different from the various rhetorical conceptions of metaphor, even though they may at times coincide. This is a paraphrase of sacred texts in the sense not of putting them into a modern style, but of consolidating and concentrating them. The artistic method is enumeratory, each prosodic section being a parallel unit, and a play of sound and repetition occurs. If we compare this style to Chassignet's syntax and sound figures, we see that the basic idea is the same, but La Ceppède's art suggests liturgical formality rather than secular mannerism.

Sometimes the thought, always based on sources of authority, seems to reflect rather bizarrely detailed interpretations of sacred history, as in the passage I have mentioned on Christ's wounds:

> Deux de cés trous gardez en l'immortalité
> Nous marquent de vos mains la liberalité,
> Par eux cherront sur nous tous vos riches hyacinthes.
>
> Et les trois serviront de trois jours à nos yeux
> Pour (mesme avant sortir des mortels Labyrinthes)
> Par iceux oeillader vos secrets dans les Cieux.　(II, 2, 60)

> Two of these holes which you will keep in your immortal form are the sign for us of your hands' generosity: through them will fall on us all your rich hyacinths. And the three holes will serve as three windows for our eyes, so that (even before passing through death's labyrinth) we may glimpse through them your secrets in Heaven.

At the last judgment, Christ will still have punctures in his hands, symbols of generosity. The other punctures are peepholes through which we can glimpse divine wisdom and love while still in this life. The oldish or unusual words and forms, *iceux, cherront, oeillader*, the rare and heavy rimes (*-inthes, -alité*), and the striking isolated image of the hyacinths give that not infrequent impression that La Ceppède has put together his poem of very diverse elements, so much so that the reader's first impression may be one of unpleasant surprise. This is an effect that is countered by wide reading in *Les Théorèmes* and greater understanding of the peculiar stylistic synthesis his verse represents.

We have observed the inappropriateness of the term *conceit* in describing such an image as peering through Christ's wounds. Wit and conceit depend on one's sensing tension and disparity between concrete reality and the purely intellectual act of making a rhetorical figure, whereas La Ceppède's view of language is considerably less nominalist. All senses of words are quite real. The sacred use of words may resemble a pun or paronomasia in form, but it is not the same as the secular figure:

> Pour delivrer Juda le Pere descendant
> D'épines entouré dans un halier ardant
> Fit l'effort merveilleux de sa forte puissante.
>
> Et le Fils descendant du sejour paternel,
> Bruslant dans cet halier d'un amour eternel,
> Fait l'épineux effort de nostre delivrance.   (I, 2, 64)

> To free Judah, the Father, descending into a burning bramble surrounded by thorns, undertook the miraculous effort of his great power. And the Son, descending from his Father's abode, burning in this bramble with eternal love, began the thorny enterprise of freeing us.

Here the *épineux effort* is not the figurative use of an adjective from *épine*, but a reference to the crown of thorns, and the *épines* surrounding the fire are not accidental but have the same symbolic sense as the crown. Again, the concrete and the figurative do not have the witty separation we find in conceitful poetry.

Sometimes La Ceppède develops an image beyond his sources, as seems to be the case in the last line here:

> O pourpre emplis mon test de ton jus precieux
> Et luy fay distiller mille pourprines larmes,
> A tant que meditant ton sens mysterieux,
> Du sang trait de mes yeux j'ensanglante ces Carmes.
>
> Ta sanglante couleur figure nos pechez
> Au dos de cet Agneau par le Pere attachez.
> Et ce Christ t'endossant se charge de nos crimes.
>
> O Christ, ô sainct Agneau, daigne toy de cacher
> Tous mes rouges pechez (brindelles des abysmes)
> Dans les sanglans replis du manteau de ta chair.   (I, 2, 63)

O purple, fill my head with your precious juice, and make a thousand purple tears drip from it, so that meditating on your mysterious meaning, I bloody these poems with the blood drawn from my eyes. Your bloody color figures our sins attached by the Father to the back of the Lamb. And Christ, taking you on his back, burdens himself with our crimes. O Christ, O holy Lamb, deign to hide all my red sins (tinder of hell) in the bloody folds of the cloak of your flesh.

The whole poem is an example of the personal meditation which recurs from time to time in *Les Théorèmes*, marking crucial points in the sacred narrative. Here the ambiguity of red, standing for the blood of salvation and the heritage of sin is a more familiar figure than some of La Ceppède's recondite references, and the sonnet has thus become one of his better known pieces. The garment of blood is a frequent devotional image, but the personal prayer dramatically develops it at the end.

Occasionally La Ceppède will employ one of the common secular figures much used in the late sixteenth and early seventeenth centuries. Here is anaphora joined with very overt enumeration:

> Blanc est le crespe sainct dont (pour son cher blason)
> Aux Nopces de l'Agneau l'Espouse s'advantage.
> Blanc est or' le manteau dont par mesme raison
> Cet innocent Espous se pare en son Nopçage.
>
> Blanc estoit l'ornement dont le Pontife vieux
> S'affeubloit pour devot offrir ses voeux aux Cieux:
> Blanc est le parement de ce nouveau grand Prestre.
>
> Blanche est la robbe deüe au fort victorieux.
> Ce vainqueur (bien qu'il aille à la mort se sousmettre)
> Blanc, sur la dure mort triomphe glorieux.   (I, 2, 54)

White is the holy veil with which, for her dear symbol, the Bride deco-rates herself in her marriage with the Lamb. White is also the mantle with which, for the same reason, the innocent Groom covers himself in his wedding. White was the ornament the old priest put on himself in order to offer, with devotion, his vows to heaven. White is the decoration of this new high priest. White is the robe owed to the one strong in victory. This conqueror (although he is going to submit to death) is white, and triumphs gloriously over harsh death.

The use of the pause in the last line, isolating *blanc*, shows that con-cern for poetic technique which manages to combine with La Cep-pède's theological preoccupations to produce this often strange po-etry. We find here an almost perfect ambiguity between the anaphoric sonnet of secular tradition and liturgical anaphora, which is monoto-nous and solemn, whereas the first is emphatic and even pompous in the positive, renaissance sense. Of the style of *Les Théorèmes* (meaning objects of contemplation from which principles can be de-rived), La Ceppède said that it was like a heavy gold cloth, difficult to handle and not at all shaped in the French manner. The heavy gold cloth, like an ecclesiastical adornment, would doubtless have elaborate patterns suggesting the peculiar mixture of various secular and sacred styles. Stating that his mission was to evangelize and not to Pindarize, La Ceppède allows, nonetheless, the partially profane sources of his style to be seen. Pindarization is linked with the name of Ronsard and the copious, variegated style he originated in France. There is an element of archaism and neologism, of the taste of the previous century, in *Les Théorèmes* which is unlike the general ten-dencies of seventeenth-century devotional styles in France. On the whole, the worldly standards of normal vocabulary and syntax which obtain in other devotional poets make the individuality of La Cep-pède's work stand out and separate him, as does the highly learned character of his *figurae*, from the stylistic tendencies most often iden-tified as baroque. At the same time, the strong element of color he derived from his sources generally surpasses that of poets over the centuries who had access to the same sources, giving his poetry a peculiar visual brilliance which indeed we associate with the ba-roque movement.

VI

George Herbert's poetry has been shown to be even richer in liturgical and biblical references than it appears on the surface.[15] His style,
however, is much less sumptuous than La Ceppède's. Indeed, its
color is never more than modest, and Herbert frequently exploited
the resources of low style, in the manner peculiar to English poets.
The famous opening of "The Collar" is Herbert at his most colloquial:

> I struck the board, and cry'd, No more;
> > I will abroad.
> What, shall I ever sigh and pine?
> My lines and life are free; free as the road,
> Loose as the winde, as large as store.
> > Shall I be still in suit?
> Have I no harvest but a thorn
> To let me bloud, and not restore
> What I have lost with cordiall fruit?
> > Sure there was wine
> Before my sighs did drie it; there was corn
> Before my tears did drown it;
> Is the yeare only lost to me?[16]

Herbert manages to move from a colloquial commonplace like "free
as the road" into traditional biblical symbolism with no loss of the
conversational impetus. Of course, he uses only one adjective and
very few words of more than one syllable. The English low-style
effect is furthered by the free verse with its sometimes distant rimes
(*pine/wine*; the rime for *me* does not come for many lines yet). Moreover, the dominance of four-stress lines comes closer to the natural
phrasing of English than the pentameter. While there are passages
of distinct visual interest in Herbert's poetry, the effects of sound
and prosodic structure generally draw our attention first in his better
poems. The combination of sound repetitions along with thematic
variations can be quite dense, as in "Aaron":

> Holinesse on the head,
> Light and perfections on the breast,
> Harmonious bells below, raising the dead

15. See Rosemund Tuve, *A Reading of George Herbert* (Chicago, 1952).
16. George Herbert, *The Poems of George Herbert* (London, 1961), hereinafter cited
in the text.

> To lead them unto life and rest:
>   Thus are true Aarons drest.
>
> Profanenesse in my head,
> Defects and darknesse in my breast,
> A noise of passions ringing me for dead
> Unto a place where is no rest:
>   Poore priest, thus am I drest.
>
> Onely another head
> I have, another heart and breast,
> Another musick, making live, not dead,
> Without whom I could have no rest:
>   In him I am well drest.

The subdued language of the first stanza, so different from the more elaborately visual baroque of La Ceppède, may not readily bring to mind the Old Testament, although the details of the priest's costume are strictly biblical. The Christian antitheses of the third stanza are much more readily apprehended, because of their rhetorical form.

This low-keyed intricacy is very much Herbert's mark. Christ's speech from the cross in "The Sacrifice" has a deliberate, solemn monotony in keeping with its liturgical origins; these lines illustrate rather well its stylistic character:

> Then on my head a crown of thorns I wear;
> For these are all the grapes *Sion* doth bear,
> Though I my vine planted and watred there:
>   Was ever grief like mine?
>
> So sits the earth's great curse in *Adam's* fall
> Upon my head; so I remove it all
> From th'earth unto my brows, and bear the thrall:
>   Was ever grief like mine?
>
> Then with the reed they gave to me before,
> They strike my head, the rock from whence all store
> Of heav'nly blessings issue evermore:
>   Was ever grief like mine?
>
> They bow their knees to me, and cry, *Hail King*!
> What ever scoffes or scornfulnesse can bring,
> I am the floore, the sink, where they it fling:
>   Was ever grief like mine?

Herbert compresses the *figurae* of vine, thorns, bunch of grapes, and the Edenic tree; the *rock* abruptly introduced is a precise scriptural reference, but nothing about the way the word is used would sug-

gest its origins to anyone who did not know them. The *floore* and
sink ("drain" and "depression"), on the other hand, are Herbert's
low-style metaphors, in which we note the elliptic *I am* type of comparison and the hard catachresis of "flinging a scoff into a sink." The
refrain, dismal and colorless, seems an artistic flaw at first, but its
cumulative effect in this long poem represents an esthetic wager
which is not entirely lost.

Herbert's prosody is well known to be highly varied, but his syntax, often bearing some relation to verse form, offers some interesting exceptional features as well, which have their correspondence in
other seventeenth-century poets. The sonnet "Prayer" is especially
fine in this respect:

> Prayer, the Churche's banquet, Angels' age,
>   God's breath in man returning to his birth,
>   The soul in paraphrase, heart in pilgrimage,
> The Christian plummet sounding heav'n and earth;
>
> Engine against th' Almightie, sinner's towre,
>   Reversèd thunder, Christ-side-piercing spear,
>   the six-daies-world transposing in an houre,
> A kinde of tune which all things heare and fear;
>
> Softnesse, and peace, and joy, and love, and blisse,
>   Exalted Manna, gladnesse of the best,
>   Heaven in ordinarie, man well drest,
> The milkie way, the bird of Paradise,
>
>   Church-bels beyond the starres heard, the soul's bloud,
>   The land of spices; something understood.

This is not only an enumeration of nouns, but careful study shows a
remarkable variety in the length and kind of noun phrases, for their
modifiers, when there are any, range through the genitive, the adjective, the compound epithet, participles present and past, prepositional phrases, relative clauses, and the noun itself used as modifier.
There is virtually a grammar-book demonstration here of the kinds
of noun phrase in English. The marvelous ending depends on the
contrast between nouns referring to specific things, concrete or abstract, and the indefinite *something*, implying that no words can
really express the meaning of this enumeration, in which the great
cycle of Christian history is résuméd.

Here and there in his poems, as in "Jordan (II)," for example, Herbert makes some comment on language that can usually be taken as a defense of low style, which for him is, of course, the specifically Christian variant of serious low style called *sermo humilis*. This is not to say that such an ornament as an extended comparison, as in "The Flower," cannot be found in his work, but he has a remarkable capacity for making complex figures like those of "Prayer" subdued and fitting to low style, to the point that he demands particularly great attention on the reader's part. A good share of his density, I think, comes from the prevalence of monosyllables in English, which permits small-scale, even fragile-seeming prosodic forms to contain a great deal of matter. Herbert's rhetorical figures and his scriptural *figurae* bear enough analogy, I think, to other devotional poets we have seen that he may be called, with some reason, a baroque poet, though one so heavily influenced by the English low-style lyric tradition that his range of style is variously slim or subtly florid. Donne's work, though regularly considered a major source of Herbert's style, is yet somewhat different; the two together show the surprising variety implicit in low style, especially when we include in it the *sermo humilis* or properly devotional variant of it.

VII

Donne's devotional poetry is somewhat miscellaneous, with both major and quite minor work. The small number of holy sonnets not infrequently quoted resemble European seventeenth-century poets' work more in style and theme than Donne usually does, and although they are, in part, of considerable distinction, I shall ignore them as lacking the peculiar Donnic stamp.

   Much fairly recent interest has focused on the two "Anniversaries": "An Anatomy of the World" and "The Progress of the Soule," as their subtitles accurately put their subjects. The "First Anniversary" is based on what I think it is proper to call a hyperbolic conceit: the death of a young girl (the biographical details are unimportant and may be studied in any good book on Donne) makes the world realize that it is in decay, a nice personification:

> This world, in that great earth-quake languished;
> For in a common Bath of teares it bled,

> Which drew the strongest vitall spirits out:
> But succour'd then with a perplexed doubt,
> Whether the world did loose or gaine in this,
> (Because since now no other way there is
> But goodnes, to see her, whom all would see,
> All must endeavour to be good as she,)
> This great consumption to a fever turn'd,
> And so the world had fits; it joy'd, it mourn'd.[17]

In the tears, vital spirits, bleeding emulation of goodness, fever, and alternation of joy and sorrow we recognize the Petrarchan elements of the *Songs and Sonnets,* and indeed the conception of the poem rests on a notion often found in Donne's secular poetry: a small world, the individual, provokes by analogy a reaction in the universe. Elizabeth Drury's death makes the world realize it is dying. The world's death at first is put in the Petrarchan terms noted above, and the tone of elegant hyperbole, closer to badinage than to epideictic poetry, is the familiar one of the secular works. This gives way to much eloquent musing, based on contemporary science, about the quite literal decay of the universe, a section much prized of those who would attribute changes in poetry to the new scientific thinking of the seventeenth century. We can recognize, with a little reflection, that the "First Anniversary" is actually a didactic poem, traditionally middle-style in nature, and thus employs secular ornament like the conceit, which inevitably brings to mind a poem like "The Feaver." The reinforcement of the scientific passages gives the work a more solid kind of intellectual consistency than "The Feaver," but we do not perceive the characteristic devices of devotional poetry in it. The "First Anniversary," though apparently cast in the shape of a formal meditation,[18] is, however, more impressive in the detail than as a harmonious structure, and that, I believe, can be ascribed in part to the use of the English couplet.

The couplet, rare in Italian but a basic form in French, assumes a peculiar character in English because of the simultaneous contrasting existence of blank verse. The rime, usually fuller than French rime need be,[19] gives an energy and emphaticness to the form which

17. John Donne, "An Anatomy of the Soule," in Donne, *The Elegies and the Songs and Sonnets,* ed. Helen Gardner (Oxford, 1965), hereinafter cited in the text.
18. See Martz, *The Poetry of Meditation,* 222–23.
19. Final pronounced consonants after the riming vowels are more frequent.

tends to impair continuity. The Latin elegiac couplet, though un-
rimed, had exactly this same effect, because of the differing structure of the second line, and I think that familiarity with this common
classical form—one easily imitated by anyone who made attempts at
Latin verse—encouraged the use of the couplet in English and made
of the form's limitations something of an elegance and a virtue. For
all the structural casualness of Latin poems written in it, it is difficult
not to develop an affection for this most Roman of prosodic molds.
The peculiarities of its English derivant can be felt not only in comparison with blank verse but by the study of the much greater variety of effects the alexandrine couplet is capable of in French.

The "Second Anniversary" has been said to be more carefully
composed, and it is certainly more devotional in its emphasis on
spiritual matters. Meditations alternate clearly with eulogies of the
soul released from life—about whom there are no longer any Petrarchist reactions, for this soul is a much less specific one than that
of Elizabeth Drury. Poetry about the progress of the soul must always, however, suffer a bit in comparison with the example of
Dante, who tends to make his successors sound unduly pompous,
and I find the meditations on man's condition much the more brilliant side of the poem:

> Thinke but how poore thou [the higher soul] wast,
>   how obnoxious,
> Whom a small lump of flesh could poison thus.
> This curded milke, this poore unlittered whelpe
> My body, could, beyond escape, or helpe,
> Infect thee with original sinne, and thou
> Couldst neither then refuse, nor leave it now.
> Thinke that no stubborne sullen Anchorit,
> Which fixt to'a Pillar, or a Grave doth sit
> Bedded and Bath'd in all his Ordures, dwels
> So fowly as our soules, i' their first-built Cels.
> Thinke in how poore a prison thou didst lie
> After, enabled but to sucke, and crie.
> Thinke, when 'twas growne to most, 'twas a poore Inne,
> A Province Pack'd up in two yards of skinne,
> And that usurped, or threatned with the rage
> Of sicknesses, or their true mother, Age.   (163–78)

The repetition of *thinke* stresses the somewhat enumeratory form of
the passage, and indeed, the structure of both "Anniversaries" has a

notable enumeratory aspect, relating them to the dominant new tendency in poetic structure.

The poetry of bodily degradation and the worms and rot of death is often said to be baroque, and indeed we find a more than generous share of such themes in sixteenth- and seventeenth-century verse. However, the matter itself is biblical, stoic, and medieval, as well as baroque, and occupies a prominent place in low-style preaching throughout the centuries: *inter faeces et urinas*, and similar notions. What is worth remarking on here in Donne is the power of prosody and image. The monosyllabic words like *lump, milke, whelpe* have tremendous concentration which rises to the rather Shakespearean "Province Pack'd up in two yards of skinne," in which the microcosm-world analogy is employed brilliantly and unexpectedly. There is a striking alternation between words of differing length, the longer ones clustering in the reference (of a certain theological dignity) to the anchorite, as well as in the two lines following "A Province Pack'd up." Donne shifts between the low style and the grander, if equally pejorative, severe δεινός type of eloquence. The passage is a model of English word structure in its relation to tone, and the couplet helps focus attention on the individual word through its delaying intermittencies. Such art, not unlike Shakespeare's in many respects, transforms the low-style Christian clichés, often so tediously single-minded, into a worthy point of departure for an ascension into the soul's higher destiny.

The "Anniversaries," despite their formal meditational structure, contain more of the general philosophical poem than of the devotional verse in the usual sense, which tends to focus on Christology like La Ceppède or on personal relations with God like Herbert. Donne, however, wrote one great meditational poem in the personal vein, "Goodfriday, 1613. Riding Westward." This poem contrasts strikingly with all the devotional verse we have examined up to now in that it opens in a secular, speculative vein, concerning a literal and realistic situation. Donne's low style has, at the beginning, its characteristic ornament of abstract reasoning, which is a true conceit in this case, its effect stemming from bizarre but forceful logic:

> Let man's Soule be a Spheare, and then, in this,
> The intelligence that moves, devotion is,

> And [but] as the other Spheares, by being growne
> Subject to forraigne motions, lose their owne,
> And being by others hurried every day,
> Scarce in a yeare their naturall forme obey:
> Pleasure or business, so, our Soules admit
> For their first mover, and are whirled by it.
> Hence is't, that I am carryed towards the West
> This day, when my Soules forme bends toward the East.

The character of Donne's old bemused, ironic, demonstrative-logical style shows up in the words one would use for instructing in philosophy: "Let . . ." The hypothesis gradually grows into reality as the primum mobile surrounding the physical universe, the Ptolemaic sphere turning from east to west and here representing secular concerns, is seen as having quite literally moved the soul in the wrong direction, for divine movement goes eastward.

Donne marvelously exploits the ambiguity of low style, moving from its objective, proving function to its Christian, *sermo humilis* form, in which the antithesis of spiritual and concrete meanings is not an ornament but the mere factual description of life:

> There I should see a Sunne, by rising set,
> And by that setting endlesse day beget;
> But that Christ on this Crosse, did rise and fall,
> Sinne had eternally benighted all.
> Yet dare I almost be glad, I do not see
> That spectacle of too much weight for mee.
> Who sees Gods face, that is selfe life, must dye;
> What a death were it then to see God dye?

With the question in the last line begins a series of interrogations, eloquent but in the vein of Pauline sacred rhetoric. One of the finest touches in the poem comes when, after the heightening questions, the poet returns to the simple reality of his riding westward on Good Friday, a drop in tone which introduces the final prayer:

> Though these things, as I ride, be from mine eye,
> They are present yet unto my memory,
> For that looks towards them; and thou look'st towards mee,
> O Savior, as thou hang'st upon the tree;
> I turne my backe to thee, but to receive
> Corrections, till thy mercies bid thee leave.
> O thinke mee worth thine anger, punish mee,
> Burne off my rusts, and my deformity,

>Restore thine Image, so much, by thy grace,
>That thou may'st know mee, and I'll turne my face.

The placing of the symbolism of direction in the framework of contemporary life makes Donne's poem seem many leveled and even quite modern compared with the generality of devotional poems. As the poet finds a reason for his back to be turned to Christ, so that he may in turn be scourged, the paradox of directional symbolism is elegantly resolved, and we encounter a superb example of what Bouhours prized in baroque poetry: an image which is truly a new thought, serious and enlightening, surprising, as Aristotle found the figures of high poetry often to be, but witty only in the old sense of employing acute insight and intelligence. Donne's concluding lines mark the point where *sermo humilis* rises in diction to suggest the austere style of the ancient rhetoricians. This is one of the most remarkable examples one could find of evolving style in a lyric poem, even more remarkable than the examples in *Songs and Sonnets*, for here Donne must cross the generally absolute barrier between the secular and the high devotional meditation. The traditional thinking about shifts of style had always focused on large genres. Donne, with his impeccable sense of tone, demonstrates how much more powerful the shorter poem can be with this resource and how the devotional poem, in particular, is all the more vivid for growing out of life's circumstances rather than originating in the isolated, cloistered, formal practice of meditation.

VIII

Discussions of what constitutes a baroque style have often been marked by both incompleteness and an inadequate historical perspective. The evolution of sixteenth- and seventeenth-century poetry is characterized not only by the introduction of two or three fairly new rhetorical figures but quite generally by the growing density with which the standard array of figures is used. Ronsard's *Amours* seems to represent a first stage in this inspissation of rhetoric in which lengthy comparisons, one-word metaphors, simpler periphrases, anaphora, oxymoron, metaphorical appositions, various figures of repetition of sounds and words, tropes involving the concrete and the figurative or abstract, and enumeration come together rather prominently. The *Amours* is not yet a book of baroque style, but it represents the particular kind of rhetorical self-consciousness that was to intensify in the next fifty to eighty years.

Of nontropic figures, that is, those which have nothing to do with the metaphoric process, a group that can be called enumeration in a general sense is particularly significant because it can determine the syntax and logical character of the poem. We may succinctly distinguish four types of enumeration: that of nouns (or of adjectives, though the latter kind is usually brief); that of sentences, of which the one-line sentence or other short, especially paratactic sentence in parallel arrangements is a notable case; a thematic enumeration by prosodic units, such as the four sections of a sonnet or a series of short stanzas; and juxtaposed thematic units in continuous verse forms like the alexandrine couplet with enjambment. A special form is the distributory sonnet. In the case of enumeration of nouns, it is a strikingly different matter if the nouns are metaphorical rather than literal. Petrarch's rare, nonmetaphorical enumerations of nouns are not quite the direct ancestor of Ronsard's metaphorical enumerations; the latter look forward to baroque density of figurative meanings. There is also with metaphoric noun enumeration a certain ambiguity between a series of distinct metaphors and a series of appositions constituting a metaphoric enchainment. Metaphorical vocatives usually form an appositional series. With nouns and with sentences, linkage in the form of *and*, or even the many *and*s of polysyndeton, is neutral. We may contrast *and* with the *but* and *yet* of the related figure of *correctio*, which we shall treat later. While asyndeton and *and* linkage are both possible in enumeration, forms like *for*, *therefore*, and *thus* destroy, of course, the enumerative principle of putting all members on the same plane.

Enumeration can have a distinctly dramatic character, insofar as, in the course of it, one does not know what kinds of further elements are to come. In something like the Drelincourt sonnet I quoted earlier, the dramatic quality of the enumeration turns almost enigmatic. (Naturally, there is the opposite effect of monotony, which we associate more with the solemnity of liturgical enumeration.) Enumeration constitutes an exception to customary syntax and therefore acquires some particular tonality, especially that of sharpness and brilliance. It is seldom neutral.

In the larger historical perspective, it is noteworthy that a series of three constitutes the usual Roman idea of enumeration, whereas we are dealing in the renaissance with often much longer ones. Enumerations are, in general, not prominent in Latin lyric or high style. There is also a certain kind of didactic low-style enumeration of sentences or clauses which we can find in Gascoigne or other writers antecedent to full renaissance style in France or England. While Du Bartas, and sometimes d'Aubigné, constitutes an exception, enumeration is normally a lyric-scaled or unitary technique, as in certain speeches in Shakespeare. Except occasionally, in the classical series of three elements, enumeration is foreign to Tasso's high epic style, for example. One can, in a general fashion, contrast enumeration and progression, although there may be a concealed or implicit progression present in enumeratory sequences. Nevertheless, enumeration tends to impair the conception of the lyric, especially the sonnet, as a logically progressive structure, modeled on the same principles as an oration or demonstration. The ending of an enumeration may demand some strong rhetorical unit such as sententia.

The principle of syntactic disjunctivity is visible at all enumeratory levels, from the disjunctive series within the sentence to the lack of conjunctive adverbial connections between thematic units. We are dealing here with a deep-reaching phenomenon which may have to do with basic linguistic structure, as in the Hebrew parallelism which lies behind certain types of European poetry, or with the feeling that continuous, formally indicated logical progression is an unnatural imposition on a less rigorous sentence structure. Postclassical Roman writers went through a phase of asyndetic, somewhat paratactic style, and there is some justification for the theory that the Latin sentence was short and plain in origin and that classical periodicity was a foreign pattern to which it was made to conform. The analogies often made between seventeenth-century literature and biblical style or Silver Latin (which is now even being called Roman baroque) depend in part on the principle of disjunctivity.

The amplificatory value of enumeration is obvious, but one particular form of it has another function as well. *Correctio*, which we encounter more and more as we move toward and into seventeenth-century poetry, serves as a kind of trope in addition to being enumeratory. In *correctio*, a comparison is made, an especially interesting one in that one of its elements is rejected. This is very different from the comparison as logical analogy or hyperbolic intensifier insofar as one cannot so readily explain why something should be evoked only to be discarded. There is a related series of figures like the negative modifier, so frequent in Shakespeare, which can take various forms: star disorbed, unscissored hair, printless feet, *flammes sans ardeur* (fireflies), *le soleil sans aurore* (referring to a lady's eye). Góngora constantly uses negative figures of some elaboration: the setting sun emits "luminosas de pólvera saetas, / purpúreos no cometas" (*Soledad Primera*).[20] The logical function of negative comparisons may be said to be an enhancement or intensification by contrast, but more important, I think, is the effect of imagistic density that is produced. There is a certain suggestion of unnnecessary enrichment, even of exuberance at times, which surpasses any feeling of logical justification. It is the same impression of semantic density we feel in other tropes which are specifically identified with baroque poetry.

The classic periphrasis involves two nouns in a genitive relationship: "dew" is the *pleurs de l'aurore*. There are many semantic forms of this syntactic structure, however, according to the degree of concreteness, abstraction, or figurativeness of the elements. *L'astre de mon printemps, le vol de mon âme*, and *l'arrogance des vents* represent three very different kinds of formation.[21] And as these are clear periphrases, we have not even suggested the varying degree of enigma possible, which is one of the real criteria of the baroque circumlocution. I think that it is safe to say that all these variations in periphrasis must already occur in the second half of the sixteenth century. A special syntactic form of periphrasis, however, is not easy to find before the seventeenth century, and even then, it is a prize figure, one not used all the time but brought forth for special effect. This is the noun and adjective phrase, as in *cometes rougissantes*

20. See Lowry Nelson, Jr., *Baroque Lyric Poetry* (New Haven, 1961), 94–96.
21. See Fernand Hallyn, *Formes métaphoriques dans la poésie lyrique de l'âge baroque en France* (Geneva, 1975).

(whips), *lumineuses glaces* (stars), or the liturgical *turris davidica* of the Litany of the Virgin Mary. The degree of enigmaticness is generally higher in these tighter, adjectival periphrases.

The one-word metaphor can be a simple metonymy like *arms* for *war*; a proper noun, obvious or strange like La Ceppède's use of *Atreus* for *wicked man*; or a conventionalized term like *sun*, *fire*, or *death* in Petrarchist language. It may also, through long cultural associations, cease really to be a metaphor at all and become a symbol. The language of Petrarchism in a poet like Scève is perhaps halfway between the simple replacement metaphor and the symbols of the neoplatonic philosophy of love. For all the more reason, Christianity has a rich vocabulary of one-word symbols, many of them having double meanings like the fire of punishment and the fire of purgation. One-word metaphors or symbols lend themselves particularly to word play: "In my end is my beginning" or "there was corn / Before my tears did drown it." One might say that sacred language tends to be literal, for it is the special quality of the *figura*, which can take any of the syntactic shapes of profane metaphorics, that both terms are real and historical and yet identical: Christ is the bunch of grapes in the winepress. When it comes to the Christian dialectic, the death of the body and the death of the old man within us are equally factual just as saying that death is life and life is death depends on spiritual and worldly antithetical connotations, both of which, however, are perfectly real. We cannot imagine Christian thought or feeling without these evocative double meanings, and it is quite obvious in the sacred rhetoric of Saint Paul and his successors that the writer takes pleasure in the elaborate linguistic effects obtainable without recourse to secular stylistic effects, where figurative meanings, unlike figural or spiritual ones, are secondary to the basic, concrete one.

The elliptic use of the copula for a comparison or to condense a lengthier process of thought, as in "we are all" or "I am the floore, the sink," constitutes another form of metaphoric density and may or may not have some resemblance to biblical expressions, depending on the nature of the noun involved. At this point we are obliged to recognize a large area of coincidence between tropes which can be illustrated from profane poems, in which they would seem to have

developed under the impetus of purely secular linguistic imagination, and the language of scripture, the church fathers, and various
other Christian writings. It is very difficult to imagine a devotional
poet of the seventeenth century with little consciousness of secular
rhetoric insofar as we can distinguish it from sacred expression, and
thus we find curious linguistic mixtures and variations. Crashaw's
English poems are less figural and probably owe more to previous
and contemporary profane poetry than Herbert's. The most learned
of the figural poets, La Ceppède, drew abundantly on sixteenth-
century profane style, though one tends to be able to see clearly the
line of demarcation in *Les Théorèmes* where secular ornaments are
juxtaposed to sacred imagery. Of course, the spirituality of much Petrarchist and neoplatonic poetry had given secular verse a tone which
could easily be assimilated to devotional literature. Before the emer-
gence of devotional poetry as a distinctly new or renewed genre, the
elevation of middle, ornamented lyric style from *piacevolezza* to *gravità* had taken place, as part of the general evolution of rhetorical
theory and practice. Furthermore, the epideictic theory of literature,
generalized in Europe as it had not been in antiquity, led to a broad
use, from Petrarch on, of what are hyperbolic expressions by ancient
criteria (though perhaps Petrarch and his successors would not always have liked the idea of exaggeration, inherent in hyperbole, to
be applied to their thoughts). Expressions having the apparent form
of hyperbole are, along with catachresis, most characteristic of religious expression, and devotional poetry thus has elements of continuity with the secular. Its imagistic tendencies range from the purely
sacred to the lofty embellished style emergent in love poetry.

Nevertheless, we can see devotional poetry as marking one of the
great modifications in stylistic practice in the seventeenth century.
Aside from mere embellished verse on the beauty of creation, it is
unambiguously high in subject, but its language generally has the
greatest analogy with middle-style decorative verse. The center of
the more visually elaborate poetry was France, whereas in England,
except for Crashaw, the native tradition of plain style encouraged a
drier kind of verse, given more to the play of feelings and concepts
in the *sermo humilis* manner. Italian devotional poetry contributed little to the new stylistic movement.

As for literary theory, generally weak in the seventeenth century save for neoclassical treatises and polemics, especially on drama, it took no significant notice of the baroque religious lyric, and Dominique Bouhours' discussion of literature in terms of *pensées neuves* is the only contemporary critical approach that is comprehensive enough to include devotional literature in a general examination of poetry.

Of course, it would be a mistake to insist on such a cleavage between profane and sacred thinking as we encounter in the nineteenth century or after. The motivation for imagery in renaissance poetry comes from the reinforcement of classical rhetorical theory by analogical thinking about the world, which identified kings with the sun, youth with roses, and society with the human body, in an almost endless possible series of correlations. In highly secular poets like Ronsard, we find a way of reasoning by analogies that reflects the general Christian hierarchical view of the universe, even if Christ, the focus of it, is somewhat absent. Moreover, this kind of thinking can be compared in some of its linguistic and intellectual effects with the figural reading of sacred history, though it is obviously much looser and authorized by no such great central tradition as that of scriptural interpretation. The individual variations in sensitivity to these currents of thought must have been great, and one may wonder whether Shakespeare's audience or the French court saw the sun more as a type of Christ or as the emblem of kingship. Of course, with analogical thinking such difficulties can be smoothed out, making the king an image of God, but there remains, nonetheless, a certain tension between the sacred and the secular, and we must, in our reading of devotional poetry, be aware of such differences as arise from secular elaboration of images and the minute approach of scriptural interpretation.

A last, difficult question which we must bring up somewhat tentatively is the possibility of distinguishing, in purely formal, stylistic terms, a mannerist current separate from and somewhat antecedent to the baroque. There appears to be at least some small justification for making such a separation. The extremes in sound play, word repetition, enumeration, and sometimes grammatical usage in Chassignet, the very heteroclite style of d'Aubigné, and the abundance of classical references, archaisms, neologisms, and peculiar words of all levels and origins in La Ceppède suggest, taken together, the last phase of Ronsard's influence and something we might call mannerism. This would be to define a mannerist style divorced from themes, secular or devotional, and sufficiently based on lexical matters that it is not impossible to see Shakespeare's language, especially in a play of mixed styles like *Hamlet*, as a vast elaboration, as befits Shakespeare's greater scope, of related attitudes toward poetic vocabulary. What separates this notion of style, general as it is, from the more baroque mode is the multiplication in the latter of periphrases and metaphors in series, the limitation put on odd vocabulary, and a certain diminution in the use of sound figures. The enumeratory element persists, of course, and so, as our distinction is narrowly linguistic, it offers, instead of the dramatic confrontation of a somber mannerist and an exuberant baroque world view, a much more modest scheme which emphasizes elements of continuity and development between mannerism and baroque. In our next chapter, we shall look at secular baroque poetry and its contrast with emerging neoclassical styles. One principle that obtains throughout all attempts at periodization of styles is the simultaneous existence of more than one stylistic current at any time, so we must not be surprised to discover that the beginnings of neoclassicism are antecedent to the end of mannerism or that the question of baroque secular style resolves itself into one of genres in keeping with ancient theory.

CHAPTER 7

From Baroque to Neoclassicism

I

While middle-style rhetoric was being elevated to a means of contemplating the divine intervention in human history, in the domain of secular poetry the long process of raising the decorum of various genres, including pastoral elegy, mythological tales, and bucolic narrative, was continuing and now reached a phase of considerable stylistic ingeniousness, including classic examples of secular baroque. Perhaps the most successful example of such a transformation of genre is "Lycidas," and as a whole book has been devoted to the theoretical and actual process by which Milton accomplished the raising of low-style pastoral elegy to a much higher level of seriousness and diction, I merely refer the reader to Hunt's fine study.[1]

Other poets' comparable reworkings of genres vary in importance as monuments of poetry, but the general principle involved is an important one for understanding seventeenth-century sensibility and style. One of the most famous of such attempts was Giambattista Marino's *Adone*, a vast poem now little read except in excerpts, if at all, but one which, along with Marino's other work, had an international audience and influence.[2] The *Adone* is an Ovidian narrative, such as Marlowe, Shakespeare, and others had written, swollen with digressions into twenty long cantos. Whereas Ovidian narration tends to be swift and, like much rapid telling, often rather low-style in its directness, the narrative almost vanishes under ornament

1. Clay Hunt, *"Lycidas" and the Italian Critics* (New Haven, 1979).
2. See James V. Mirollo, *The Poet of the Marvelous: Giambattista Marino* (New York, 1963), 245–55.

in Marino's work. He elevates the pastoral mythological tale to the highest level of smooth lyric middle style. Although the work is sometimes called an epic, Marino was careful to describe it as "molli versi e favolosi e vani" (I, 10); *mollis* usually refers in Latin to elegy, an elegant low style, but in this case I believe Marino meant "voluptuous" as well as "beneath high-style seriousness." Here, in the presentation of Adonis, is a fairly typical stanza:

> Era Adon ne l'età che la facella
> sente d'Amor più vigorosa e viva,
> ed avea dispostezza a la novella
> acerbità de gli anni intempestiva.
> Nè su le rose de la guancia bella
> alcun germoglio ancor d'oro fioriva;
> o, se pur vi spuntava ombra di pelo,
> era qual fiore in prato o stella in cielo.[3]

Adonis was at the age when one feels the torch of love more strongly and intensely, and he had unusually early inclinations for one so unripe in years. Nor on the roses of his cheeks did there yet flower any seed of gold, or if there appeared a shadow of hair on them, it was like a meadow flower or a star in heaven.

Description and metaphor go together in Marino as heightening elements of style; at times literal description predominates, it being felt to have an equal status as ornament, but usually the two are intermingled as here. The impression Marino's verse almost always creates is one of concreteness and color, even though his materials tend to be fairly conventional; the torch, roses, meadow flower, and star obviously derive from the Petrarchist tradition, but Marino clusters his images in such a way that his verse seems far more sensory and sensuous than that of the cinquecento poets.

Description of any length often has an enumeratory quality about it; while there exist progressive descriptions, Marino's tend to be static and to list decorative elements, both within the stanza and in larger units as well. Canto VIII, for example, continues a description of the five gates with the five gardens of pleasure begun in Canto VI. Now comes the fifth gate and fifth garden, that of touch. There are personifications to be described (sighs, glance, laughter, and so

---

3. Giuseppe Guido Ferrero (ed.), *Marino e i marinisti* (Milan, 1954), I, 41, hereinafter cited in the text.

forth). A fountain entices Adonis to bathe with Venus, and their naked contemplation of each other takes up many more stanzas. Next their abode and bed must be told of, and the lovers talk a little. With embellishments, this all adds up to 149 octaves, one of the shorter cantos.

Marino actually employs such specific enumerative constructions as a series of parallel nouns, sometimes in apposition as here:

> Quella bocca mi porgi. O cara bocca,
> de la reggia del Riso uscio gemmato,
> siepe di rose, in cui saetta e scocca
> viperetta amorosa arabo fiato,
> arca di perle, ond'ogni ben trabocca,
> cameretta purpurea, antro odorato,
> ove rifugge, ove s'asconde Amore,
> Poi ch'ha rubata un'alma, ucciso un core.   (VIII, 122)

Give me your mouth. O dear mouth, gem-covered gate of the palace of laughter, hedge of roses, in which an amorous little viper shoots the arrows of a breath bearing Arabian scents, ark of pearls, from which every treasure pours forth, little purple chamber, odoriferous cave, in which Love hides when he has stolen a soul or killed a heart.

It is notable that Marino makes only the most elementary use of hyperbaton on the whole; excessively unusual or developed sentence structure would detract from the direct and voluptuous effect he aims at. His rhetorical figures are mostly commonplace, inconspicuous ones, save for enumeration and sound repetitions:

> Bacia, e dopo 'l baciar mira e rimira
> le baciate bellezze, or questi, or quella.
> Ribacia, e poi sospira e risospira
> le gustate dolcezze or egli, or ella.
> Vivon due vite in una vita, e spira
> confusa in due favelle una favella,
> giungono i cori in su le labra estreme,
> corrono l'alme ad intrecciarsi insieme.   (VIII, 124)

Now he, now she kisses, and after kissing looks and looks again at the beautiful kissed parts. Now he, now she kisses again, and then longs and longs again for the tasted sweets. They live two lives in one and breathe out two languages mingled into one; they join their hearts on the tips of their lips; their souls run to intwine themselves.

Sound plays do not figure so prominently in the cinquecento Bembist tradition as they do in French poetry of the period, so that Marino is actually reintroducing into Italian effects which had largely been neglected for some time. Sound figures had played a small role in Petrarch's work, and hence they had occurred only sporadically among his most direct imitators.

The simplifying of syntax in Marino is accompanied by a less frequent use of recondite Latinisms than in previous Italian poets. From time to time, he uses a rare word, but on the whole, his language seems more modern, less given to metaplasm or other peculiar poetic forms, while remaining recognizably the artificial idiom of Italian verse.

In this *poésie de style*, as the French called elegant but empty verse, the conceit tends to be based on hyperbole or antithesis more than on catachresis. The conceit is not, however, constantly present; as we have noted, Marino favors nonmetaphoric description as well. It appears that he did not have a rigorous esthetic of the conceit, despite what the term *Marinism* came to mean in French and English. There is an interesting dialogue, the first work devoted to the conceit, in which Marino, appearing as one of the interlocutors, defines the concetto as almost any figure or interesting use of words.[4] This is an example of the extremely casual, even slovenly, thinking about the conceit typical of the seventeenth century. Even the famous *Cannochiale Aristotelico* (1654) of Emmanuele Tesauro, the only long work devoted to the conceit, is an appallingly weak piece of writing in which one thing after another is assimilated to the conceit with no sense of distinctions, much less any of the intellectual acumen of the really superior rhetorical treatises of the previous century. The general notions of ingeniousness, *meraviglia*, or "wonder," and novelty are the closest one gets to a definition of the conceit, and I observe here as before, these are effects that can be produced by a number of figures and whose impact will vary from reader to reader. Such criteria have none of the objectivity present in the definition of anaphora, say, or simile.

The *Adone* is a kind of success in the sense that its style is fairly even—to the point of monotony, one might add—with systematic use of words and metaphors which make it very easy to imitate.

4. *Ibid.*, 172–73. See also Bernard Weinberg, *A History of Literary Criticism in the Italian Renaissance* (2 vols.; Chicago, 1974), I, 235–37, 242–44.

From it derives a particular kind of color and wit which is sometimes mistaken for the essence of baroque poetry itself but which is very one-sided. An interesting comparison can be made with the witty conceits of Shakespeare's *Venus and Adonis*, particularly at the high point of the narrative when Adonis is gored. In the *Adone*, the action is obscured by periphrastic language, but Shakespeare uses a catachretic, or extremely ingenious, thought:

> 'Tis true, 'tis true! thus was Adonis slain:
> He ran upon the boar with his sharp spear,
> Who did not whet his teeth at him again,
> But by a kiss thought to persuade him there;
> And nuzzling in his flank, the loving swine
> Sheathed unaware the tusk in his soft groin.[5]

This is not to say that Shakespeare's poem is not also decorative and sensual, but the varying effects of style in Shakespeare remind us that conceit poetry can comprise a greater range than merely the idealized, sensory register of the smooth middle-style. The fact that Shakespeare's Adonis is sexually bashful and unwilling, unlike the precocious Adone, means that wit has a greater opportunity for display, and the sensuality of Shakespeare's poem, as Venus forces herself on Adonis, has a more intense quality, despite all periphrases and ornaments, than do Marino's prettified descriptions of Adone's erections. The conception of language in Shakepeare's early piece is as baroque as Marino's, but the subject matter is handled with less idealization, just as Marino himself, in his once famous "Amori Notturni," handled impotence quite directly. The fact is that Marino is often less Marinist than one might imagine and that superabundant description, rather than the striking conceit, is perhaps his most baroque quality.

The kind of colorful idealizing style Marino devised for the *Adone* has certain Petrarchist antecedents and seems especially to suit the romance languages with their small poetic vocabulary. In many ways the most remarkable exponent of it was not Marino at all but Góngora. The latter represents the culmination of the Italianate phase of Spanish verse. The similarities in phonetic structure of the two languages and the constant cultural contacts brought about by

5. William Shakespeare, *The Complete Works*, ed. G. B. Harrison (New York, 1948).

the Spanish occupation of large parts of Italy had resulted, beginning with Garcilaso de la Vega, in an important rapprochement of the two literatures, with the native Spanish tradition being partly occluded by Petrarchist influences. This is not one of those dull matters of influence, but the stimulus toward a certain amount of distinctive, original poetry, whose character is at once Spanish and unmistakably Italianate. Góngora, drawing on the Italian tradition, created one of the most memorable of baroque styles.[6]

In his two major works, *Polifemo y Galatea* and the *Soledades*, Góngora used classical subject matter as did Marino. The *Soledades* (of which only the first of four parts was completed) tells a kind of pastoral story such as the Greek novel had used. A young man of high birth is shipwrecked, struggles ashore, and finds himself in a community of goatherds and shepherds; the material is quintessentially low-style. Góngora raises his poem stylistically but not, as Milton did with the pastoral death elegy, by a subtle interweaving of traditional vocabulary and motifs with a new high manner; Góngora employs an elaborate diction right from the beginning:

> Era del año la estación florida
> en que el mentido robador de Europa
> (media luna las armas de su frente,
> y el Sol todos los rayos de su pelo),
>   luciente honor del cielo,
> en campos de zafiro pace estrellas,
> cuando el que ministrar podía la copa
> a Júpiter mejor que el garzón de Ida,
> náufrago, y desdeñado sobre ausente,
> lagrimosas de amor dulces querellas
>   da al mar; que condolido,
>   fué a las ondas, fué al viento
>   el mísero gemido
> segundo de Arión dulce instrumento.   (1-14)

It was the flowery season of the year, in which Taurus, like the bull Jupiter disguised himself as to ravish Europa—the horns of his forehead are a half moon; his shining hide is made of sunbeams—Taurus, the gleaming ornament of heaven, pastures on stars in sapphire fields, when a young man who could better serve Jupiter as cupbearer than Ganymede, both

---

6. For style in general, see Dámaso Alonso, *La Lengua poética de Góngora*, Revista de Filologiá Española, XX (Madrid, 1935). For interpretation of specific difficult passages, see Luis de Góngora, *Soledades*, ed. John Beverly (Madrid, 1979); Luis de Góngora, *Poems of Góngora*, ed. R. O. Jones (Cambridge, 1966).

shipwrecked and missing, makes sweet amorous complaint to the sea, which took pity on him, for his wretched moaning moved the wind and waves like the instrument of a new Arion saved from drowning.

The *chronographia* with which the poem opens is of unusual development and brilliance, managing to give both sensory immediacy and mythological depth to the image of the constellation Taurus. The sentence structure is of a periodic type in which the subordinate *when* clause contains the main subject matter. The process of leading up to it involves syntactic suspensions, two parenthetical, absolute nominal constructions (*media luna* and *y el Sol*), an apposition, and a verb placed late in the clause: *pace estrellas*. This indirect kind of sentence, putting the main matter in the subordinate clause, is reinforced by the indirection of a periphrasis which is also a negative or at least unequal comparison. *Que condolido* represents a rather extreme use of the absolute clause, involving the continuous relative, and introduces the final clause, which, like others, contains the simplest, minimal verb; thus nominal syntax of a high-style, Latinate sort is created. The displacement of adjectives from their nouns is carried further than what is customary even in Tasso's high, hyperbatic style and has some uniquely Spanish antecedents.

High-style, hypotactic syntax is often avoided by poets for purely narrative moments. The delaying effect it tends to have risks putting the static and the narrative on the same plane, instead of varying the pace. Góngora, however, is resolutely hypotactic and hyperbatic in depicting actions:

> No bien pues de su luz los horizontes,
> que hacían desigual, confusamente,
> montes de agua y piélagos de montes,
>   desdorados los siente,
> cuando entregado el mísero extranjero
> en lo que ya del mar redimió fiero,
> entre espinas crepúsculos pisando,
> riscos que aun igualara mal volando
>   veloz, intrépida ala,
> menos cansado que confuso, escala.   (42–51)

Hardly has he seen the horizons deprived of their golden light—the horizons which confusedly look like uneven mountains of water and seas of mountains—when, having put on the clothes he had saved from the fierce sea, less tired than confused, he climbs up crags, treading twilit ground, among thorns, crags to whose top even a swift, intrepid bird could with difficulty rise up in flying.

The visual paradox of the mountains of water and seas of mountains suits the crepuscular atmosphere and Góngora's fondness for unusual figures; the periphrasis for clothes, the metonymic "walking on twilights," and the seminegative comparison with the bird all create again an effect of syntactic suspension, for the verbs *siente* and *escala* are placed at the very end of their clauses. We observe here a kind of ponderous sentence structure favored in romance renaissance prose much more than in verse, and the irregular movement of the *silvas* (freely combined eleven- and seven-syllable lines) accentuates its involved character. The choice of a hyperbatic style, which is not only of epic elevation but also has, from time to time, the air of complicated prose, is best interpreted, I think, as a form of conceit. The disparity between the actions accomplished and the manner of telling is at once charming and witty. We perceive a grand sensibility at work on slim material, but the lyric, sensory aspect of the vocabulary prevents the contrast from seeming grossly heroi-comic; rather, the effect is one of subdued humor and ingenuity.

The narrative of the first *Soledad* involves a number of set speeches. The first is the long encomium pronounced by the stranger to the goatherd's hut. Such a set piece is intended obviously to suggest epic or primitive simplicity and formalized, not to say formulaic, manners, for the whole speech is shaped by the repetition of the last lines of the following excerpt:

> "Tus umbrales ignora
> la adulación, Sirena
> de Rëales Palacios, cuya arena
> besó ya tanto leño:
> trofeos dulces de un canoro sueño.
> No a la soberbia está aquí la mentira
> dorándole los pies, en cuanto gira
> la esfera de sus plumas,
> ni de los rayos baja a las espumas
> favor de cera alado.
> ¡O bienaventurado
> albergue a cualquier hora!"   (124–35)

Your thresholds know not adulation, the siren of royal palaces, who has drawn to her sands many ships: the siren's sweet trophies attracted by her sonorous dream spell. Nor does mendacity here serve haughtiness, gilding her feet as she spreads her peacock tail of plumes, nor does Icarus, with his waxen wings, fall from favor and sunlight into the sea. O happy abode at any hour!

The interesting thing about the encomium is that it consists of negative comparisons, mythological or symbolic as in the case of the periphrastically designated peacock. Góngora's fondness for negative constructions produces, on the one hand, an indirect kind of line of thought and narrative and, on the other, the superposition of images of court life upon this, its pastoral opposite. We find more of the same double reference in a passage echoing the simple hospitality of ancient narrative:

> Limpio sayal, en vez de blanco lino,
> 　　cubrió el cuadrado pino,
> y en boj, aunque rebelde, a quien el torno
> forma elegante dió sin culto adorno,
> leche que exprimir vió la Alba aquel día,
> 　　mientras perdían con ella
> 　　los blancos lilios de su Frente bella,
> gruesa le dan y fría,
> impenetrable casi a la cuchara,
> del sabio Alcimedón invención rara.　(143–52)

Pure homespun, instead of white linen, covered the square pine table, and in the cup of boxwood, to which, however resistent, the lathe gave an elegant form without ornate fashion, they gave him thick, cold milk, which the dawn saw gathered while the white lilies of her brow died with her, milk which the spoon can hardly press into, the spoon which Virgil's Alcimedon invented.

The negative mention of linen and ornate objects, the implied comparison with wine, and the courtly-poetic personification of the dawn may be justified on the grounds that we are perceiving everything through the eyes of the high-born stranger. The mechanics of this style, as we observe it here and in the preceding quotation, involve a great deal of ellipsis. The mythological allusions are not only indirect but may employ such a device as the concise periphrasis of *favor de cera alado*. The abstract noun means "him who has been favored with," and the adjective modifies *favor* not *cera*, so that we have an enigmatic adjective and noun circumlocution "winged favor of wax," for Icarus. The technique of using abstract nouns as concrete ones is also illustrated by *soberbia*, which is then given the attributes of the peacock: pride with its gilded foot and plumes. The Petrarchisms like the description of the dawn personified further contribute to this effect of learned elegance. Even the clichés involved in the Petrarchist expressions have a positive value in suggesting the commonplaces of those who live in "Rëales Palacios."

In epic fashion, a sage old man delivers himself of wisdom which consists of the traditional classical complaint against the invention of the ship (see Horace, *Odes* I, 3, for example):

> "¿Cuál tigre, la más fiera
> que clima infamó Hircano,
> dió el primer alimento
> al que, ya deste o de aquel mar, primero
>   surcó labrador fiero
> el campo undoso en mal nacido pino,
>   vaga Clicie del viento,
> en telas hecho antes que en flor el lino?" (366–73)

What tiger, the fiercest that the Hyrcanian land bred in its infamy, nurtured the man who first ploughed, like a haughty man of the land, the watery field of this or that ocean in a boat made of pine planks cursed in their origin? He was a wandering sunflower in the wind, with his flax turned into sails not flowers.

This formal speech appropriately begins with a hyperbolic and proverbial comparison: Hyrcanian tigers are the fiercest, and cruel men were often said to have been nursed by tigers. The fact that the material of the ship, the pine tree, comes from the land introduces the elegant sustained comparison between agriculture and seafaring, which has classical metaphors behind it. The reference to the boat as Clytie, who was turned into a sunflower by a god, suggests the powerlessness of the boat at the hands of divine forces, and the contrast of sea and land is completed by the comparison of the sunflower with ordinary flax flowers growing in a field.

The depths of classical allusion in the *Soledades*, in theme, syntax, and imagery, is such that one feels it is impossible to take it all in without some exhaustive study of sources. Often the allusion is made without the key word, as in the reference to Icarus earlier, or as in the following lines, where the peasant girls, singing like sirens, might bring the same uprooting of the forest, following in fascination their song, as we encounter in the Orpheus myth:

Sirenas de los montes su concento,
a la que menos del sañudo viento
    pudiera antigua planta
temer rüina o recelar fracaso,
pasos hiciera dar el menor paso
    de su pie o su garganta.
Pintadas aves, cítaras de pluma,
coronaban la bárbara capilla,
mientras el arroyuelo para oílla
    hace de blanca espuma
tantas orejas cuantas guijas lava,
de donde es fuente a donde arroyo acaba.   (550–61)

Sirens of the mountain, like Orpheus in their harmonies, their slightest step or movement of the throat would uproot the ancient trees which least feared ruin or dreaded shattering from the angry winds. Painted birds, feathered citharas crowned their barbarous choir, while the stream, to hear it, made as many ears of white foam as the pebbles it washed, from where it rose as a spring to where it ended in the sea.

The seemingly idle line about the stream refers to Virgil's account of the Orpheus legend, ending with the river repeating Orpheus' words. In syntax, the passage contains two characteristic Gongorisms: the article *la* is separated by a relative clause from its noun *planta*, through an ambiguity in Spanish grammar which permits *el*, *la*, and *lo* to be demonstrative pronouns followed by clauses as well as articles. The typical comparison involving the river is this time one of equality; Góngora so favors comparisons that he uses those of all orders: inequality, equality, near equality, or negativity. The comparison is one of his preferred amplificatory devices in that it tends to distract one at first from the initial term of the comparison only to draw a great abundance of material into the poem.

A rustic wedding concludes the first *Soledad*, involving heroic games as in Homer or Virgil, epithalamic choruses suggested probably by Catullus, and a very Horatian speech wishing the couple a life of *mediocritas* of fortune, the golden mean. In the course of this, the high-born stranger meets the bride, who brings back memories of his beloved:

Este pues Sol que a olvido le condena,
cenizas hizo las que su memoria
negras plumas vistió, que infelizmente
sordo engendran gusano, cuyo diente,

minador antes lento de su gloria,
inmortal arador fué de su pena,
y en la sombra no más de la azucena,
que del clavel procura acompañada
imitar en la bella labradora
el templado color de la que adora,
víbora pisa tal el pensamiento,
que el alma por los ojos desatada
señas diera de su arrebatamiento
    si de zampoñas ciento . . .   (737–50)

For the sun of the woman who has consigned him to oblivion made ashes of the black feathers his memory was clad in, but they unhappily begot the silent worm of despair, whose tooth, which once slowly undermined his glory, now became the immortal ploughman of his sorrow, and in the shade of the peasant girl's face, equally of lilies and carnations, he tries to recreate in her the refined color of the woman he worships, but in this adumbration, his thoughts tread on a viper such that his soul, pouring through his eyes, would have given signs of his violent emotion if a hundred pipes had not . . .

A most elaborate series of psychological images link the concrete and abstract. The resurrection myth of the phoenix is transformed so that a worm, rather than a new phoenix, is born from the ashes into which the past has been reduced. This worm is the basis on which Góngora shifts to a metaphor of mind as field, and then the worm becomes the snake of the Latin proverb (*latet anguis in herba*) which, however, here lies in the shade or adumbration of memory provoked by the peasant bride's Petrarchist features. The passage ends with a contrary-to-fact condition: he would have wept, if the next part of the entertainment had not appeared. We see here a perfect example of tangential, indirect narrative linkage.

The relations of the concrete and figurative in the passage on the stranger's memory of his lady are especially revealing of Góngora's technique at its most complex. The metonymy *Sol* means both lady and phoenix; the black plumes attached to his memory are the literal signs of mourning used on doors and coaches at funerals. The worm that emerges from the pyre is a literal attribute of dead bodies, much dwelt on in some poetry. Death, symbolized by the worm, diminishes one's earthly glory in a commonplace of heroic thought (as Ulysses reminds Achilles in *Troilus and Cressida*). The worm as ploughman is the stranger's thought that he is considered dead. The prick of the ploughshare (comparable to the bite of the viper in the next lines) is probably the justification for the image. The shadow of the lilies and carnations has no literal meaning but provides a suitable place for the metonymic viper (bitterness) to hide. In all this passage the abstract nouns are literal: *olvido, memoria, gloria, pena,* and *color,* as well as the concrete ones *labradora* and *ojos,* so that they serve as a guide through the changing, dense metaphoric expressions. The whole is a semantically complex development on the Petrarchist habit of juxtaposing the concrete, figurative, and abstract. In this sense, a characteristic side of baroque style derives from Petrarchist technique but, greatly expanding the metaphoric vocabulary and condensing the imagery, goes well beyond it. The filiation from Petrarchism does not mean the equivalence of baroque metaphorics and Petrarchism, as is sometimes asserted.

We have observed a number of peculiar elements in Góngora's style: hyperbatic narrative, comparisons negative and otherwise, periodic syntax in the manner of renaissance romance prose, drawing many sorts of things into the sentence, covert mythological allusions, and periphrases of all kinds. All this adds up to a style of great indirection, by which we perceive a pastoral ideal through a courtly and erudite baroque style. The values of grandeur and simplicity are both present. There is less of an invidious contrast between noble life and humbleness (despite the slighting remarks about court life in the encomium to the hut) than a synthesis, which Góngora's rhetoric makes possible. Hyperbaton, a characteristic high-style figure, joins with elaborate middle-style lyrical language and low-style narrative elements to create a poem which at first may seem bizarre in its stylistic mixture but in the end proves to convey a tone, wit, and sensibility which none of the three traditional styles alone could impart.

References to color and to what the French call *matières nobles,* precious metals, gems, ivory, and so forth, issue from late Petrarchism and give a special tone to much romance baroque poetry (and to Crashaw's work in English). One often-anthologized French ode represents an extreme point of this tendency. The author, Hippolyte de La Mesnardière, was known primarily as a literary theorist, and most of his verse is in the light, précieux mode. One of his odes, however, "Le Soleil couchant," demonstrates how poetic originality occasionally arises in unlikely circumstances. An elegant personification opens the poem:

> Le GRAND ASTRE va lentement
> Vers les Sapphirs de l'Onde amére.
> Et Vénus dans l'autre Hémisphére,
> Donne ordre à leur Appartement.
>
> De celui dont il va sortir,
> L'Air est pompeux & magnifique.
> Je doute que soûs l'Amérique
> On puisse aussi bien l'assortir.
>
> Ces grans Rideaux à fond vermeil,
> Dont l'Or petille dans la Nuë,
> Sont d'une Estoffe peu connuë
> Aux Païs où va le Soleil.
>
> Estans sans doute moins polis,
> Il s'y néglige davantage;
> Et ne sort en grand Equippage,
> Que pour charmer la FLEUR DE LIS.[7]

The great heavenly body slowly goes toward the sapphires of the bitter wave. And Venus, in the other hemisphere, straightens up their apartment. In the place he is leaving the air is pompous and magnificent. I doubt that down in America they can match it. These great curtains with their gilded background, whose gold sputters in the clouds, are made of a material scarcely known in the countries where the sun is going. Since they are doubtless less civilized, the sun is less ceremonious and takes out his great equipage only to charm France.

The center of the poem is a very long series of descriptive stanzas in which the poet draws the attention of his companion to the colors of the sunset:

> DIEUX! la merveilleuse clarté!
> ALCESTE, admirez la Nüance
> De ce Jaune-clair, qui s'avance
> Soûs cét Incarnat veloûté.
>
> L'OEILLET d'Inde seroit ainsi
> Dans sa douce & sombre dorûre:
> Si sur les pans de sa bordûre
> La Rose trenchoit le Souci.
>
> Mais voilà cét esclat changé
> En un meslange plus modeste.

7. Hippolyte de La Mesnardière, *Les Poésies* (Paris, 1656).

> Voyez ce Rocher bleu-céleste,
> Où deborde un pasle-Orangé.

Gods! the marvellous brilliance! Alcestis, admire the shade of that bright yellow which is moving up under that velvety pale red. The marigold would be like that, in its soft, dark gold, if on its edging, pink would be stronger than yellow. But now that burst of color has changed to a more modest mixture: look at that skyblue cliff, where pale orange is pouring down.

Many stanzas develop the idea of the beauty of the sun before he joins Thetis, his loved one, in their ocean bed. At the end, the poet invites Alcestis to go indoors so that the stars will not be jealous of her.

The idea of painting in words has a long history, beginning in antiquity, but we should note that the vocabulary of color is vague and limited in classical and medieval languages, whereas in the sixteenth and seventeenth centuries, doubtless owing something to high renaissance painting, the increasing number of words designating colors and the discriminations among them gave poetry a great new technical resource. Furthermore, European painting, from the Venetian school through Italian baroque, made the association of color and emotion much stronger. Poetry passed beyond the rather limited stage of traditional color symbolism (white is purity; green is hope, and so forth), so that a description like La Mesnardière's or an expression like Marvell's "green thought in a green shade" can no longer be interpreted univocally as symbolizing this or that abstraction. A rich emotive ambiance replaces the schematic earlier use of color and is closely connected with the baroque celebration of the world's beauty.

The display of color vocabulary in La Mesnardière's poem exemplifies and condenses to a paroxysm one aspect of baroque style. What is equally curious about this poem, however, is that La Mesnardière, who was an exact theorist of the drama, called it an ode, whereas the style is middle, decorative, and lyrical rather than sublime, as the French were beginning to call high style. That there is some shift in conception, if not confusion, here becomes evident when we study La Mesnardière's preface to his poems. La Mesnardière starts out in the tone of one who adheres to the best ancient notions on art, but gradually, peculiar views slip in: Vincent Voiture combines the best of Horace, Catullus, and Ovid; although naturally idylls should be in the simple style, he has made his elevated and *pompeux*. It is quite clear that the system of styles, genres, and taste which the renaissance took over as best it could is being overturned by new attitudes. Voiture's slight epigrams are assimilated to more substantial poetry; the grandiose is creeping into low-style genres, and conversely, the ode is being lowered to the précieux personification and an elaborate form of middle-style description. The confusion that we often find in seventeenth-century literary theory, other than on the theater, is exemplified by La Mesnardière's remarks and practice. Behind it all is an increasing sense of the value of contemporary literature and a perhaps unconscious, rarely stated devaluation of Greek and Roman exemplarity in art. La Mesnardière's ode on the setting sun quite boldly ignores the well-established conventions of the ode in France and offers something new instead.

Mainly, however, it is the low-style genres that we find affected in the seventeenth century by the pervasive love of pomp, ornament, or wit. The French elegies of the earlier seventeenth century sometimes show a new cleverness and range of imagery which separates them from the Petrarchism of the preceding century; the best one in this respect is François Maynard's "La Belle Vieille," the very title of which suggests a renovation of love poetry. But the greatest love elegy in the new mode is unquestionably Andrew Marvell's "To His Coy Mistress," in which the traditional elegiac commonplaces are evoked and splendidly transformed through new imagery and wit:

> Now therefore, while the youthful hue
> Sits on thy skin like morning dew,
> And while thy willing soul transpires
> At every pore with instant fires,
> Now let us sport us while we may;
> And now, like amorous birds of prey,
> Rather at once our time devour,
> Than languish in his slow-chapped power.
> Let us roll all our strength, and all
> Our sweetness, up into one ball:
> And tear our pleasures with rough strife,
> Through the iron gates of life.
> Thus, though we cannot make our sun
> Stand still, yet we will make him run.[8]

8. Andrew Marvell, *The Complete Poems*, ed. Elizabeth Story Donno (Baltimore, 1972), hereinafter cited in the text.

This is, of course, a very different conception from that of the *mollis* elegy. Marvell's choice of meter contributes as much as the imagery to the incision of his lines. The tendency of English couplets to end in closed monosyllables provides a special sharpness and emphasis romance riming does not so readily attain. This is especially true of the shorter tetrametric couplet, to which nothing in Italian or French corresponds. Within this metrical framework, then, the vocabulary of willful, delighted, and even violent activity rejects the whole languid and plangent elegiac strain. The low but elegant style traditionally attributed to elegy is replaced by something akin to the vigorous note of satire. Terms like *birds of prey, devour, rough strife,* and *iron gates* suggest the harsh, αὐστηρός style, yet employed in an essentially positive way.

The transformation of genres we have been observing is an exceedingly delicate matter. While "To His Coy Mistress" and "Lycidas" are completely successful, the scale of the *Adone* and the projected form of the *Soledades* resulted in shapelessness in the case of Marino and in abandonment of his poem by Góngora. "Le Soleil couchant" is merely a brilliant eccentricity with no particular consequences. The opinion has been expressed more than once that the sonnet or short poem is the most successful form of baroque poetry, the one in which there is no tension between elaboration of detail and structured wholeness. We shall explore that notion now by looking at a few of the finest short pieces of the seventeenth century which correspond to general notions of baroque style.

II

There is a whole school of charming Marinist verse writers in seventeenth-century Italy, much of whose work, however, tends to be lightweight. These poets wrote madrigals and sonnets, both equivalents of the ancient epigram, and unexpected turns on Petrarchan themes and images form the basis of their inspiration. This is what we might call the low secular baroque style, *genus subtile floridius,* related to the précieux poetry of contemporary France, but we must keep in mind that the brief witty poem is a common ancient form, much illustrated in the *Greek Anthology,* which was widely known and imitated. However, the Petrarchist sources of this poetry, its constant use of titles like "To a Lady," "To a Blond Lady," and "To a Lady Wearing Blue," put Italian baroque epigrams definitely in the stylistic ambit of European poetry. The lyric production of Marino himself is enormous, but we may single out of this uneven mass of verse certain pieces like "La Bella Vedova" or "Schiava," which have a bit more than passing epigrammatic charm. "Schiava" opens with an allusion to the Song of Songs:

> Nera sì, ma se' bella, o di natura
> fra le belle d'amor leggiadro mostro;
> fosca è l'alba appo te, perde e s'oscura
> presso l'ebeno tuo l'avorio e l'ostro.
>
> Or quando, or dove il mondo antico o il nostro
> vide sì viva mai, sentì sì pura,
> o luce uscir di tenebroso inchiostro
> o di spento carbon nascere arsura?
>
> Servo di chi m'è serva, ecco ch'avolto
> porto di bruno laccio il core intorno,
> che per candida man non fia mai sciolto.
>
> Là 've più ardi, o Sol, sol per tuo scorno
> un sole è nato; un sol, che nel bel volto
> porta la notte, ed ha negli occhi il giorno.

You are black but beautiful, O miracle of nature among love's beauties. Dark is the dawn compared with you; ivory and purple dim and darken beside your ebony. Now when or where did the ancient world or ours see so brilliant a light, feel such a pure light come from shadowy ink, or from burnt-out coals rise such a fire? I am the servant of my servant: see how I bear a dark bond wrapped around my heart, which no white hand shall ever loosen. O Sun, where you burn brightest, another sun is born to cast scorn on you, another sun who in her beautiful face bears night and has day in her eyes.

Marino's gift for using conventional images in such a way as to produce a rich impression of color is nicely illustrated in these antitheses and paradoxes. But there is something much more important here than elegant figures of thought and sound. Marino's sonnet has a general esthetic implication, for it is about what the French called "irregular beauty," that is to say, a form of beauty unforeseen by the guiding rules and principles of classicizing art. Irregular beauty is closely related to the Marinesque ideas of wonder, surprise, and ingenuity and to the unexpected marvels of nature, which, as part of universal correspondences, have something to teach us. This kind of poetry is dependent on the prior existence of the classical cinquecento manner and ultimately of Petrarch. It is often said, in the attempt to disparage the defining of baroque poetry solely in terms of imagery, that paradoxes, catachreses, and violent antitheses are found in generous supply in medieval Latin and vernacular verse. However, despite the existence of a kind of eternal, recurrent mannerism or baroque,[9] a poem like Marino's lies in a very specific historical stylistic context, and we would do wrong to ignore the fact that it is part of a careful elaboration of renaissance esthetic ideas, here inverted, as far as the imagery goes. In other respects, Marino's sonnet tends, like other short Italian baroque poems, to use a simpler sentence structure than the cinquecento sonneteers and to multiply finite verbs in a way that contrasts with many examples of baroque poetry in French.

The serious esthetic implications of "Schiava" are paralleled elsewhere by a didactic moral seriousness which was inherited from earlier centuries and takes the form of symbolic illustrations. The following poem is one of the best by Tristan L'Hermite; it is a reworking of one of the sonnets in Marino's "moral" verse but is far more attractive than the original, thanks to the greater sententiousness produced by the phrasing of the French:

> Aux rayons du Soleil, le Pan audacieux,
> Cét Avril animé, ce firmament volage,
> Estalle avec orgueil en son riche plumage
> Et les fleurs du Printemps & les Astres des Cieux.
>
> Mais comme il fait le vain sous cét arc gracieux
> Qui nous forme d'Iris une nouvelle Image,
> Il rabat tout à coup sa plume & son courage
> Si tost que sur ses pieds il a porté les yeux.
>
> Homme, à qui tes desirs font sans cesse la guerre,
> Et qui veux posseder tout le rond de la Terre:
> Voy le peu qu'il en faut pour faire un Monument.
>
> Tu n'es rien que l'Idole agreable & fragile
> Qu'un Roy de Babylone avoit veuë en dormant,
> Ta teste est toute d'or, mais tes pieds sont d'argile.[10]

9. See Ernst Robert Curtius, *European Literature and the Latin Middle Ages,* tr. Willard R. Trask (New York, 1953), 273–301.

10. François Tristan L'Hermite, "L'Ambition tancée," in Tristan L'Hermite, *La Lyre,* ed. Jean-Pierre Chauveau (Geneva, 1977), hereinafter cited in the text.

In the sunbeams, the bold peacock, that animated April, that fluttering firmament, spreads out with pride on his rich feathers both springtime's flowers and the stars of heaven. But as he poses vainly beneath the gracious arch of his tail, which gives us a new image of the rainbow, his feathers and spirits collapse once he has glimpsed his own feet. Man, besieged by your desires and yearning to own the whole terrestrial globe, see how little is needed to make a tomb. You are but the charming, fragile idol that a Babylonian King saw in his sleep; your head is all gold, but your feet are clay.

The appositions of the first quatrain illustrate the essentially baroque figure of the adjective and noun periphrasis, and the combination of the symbol of natural correspondences, the peacock, with the biblical *allegoria* (introduced by the characteristic *n'être que* comparison), show the way in which secular and sacred metaphor mingle in seventeenth-century verse. The theme is that of vanity, *grandeur et misère*, which generally preoccupied seventeenth-century thinking (one could compare the sonnet with Góngora's work and Bossuet's, as well as with Pascal's) but found a particularly nice expression in the highly colored contrasts of baroque poetry.

Closely related to the imagistic illustration of grandeur and emptiness is the baroque use of encomiastic description. Usually description, as a rhetorical figure, is particularly marked by the epideictic idea so strong in European lyric; the greater linguistic elaboration of description in the seventeenth-century heightens its moral significance, as in Saint-Amant's "L'Hiver des Alpes":

> Ces atômes de feu, qui sur la Neige brillent,
> Ces estincelles d'or, d'azur, et de cristal,
> Dont l'Hiver, au Soleil, d'un lustre oriental
> Pare ses Cheveux blancs, que les Vents esparpillent:

> Ce beau Cotton du Ciel, dequoy les monts s'habillent,
> Ce pavé transparant, fait du second metal,
> Et cet Air net, et sain, propre à l'esprit vital,
> Sont si doux à mes yeux, que d'aise ils en pétillent.

> Cette Saison me plaist, j'en ayme la froideur,
> Sa Robbe d'innocence, et de pure splendeur,
> Couvre en quelque façon les crimes de la Terre:

> Au prix du dernier chaut ce temps m'est gracieux;
> Et si la Mort m'atrappe en ce chemin de verre,
> Je ne sçaurois avoir qu'un Tombeau precieux.[11]

---

11. Marc-Antoine de Saint-Amant, *Oeuvres*, eds. Jacques Bailbé and Jean Lagny (4 vols.; Paris, 1967–71), II, hereinafter cited in the text.

These atoms of fire shining on the snow, these sparks of gold, azure, and crystal, with which winter, in the sunlight, decorates in oriental splendor her wind-scattered hair, this beautiful heavenly cotton the mountains are clad in, this transparent floor made of the second metal, silver, and this clear and wholesome air, suitable for the vital spirits, are so sweet to my eyes that they sparkle with the delight of it. This season I like; I like its coldness. Its robe of innocence and pure brightness covers in its way the earth's crimes. Compared with the late heat, this time of year is gracious; and if Death comes upon me in this glassy road, I would merely have a precious tomb.

Multiple periphrases and personification constitute the elements of baroque rhetoric here, especially characteristic in that all the figures tend to illustrate the same quality of glittering whiteness and purity. The sonnet demonstrates irregular beauty in that snow and mountains were not for a long time yet to come to be considered objects of esthetic admiration. They were generally associated with the dismal side of winter and with horrid, inhuman shapes. Saint-Amant makes of his landscape a symbol of moral purification, of casting off sullied earthly concerns before death, as final rites are a kind of purging of the various parts of the body in preparation for their resurrection. Even in a poet like Saint-Amant, whose concerns are so often worldly, we encounter very orthodox religious undertones. This use of encomiastic description is handled in such a way that we perceive at first mainly the striking esthetic novelty of it, only upon reflection to see its moral associations; this is again a frequent aspect of baroque rhetoric relating secular and devotional poetry.

Andrew Marvell is an ambiguous poet through temperament and the greater moral indirection Protestant poets sometimes show in the seventeenth-century. They were more accustomed to private and individual moral reflections than were Catholic poets, for whom accusations of heresy and immorality were a real problem in the early and middle seventeenth century. Marvell wrote a group of poems on the mower with pastoral and Petrarchist images and phraseology that have encouraged modern commentators to see more in them than merely wit and the renovation of bucolic imagery. One of these poems, "The Mower to the Glowworms," which is short, is especially suggestive:

> Ye living lamps, by whose dear light
> The nightingale does sit so late,

And studying all the summer night,
Her matchless songs does meditate;

Ye country comets, that portend
No war, nor prince's funeral,
Shining unto no higher end
Than to presage the grass's fall;

Ye glowworms, whose officious flame
To wandering mowers shows the way,
That in the night have lost their aim,
And after foolish fires do stray;

Your courteous lights in vain you waste,
Since Juliana here is come,
For she my mind has so displaced
That I shall never find my home.

The two apostrophic periphrases are the baroque rhetorical feature here. Fireflies, moreover, especially fascinated French and Italian poets of the period as marvels of nature worthy of an elaborate descriptive style. The third stanza, with its strong Christian associations of loss of grace, pursuit of false gods, and the ever-present potential of salvation, is countered by the Petrarchist interpretation put on the poem by the conclusion. The undertones of the third stanza persist, however, and we see the concluding one as a limited, false, worldly reading of the symbolic situation. Such sophistication in structuring a poem reminds us of the favorite baroque device of *correctio*, in which alternatives are envisaged. Here, however, we have, so to speak, *abusio*, or "mischoice" (the opposite of *correctio*) in which the second alternative is the less valid one. The other mower poems are likewise suggestive of moral-religious interpretation.

The elaborate imagery of the world in baroque poetry has several shades of meaning. It may represent the idea that the world, as God's handiwork, is worthy of praise, which is the most general notion. More specifically, the elements of nature constitute a system of correspondences between the moral and the physical; this is the old idea of the book of nature, a kind of other Bible. Finally, in the book of nature there are negative symbols like those of vanity and worldliness. The motivation for highly sensory imagery is thus connected, in many cases, with a fairly overt form of ethical and even theological thinking.

In rhetorical theory, there corresponds a vituperative or denigra-

tory genre to every laudatory one. This means that the typical figures of baroque description and metaphor can be used for what one
might loosely call satiric purposes. I say loosely because the idea of
negative encomium is closely involved with the seventeenth-century
idea of the irregular, the strange as a subject of poetry, which leads
by degrees to the ugly and the horrible, and in every case we cannot
precisely define a satiric aim. Vituperation of the ugly and delight in
the grotesque have an ambiguous relationship. Ornamented satire
has antecedents in the "Princes" and "Chambre doree," books of *Les
Tragiques,* and a certain number of examples are encountered later
on. Here is a piece by the obscure Laugier de Porchères, which describes the end of a military man, a man who was all show and
fierceness, while being utterly incompetent:

> Traict de poudre enflammé, qu'un peu de feu desserre,
> A qui le luire est vivre, et le vivre est monter,
> Que l'on voit resplendir, qu'on voit esclater,
> Or' comme une Comete, ores comme un tonnerre.
>
> Brave dragon de feu, qui sifflant loing de terre
> Te voudrais comme un astre au ciel faire adopter,
> A l'entreprendre hardi, foible à l'exécuter,
> En aspirant heureux, mourant tu fais la guerre.[12]

Arrow of flaming powder, which a bit of fire sets off, for whom shining is
life, and life is rising, whom you see gleaming forth, whom you see burst,
now like a comet, now like a thunderbolt; brave fiery dragon-dragoon,
who, whistling far from earth, would like to be taken for a star in the sky,
bold in enterprise, weak in execution, you rose in joy but falling engaged
in combat.

On a lower level, we find these opening lines of Saint-Amant's "La
Berne":

> Excroqueuse de gringuenaude
> Avec ton nez à chiquenaude,
> Où tend pour enseigne un morveau,
> Que ton gros cocu, Jean le Veau,
> Avalle en guise d'huistre verte . . .

Thief of bodily excretions, with your nose one longs to snap, where your
establishment is symbolized by a big piece of snot, that your big cuckold,
Jean the Calf, swallows up in lieu of a green oyster . . .

12. Laugier de Porchères, "Sur la mort de Polemandre comparée à une fuzée," in
Jean Rousset (ed.), *Anthologie de la poésie baroque française* (2 vols.; Paris, 1961), I.

This vein of verse has analogues in Italian satire (the *capitoli* of the cinquecento), in *capricci* like Marino's description of mating fish ("Amor di pesci"), in burlesque and heroicomical literature, and in other works where ugliness, verbal exuberance, grotesquerie, and humor mingle. It is not my purpose to explore this large general area, usually designated as satiric, or as the French used to put it, "satyric," but an example is necessary to illustrate the direction which irregular beauty, leading to the irregular *tout court*, could take in baroque esthetics. It would appear that the freedom of imagistic invention in baroque literature led some poets by a quite natural evolution to devise elaborate images which were ambiguous as praise or were downright ugly, except of course, that even in dealing with the ugly the same delight in creative linguistic play persists. The separation of genres also becomes problematic when middle style, the one devoted to the idealized and the beautiful, accepts wit in the form of conceits like beauty's issuing from "shadowy ink" and "dead coals," as in Marino's "Schiava," or admits the comparison of an adored lady to a hydra, which Desportes made in one of his odd pieces anticipating seventeenth-century rhetoric. The essentially middle-style character of baroque secular poetry becomes altered through that very free tendency toward ornament and elaboration which makes it middle style.

III

The irregular has a further important sense in seventeenth-century poetry. While it is common to use a sonnet or other conventionally developed lyric form to present irregular beauty or frank ugliness, there is also the possibility of using irregular composition, dispositio, or structuring, especially in a longer work. This is not the same thing as Marino's digressions or long developments in the *Adone*, which are merely a hypertrophic form of ordinary structural elements and give an impression of slovenly, monotonous composition more than of calculated irregularity.

Saint-Amant's "La Solitude" (before 1619) was his first important poem and received much admiring attention both in and out of France. It seemed like a new kind of poetry, and source hunters have not been able to make it derive as a whole from any tradition; Saint-Amant, though not possessed of the highest poetic gifts, nevertheless displayed originality throughout his career. "La Solitude," which the poet described with such terms as *fantasque, ardeur,* and *licence* is a two-hundred-line poem about an island which the poet had occasion to visit. He moves from one subject to another: steep hills, streams, birds, ruins, graves, a grotto, the sea. The diction is not especially baroque; what is new is the capricious movement of the poem, which cannot easily be assimilated to enumeration, for the elements of his description are varyingly presented, whereas the members of an enumeration should be on the same plane. Some unifying features have been found in the poem—images of verticality, darkness and light, death and immortality, reality and reflection—and one commentator has insisted especially on the "grotto experience."[13] A great deal of ingenuity has gone into defining the unity of the poem, but unity is one of those elastic concepts that with some thought can be made to envelop the most disparate things. The point seems rather to be that the poem takes place on an island, for generally islands are settings of uncommon experiences. I think if we go beyond this to narrowly define a theme in the customary literary sense, we are misreading a poem which charmed its contemporaries because it seemed to have no literary wholeness; it pleasantly violated the familiar rhetorical notions.

Some years after "La Solitude," Saint-Amant revisited Belle-Isle and wrote another poem, "Le Contemplateur" (1628), similar in movement, in which he refers specifically to "La Solitude." The suggestions of consciousness of good and evil and of origins that we find in the earlier poem are clearer here, where each sight brings forth some thought of a Christian nature. The air of improvisation is similar, however, the poem including such disparate elements as dinner table conversation and a vision of the Resurrection. The style is more baroque than that in the earlier poem:

> O bon Dieu! m'escriay-je alors,
> Que ta puissance est nompareille,

---

13. See Robert T. Corum, Jr., *Other Worlds and Other Seas: Art and Vision in Saint-Amant's Nature Poetry* (Lexington, Ky., 1979), 31; Samuel L. Borton, *Six Modes of Sensibility in Saint-Amant* (The Hague, 1966), 63.

> D'avoir en un si petit corps
> Fait une si grande merveille!
> O feu! qui tousjours allumé,
> Brusles sans estre consumé!
> Belle Escarboucle qui chemines!
> Ton éclat me plaist beaucoup mieux
> Que celuy qu'on tire des mines
> Afin d'ensorceler nos yeux!   (221–30)

O good God, I cried then, how unmatched your power is, to have made such a great marvel of so little a body! O fire! who, always lit, burn without being exhausted! Beautiful carbuncle in movement! Your gleam charms me much more than that of the stone they take from mines to enchant our eyes!

Here is the favorite baroque insect, the firefly, with suitable circumlocutions.

A *grand Homme marin* appears at one point:

> Il a le corps fait comme nous,
> Sa teste à la nostre est pareille,
> Je l'ay veu jusques aux genous,
> Sa voix a frappé mon oreille;
> Son bras d'escailles est couvert,
> Son teint est blanc, son oeil est vert,
> Sa chevelure est azurée;
> Il m'a regardé fixement,
> Et sa contenance assurée
> M'a donné de l'estonnement.
> . . . .
> De mainte branche de coral
> Qui croist sous l'eau comme de l'herbe,
> Et dont Neptune est libéral,
> Il porte un pennache superbe;
> Vingt tours de perles d'Orient
> Riches d'un lustre variant
> En guise d'écharpe le ceignent;
> D'ambre son chef est parfumé,
> Et quoy que les ondes le creignent
> Il en est pourtant bien aymé.   (161–70, 181–90)

His body is like ours, his head similar to ours. I saw him down to the knees. His voice struck my ear; his arm is covered with scales, his skin white, his eye green, his hair azure. He stared at me, and his look of assurance astonished me. He bears a headdress of many branches of coral, which grows like grass under the water and which Neptune is generous with. Twenty strands of Oriental pearls, rich with varying luster, are wrapped around him like a scarf. His head smells of amber, and although the waves fear him, they love him still.

The enumeratory descriptive style is exemplified in this apparition, whose significance is far from evident. Again, as in "La Solitude," despite a good deal of Christian and moral reference, the subject of the poem is hard to define in the traditional rhetorical way. It is a meditation, but not a structured one in the devotional manner. We can say that the unity of the poem lies in the mind of the speaker, his exploratory fascination, and his reminiscences of the Christian scheme of the world, but this kind of psychological unity is not a rhetorical one in the renaissance or seventeenth-century sense. The pleasure of the poem would seem to reside in a deliberate elusiveness, so far as the traditional rules of composition go.

"La Solitude" appears to have been known to Marvell, whose long "Upon Appleton House" reflects some of the same difficulties in interpretation. There is an ancient tradition of encomia on places; Jonson's "To Penshurst" is an earlier English example, and there are a number of poems in seventeenth-century France which celebrate great houses. However, the curious thing is that the Appleton House which Marvell knew and stayed in was a modest dwelling, with nothing of the stately manor about it.[14] Consequently, his laudatory poem moves in the realm of the past and of fantasy to a large extent. The early part of the poem tells of the nunnery which once stood on the spot and of how the mother of General Fairfax, the house's proprietor, was forcibly taken from the nunnery to be married. Then we have a picture of the retired general directing his army of flowers:

> When in the east the morning ray
> Hangs out the colours of the day,
> The bee through these known alleys hums,
> Beating the *dian* with its drums.
> Then flowers their drowsy eyelids raise,
> Their silken ensigns each displays,
> And dries its pan yet dank with dew,
> And fills its flask with odours new.
> . . . .
> Well shot, ye firemen! Oh how sweet,
> And round your equal fire do meet,
> Whose shrill report no ear can tell,
> But echoes to the eye and smell.
> See how the flowers, as at parade,

14. See John Dixon Hunt, *Andrew Marvell: His Life and Writings* (Ithaca, 1978), 80–112.

> Under their colours stand displayed:
> Each regiment in order grows,
> That of the tulip, pink, and rose.   (289–96, 305–12)

Marvell drops not so much to the précieux tone as to the mock-heroic one, a mode Saint-Amant has sometimes been credited with inventing. Still with a certain lightness of touch, the poet thinks of Eden, an "isle," and next "passes" (note the rhetorical insouciance of the connective verb) to the tall grass:

> And now to the abyss I pass
> Of that unfathomable grass,
> Where men like grasshoppers appear,
> But grasshoppers are giants there:
> They, in their squeaking laugh, contemn
> Us as we walk more low than them:
> And, from the precipices tall
> Of the green spires to us do call.   (369–76)

Marvell has a way of introducing words like *abyss* and *unfathomable* which have rich moral connotations, but he allows these connotations to be undertones, not immediately caught up or sustained.

> To see men through this meadow dive,
> We wonder how they rise alive,
> As, under water, none does know
> Whether he fall through it or go.
> But, as the mariners that sound,
> And show upon their lead the ground,
> They bring up flowers so to be seen,
> And prove they've at the bottom been.
>
> No scene that turns with engines strange
> Does oftener than these meadows change.
> For when the sun the grass hath vexed,
> The tawny mowers enter next;
> Who seem like Israelites to be,
> Walking on foot through a green sea.
> To them the grassy deeps divide,
> And crowd a lane to either side.   (377–92)

From the reversal of sizes in the passage about the grasshoppers and men through the theatrical metaphor and underwater imagery, we find characteristic baroque visions of reality transformed. There is, of course, a certain ambiguity, for both fanciful poets and biblical prophets have visions, and further sea imagery culminates in an apocalyptic flood being released from an estate upstream, offended at the general's long absence:

> Then, to conclude these pleasant acts,
> Denton sets ope its cataracts,
> And makes the meadow truly be
> (Which it but seemed before) a sea.
> For, jealous of its Lord's long stay,
> It tries t'invite him thus away.
> The river in itself is drowned,
> And isles the astonished cattle round.   (465–72)

Such references as those to the dividing of the Red Sea and to the Flood constitute the kind of conceit which derives from hyperbole, anachronism, and parallels between the sacred and profane. It is arguable whether the biblical allusions form a serious thematic ground for the poem or exist as playful enhancements to complimentary verse. Joking with the sacred is not, we should remember, out of keeping with the intensely religious culture of the seventeenth century.

The notion of the half-sacred play ("these pleasant acts") is continued in the poet's taking refuge in an ark, where he meditates on birds until suddenly the deluge is over:

> For now the waves are fall'n and dried,
> And now the meadows fresher dyed,
> Whose grass, with moister colour dashed,
> Seems as green silks but newly washed.
> No serpent new nor crocodile
> Remains behind our little Nile,
> Unless itself you will mistake,
> Among these meads the only snake.   (625–32)

The day, which began with the general reviewing his flowers, is drawing to an end, and a long hyperbolic compliment to Fairfax' daughter Maria, Marvell's pupil, takes up the rest of the poem; she is compared to the nun of the opening, and so a superficial circularity is established. But Marvell does something very interesting here; instead of bringing the poem to a rhetorical climax with the praise of the daughter, Marvell adds one final stanza, quite unrelated to her:

> But now the salmon-fishers moist
> Their leathern boats begin to hoist,
> And like Antipodes in shoes,

Have shod their heads in their canoes.
How tortoise-like, but not so slow,
These rational amphibii go!
Let's in: for the dark hemisphere
Does now like one of them appear.   (769–76)

The last thing we perceive is the bizarre, delightful conceit about the fishermen carrying canoes over their heads, which seems to be a way of reaffirming the fact that the poem is conceit and fantasy, for all its complimentary reference to the house and its inhabitants. This oddly shaped poem has, after long neglect, excited modern attempts at interpretation.[15] The complex of references to sacred history, religion, and retirement (both the nuns and the general are, in a sense, in retirement) gives a certain teasing impression of a sustaining idea behind the poem, but the succession of events is very hard to interpret without recourse to the idea of the associational structures found in twentieth-century poetry. There seems to be a determined attempt on Marvell's part, as on Saint-Amant's in "La Solitude" and "Le Contemplateur," to create something of an enigma, by the rhetorical criteria of their day. The study of these longer poems gives us a much richer idea of the baroque imagination than sonnets, however excellent, can provide. Such poems also impair the frequent and needlessly literal comparisons between baroque poetry and the fine arts. The *ut pictura poesis* notion certainly flourished, but as with many phrases from classical treatises (this one is a misinterpretation of a line of Horace' *Ars Poetica*) we must be careful of simple-minded applications of it. While on the one hand, there are a great many static descriptions of art works (Marino's *La Galleria*, for example), they do not, on the whole, rank high among seventeenth-century poems, and such longer, mysterious, ever-changing works as Marvell's or Saint-Amant's constitute a much more original, more particularly baroque, conception of descriptive poetry.

IV

We cannot really sum up our notion of baroque poetry without some idea of its total literary context. At the end of the sixteenth century,

15. See, for example, Rosalie L. Colie, *My Echoing Song: Andrew Marvell's Poetry of Criticism* (Princeton, 1970), 181–238.

where we may situate a mannerist current of style, if we wish to make the distinction, and the beginnings of a baroque mode, still another kind of poetry was coming into being. This is the French neoclassical style, which we must not see as a simple antithesis to baroque poetry, but as a parallel and in some ways related style. The rhetorical education of poets writing in different manners was essentially the same, and as they had written the same kind of orational exercises, studied the same figures, and read the same Latin classics, there are subtle bonds between seemingly diverse or opposed stylistic practices.

François de Malherbe, with whom the beginnings of French neoclassicism are always associated, was a reasonably close contemporary of Ben Jonson's, but their conceptions of style, though both are always called classical or neoclassical, have interesting differences. Malherbe, for one thing, focused on, or was most famous for, high style, whereas Jonson's neo-Roman manner expressed itself primarily in low-style genres. In some ways, Malherbe's classicism, though one may care less for it, was more original, more independent of Latin practice than Jonson's.

Malherbe's characteristic idea of style expressed itself early in a poem called "Les Larmes de Saint-Pierre" (1587), which is often called baroque for no very good reason other than that the tears of figures in sacred history were often the subject of baroque elaboration. Malherbe's poem is a free adaptation of a work by Luigi Tansillo, and we are fortunate in that we can isolate, by comparison of the two very different texts, the peculiar quality of Malherbe's French neoclassicism, which profoundly separates it from cinquecento Italian ideas of classicizing style. One of Tansillo's stanzas that Malherbe more or less adapts to his poem is the following:

> Come padre dolente, che sotterra
> Lasciando il morto figlio, esce del Tempio;
> E mentre incerto suspirando egli erra,
> Giunge a la piazza, ove'l dì stesso l'empio
> Ferro l'uccise, e rossegiar la terra
> Vede del fresco sangue; al crudo scempio
> Rinova il grido, e più, che prima piange
> Tal, che la doglia par, che'n rabbia cangia.[16]

16. Luigi Tansillo, *Le Lagrime di San Pietro*, II, 2, quoted in François de Malherbe, *Oeuvres*, ed. M. L. Lalanne (5 vols.; Paris, 1862), I, hereinafter cited in the text.

As a sorrowing father, who has left his son in the grave, leaves the church and while sighing and uncertain of his way he wanders, he comes upon the square where that very day the impious sword had killed him, and he sees the ground red with fresh blood; at the sight of the untimely slaughter he renews his cries, and weeps more than before, so much that his sorrow seems to change into rage.

This is a comparison made when Saint Peter is wandering about in distraction and despair at having denied Christ. It is clearly written and pictorial, within the limits of Italian poetic diction, of which there are only two metonymic examples: *Tempio* for church, and *ferro* for sword, both commonplace. Malherbe, however, eliminated much of what was literal or precisely visual in his reworking:

> Comme un homme dolent, que le glaive contraire
> A privé de son fils, et du tiltre du pere,
> Plaignant deçà delà son mal-heur advenu,
> S'il arrive à la place où s'est faict le dommage,
> L'ennui renouvelé plus rudement l'outrage,
> En voyant le sujet a ses yeux revenu.
>
> Le vieillard qui n'attend une telle rencontre,
> Si tost qu'au despourveu sa fortune luy monstre
> Le lieu qui fut tesmoin d'un si lasche meffaict,
> De nouvelles fureurs se deschire et s'entame,
> Et de tous les pensers qui travaillent son ame
> L'extresme cruauté plus cruelle se faict.   (283–94)

Like a sorrowing man, whom an enemy's opposing sword has deprived of his son and of his title of father, lamenting here and there the misfortune that has occurred, if he happens on the square where the destruction took place, a renewed pain outrages him more roughly, seeing the matter come back before his eyes. The old man who is not expecting such an encounter, as soon as, unexpectedly, his ill-fortune shows him the spot which witnessed such a cowardly misdeed, is torn and cut by new fury, and the great cruelty of all the thoughts exercising his soul becomes even crueler.

The *glaive contraire* is at once a more condensed expression than Tansillo's and a periphrastic one; it is a fine example of concision, whereas almost everything that follows dilutes the material. The *tiltre de pere* repeats, with an abstraction, the preceding words; *où s'est faict le dommage* is almost obscure in its use of the metonymy *dommage* for murder; and *le sujet* is the vaguest of words, a part of the abstraction *sujet de sa pensée* lifted from its normal context and made to function with *voir*, which means "seeing in the mind," *reve-*

nue being somewhat pleonastic. *Rencontre* is usually used for people; *sa fortune luy monstre* is a periphrasis for "sees by chance," in which the word *fortune* is somewhat trivialized; like *fortune, lieu* is person-ified; *lasche meffaict* is vague but understandable in the context; *s'en-tame* adds nothing to *se dechire*; and finally, the last lines are very wordy.

This passage is not representative of Malherbe's mature work or of French neoclassicism in its ultimate form, but it shows the mechanisms involved. Personifications and metonymies, or one-word metaphors, of little vividness play a large role, and some abstract terms are used very loosely. The riper form of Malherbe's more abstract diction can be seen in the opening of the "Prière pour le Roy allant en Limozin":

> O Dieu, dont les bontez, de nos larmes touchees,
> Ont aux vaines fureurs les armes arrachees,
> Et rangé l'insolence aux piez de la raison,
> Puis qu'à rien d'imparfaict ta loüange n'aspire,
> Acheve ton ouvrage au bien de cét empire,
> Et nous rends l'embonpoint comme la guerison.

O God, whose goodness, touched by our tears, has torn its weapons from vain fury and brought insolence to the foot of reason, since your praiseworthy actions aspire only to what is perfect, finish your task for the good of this empire and give us back flesh with health.

It is not God or persons who act here; instead, their qualities serve as subjects and complements of the verbs: *bontez* in the poetic plural (not God), *vaines fureurs* (not insane, raging men), *insolence* (not the insolent rebels), *raison* (not the reasonable king sitting on his throne and possessing feet, unlike reason). The other figures are the commonplace metonymy in which a concrete word becomes general and vaguely abstract (*larmes*), the concise *ta loüange*, which might be called the opposite of a periphrasis since it tightens the wording, and the unusual conversion of *embonpoint* into an abstraction meaning "health." Most of this diction is a justified and reasonably effective form of high style, with its emphasis on nouns. It is a peculiar form of diction in its transformation of everything into abstractions, and its sources are doubtless varied, but one should note that classical Latin makes very little, very sporadic use of such abstractions and that abstractions are also limited in Italian high style. This is a peculiarly French kind of diction, reflecting the idea that the general term, the abstract term, the periphrasis employing abstractions, and the metonymic conversion of the concrete into the abstract represent grandeur in language.

Malherbe wrote fewer than ten major odes, and their styles vary, so that the mythological parts of the ode welcoming Marie de Médicis to France or the "Ode sur l'attentat" move in a world where hints of the concrete are greater. Malherbe's style was less theoretically worked out, less consistent than my examples up to now might lead one to think. In his early poem, in a passage not found in Tansillo, Saint Peter is said to "se mettre au visage / Sur le feu de sa honte, une cendre d'ennui" (47–48). French neoclassical style does not absolutely reject concrete terms but tends to use them figuratively and in combination with abstractions, as here. Obviously such a line would not be out of place in a baroque poem, where the concrete and the abstract are often juxtaposed; we see here a typical example of the close relation of the two styles, based on the cultivation of figures, which are, after all, limited in number. However, a perhaps more typical, certainly more exclusively neoclassical expression can be found in the periphrasis *l'honneur ravi de sa pudicité* referring to Ariadne, in the introduction to "Les Larmes de Saint Pierre." Here two abstract nouns are metonymically substituted for two other abstractions (*l'ornement de sa virginité*), so that you have a secondary level of abstraction in the process of avoiding the ordinary word.

We perceive in all this a consciousness of transferred meanings which is not at all unlike the baroque rhetorical consciousness, although Malherbe prefers to play with abstractions rather than contrast them with the concrete. But in the larger rhetorical perspective we see the reason for Malherbe's style: he is addressing royalty or nobility in high-style odes, whereas all our secular examples of baroque diction belong to an elaborate register of middle style. The distinctions between baroque and neoclassical styles are not necessarily subjective ones involving some world view or metaphysical principle. They are often carefully bound to the classical genre distinctions.

An interesting illustration of this distinction occurs in Saint-Amant's narrative *Moïse sauvé*. Saint-Amant is commonly thought of as the antithesis of Malherbe, but actually his various styles include a neoclassical one. *Moïse sauvé* is ambiguously subtitled *Idylle heroïque,* and we can see in this story of Moses' infancy, extended with dreams and visions of his future destiny, how the heroic or high-style manner obtrudes in the verse when a subject like Pharaoh is treated:

> Mais, helas! un dur prince, un tygre espouventable,
> Diffamant par son regne un lieu si delectable,
> Le rendoit aux Hebreux, lors esclaves sous luy,
> Un triste et sombre enfer plein d'horreur et d'ennuy.
> Et bien que sur ces bords, depuis que dans les chaisnes,
> Ils souffroyent la rigueur des plus sanglantes gesnes,
> Par plus de trois fois le ravage annuel
> Eust couvert tous les champs d'un bien-fait ponctuel,
> Toutesfois le long cours de cette servitude,
> Pour cette nation n'avoit eu rien de rude,
> Au prix de l'aspre joug, dont cet homme inhumain
> Luy surchargeait le col, de sa terrible main.[17]

But alas, a harsh prince, a terrible tiger, defaming by his reign such a delightful spot, made it for the Hebrews, at that time slaves under him, a sad and dark hell full of horror and sorrow. And although on these banks, since, in chains, they suffered the rigor of the bloodiest torments, more than three times the yearly ravage of the waters had covered all the fields with their timely benevolence, yet the long duration of this servitude had had nothing harsh for this nation, compared with the bitter yoke which this inhuman man placed on their necks with his terrible hand.

Since this is not an ode but epic narration, we do not find the extreme abstraction we have seen previously. Nevertheless, the diction tends toward the conventionally figurative or metonymic; it is removed from the concrete. *Tygre* is a commonplace term of opprobrium of no visual value; the "delightful place" and "sad dark hell" are very general; "suffering the rigor of torments" is more roundabout than "suffering rigorous torments." It is difficult to decide whether words like *gesnes, servitude,* or *chaisnes* have a precise meaning because they are common figurative words in the seventeenth century. The periphrasis about the Nile's annual floods is purely abstract, but Saint-Amant has taken one common abstract

---

17. Marc-Antoine de Saint-Amant, *Oeuvres complètes,* ed. Ch.-L. Livet (2 vols.; Paris, 1855), II, Premiere Partie, hereinafter cited in the text.

metonymy, *joug*, and given it figurative value by adding *surchargeait* and *main*. One can see how certain admirers of the abstract style found the ode an even higher genre than the epic; the ode was free of the requirement of much narrative detail.

The idyllic aspect of *moïse sauvé* concerns Moses' humble parents and background. It often tends to be idyll raised to an elaborate, baroque middle style, as in a number of famous descriptions. Perhaps the most interesting of these, because it is used to close the poem, is that of night:

> Quand tout fut accomply, les heures tenebreuses
> Ornoyent le firmament de lumieres nombreuses;
> On descouvroit la lune, et de feux animez
> Et les champs et les airs estoyent déjà semez.
> Ces miracles volans, ces astres de la terre,
> Qui de leurs rayons d'or font aux ombres la guerre,
> Ces tresors ou reluit la divine splendeur,
> Faisoyent deja briller leurs flames sans ardeur;
> . . . .
> Le silence paisible et l'horreur solitaire
> Contraignoyent doucement les hommes à se taire.
> Taisons-nous donc, ô Muse! et jurons en ce lieu
> De ne parler jamais qu'à la gloire de Dieu.
> (Douzième Partie)

When all was accomplished, the shadowy hours decorated the firmament with numerous lights; you could see the moon, and the fields and air were already sown with animated fires. These flying miracles, these stars of the earth, who with their beams of gold make war on shadows, these treasures in which the divine splendor gleams, already made their heatless flames shine. The peaceful silence and the solitary dread gently forced men to fall silent. Let us fall silent, o Muse, and swear in this place never to speak but of the glory of God.

The modern reader may be tempted to see in a passage like this one the results of a double esthetic, by which moral and narrative sections of the poem contrast with sensory, lyric ones. Such a reading, however, derives from the modern prejudice in favor of imagery and from the tendency to see the latter as the essence of poetry. But here, on the contrary, we find an excellent illustration of the way morality and *meraviglia* mingle in baroque writing. My earlier examples from Saint-Amant and Tristan demonstrated the way in which the imagery of correspondences proves to be subtly didactic; in these lines, however, the spectacular and the ethical are superimposed in a quite overt fashion, the key to which is the prominently placed word *glory*. *Glory* is an ambiguous term in that it suggests visual splendor, especially radiance, while remaining quite ethical in import: God's glory consists in his praiseworthy and total goodness. The fireflies so beloved of baroque poets embody the moral significance inherent in description according to classical doctrine, where the praise of the beautiful tends to imply laudation of the good. Rhetorical theory seeks not fragmentation but unity in such superficially disparate stylistic phenomena as epic narrative and epic description or simile. Saint-Amant is investing his descriptive passages with the ethical elevation of devotional verse, in keeping with his sacred narrative.

A curious thing about *Moïse sauvé* is that, while one might expect an association between baroque style and religious subjects, the most baroque parts have nothing specifically to do with details of religion; they are part of the idyllic aspect of the work. A clearer generic division between the baroque as a religious style and secular neoclassicism is to be found in a less well known work, Du Bois-Hus' *La Nuict des nuicts et le jour des jours*, which presents, in an implicit comparison, the births of Christ and Louis XIV. The sacred part of the work, the night of nights, inclines toward baroque description:

> Le visage du firmament
> Descendu dans cet element [water]
> Y fait voir sa figure peinte,
> Les feux du Ciel sans peur nagent dedans la mer,
>   Et les poissons sans crainte
> Glissent parmy ces feux qui semblent les aymer.
>
> Dans le fond de ce grand miroir
> La nature se plaist à voir
> L'onde et la flamme si voisines,
> Et les astres tombez en ces païs nouveaux,
>   Salamandres marines,
> Se baignent à plaisir dans le giron des eaux.
>
> L'illustre Deesse des mois
> Quittant son arc et son carquois
> Descend avecque eux dedans l'onde,
> Son croissant est sa barque, où l'hameçon en main
>   Fait de sa tresse blonde,
> Elle pesche à loisir les perles du Jourdain.[18]

18. Gabriel Du Bois-Hus, *La Nuict des nuicts et le jour des jours,* ed. Annarosa Poli (Bologna, 1967), 1828–45.

The face of the firmament, descending into the water, makes her painted features seen in a reflection. The sky's fires fearlessly swim in the sea, and the fearless fish slip among these fires which seem to love them. In the depths of this great mirror, nature likes to see the wave and the flame so close, and the stars fallen into these new countries, like marine salamanders, bathe with delight in the bosom of the waters. The illustrious goddess of months, leaving her bow and quiver, goes down with them into the water; her half moon is her boat, where, hook in hand, made of her blond hair, she fishes at leisure for the Jordan's pearls.

All these baroque devices are felt to be a suitable prelude to Christ's birth, and the reason for it doubtless is that the nativity has a pastoral setting. Du Bois-Hus accordingly follows the seventeenth-century tendency and raises the idyllic and pastoral to an ornate middle style. The birth of Louis XIV, on the other hand, tends to call forth a more abstract, odelike style:

> Le visage de l'horizon
> Durant sa plus belle saison
> N'eut jamais la mine si leste,
> Vous diriez à le voir qu'il se pare à dessein,
> Et la voute celeste
> N'a jamais decouvert un plus aimable sein.   (4755–60)

The face of the horizon in its most beautiful season never had so eager a look; she appears to adorn herself on purpose, and the heavenly vault never showed a more gracious bosom.

Although there is a good deal of description of the day on which Louis was born and of the festivities, the concrete details are constantly ennobled by juxtaposition with rather abstract personifications or metonymies like *voute celeste* and *sein*. There is clearly a devotional-secular opposition of styles in the poet's mind, although just enough parallels occur in the two styles (the use of personification, for example) to avoid an abrupt, inartistic clash between the two parts of the poem.

The principle of double styles—middle-level baroque description and high neoclassical kingly praise—is widely encountered. Saint-Amant's poems connected with his position at the Polish court tend to be neoclassical, for example. Georges de Scudéry's famous baroque sonnets on the fountain of Vaucluse and on the gypsy woman are followed by neoclassical addresses to noble or royal patrons. Tristan L'Hermite, often called a French Marinist, was a great writer of high-style odes, and since he was one of the most gifted poets of the period, his odes show some interesting aspects of neoclassical style. Here the Prince de Bourbon is praised for military valor:

> O que vostre valeur insigne,
> D'un art dont vous seul estes digne,
> Donna de coeur à nos guerriers
> Quand vos bras lancerent la foudre,
> Et parmy le sang et la poudre
> Firent des moissons de lauriers.
>
> ("À Monseigneur le Prince")

Oh how your signal valor, with an art worthy of you alone, gave courage to our warriors, when your arms cast thunderbolts and amidst blood and powder made a harvest of laurels.

Neoclassical style tends to use less metaphor than common metonymies of abstract value. However, the juxtaposition of two such metonymies revives their concrete origins, and we then have a catachresis or peculiar mixed metaphor. This is not a conceit but a bold, high-style, elliptical expression. However, the closeness of neoclassical style at times to baroque metaphorics can be seen in the following lines addressed to Cardinal Mazarin:

> Le Tybre pour l'amour de vous
> A bien sujet d'estre jaloux
> Des felicitez de la Seyne;
> Depuis que vostre esprit gouverne sur ses eaux,
> Elle dérobe un astre à la grandeur romaine,
> Et gagne des lauriers plus qu'il n'a de roseaux.
> Si nos heros victorieux
> Portent la terreur en tous lieux,
> Et font de si hautes merveilles,
> Tant de fameux succès en deux ans arivez
> Ne doivent s'apeler que les fruits de vos veilles,
> Que dans le cabinet vous avez cultivez.
>
> ("À Son Eminence")

The Tiber, for the love of you, has good reason to be jealous of the Seine's happiness; since your mind governs on her waters, she has stolen a star from Roman grandeur and wins more laurels than she has reeds on her banks. If our victorious heroes bear terror everywhere and perform such high marvels, so many successful actions accomplished in two years can only be called the fruit of your vigils, which you cultivated in your study.

Here we have an ambiguous style in some ways. The opening personification belongs to both baroque and neoclassical diction, and the star image, while seeming perhaps more like a metaphor than a metonymic abstraction, is joined to the abstract *grandeur romaine*.

However, a phrase like *dérobe un astre au ciel de Rome* is closer to true metaphor. The spirit presiding over the waters involves a metonymy of *waters* for *region*, which is the opposite of the usual neoclassical practice of going from the concrete to the abstract in metonymy. The juxtaposition of figurative laurels and real reeds could be read as a conceit or as an elliptical high-style expression, devoid of cleverness. In the second stanza, the style is purely abstract until we come to *fruits* and *cabinet*. *Fruit* is one of the commonest abstract metonymies in neoclassical language, and we may or may not feel that *cultiver* brings its literal meaning back; if it does, of course, we have either a conceit or an elevated catachresis in the idea of growing fruit in a study. A later stanza has a similar movement:

> Sous ses auspices bien-heureux,
> Nos conquerans avantureux
> Produisent de si belles choses
> Que les peuples d'Ibere et les peuples Germains
> Sont contraints d'avouer qu'à l'ombre de vos roses
> Les palmes tous les jours croissent entre nos mains.

Under the blessed auspices of your cardinal's purple, our adventurous conquerors produce such fine things that the Iberian and German peoples are obliged to admit that in the shadow of your roses, palms grow daily in our hands.

The *si belles choses*, the ultimate in generality, has no place in real baroque style. The palms growing daily to indicate victories is, joined with *hands*, a solemn catachresis, but the preceding word *roses*, seems to provoke a bizarre feeling of mixed metaphor, especially since these roses are not the common metonymy for a lady's cheeks and lips but rather an unusual designation of the cardinal's purple robe and thus the cardinal himself. However, we might note that all these words are on a figurative level, whereas the characteristic baroque effect is rather to bring out a contrast between a figurative and a concrete word. Ultimately, of course, it is the tone or level which determines the effect of the words, and an address to Cardinal Mazarin should be sufficiently solemn to make us see all these devices as high-style boldness of expression, rather than the sort of clever compliment one would make to a lady. Still, one sees how the line between baroque and neoclassical expression can be ambiguous unless we carefully observe the rhetorical situation.

Although neoclassical diction normally uses a fairly conventional

amount of subordination and sentence linkage, we occasionally find
a descriptive enumeration:

> Plaisant climat, divin sejour
> Eloigné du grand monde et de ses artifices,
> Paisible empire, et bien-heureuse cour
> Où regnent les Vertus au milieux des delices,
> Grands et merveilleux bâtimens,
> Agreables compartimens,
> Bois si doux, si frais, et si sombre,
> Claires eaux, belles fleurs, admirable maison,
> Comme vos apas sont sans nombre,
> Ils sont aussi sans prix et sans comparaison.[19]

Charming climate, divine place, far from the great world and its artifice,
peaceful empire, and blessed court where Virtues reign amid delights,
great and wonderful edifices, charming apartments, a wood so mild, so
cool, and so dark, clear waters, beautiful flowers, admirable house, as your
charms are without number, they are also priceless and incomparable.

This ode to the "Maison d'Astrée," actually the chateau of a real
lady, shows the extension of neoclassical style down into the descriptive middle range. Ultimately, with the generalization of neoclassical style in the later seventeenth century in France, the middle-
style lyric virtually disappeared. There are no generally known
collections of lyric poetry, such as it had existed since Petrarch, in
the high French neoclassical era.

V

We can note some of the same ambiguity of style we found in Tristan's ode to Mazarin at the beginning of the career of one of the great
English neoclassicists, Dryden. In his poem "Upon the Death of
Lord Hastings," where the tone must be serious and high, as befits
the man celebrated, rhetorical ostentation sometimes leads Dryden
into figures which border on the clever tone: "To bring a *winding* for
a *wedding sheet*" is a comment on Hastings' youthful death, and
would be an almost Shakespearean figure, had Dryden not un-
derscored the alliterative expressions, in an unnecessary act of self-
consciousness. Later, the consolation to Hastings' widow has what

19. François Tristan L'Hermite, *Les Vers héoriques*, ed. Catherine M. Grisé (Geneva, 1967).

may seem like a merely ingenious conclusion, but actually belongs
to the high neoclassical decorum by its abstractions and generality:

> O wed
> His soul, tho' not his body to thy bed:
> Let that make thee a mother; bring thou forth
> Th'Ideas of his virtue, knowledge, worth;
> Transcribe th'original in new copies: give
> Hastings o' th' better part: so shall he live
> In 's nobler half; and the great grandsire be
> Of an heroic divine progeny.[20]

As happens at times in neoclassical elevated language, we cannot be
too sure what this posthumous progeny of ideas consists of, but as
for the mothering image, it seems nicely to fall into the category of
the bold, high-style figurative expression. Nonetheless, *body* and *bed*
in their concreteness seem to make a baroque contrast between the
literal and the figurative. This is a borderline style and remote from
the much simpler-seeming high diction Dryden ultimately devised.

Dryden has the distinction of having written in 1694 one of the
rare fine lyrical poems of the late seventeenth century in a neoclassical style. It is a death elegy in which the pastoral convention is replaced by reference to the *Aeneid*, thus heightening the style above
the traditional lower category of the genre:

> Farewell, too little, and too lately known,
> Whom I began to think and call my own:
> For sure our souls were near allied, and thine
> Cast in the same poetic mold with mine.
> . . . .
> The last set out the soonest did arrive.
> Thus Nisus fell upon the slippery place,
> While his young friend perform'd and won the race.
> ("To the Memory of Mr. Oldham")

The allusion is to the footrace during the funeral games in *Aeneid*, V.
A phrase from Catullus' poem on the death of his brother introduces
a reminiscence of the famous passage on Marcellus near the end of
Aeneid, VI:

> Once more, hail and farewell; farewell, thou young,
> But ah too short, Marcellus of our tongue;

---

20. Louis I. Bredvold (ed.), *The Best of Dryden* (New York, 1933), hereinafter cited
in the text.

> Thy brows with ivy, and with laurels bound;
> But fate and gloomy night encompass thee around.

Dryden avoids metaphor by using literary allusion, which is another form of comparison. The diction has a few mild metonymies but the principle attraction of it is its great concision. There is nothing in French neoclassicism in any way like it, for the lyric had dwindled into triviality by then in France, and French neoclassicism had by and large cut itself off from the classical sources of diction, so that discreet evocations of stately, sententious Latin were no longer possible.

VI

We can observe a large area of coincidence between baroque and neoclassical styles when it comes to figures: hyperbole, catachresis, metonymy, personification, periphrasis, and the conversion of adjectives into nouns as in "suffer the rigors of torments" for "rigorous torments." With most of these, however, it is possible to employ a more rather than less abstract vocabulary or to avoid making a startling juxtaposition of the abstract and the concrete. Such is the neoclassical tendency, especially as we see it in the ode. We must be careful, however, not to make baroque poetry the antithesis of neoclassical elevation, abstraction, and generality; there is a plurality of styles in rhetorical theory, each with some relation to others, and certainly the elaborate baroque middle style is not simply the contrary of Malherbe's manner. It is true that some poems may appear such. One could easily make an antithetical system contrasting Saint-Amant's "La Solitude" with a royal ode. But Saint-Amant and "La Solitude" are not all of European baroque poetry or even all of French, for that matter. It is important above all to remember that much of baroque poetry is not sheer fantasy but has behind it a great deal of complex culture—religious, ethical, and even scientific. Paradox, merely to take an obvious example, has a long history as a philosophical problem and exercise in analysis. Even the omnipresent firefly is as much a scientific problem and demonstration of the significance of nature as it is a delight to the eye. Vistas of forgotten learning are liable to open up when one tries to determine the motivation for baroque imagery. Nor can the conceitful character of baroque figures be simply contrasted with the high seriousness of neo-classicism, although for purposes of analysis, I have perhaps made them appear quite antithetical. The conceit is the more decorative, self-consciously ostentatious form of the bold thought or compressed expression of high style, Dominique Bouhours' *pensée neuve* being a neutral term covering both.

Finally, it would be ill-advised to make baroque and neoclassical styles the absolute expression of successive historical periods. There is a temporal development of the neoclassical ode from Malherbe through Théophile de Viau, Tristan L'Hermite, and others, parallel with the baroque movement in style. The two genres constitute two separate layers of literature for a long time. And even during what we think of as the high neoclassical period in France, while lyric poetry may have dwindled, the reading public continued to look into the books of earlier generations, and there was an abundance of ballet and spectacular theater, which had little to do with the culture represented by Boileau and Racine. After 1670 the opera surpassed tragedy in popularity, and in general, the broad characteristic tendency of art in Louis XIV's time was toward *meraviglia* in the theatre and the novel, so that strict neoclassical or neo-Aristotelian art was a comparatively small area of esthetic expression. We remember it because of its greatness, but again must not be misled into any false concept of periodization.

CHAPTER 8

Racine and French Neoclassicism

I

Examples of skillfully written French neoclassical odes and related poems could be endlessly multiplied, but their art is rather schematized, and we would not advance much further in the study of high neoclassical style. It is in the theater that we find greater diversity of stylistic conceptions, and Racine's work, most of all, readily illustrates how, within what appears to be a relatively narrow range of diction, various distinctive styles are possible.

From the standpoint of style, French drama observes a fairly steady evolution from the renaissance tragedies of Garnier through Racine. One attempt to sample key rhetorical figures throughout this period reveals a decrease in the length of anaphoric passages and in the length and frequency of enumerations, a tendency to reduce metaphoric developments of Petrarchist love-fire and love-war images to simple one-word metonymies, the virtual disappearance of similes of any length, greater precision in the use of interrogation, and the gradual abandonment of stichomythia and abundant sententiae.[1] This general picture is clear and is notable for not showing any distinctive baroque variation in the early seventeenth century. It is difficult, actually, to isolate a significant baroque phase of French tragedy with well-defined rhetorical characteristics, although Corneille's sententiae and stichomythia do seem to work with the thematics of his plays to suggest to some degree such a phase.

The stylistic aspect of the so-called *querelle du Cid*, however, is important in the criticism made of Corneille's bold metaphors, such as

---

1. See Kay Ellen Cushman, "The Evolution of Dramatic Rhetoric in France: The Phaedra Plays, 1573–1677" (Ph.D. dissertation, Indiana University, 1968).

the one in which the count's wounds become mouths crying out for vengeance (II, viii, 679–80). This was not a new metaphor—it was in Corneille's Spanish source and can be found in Shakespeare—but it offended literary sensibilities for whom the *audacior ornatus* of the Greeks and the renaissance seemed not to belong to dramatic decorum. The metaphor in question is one of a very few elaborate ones in *Le Cid* and is interesting for us in that it demonstrates the ambiguity of stylistic conceptions that prevailed during the first half of the seventeenth century in France. We risk thinking of *Le Cid* as a neoclassical play with baroque patches, although Corneille could hardly have thought of it in those terms. The notion of a baroque-neoclassical antithesis was not completely formed for many readers and perhaps was never conceived of with the rigor later centuries could distinguish in it. The key role of the theater for the literary public is also made apparent in the *querelle du Cid*, in any case. Baroque lyrics or long poems were less exposed to intense discussion and did not bring to light major directions in taste in the same way as did the discriminating spectators' reactions to plays.

All attempts to distinguish a baroque phase in French tragedy must ultimately rely more on thematic than on stylistic notions of the baroque. To emphasize this, I should like to turn briefly to a totally unambiguous example of baroque drama, Calderón's *La Vida es sueño* (1636), which is more or less contemporaneous with *Le Cid* and which must stand as a major point of reference in any argument over the baroque character of this or that French or English drama. The first speech in Calderon's play is delivered by a disguised character who has been thrown from her horse:

> Hipogrifo violento
> que corriste parejas con el viento,
> ¿dónde rayo sin llama,
> pájaro sin matiz, pez sin escama,
> y bruto sin instinto
> natural, al confuso laberinto
> de esas desnudas peñas
> te desbocas, te arrastras y despeñas?
> Quédate en este monte,
> donde tengan los brutos su Faetonte;
> que yo, sin más camino
> que el que me dan las leyes del destino,
> ciega y desesperada,

> bajaré la cabeza enmarañada
> deste monte eminente
> que abrasa al sol el ceño de la frente.
> Mal, Polonia, recibes
> a un extranjero, pues con sangre escribes
> su entrada en tus arenas;
> y a penas llega, cuando llega apenas.
> Bien mi suerte lo dice;
> mas ¿dónde halló piedad un infelice?[2]

Violent hippogriff, who ran like the wind, where, like a beam without flame, a bird without color, a fish without scales, and a beast without instinctive love of your natural matter, the earth, are you running away, creeping off, throwing yourself headlong, in the mazy labyrinth of these bare rocks? Remain on this mountain, like Phaeton thunderstruck by Zeus, while I, with only the path granted to me by the laws of destiny, climb down, blind and desperate, the tangled head of this high mountain whose supercilious brow kisses the sun. Poland, you receive a stranger badly, since you inscribe in blood his entrance into your sands; and hardly has he arrived, when he receives hard pains. My luck assured me of it, but where can an unhappy man find pity?

The series of four negatives, referring to fire, air, water, and earth, suggest that the horse was going so fast as to be dematerialized; the fourth element in the hyperbole has to be guessed at from the others. The bleeding stranger, injured on the rocks as she fell, climbs down the long locks of the mountain's head. The apostrophe to Poland, on whose borders Rosaura has arrived, is accompanied by a play on words (*a penas, apenas*) and sententious reflections; the intricate rhetoric is wedded to philosophical generality. Rosaura then finds the imprisoned heir to the Polish throne singing a long, enumeratory lyric about free will:

> Nace el pez, que no respira,
> aborto de ovas y lamas,
> y apenas bajel de escamas
> sobre las ondas se mira,
> cuando a todas partes gira,
> midiendo la inmensidad
> de tanta capacidad
> como le da el centro frío:
> ¿y yo con más albedrío
> tengo menos libertad?
>
> Nace el arroyo, culebra

2. Pedro Calderón de la Barca, *La Vida es sueño*, ed. Ciriaco Morón (Madrid, 1977).

> que entre flores se desata,
> y apenas, sierpe de plata,
> entre las flores se quiebra,
> cuando músico celebra
> de las flores la piedad
> que le dan la majestad,
> el campo abierto a su ida:
> ¿y teniendo yo más vida
> tengo menos libertad?

The unbreathing fish is born of waterweeds and mud and, scarcely a shiplet of scales, is reflected on the waters when it turns about, measuring the immensity of such capacity as the ocean gives it, and I, with more free will, have less freedom? The stream is born, a viper breaking away amid flowers, and hardly, like a silver serpent, is it broken among the flowers than it celebrates in music the piety of the flowers who gave it majesty, as it flows in the open field, and having more life, do I have less freedom?

It is not uncharacteristic of baroque metaphorics that, in a comparison between the speaking *I* and a fish or stream, a further parallel is introduced between the fish or stream and a boat or snake. The exploratory secondary similes emphasize more than one point of comparison. In the second stanza above, the viper-stream rises, curves sinuously among flowers, sings of the latter, and is treated reverently by them in turn. It is quite clear from the style that *La Vida es sueño* belongs to an entirely different conception of the theater from the English and French tragedy. The prosody is lyrical; the thematics, overtly theological; and the mode of the play, purely symbolic.

Segismundo has been imprisoned because his horoscope had forecast a violent, tyrannical future for him as king. He is finally given a chance to reign and, after brutal behavior, is put back in confinement, where he reflects in the play's most famous passage about the unreal quality of his experience:

> Yo sueño que estoy aquí
> destas prisiones cargado,
> y soñé que en otro estado
> más lisonjero me vi.
> ¿Qué es la vida? Un frenesí.
> ¿Qué es la vida? Una ilusión,
> una sombra, una ficción,
> y el mayor bien es pequeño;
> que toda la vida es sueño,
> y los sueños sueños son.

> I am dreaming I am here, laden with chains, and I dreamed that I was in another, more agreeable state. What is life? A frenzy. What is life? An illusion, a shadow, a fiction, and the greatest good is slight, for all life is a dream, and dreams are only dreams.

The rhetoric is enumeratory again and employs the characteristic baroque metaphor formed by the verb *to be* joined to a noun with no connective. The parable of the play continues as Segismundo's free will is again tested by a new release.

La Vida es sueño is purely baroque in both style and theme, and with it in mind, we see that the baroqueness of Shakespeare, Corneille, or other English and French tragic poets is a distinctly relative matter if style is any consideration. Once we dispose of the notion that one or two unusual metaphors make a whole play baroque, we can more securely examine Racine's distinctive styles, which, representing the highest achievement of French neoclassical verse, are sufficiently complex and varied as to have attracted numerous favorable and unfavorable judgments and characterizations.

II

In *Andromaque*, after two less-distinguished earlier plays, we see for the first time a style which is quite peculiar to Racine, even though its elements have been drawn together from various devices and tendencies to be found in earlier seventeenth-century playwrights. The grammar of the first speech indicates a good deal about what will follow; Orestes, meeting Pylades unexpectedly in Epirus, says:

> Oui, puisque je retrouve un ami si fidèle,
> Ma fortune va prendre une face nouvelle;
> Et déjà son courroux semble s'être adouci,
> Depuis qu'elle a pris soin de nous rejoindre ici.
> Qui l'eût dit, qu'un rivage à mes voeux si funeste
> Présenterait d'abord Pylade aux yeux d'Oreste?
> Qu'après plus de six mois que je t'avais perdu,
> A la cour de Pyrrhus tu me serais rendu?[3]

Yes, since I find again so faithful a friend, my fortune is going to take a new turn, and already its anger seems to have lessened, since it found a

---

3. Jean Racine, *Oeuvres complètes*, ed. Raymond Picard, Bibliotheque de la Pléiade (2 vols.; Paris, 1950), I, i, 1–8, hereinafter cited in the text.

way to join us here. Who would have thought that a shore so fatal to my wishes would first of all present Pylades to Orestes' eyes? That after I had lost sight of you for six months, you would be given back to me at Pyrrhus' court?

Un ami si fidèle is an understatement for the friend whom Orestes obviously prizes most. The use of the indefinite article (*cf.* "Je ne condamne pas un courroux légitime" [II, iv, 613]) is in this case a form of poetic grammar which objectivizes, exteriorizes, and has less emotive tension than *mon meilleur ami*. Furthermore, Orestes goes on to mix *je* and *vous* with the third-person substitutes, their proper names, for the more immediate pronouns. This is an important method of varying diction in a play where characters are constantly faced with discussions of the relations of *je* and *vous*, but it also slightly exteriorizes and dramatizes the style. This curious way of mingling the understated *un ami fidèle* with the more emphatic *Pylade* is typical of the microvariations of tone in Racine's style.

Orestes speaks of *ma fortune*, and this ordinary personification (made sharper by being the subject of the verb, as is often the case with personification) serves as a point of departure for a more surprising one: *Son courroux*. *Ma fortune* has become so exterior and objective as to have its own emotions (*le courroux de ma fortune*) talked of in the third person. The *elle a pris soin* further intensifies the personification; when a pronoun can be substituted for a personification we have more than a mere passing expression like "my bad luck." *Un rivage*, which in less poetic grammar would be at least *ce rivage*, has the degree of vagueness which is part of understatement, but this vague place is the active subject of a verb, whereas the two men are merely passive objects; the passive voice in *tu me serais rendu* continues the same mode of expression. In the preceding sentence, it is, furthermore, not Orestes to whom this foreign shore is fatal, but his wishes; this is less strong than "fatal to me" and, along with the understatement, separates Orestes from his emotions, as he had been separated from the forces at work in his life in the first four lines.

Obviously the grammar of this speech is designed to suggest the idea that fate controls the characters of the play, and Orestes' use of the indefinite article with *ami* and *rivage* conveys a certain detachment, an inability to dominate, specify, and point out (by the deictic *ce*) which will mark much of his behavior. However, we must not overinterpret the grammar so that it reflects solely the character of Orestes. These devices form a part of a whole rhetoric in the play which represents the varying tones as the four main characters, Orestes, Hermione, Andromache, and Pyrrhus, confront one another with their changing indifference, their intermittent will to impose themselves on the other characters, their withdrawal from a situation and their anger at their inability to force another character to act. *Andromaque* is a very curious play in that its general idea, that of fate, is not the object of the characters' discussion, by and large. They have no ideas, only rhetorical stratagems to represent themselves in such a way as to try to obtain from one another what they most wish.

It is common idiom to say, as one character does of Andromache, "Sa beauté la rassure." There are certain abstract words which we use freely as subjects of verbs, without feeling any strong sense of personification. Likewise we can say in ordinary speech that the presence of the Greeks would enhance the splendor of Pyrrhus' wedding ("dussent de son hymen relever la splendeur" [V, iii, 1504]). But if we refer, as Pylades does (I, i, 11) to *la fureur des eaux* separating two ships, we are using the abstract noun in an ambiguous way, suggesting either strong personification or a periphrastic emphatic replacement for *les eaux furieuses*, which is a milder personification. We find in *Andromaque* a tremendous range of constructions involving abstractions, abstract words designating emotions, half-abstract metonymies (*ma flamme*, "my love"), words of abstract form designating actions (*ma vengeance*), and psychological abstractions (*mon âme*). Here are some characteristic phrases:

> Votre âme à l'amour en esclave asservie
> Se repose sur lui du soin de votre vie.   (I, i, 29–30)

Your soul enslaved to love, relies on it to take care of your life.

> Comment lui rendre un coeur que vous me retenez?
>   (I, iv, 344)

How can I give back to her a heart which you are keeping from me?

> Votre amour plus timide
> Ne prendra pas toujours sa colère pour guide.   (I, iv, 381–82)

Your love grown more timid will not always take its anger as its guide.

J'ai donné des larmes à vos malheurs.   (I, i, 14)

I have given tears to your sorrows.

Mais que ma cruauté survive à ma colère?   (I, ii, 214)

But should my cruelty outlive my anger?

Je n'ai trouvé que pleurs mêlés d'emportements.   (II, v, 648)

I found only tears mingled with bursts of anger.

Par quelle erreur veux-tu toujours sur toi
Détourner un courroux qui ne cherche que moi?
(III, i, 779–80)

By what false notion do you always try to turn aside onto yourself an anger which aims only at me?

Pardonnez à l'éclat d'une illustre fortune
Ce reste de fierté qui craint d'être importune.   (III, vi, 913–14)

Pardon the brilliance of an illustrious station for this remnant of pride which fears to make itself importunate.

Vos bontés, Madame,
Ont gravé trop avant ses crimes dans mon âme.
(IV, iii, 1177–78)

Your kindnesses, Madame, have too deeply imprinted his crimes in my soul.

Le coeur est pour Pyrrhus et les voeux pour Oreste.
(II, ii, 538)

The heart is for Pyrrhus, the good wishes for Orestes.

Doutez, jusqu' à sa mort, d'un courroux incertain.
(IV, iii, 1999)

Be uncertain, until he is dead, of a doubtful anger.

The variables in these expressions are, first, the category of noun involved, ranging as we remarked before from the concrete (*coeur*) used as a semiabstract word to the pure abstract word; next, the use of the noun as subject or object is a further consideration; poetic plurals occur with a sense of profusion, frequency, or vagueness to complicate some expressions; the degree to which the verb lends itself to personification is yet another element; and finally, the variations between indefinite article, partitive article, definite article, possessive adjective, and demonstrative adjective provide an extraordinary array of effects.

The general value of this rhetoric lies in the way the character, concerned primarily with his own emotions and situations, dramatizes them for his sake or for his interlocutor's. Sometimes the character presents his feelings with pseudoobjectivity in an attempt to persuade; sometimes he behaves as if he had no responsibility for them; on other occasions he is deeply involved with uncontrollable parts of himself ("Mon coeur, mon lâche coeur, s'intéresse pour lui" [V, i, 1404]). There are both understatement and overstatement in these various constructions, providing that constant sense of studied, varying rhetorical effect we encounter in Racine. The greatest grammatical inventiveness is present; much of the peculiar literary syntax of noun determinatives in French can be better illustrated in *Andromaque* than almost anywhere else.

One key word related to the expression we have just examined is *eyes*. Among the metonymic uses of parts of the body (*bras* means help, *tête* means the whole person), eyes have the preponderant role for several reasons. The emphasis on eyes in Latin poetry and poetry since Petrarch is not arbitrary. The eyes in classical esthetics are felt to be not only the most beautiful but also the most expressive part of the body, and further, they are identified with life itself. (In ancient and still in seventeenth-century optics, the eyes were thought to emit light, the sign of life, and the gods were recognized by their eyes.) The word *yeux* and related words lend themselves to the most varied semantic and grammatic treatment:

> Ses yeux s'opposeront entre son père et vous.   (I, ii, 240)

Her eyes will interpose themselves between you and her father.

> Vous pensez que des yeux toujours ouverts aux larmes
> Se plaisent à troubler le pouvoir de vos charmes?
> (II, i, 449–50)

Do you think that eyes ever open to tears enjoy disturbing the power of your charms?

> Venez dans tous les coeurs faire parler vos yeux.   (II, ii, 568)

Come make your eyes speak in all hearts.

> Je sais que vos regards vont rouvrir mes blessures.   (II, ii, 445)

I know your glances will reopen my wounds.

> Commandez à vos yeux de garder le secret.   (III, i, 720)

Order your eyes to keep the secret.

>   Vox yeux, à la fin désarmés.   (IV, iii, 1151)

Your eyes, finally disarmed.

>   À chercher dans vos yeux une mort qui me fuit.   (II, ii, 496)

To look in your eyes for a death that flees me.

Expressions like *à sa vue, à ma vue,* are also frequent, for the characters observe one another closely for signs of resistance or submission. The eyes are always quite literally a part of the body, unlike the heart, but they are given the attributes of the whole person and so form part of figurative expressions. Of all the words pertaining to psychology in *Andromaque,* the eyes constitute the strongest link to the physical world, but by processes of personification and metaphor, they initiate the chain of terms rising through heart and *flamme,* to abstract terms of emotion and complete abstractions like fortune or destiny. The elements of metaphor, metonymy, concreteness, figurativeness, and abstraction are much more elaborately combined in *Andromaque* than in the language of the neoclassical ode. Whereas with the ode, we tend to encounter again and again the same use of figures, Racine's lines are full of odd surprises and offer a worthy subject to fairly detailed explication.

It is this complex vocabulary, with its continuum between the tangible and the conceptual, that gives *Andromaque* its peculiar stylistic color. The characters acquire greater stature, the grandeur befitting their worldly positions, through the diction Racine devises for them. We may find *son coeur* personified to some extent in earlier neoclassical plays, but it is with Racine that this and analogous expressions reach their full development. And this development is a peculiarly French one; Italian, as we have seen, is more sparing in abstracts, and in classical Latin poetry there are only occasional, vaguely comparable expressions like "Sic animis iuvenum furor additus" (*Aeneid,* II, 355). The lack of articles in Latin makes many of the nuances of Racine's usage impossible, and there is a tendency toward the concrete *me miserum* where French would say *ma misère.* However, one classical rhetorical device does complement the objectifying of emotion in Racine: the periphrastic denomination of characters (*l'époux d'une Troyenne, la veuve d'Hector, cet amant irrité*) tends toward the same effect, at once distancing and emphatic in its frequent irony or distaste.

It has been said that there are more verb metaphors in Racine than noun ones, but these are most often merely colorless metonymies like the frequent use of *payer, prix, salaire, acheter,* and so forth in *Andromaque,* which are isolated in context and add little semantic richness to the style. Perhaps only the verb *arracher,* a favorite of Racine's, conserves its natural connotations of violence. It is clear from my discussion of nouns, on the other hand, how prominent they are in their curious usages. Two famous passages will indicate more exactly how parts of speech are related in *Andromaque.* Pyrrhus speaks:

> J'ai fait des malheureux, sans doute; et la Phrygie
> Cent fois de votre sang a vu ma main rougie.
> Mais que vos yeux sur moi se sont bien exercés!
> Qu'ils m'ont vendu bien cher les pleurs qu'ils ont versés!
> De combien de remords m'ont-ils rendu la proie!
> Je souffre tous les maux que j'ai faits devant Troie.
> Vaincu, chargé de fers, de regrets consumé,
> Brûlé de plus de feux que je n'en allumai,
> Tant de soins, tant de pleurs, tant d'ardeurs inquiètes.
>
> (I, iv, 313–21)

I doubtless made wretches of men, and Phrygia saw a hundred times my hand reddened with your blood. But how your eyes have worked on me! How dearly they have sold me the tears they have wept! Of what great remorse I am the prey! I suffer all the evils I committed in Troy. Conquered, laden with chains, consumed with regrets, burned by more fires than I lit in Troy, so many cares, so many tears, such uneasy burning.

A vu acquires vividness from the personification, which, moreover, is a proper noun, but the dominant words are the half-metonymic *sang* ("your blood" for "your people's blood") and the infrequent color term. *Exercés* is an all-purpose verb to which *vos yeux* gives meaning, whereas *vendu* acquires some intensity from the increasingly forceful, violent character of the nouns, like *proie,* one of Racine's favorites and always powerful. *Brûlé* and *allumai* are dependent on the two senses of *feux* for their effect, and the passage concludes with modifiers to *feux.* The richness of the verbs here cannot be isolated from the nouns they are joined to. This impossibility of taking the word in isolation is true, in quite another sense, of the nouns and adjectives, for we have here one of the finest examples of

Racine's use of allusion in *Andromaque*, by which a vast amount of emotive content is succinctly summoned up. The love-war-fire imagery sheds much of its Petrarchist effect in key passages, where it brings to mind the destruction of Troy, as seen in the *Aeneid*. The famous *brûlé de plus de feux* is not précieux, as those with little sense of rhetorical distinctions are wont to say, but an *audacior ornatus* of the most high-style effect; it has nothing to do with middle-style baroque compliments. The whole passage, with its proper nouns, unusually frequent in *Andromaque*, and its references to real as well as figurative slavery and to the tears of the vanquished magnificently transforms Petrarchist imagery by allusion to something concrete and prepares us for the final ironic allusion of the play, where Pyrrhus is killed at an altar, the same kind of place as the one in which he had killed Priam. It is very typical of Racine's rhetorical subtlety to reconvert the metonymies of fire and chains into concrete terms, countering the neoclassical tendency—his own usual tendency—to metonymize concrete words into abstracts. This double movement, like the one by which distancing and understatement often create emphasis, is a phenomenon we shall see more of in Racine's style. It is a way of exploiting neoclassical rhetoric that we do not find in the ode, or if we find in it some analogous handling of figures, the monotony of tone fails to give the figures any salience.

The second passage in which I wish to point out the dominance of nouns is related to the one we have just considered. It is Andromache's lament over Troy:

> Dois-je les oublier, s'il ne s'en souvient plus?
> Dois-je oublier Hector privé de funérailles,
> Et traîné sans honneur autour de nos murailles?
> Dois-je oublier son père à mes pieds renversé,
> Ensanglantant l'autel qu'il tenait embrassé?
> Songe, songe, Céphise, à cette nuit cruelle
> Qui fut pour tout un peuple une nuit éternelle.
> Figure-toi Pyrrhus, les yeux étincelants,
> Entrant à la lueur de nos palais brûlants
> Sur tous mes frères morts se faisant un passage,
> Et de sang tout couvert échauffant le carnage.
>   (III, viii, 992–1002)

Must I forget them, if Pyrrhus no longer remembers them? Must I forget Hector deprived of funeral rites and dragged, dishonored, around the city walls? Must I forget his father lying at my feet, bleeding on the altar he embraced? Think, think, Cephisa, of that cruel night that was an eternal night for a whole people. Imagine Pyrrhus, with his eyes sparkling, entering the glow of our burning palaces, pushing through the heap of all my dead brothers and covered with blood, encouraging the slaughter.

Here Racine uses the Latin device which commonly replaces clausal narrative; a noun with participle is concisely substituted for a finite clause: "forget that Hector was deprived of funeral rites." This small grammatical adjustment over Racine's customary clausal syntax has great density and a kind of syntactic solemnity. The general rhetorical feature of the description is that it is classicizing in choice of significant detail. It is often fancifully said that *Andromaque* is a Virgilian play, a statement which is stylistically absurd in any exact sense, but the art of description in Racine comes closer to that of classical high style than anything we have seen in French. The general classical principle governing descriptions occurring in the midst of works is the πρέπον or *aptum*, which refers to the proper structure and proportion of parts, so as to make a harmonious whole. The Latin and Greek words are usually translated as decorum or *convenance*, which suggest to us more an ethical than an esthetic sense, but the classical terms have no such necessary connotations. The specific function of a description like this one of the fall of Troy is to give evidence supporting an argument. It is therefore part of a whole, like evidence in a judicial oration. The baroque idea of description corresponds to a completely different rhetorical concept, that of ecphrasis—laudatory or epideictic detailing of the qualities of a person, place, or thing which is an end in itself.

The question of description as evidence brings us to one of the most significant aspects of the rhetoric of *Andromaque* and of neoclassical tragedies in general. While there is a great deal of effective use in the play of figures like zeugma, oxymoron, *correctio*, or imaginative hyperbaton, these are incidental details of Racine's art which, excellent as they are, cannot provide a total rhetorical account of the work.[4] For that we must examine, in at least part of the play, Racine's use of the topics of invention. Therein lies the great difference be-

---

4. For figures in general in Racine, see Peter France, *Racine's Rhetoric* (Oxford, 1965).

tween the static French renaissance tragedy and the plays of Corneille and Racine. The topics of invention belong more to judicial
rhetoric than to the epideictic variety, and while they play some role
in lyric poetry, it is in the theater that the development of the verse
most relies on them. They are as present in Shakespeare as in the
French tragic poets, but the density of Shakespeare's stylistic texture
tends to conceal them somewhat from modern readers unskilled in
the analysis of ancient oratory.[5] In *Andromaque* they stand out with
special clarity in that most of the action of the play consists in attempts to persuade through argument. Not all of these devices are
logical, moreover, it being part of ancient tradition to resort to all
forms of scorn, concealment, false praise, ironic declarations, sup-
pression of the truth, and so forth. The terms for the various topics
of invention are much less familiar than the Greek and Latin words
for verbal ornaments, and I shall use certain ones, with explana-
tions, to demonstrate an area of rhetorical learning and practice
which, we have largely forgotten, constituted an important disci-
pline for the playwright as well as the lawyer.

IV

There is a large body of doctrine, ancient and renaissance, on judicial rhetoric, with various authors adducing somewhat different systems of tactics and proofs; basically, since the situations described by
these systems are the same, one can proceed a bit eclectically in the
analysis of texts. One word in particular should be said about the
flexibility of the syllogism or, in its more reduced form, the enthymeme. Much argument in plays has behind it more or less explicit syllogisms, which amplification and ornament conceal to the
casual reader but whose structural value the playwright was most
assuredly aware of and which his education fitted him to classify
and analyse with great accuracy.

   The first confrontation occurs at the beginning of *Andromaque* after
the expository narrative when Orestes presents himself to Pyrrhus
as ambassador of the Greeks, asking for the life of Astyanax (I, ii).

---

   5. See Sister Miriam Joseph, *Shakespeare's Use of the Arts of Language* (New York,
1966), 18, 22–31, 338.

He begins by a flattering compliment to Pyrrhus (*captatio benevolentiae*), which is a form of exordium (143–46). The customary brief narrative and main point follow, but he also adds a prediction (*diabole*) about Astyanax as a future danger, which is a threat to Pyrrhus. Essentially, these lines (161–68) are an anticipation of objections (*procatalepsis*). An exhortation in the form of an imperative constitutes the peroration of this miniature classical oration. Pyrrhus' whole reply is a rejection of the argument as absurd (*apodioxis*). First he is scornful about the Greeks' excessive concern (*mycterismus*, 173–80). Arguing from equality, a technical distinction, he says he need not give up his captive any more than the other Greeks theirs' (181–91). He concludes with an elliptic hypothetical syllogism: at the fall of Troy it would have been just to kill Astyanax, but it is no longer so (205–10). After this *argumentum a tempore*, he dismisses the Greek claims. Orestes uses *definitio* to press the Greek cause: they wish to punish Hector, and Hector's son represents Hector (224–27). The Greeks might even invade Epirus (*cataplexis*, a threat). Let them invade, says Pyrrhus, turning Orestes' argument against him (*metastasis*, 229–30). Orestes argues from general experience (*apodixis*, 239–40) that Hermione will prevail over Pyrrhus. "Hermione, seigneur, peut m'être toujours chère," Pyrrhus declares in a *concessio* (241), which, seeming to grant a point, actually, as he develops the theme of his independence from Hermione, injures Orestes' argument. The next confrontation is between Pyrrhus and Andromache (I, 4). He swears an oath (*orcos*, 283–92) to defend Astyanax, but in a hypothetical, fragmentary syllogism or enthymeme, wishes to conclude that in return Andromache should be grateful. The statement is made with litotes and antithesis: "En combattant pour vous, me sera-t-il permis / De ne vous point compter parmi mes ennemis?" (295–96). Rhetorical questions (*erotesis*) with a strong negative implication reject this argument, and Andromache concludes with a sententia about Pyrrhus' proper duty toward her son. (310). Pyrrhus reproaches her with ingratitude (*onedismus*, 311–12), admits his wrongs in the war (*paromologia*, 313–14), but recites his woes at the hands of Andromache (*brûlé de plus de feux*, 315–22), which need redress (*mempsis*). Andromache rejects his false arguments (*antirrhesis*, 333–41). Pyrrhus concedes that he should marry Hermione, which only strengthens his emotional argument (*concessio*, 343–54). Again, Andromache rejects his foolish argument (*antirrhesis*, 355–56), comparing herself with Helen (a comparison of inequality). Pyrrhus, exasperated, says Astyanax must die, pretexting absolute necessity (*dicaeologia*); there is an argument with excluded middle here: Andromache marries Pyrrhus or Astyanax dies.

Act II begins with Hermione and her *confidente* exploring a dilemma, a situation in which all solutions are unacceptable. The *confident*'s role in *Andromaque* is often to supply evidence or make counterarguments. Hermione recites her past woes (*mempsis*) and justifies her speech and actions (*proecthesis*, 456–70). She indulges, as well, in a certain amount of feigning, known as *dissimulatio*. Orestes arrives with the tale of his misfortunes (*mempsis*, 481–504) brought about by Hermione, but she digresses to evade the question (*apoplanesis*, 505–511). Her urging Orestes to occupy himself with his embassy is turned against her (*metastasis*) since Pyrrhus has dismissed him, and Orestes returns to his complaints against Hermione (*reditus ad propositum*, 512–18). She justifies her past actions (*proecthesis*) with rhetorical questions (*erotesis*, 519–28) and confesses frankly (*parrhesia*, 532–36) that she really would like to love Orestes, whom she has longed to see. Orestes examines the paradox of her both loving and hating Pyrrhus, who scorns her. "Qui vous l'a dit, seigneur, qu'il me méprise?" she replies with a reproachful question (*epiplexis*, 551), the figure especially associated with Hermione. Orestes answers with *sarcasmus* (555–60); Hermione digresses to evade the subject (*apoplanesis*) and suggests Orestes should lead the Greeks against Pyrrhus (561–65). With *peristrophe*, that is, converting an opponent's argument to one's own use, Orestes urges Hermione to leave Epirus and join him in rousing the Greeks to wage war on Pyrrhus (566–69). The scene concludes with Hermione's objection, with Orestes' turning Hermione's words against her and accusing her (*metastasis*), and with her self-justification (*proecthesis*, 570–90). When Pyrrhus sees Orestes again (II, 4) he retracts his earlier argument, but Orestes, taking exactly the opposite of his previous position, rejects the retraction on moral grounds (*antirrhesis*, 605–16). When Pyrrhus is alone with his *confident*, he affirms his intention to marry Hermione, but constantly returns to the thought of

Andromache and how she will react (*commoratio*, harping on a point, 633–704).

This protracted analysis of argumentation in the first two acts of *Andromaque* is perhaps tedious in its detail, but I wish to demonstrate the manner in which Racine composes by rhetorical units. The topics of invention (of which he uses only a small number, others being suited primarily to the courtroom) stand ready to be combined in such a way as to make a continuous dialectical movement. It is interesting to note that Hermione's famous lines mostly represent epiplexis: "Ne vous suffit-il pas que je l'aie condamné?" (IV, iii, 1188); "Je ne t'ai point aimé, cruel, qu'ai-je donc fait?" (IV, v, 1356); "Je t'aimais inconstant, qu'aurais-je fait fidèle" (IV, v, 1365); "Qu'a-t-il fait? A quel titre? / Qui te l'a dit?" (V, iii, 542–43). There are, therefore, possibilities of characterization in the use of the topics of invention. The particular choice of topics will, of course, color the play as a whole. Antithetical movements of emotion are stronger in *Andromaque* perhaps than in most of Racine's plays. On the other hand, there are no courtroom scenes in his tragedies where the king metes out justice to plaintiff and defendant, as are found in Corneille's plays. The latter is famous for his legalistic development of scenes, but actually his rhetoric comes from the same general sources as Racine's, despite the very different effects in the two dramatists. The topics of invention as laid down by Aristotle and Cicero, with embellishments added by others, are the units out of which a play like *Andromaque* or *Le Cid* is built.

V

The study of Racine's work, more than any other, brings up basic questions about the theory and practice of French neoclassical styles. We have already observed, in the last chapter, certain ambiguous-seeming relations of neoclassical with baroque style and shall not reconsider those at this point; rather, we must refer more specifically to certain points of classical theory and of seventeenth-century stylistic reformers. There are four general rules of style to be found in ancient rhetoric which precede remarks on specific levels or forms of style. They are purity (*latinitas*), clarity (*perspicuitas*), ornament, and decorum. Naturally, these very general ideas are much modified by the needs of writers working in this or that genre, but they are not to be idly transgressed. French neoclassicism took the ideas of purity, clarity, and decorum and exploited them more tenaciously than had been usual, but the results are not so simple as the abstract statement of these principles would seem to imply. In Malherbe, whose oral teachings (recorded by a younger poet, Racan) and actual stylistic practice were both of great influence, we already find contradictions. While Malherbe claimed that clarity was the virtue lacking in the *galimatias* of earlier poets and expounded a radical doctrine of purity (use the words that the uneducated could understand), his own mature work is far from lacking in problematic periphrases, ornate terms, and high fictions about royalty that are extremely bold, if not always very moving.

The theory of idiomaticness and clarity in style was pursued most famously perhaps by the grammarian Vaugelas, but his theories came to be so generalized as to be the property of all literary critics. If we follow these principles through in the framework of classical rhetorical theory, we find that a plain style or low style is the only one which suits French neoclassical prescriptions, but from Malherbe on, the ode certainly suggests that clarity and idiomaticness were interpreted on a rather learned plane and that, in fact, the avoidance of certain kinds of ornament seems more central to neoclassical concerns.

Tragic poetry, however, was the place where neoclassical thinking found its greatest scope, and a new stylistic term entered the critical vocabulary, *langue noble*, which is a heightened, refined diction, yet pitched beneath the high odic manner and less showy in its ornaments. There was also a place for plain diction in the *langue noble*, solving the old renaissance dilemma of whether kings and queens should speak ornately when overcome by emotion. In many ways, *Andromaque* is an excellent example of *langue noble*, free of archaism and neologism, containing numerous tropes, whose unidiomaticness is defensible on the grounds of poetic tradition, and exhibiting many examples of plain diction used under the stress of emotion, like Hermione's famous *epiplexes*. The paradox of Racine's simultaneously complex and simple style is already embodied in *An-*

dromaque, but applying the old criterion of *galimatias*, or poetic jargon, which Malherbe used in judging others if not himself, the metonymies and personifications of *Andromaque* are perhaps excessively contorted at times in their individual conception and in their frequency as a whole.

That Racine was concerned with this problem of diction is evident from the preface to *Bérénice* (1670, three years after *Andromaque*) and from the style of the play itself. The preface succinctly puts Racine's ideal of style as consisting of "la violence des passions . . . la beauté des sentiments et . . . l'élégance de l'expression." If we begin with the third phrase and look for its antecedents in classical rhetorical theory, we find that elegance is a term usually applied to a pure, clear, low style, typically that of Roman love elegy. And of course violent passions and beautiful feelings are also part of elegiac tradition. This is a distinctly new conception of tragedy but evidently not idiosyncratic since, if we look up what Boileau has to say about tragedy in his *Art poétique*, he seems to share much the same elegiac ideal, and *Bérénice* was called elegiac by its contemporary admirers. Looking at *Andromaque* in retrospect, we can see that the subject matter of the dialogue has something of the bitter Roman elegies and that only the most elaborate figures of style seemed opposed to it.

Racine was very proud of having made a five-act tragedy out of the simple matter of the new Emperor Titus' telling Berenice, the queen of Palestine, that he could not marry her, the Romans being by tradition opposed to the titles of *rex* and *regina* since they drove out their own kings. There is relatively little bitterness and much lamenting in the play. As nearly as one can establish such things by counting, there are fewer tropes in *Bérénice* than in *Andromaque*, and the ones we do find are generally more discreet. These lines, where Titus directs Antiochus to explain the situation to the queen are a fairly good example of the elegiac style in its syntactically expanded form:

> Si l'espoir de régner et de vivre en mon coeur
> Peut de son infortune adoucir la rigueur,
> Ah! Prince, jurez-lui que toujours trop fidèle,
> Gémissant dans ma cour, et plus exilé qu'elle,

> Portant jusqu'au tombeau le nom de son amant,
> Mon règne ne sera qu'un long banissement.   (III, i, 749–54)

If the hope of reigning and living in my heart can soften the harshness of her misfortune, swear to her, prince, that, too faithful forever, moaning in my court, and more exiled than she is, I will bear to the grave the title of her lover, and my reign will be only a long banishment.

The paradox of his reign being an exile is abstract enough not to be ostentatious, and in general, lines do not stand out as they do in the more conflictual situations of *Andromaque*. The general opposition of public and private life is, moreover, one the Roman elegists often touch on.

Of course, the greatest significance of *Bérénice* for our purposes here is that it represents a quite overt abandonment of the stricter ideal of high style in tragedy and the formation of a *langue noble* which is closely related to the modestly ornamented, elegant form of low style, the *genus subtile floridius*. The neoclassical theory of purity and clarity as governing all styles is realized. The idea that classicism naturally tends toward a moderately low if quite refined style, which is implicit in Ben Jonson's work, receives its most remarkable embodiment in *Bérénice*. In a sense, all the French neoclassical strictures about decorum of action and language tended to counter the traditions of high style as bold in vocabulary, sentence structure, and ornament. It has been speculated that one of the most abiding influences on Racine was Ovid, the Ovid of the tragic elegies of the *Heroides*.[6] We are reminded in *Bérénice* more than ever of the analogies between the Latin elegiac couplet and Racine's handling of the couplet:

> Non ego dedignor supplex humilisque precari.
>   Heu! ubi nunc fastus altaque verba? Iacent.
> Et pugnare diu nec me submittere culpae
>   Certa fui, certi siquid haberet amor;
> Victa precor genibusque tuis regalia tendo
>   Bracchia. Quid deceat, non videt ullus amans.[7]

I do not disdain, begging and humble, to implore you. Alas, where now are my pride and haughty words? They lie fallen. For a long time I was

6. See Georges May, *D'Ovide à Racine* (New Haven, 1949).
7. Ovid, *Heroides and Amores* (Cambridge, Mass., 1977), IV, 149–54.

certain I could struggle and not succumb to any fault. As if there were certainty in love! Overcome, I beg; I stretch my queenly arms to your knees. No one in love can see what is fitting or not.

Here is a prototype of the succinct, intense, introspective style, with its passionate yet general and slightly abstract vocabulary. The couplet condenses the emotions rather than letting them pour out and dissipate their power. This is the great beauty Racine sensed in the couplet which led him to use, as the basis of his poetic texture, one or two-line sentences, in which reticence or pent-up emotion is the more powerful for being constrained. Ovid's work is not rich in such inwardly turned passages; the Roman elegy too often tends to wander, narrate, describe, and draw in miscellaneous ornaments. Racine saw what was potentially most vital in classical elegy and developed it into a consistent style.

It is often imagined by those with an inadequate sense of French (or Latin) poetry that the generally closed couplet is some sort of wearisome constraint that poets merely submitted to as passive members of the police state of French neoclassicism to bring out the image underlying such thinking. The closed couplet was not, indeed, a particularly apt instrument for extended narration, but it had great potential virtues for the stage, if only Corneille and Racine actually realized them. While French cannot easily imitate the centripetal, tight character of Latin syntax, the couplet is one of those fruitful conventions that make the poet achieve effects he might otherwise not have attained, and the density of Racine's diction, its reliance on small but significant variations, are a great justification of the form.

VI

With *Phèdre*, Racine moved beyond the more austere conception of neoclassical tragic verse; there are new ornaments in the style, as well as the fullest realization of certain tendencies he had shown since *Andromaque*. The first speech, in which Hippolytus addresses his tutor, is revelatory:

> Le dessein en est pris: je pars, cher Théramène,
> Et quitte le séjour de l'aimable Trézène.

Dans le doute mortel dont je suis agité,
Je commence à rougir de mon oisiveté.
Depuis plus de six mois éloigné de mon père,
J'ignore le destin d'une tête si chère;
J'ignore jusqu'aux lieux qui le peuvent cacher.   (I, i, 1–7)

The decision is made; I am leaving, dear Theramenes, and abandoning lovely Troezen. In the mortal doubt which agitates me, I am beginning to grow ashamed of my idleness. In the six months my father has been away, I do not know the destiny of so dear a one. I do not even know what places he might be hidden in.

It is often interesting to translate Racine's expressions into prosaic language to illustrate the slight deviation from ordinary idiom which he cultivates: *ma décision est faite* would be the equivalent of the first hemistich. We note that you cannot say so elegantly *mon dessein est pris*; Racine has chosen an impersonal, absolute-sounding article. The *en* is present because the full expression is *prendre le dessein de*, and in Racine we see the culmination of a tendency at work even in the more elegant prose of the late seventeenth century. A colorless verb is joined to a noun (often a verbal noun) to replace a shorter, more vigorous verb: *je l'ai décidé*. The second line contains a further development of this syntactic habit; an adjective is added to one of the two complementary nouns: *quitter le séjour de l'aimable Trézène*. Both *séjour* and *aimable* are pleonastic from a commonsense point of view, but Racine's intentions here are both interesting and evident. *Quitter le séjour de* is a long periphrasis after the curt *je pars*, and the epithet is an imitation of the classical use of conventional adjectives with proper names. The whole adds up to a double, complementary movement, in which a short, direct expression, such as might be found in ordinary prose, is balanced by a longer one, in which the possible wordiness of the periphrasis is compensated for by its weight. Racine shows himself most aware in *Phèdre* of the relative rapidity and lightness of French and attempts to counter them intermittently. The third line, again, appears to be a periphrasis for *plein d'inquiétude*. *Agiter* is an all-purpose verb of a general character; *mortel*, however, which means fatal or "pertaining to death," is a very compressed expression since *doute*, with perhaps its older sense of "fear," taken with the adjective, means "fear or doubt that Theseus is dead." So Racine's periphrasis actually turns out to be not entirely an expansion of a simple expression; within it, he has reduced a whole clause to an adjective. Again the double movement toward condensation and expansion is revealed to be an essential part of Racine's linguistic imagination. We have encountered the mannerist or decadent Latin version of the double movement in d'Aubigné, where each tendency, curtness and expansion, is greatly exaggerated. Racine's use of brevity and amplification is not, it seems to me, classical in the sense that he has imitated it from Virgil or Cicero but is a distinctive working out of the problems of weight and swiftness, polysyllabism and monosyllabism, in French. Styles must always to some extent depend on the structure of a language, and French presents problems in word length different from Latin.

The fourth line of our passage from the beginning of *Phèdre*, *je commence à rougir*, is perfectly straightforward and unsusceptible of prosaic reduction. Typically *mon père* is next juxtaposed by rime with the metonymy *une tête si chère*, with its distancing, elevating substitution of the indefinite article for the possessive *mon* and its mandatory adjective: plainness and elaborateness alternate. *Qui le peuvent cacher* is a much more interesting expression than it may seem at first. Its important aspect is perhaps not so much the relatively weak personification of *lieux* as it is the placing of the pronoun in the accusative; *où il peut se cacher* or *être caché* would be the prosaic form. The use of what in normal thought sequence would be the subject ("he," Theseus) as an object continues the syntactic tendency seen in the passive *le dessein en est pris* and in the passive participle *éloigné*; in this last case Racine perhaps forces the sense a bit in his desire for a passive construction since it is usually the person or thing absent which is *éloigné* from the speaker's point of view. But these passive constructions all add up to the tendency to avoid, when a certain stately smoothness is needed, the highly sequential, progressive effect of a series of active verbs with persons as subjects. The latter is a characteristic of rapid narrative, and Racine carefully saves such effect for special passages like Phaedra's narrative in act I, scene 3.

Theramenes' reply to Hippolytus does indeed have an active verb narrative, but excited sequentiality is mitigated by the use of geographical periphrases highly reminiscent of classical poetry:

> Déjà, pour satisfaire à votre juste crainte,
> J'ai couru les deux mers que sépare Corinthe;

J'ai demandé Thésée aux peuples de ces bords
Où l'on voit l'Achéron se perdre chez les morts;
J'ai visité l'Elide, et laissant le Ténare,
Passé jusqu'à la mer qui vit tomber Icare.   (I, i, 9–14)

Already to satisfy your reasonable fear, I have gone along the two seas which Corinth separates. I have asked for Theseus of the peoples of those banks where the Acheron sinks down to the land of the dead. I have visited Elis and, leaving Cape Taenarus, gone over to the sea where Icarus fell.

We note here a balance between verbs with *je* as a subject and those with slightly personified places as subject. This alternation also softens the narrational-sequential effect. While periphrasis in baroque poetry tends to be limited to connotations of praise and wonder or occasionally vituperation, Racine's periphrases demonstrate more diverse associations, for a periphrasis always has an emotional burden that the proper term does not. Within the general area of grandeur for which geographical periphrases are used in classical poetry, we can distinguish here the imposing presence of the sea, the awe inspired by the dead, and the perilous aspirations of mortals in regard to the gods.

It is quite clear from the opening of *Phèdre* that Racine has completely rejected the antiornamental prejudices of neoclassical esthetics in his search for a genuinely classical effect. He is using more figures "for the eye," as Aristotle recommended (*Rhetoric* 1411b). One might compare the opening of *Phèdre* with the priest's speech at the beginning of *Oedipus Rex* for a similarly stately, protracted exposition. However, Racine also uses his devices to some extent for character portrayal.[8] Periphrasis can be a means of understatement and reticence, as at the end of these lines of Hippolytus':

Cher Théramène, arrête, et respecte Thésée.
De ces jeunes erreurs désormais revenu,
Par un indigne obstacle il n'est point retenu;
Et fixant de ses voix l'inconstance fatale,
Phèdre depuis longtemps ne craint plus de rivale.
Enfin en le cherchant je suivrai mon devoir,
Et je fuirai ces lieux que je n'ose plus voir.   (I, i, 22–28)

Dear Theramenes, cease, and show respect for Theseus. Having gotten

---

8. For sentence structure and character portrayal, see Mary Lynne Flowers, *Sentence Structure and Characterization in the Tragedies of Jean Racine* (Rutherford, N.J., 1979).

over his youthful errors, he is not detained by some unworthy attachment. And Phaedra, having put an end to his fated inconstancy, has had, for a long time now, no fear of a rival. Finally, by looking for him, I will be following my duty, and I will escape from this place which I no longer dare look upon.

The first line asks Theramenes not to suggest that Theseus is lost in erotic adventures. *Respecte* as a simple imperative is a fine example of obtaining maximum force from a word through brevity. The next lines continue the passive presentation of Theseus (*point retenu*; his wandering desires having been held in one place by Phaedra) and employ periphrases, *indigne obstacle*, which shows Hippolytus' prudish euphemism, and *rivale*, a nobler, more distant, and shorter way of saying "any other woman." Finally, *que je n'ose plus voir*, a deliberately mysterious phrase, gives rise to the discussion occupying the rest of the scene.

Two kinds of periphrases are illustrated in the lines immediately following:

> Théramène: Hé! depuis quand, Seigneur, craignez-vous la présence
> De ces paisibles lieux, si chers à votre enfance,
> Et dont je vous ai vu préférer le séjour
> Au tumulte pompeux d'Athène et de la cour?
> Quel péril, ou plutôt quel chagrin vous en chasse?
>
> Hippolyte: Cet heureux temps n'est plus. Tout a changé de face
> Depuis que sur ces bords les Dieux ont envoyé
> La fille de Minos et de Pasiphaé.   (I, ii, 29–36)

Theramenes: Well, since when, dear lord, do you fear the presence of this peaceful spot, so dear to your childhood, and which I have seen you prefer to the grandiose tumult of Athens and the court? What danger, or rather what sorrow drives you away? *Hippolytus*: Those happy times are no more. Everything has changed since the gods sent the daughter of Minos and Pasiphae to these shores.

Craindre la présence and *préférer le séjour* are typical verb-noun combinations used instead of verbs, but here they are distinctly on the wordy side, as is the *correctio* in Theramenes' last line above; Theramenes is a Nestorian figure, eloquent in his prolix fashion but withdrawn from the agitations of youth by reason of his age. Hippolytus answers him with a supremely concise phrase, then elaborates. All of Hippolytus' periphrasis, the image of arrival on a shore and the references to gods and to the parentage of Phaedra are tightly proleptic and thematic. We note the element of euphemism again in Hippolytus' use of periphrasis, to be balanced later by Phaedra's reticence to speak openly. The periphrasis is used to designate menaces.

Theramenes replies with a double expression, saying the same thing in prosaic language and then in a protracting passive construction: "J'entends. De vos douleurs la cause m'est connue." But again, there are constructions which seem periphrastic from the viewpoint of ordinary idiom but actually turn out to be far more concise and expressive than any translation one could make of them into plain French:

> Dangereuse marâtre, à peine elle vous vit,
> Que votre exil d'abord signala son crédit.　(I, i, 39–40)

She is a dangerous stepmother, and hardly had she seen you than your banishment demonstrated how powerful she was.

Crédit has nice associations of influence, palace intrigue, power, and rivalry; *signala* is a stronger, sharper verb, at least in the preterite, than many of Racine's. Again we find a reversal of the normal sequence of ideas, which would be "her influence caused you to be exiled." The deviation from ordinary expression gives the line a vivid quality and is based on the principle of turning about ideas which obtains not rarely in Greek and Latin poetry: *fuso crateres olivo* (*Aeneid*, VI, 225), which is oil poured out from bowls, not bowls of outpoured oil; *ibant obscuri sola sub nocte per umbram* (*Aeneid*, VI, 266), where it is the wayfarers who are actually *soli* and the night *obscura*, not the other way round; *et totidem flavas numerabant horrea messes* (Milton, "Epitaphium Damonis"), where in reality men count the harvests not the barn. Hypallage and personification are just two types of idea reversal, one of the most valuable tools, as Racine discovered, for altering idiom in search of power of expression.

The *dangereuse marâtre* of the above lines deserves commentary in itself, for it anticipates a whole distinctive aspect of the syntax of *Phèdre*. It is an antecedent apposition, an expressive construction with no equivalent in English, but its density is shared by even the normal postpositive apposition: appositions can be substitutes for whole clauses. However, their concision is counterbalanced by the weighty, prolonged effect they give the sentence into which they are inserted:

> Je fuis, je l'avoûrai, cette jeune Aricie,
> Reste d'un sang fatal conjuré contre nous.   (I, i, 50–51)

I am fleeing, I must admit, the young Aricia, who is the last remnant of a house fated to conspire against us.

Appositions, like epithets, create expanded sentences in order to permit a contrast by the most direct expression, as occurs in the sequel to the lines above: "Si je la haïssais, je ne la fuirais pas." Normally, the apposition might seem too ponderous a syntactic device for the generally rapid pace of French neoclassical tragedy, but as in the case of geographical periphrases, Racine employs exceptional effects in *Phèdre* in order to draw closer to the noun-laden classical ideal of high style.

All the stylistic devices we have noted recur with slight variations in the rest of the first scene of *Phèdre*. A nice example of condensation and expansion occurs in Hippolytus' answer to the brief *Aimeriez-vous?* of Theramenes:

> Ami, qu'oses-tu dire?
> Toi qui connais mon coeur depuis que je respire,
> Des sentiments d'un coeur si fier, si dédaigneux,
> Peux-tu me demander le désaveu honteux?   (I, i, 65–68)

Friend, what are you daring to say? You who know my heart since my birth, can you ask me to disavow shamefully the feelings of so proud, so disdainful a heart?

The first line is plain, but in the three-line sentence which follows, we have a typical mixture of expansion and the unexpectedly tight *demander le désaveu honteux*, which follows the rule of joining a verbal noun to a colorless verb and adding an adjective for fullness. The normal *demander que je désavoue honteusement*, though not much longer, is wordier, and we see that the verb-noun expressions can be a way of avoiding a clause and thereby approximating the more stately Latin habit of circumventing the use of finite verbs. Similarly, *depuis que je respire* is one word shorter than *depuis que je suis né*, so rime is not the sole motivation for the expression.

The psychological phraseology of *Phèdre*, like that of *Andromaque*, alternates the use of the personal pronoun with metonymies, personifications, and periphrases, but the odder personifications and the insistence on the rather Petrarchist eyes and heart have grown rare. The idiom is graver, even though the grammatical mechanisms are often the same. The nurse describes Phaedra:

> Elle meurt dans mes bras d'un mal qu'elle me cache.
> Un désordre éternel règne dans son esprit.
> Son chagrin inquiet l'arrache de son lit.
> Elle veut voir le jour; et sa douleur profonde
> M'ordonne toutefois d'écarter tout le monde.   (I, ii, 146–50)

She is dying in my arms from an ill which she keeps hidden. A vast disarray fills her mind. Her unquiet sorrow tears her from her bed. She wishes to see daylight; and her deep suffering orders me to disperse any people at hand.

Although the pattern of varying the subjects of the verbs in psychological description is the same, there is less development of the abstract subjects. However, there is no loss of intensity. *Désordre* is one of the richest of Racine's negative or litotic expressions; *éternel*, one of his few hyperboles; and the yoking of such different types of words is a fine example of rhetorical invention. The whole complex of eyes-sight-light common in *Andromaque* and recurring in these lines has been turned in *Phèdre* into a symbolism of life and death, purity and guilt. Although the example of Shakespearean criticism has encouraged a quest for image chains and symbols in Racine, this endeavor too often proves to be a vain attempt to overinterpret metonymies and to make Racine more "interesting," more modern in intent than he actually is. *Phèdre* does employ symbolism, but of a more Greek than Shakespearean type. Like the wandering road and sterile fields of *Oedipus Rex*, Racine's symbolism is taken from actual physical circumstances: the sunlight, the fact that Pasiphae has given birth to one monster already, and the poison that Phaedra eventually drinks.

Some of the best effects of Phaedra's confession to Oenone are based on Racine's classical sources. The style continues to be epithetical and periphrastic, and as in the way Hippolytus' name is brought out, circumlocution again shows its value as euphemism. With Phaedra's narrative, however, a style that contrasts with the exclamations and somewhat disconnected earlier texture sets in. One periphrasis, *sous les lois de l'hymen*, represents Phaedra's period of calm; then one-line or half-line sentences provide a multiplicity of verbs in a direct, pronoun-dominated narrative movement we have not seen up to this point:

> Mon mal vient de plus loin. À peine au fils d'Egée
> Sous les lois de l'hymen je m'étais engagée,
> Mon repos, mon bonheur semblait être affermi,
> Athènes me montra mon superbe ennemi.
> Je le vis, je rougis, je pâlis à sa vue;
> Un trouble s'éleva dans mon âme éperdue;
> Mes yeux ne voyaient plus, je ne pouvais parler;
> Je sentis tout mon corps et transir et brûler.
> Je reconnus Vénus et ses feux redoutables,
> D'un sang qu'elle poursuit tourments inévitables.
>   (I, iii, 269–78)

My suffering goes back further. Hardly had I pledged myself to Theseus by the laws of marriage than my calm, my happiness seemed certain. Athens showed my haughty enemy. I saw him, I blushed, I grew pale before him. An upheaval took place in my frantic soul. My eyes could see no more, I could no longer speak; I felt my whole body chill and burn; I recognized Venus and her dread flames, the inevitable torments of a race she persecutes.

The key line *Athènes me montra* employs the recurrent and striking device of reversal of natural subject and complement: *je vis à Athènes mon ennemi. Montra* is worthy of note, not only because it is more active than forms of *voir*, but also because it is the first *passé simple* for many lines and makes the strongest contrast with the statal *semblait* just before it. The manipulation of tenses is one of Racine's less frequent but very striking effects.[9] The passage concludes with an appropriate grammatical device: an apposition stops the regular forward line-by-line movement.

Two of Racine's bold figures occur in Phaedra's narrative. In speaking of the temple she built and the sacrifices she directed, she says, "Je cherchais dans leurs flancs ma raison égarée," a startling catachresis. The famous oxymoron *flamme si noire* follows somewhat later. Again, we should not think of these figures as belonging to

---

9. See J. B. Ratermanis, *Essai sur les formes verbales dans les tragédies de Racine* (Paris, 1972).

another order of style from the rest of the play, but as peaks of high style, which cannot be too numerous, for the most effective classicizing styles aim at a certain rise and fall of tension and effect, so unlike the baroque ideal of sustained, unvaried brilliance. This care for variation accounts for the irregular distribution of the more special ornaments in *Phèdre*. However, the total effect is not one of unevenness, as we can see from the relationships of images to each other. For example, Aricia at one point uses a metaphor rather condensed in its reference:

> J'ai perdu, dans la fleur de leur jeune saison,
> Six frères, quel espoir d'une illustre maison!
> Le fer moissonna tout, et la terre humectée
> But à regret le sang des neveux d'Erechthée.   (II, i, 423–26)

I lost, in the flower of their young season, six brothers—what a hope for an illustrious line! The sword reaped them all, and the dampened earth drank regretfully the blood of the grandsons of Erechtheus.

Hippolytus then picks up the theme:

> Assez dans ses sillons votre sang englouti
> A fait fumer le champ dont il était sorti.   (II, ii, 503–504)

Your blood seeped into the furrows has long enough made fruitful the fields from which it had risen.

Blood, earth, sunlight, the sea, darkness, air, and fire, the basic kind of images of the world one finds in the *Aeneid* or in Homer, create the sense of fundamental forces that so distinguishes the art of *Phèdre* from Racine's previous neoclassical world of more exclusively human and psychological conflicts.

The most famous scene in *Phèdre* is the meeting of Phaedra and Hippolytus in act II, scene v. In it Racine deploys an extraordinary example of invention which comes under the category of bold *ornatus*. Phaedra prepares the ground with a notion that is basically a commonplace but surprising in the circumstances:

> Que dis-je, Il [Thésée] n'est pas mort, puisqu'il
>   respire en vous.
> Toujours devant mes yeux je crois voir mon époux.   (II, v, 627–28)

But I am wrong. Theseus is not dead for he lives in you. I seem always before me to see my husband.

Then a *correctio* follows; a sentence is developed with a remarkable example of accumulating postpositional modifiers of a rather bland character until the last one is reached:

> Je l'aime [Thésée], non point tel que l'ont vu les enfers,
> Volage adorateur de mille objets divers,
> Qui va du Dieu des morts déshonorer la couche;
> Mais fidèle, mais fier, et même un peu farouche,
> Charmant, jeune, traînant tous les coeurs après soi,
> Tel qu'on dépeint nos Dieux, ou tel que je vous vois.
> (II, v, 635–40)

I love Theseus, not as hell saw him, the fickle worshipper of a thousand faces, going to dishonor the bed of the god of the dead, but faithful, proud, even a little timid, charming, attracting all hearts, just as our gods are depicted, or just as you appear.

This rather loose sentence structure runs counter to Racine's general practice and achieves the effect, more difficult in French than in Latin, of postponing the key word *vous* till almost the end of the sentence. The casual-seeming indirection of what precedes culminates in a phrase of great force.

As the speech builds to a climax, Phaedra introduces what we might analyze as a hypothetical, fragmentary syllogism:

> Par vous aurait péri le monstre de la Crète,
> Malgré tous les détours de sa vaste retraite.
> Pour en developper l'embarras incertain,
> Ma soeur du fil fatal eût armé votre main.   (II, v, 649–52)

By your hand the monster of Crete would have perished, despite the maze of his vast den. To trace a path through its confusing, tangled corridors, my sister would have provided you with the thread destined to make you victorious.

Since Hippolytus is like Theseus, Ariadne would have aided him in the labyrinth. But since Phaedra loves Theseus in Hippolytus, she would have come to his help instead; a *correctio* follows:

> Mais non, dans ce dessein, je l'aurais devancée:
> L'amour m'en eût d'abord inspiré la pensée.
> C'est moi, Prince, c'est moi dont l'utile secours
> Vous eût du Labyrinthe enseigné les détours.   (II, v, 653–56)

But no, I would have anticipated her intentions; love would have made me think of it. I am the one, Prince, whose useful help would have shown you the intricacies of the labyrinth.

Suddenly the comparison of Phaedra and Ariadne ceases, and the past is transformed into a fantasy:

> Et Phèdre au Labyrinthe avec vous descendue,
> Se serait avec vous retrouvée, ou perdue.   (II, v, 661–62)

And Phaedra, going down into the Labyrinth with you, would have, with you, found her way, or been lost.

This tortuous reasoning is based on the questions of identity, equivalence, and conclusion which syllogisms use, but it is highly elliptic as suits the *audacior ornatus* of high style. The conditional perfect is the rare tense of longings and regrets and bears a heavy emotional burden here, especially as the labyrinth is referred to with a verb suitable for the underworld (*descendre*); Phaedra is thinking of leading Hippolytus down into her darkness. This fantasy is cast in elegant phrases. *Devancer dans ce dessein* serves for "would have thought of it first," a typical concise replacement for a finite clause; *inspirer la pensée de* uses verb and noun in Racine's typical fashion for *faire songer à*; *utile secours* substitutes for the personal pronoun. The postponement of the past participles to the end of the last line, allowing prepositional phrases to intervene between them and the subject, illustrates a delicate sense of word order for a crucial statement, whereas Racine usually observes a fairly normal sequence of sentence elements. All this is calculated as a contrast with Phaedra's bald statement, which follows shortly:

> Ah! cruel, tu m'as trop entendue.
> Je t'en ai dit assez pour te tirer d'erreur.   (II, v, 671–72)

Ah, cruel one, you have understood only too well. I have said enough to undeceive you.

The double style here, representing fantasy and reality, shows its most vivid contrastive effect. Racine never uses the plain, outspoken style for very long though; otherwise the prosaic would lose its value. He modulates very carefully back into a more literary idiom with a line whose beginning is colloquial, whose imperative is blunt, but whose double object is more literary in idiom: "Hé bien! connais donc Phèdre et toute sa fureur" (672). The whole following speech oscillates between the direct and even colloquial and the stylized use of appositions, litotes, and other figures, to conclude with one of the most remarkable of verbal inventions as Phaedra demands Hippolytus' sword, *Donne*. This bare imperative closing a speech demonstrates that Racine's syntactic imagination is as great as his invention of phrases.

There is a great deal in the declaration scene which violates the principles of decorum observed regularly in French neoclassical theater. The actual shifts of level of phrase and vocabulary run quite counter to the notions of homogeneous style and sustained tone which most playwrights found easy and natural to observe, drawing as they did on stock expressions. *Phèdre* is, in fact, so spectacular in its combination of styles that the play may appear to be impaired by it as a whole. The use of styles to characterize speakers makes the roles of Phaedra and Oenone stand out very sharply from the others. Another quite unexpected shift of style comes with Theramenes' narrative of Hippolytus' death. Messengers' speeches often had distinctive features in Greek tragedy, and Giraldi Cinthio in the sixteenth century had proposed that the highest degree of ornamentation be reserved for the narration of off-stage events. Racine chose to write the *récit de Théramène* in a form of epic style, and as Racine was the most gifted of the French neoclassical poets, we can gather from this passage why epic in France was a less successful genre than others in the seventeenth century. Despite intermittent enjambment, the couplet produces little of the effect of continuity judged essential to the epic form of high style. As the monster who kills Hippolytus emerges from the sea,

> Ses longs mugissements font trembler le rivage.
> Le ciel avec horreur voit ce monstre sauvage.
> La terre s'en émeut, l'air en est infecté,
> Le flot qui l'apporta recule épouvanté.   (V, vi, 1521–24)

Its long roars make the shore tremble. The sky sees this savage monster with horror; the earth is shaken; the air is infected by it. The wave which brought it to the shore rolls back in terror.

The verse form is distinctly monotonous in external rather than psychological narration. The diction, with its general terms, tends to be at once exaggerated and colorless. One sees the precise motivation behind these lines. A *monstrum* is a thing which does not follow nature's rules, which is out of nature, and so the elements draw back from it. This is the reason that Phaedra, as a moral *monstrum*, hides in the dark as did the Minotaur. Nature is repelled by such creatures. All this is very carefully thought out; Racine's poetic plans were excellent in principle, but the narrative gift is lacking.[10]

In the final scene of the play, we become especially aware of the fact that Theseus has little more than refined rant in his role: he is a Senecan figure, whereas Phaedra, always given impressive lines, concludes her part and her life with the last great audacious stylistic invention of the play:

> J'ai voulu, devant vous exposant mes remords,
> Par un chemin plus lent descendre chez les morts.
> J'ai pris, j'ai fait couler dans mes brûlantes veines
> Un poison que Médée apporta dans Athènes.
> Déjà jusqu'à mon coeur le venin parvenu
> Dans ce coeur expirant jette un froid inconnu;
> Déjà je ne vois plus qu'à travers un nuage
> Et le ciel, et l'époux que ma présence outrage;
> Et la mort, à mes yeux dérobant la clarté,
> Rend au jour, qu'ils souillaient, toute sa pureté.
> (V, vii, 1635–44)

I insisted, in order to present my remorse to you, on taking a longer road to the house of death. I drank, I injected into my burning veins a poison that Medea had brought to Athens. Already the poison reaching my heart casts an unknown chill into my dying heart. Already I can no longer see, except through a cloud, both the sky and my husband whom my presence dishonors. And death, stealing the brightness from my eyes, gives back to the light they sullied all its purity.

Carefully using various devices of repetition, Racine brings together here the major images of the play: the descent into darkness, the fire in the body, the poison which was destroying Phaedra in the first act, and the *monstrum* who has infected the air. The metaphor *souiller le jour* is a very amazing one, if we remember that eyes were always represented as giving out some kind of light. Phaedra obscured nature's light with the dull dark glow of her eyebeams, the outer form of her *flamme si noire*.

From its conception as a Christian parable of the soul deprived of grace to its stylistic detail, *Phèdre* belongs to a higher style than most

10. For a justification of the *récit de Théramène*, see Leo Spitzer, *Linguistics and Literary History: Essays in Stylistics* (Princeton, 1948), 87–125.

neoclassical tragedies. The emphasis on noun phrases—through epitheton, periphrases, and verb and noun substitutes for ordinary verbs—is a notable high-style feature, whereas generally the balance among nouns, adjectives, and verbs in French neoclassical tragedy tends to give the verb somewhat more weight. The tendency to use passives or to use persons as the object rather than the subject of verbs constitutes a stately deviation from normal idiom. Even hyperbaton, usually so mechanical in neoclassical style, is at times quite expressively handled. Finally—and this is perhaps the most important point about the play's style—the one-word metaphors or metonymies—(even *feux* and *flamme*) tend to come fully to life because of the plentitude of imagery. We do not experience them as mere half images, elegant variations in an abstract style, as so often happens in French neoclassicism, but feel them as part of an imagistic description of the world. The range of images is also strongly reminiscent of Virgilian epic. There is nothing of baroque technique in *Phèdre*; *delectatio* plays no role in this forceful style. At the same time, the play is no more epideictic and hyperbolic in the manner of the neoclassical ode than it is elegiac in the fashion of *Bérénice*. Racine realized a style proper to tragedy.[11]

VII

Given the existence in the seventeenth-century French theater of a strongly conventionalized poetic diction, readers who are principally familiar with the major work of Corneille and Racine are often curious as to how their work differs from that of other poets of the common style, the *langue noble*, of the period. Rather than further investigating the variations of Racine's style, in *Britannicus* or *Athalie*, say, I think it appropriate to attempt to suggest briefly in what way Racine may be distinguished from his fellow tragic poets and contemporary rivals as a major poet. Pradon's *Phèdre et Hippolyte*, which was written as a rival play to Racine's in one of those complicated intrigues where literature and society were too closely mingled

---

11. For two further studies on Racine's style, see Leo Spitzer, "The Muting Effect of Classical Style in Racine," in R. C. Knight (ed.), *Racine: Modern Judgements* (Nashville, 1970), 117–31; Jacques-Gabriel Cahen, *Le Vocabulaire de Racine* (Paris, 1946).

for the good of either, will serve to illustrate what Racine did and did not do as a poet and playwright.

I say as a poet and playwright because more questions of plot structure are involved here than in a comparison of two sonnets. Indeed, the first thing that strikes one about Pradon's play is that some of Phaedra's feelings and actions, for which Racine rose to his greatest inventiveness, are merely recounted by other characters in Pradon. Here Aricia is talking to Hippolytus about Phaedra's fondness for him, which he is annoyed at:

> Cette Phèdre pourtant si charmante & si fiere
> Fait voir une amitié pour vous tendre et sincere;
> Oui, Seigneur, tous les jours mes yeux en sont témoins:
> Peut-être pour Thésée en auroit-elle moins.
> Dans votre air, de Thésée elle trouve l'image:
> Ces traits qui lui sont chers sont sur votre visage.
> Je l'écoute avec joie, hélas! je m'applaudis
> Qu'en brûlant pour le pere elle adore le fils.
> Tous ses soins vont pour vous jusqu'à l'inquiétude;
> Et je rougis, Seigneur, de votre ingratitude.[12]

Nonetheless, Phaedra, so charming and proud, shows sincere and tender friendship toward you. Yes, sir, I witness it every day. Perhaps she has less feeling for Theseus. She discovers Theseus' look in your aspect; those features dear to her can be found in your face. Alas, I listen joyfully to her and I congratulate myself that through loving the father, she adores the son. She is so concerned with you as to be really worried. And I blush for you, sir, at your thanklessness.

This is the material with which the declaration scene opens in *Phèdre* and for which Racine devised among other things the elaborately winding, indirect sentence I quoted earlier. Pradon merely summarizes, in invaried couplets, as suits the casual onlooker that Aricia seems to be here, some plot material of no great intensity for which his language assumes the perfunctory, edulcorated neoclassical vein. Not a single expression goes beyond the most ordinary neoclassical grammar or vocabulary.

When Phaedra admits her love for Hippolytus to Oenone in *Phèdre*, elaborate resources are brought into play. Phaedra's mind wanders in revery; her thoughts are incoherent; lines are broken up; and

---

12. Nicolas Pradon, *Phèdre et Hippolyte*, in Pradon, *Oeuvres* (2 vols.; Paris, 1744), I, ii, hereinafter cited in the text.

periphrasis is used to bring out step by step the adored, secret and guilt-laden name of Hippolytus. Pradon merely has Phaedra tell Aricia, at the mention of Theseus' return, what preoccupies her:

> A ce fatal retour,
> Pour Rival à sa Gloire il trouvera l'Amour;
> Mais peut-être un Amour qui nous sera funeste,
> Un Amour malheureux que ma vertu déteste.
> Aricie, il est temps de vous tirer d'erreur;
> Je vous aime, apprenez le secret de mon coeur;
> Et les soupirs de Phedre & le feu qui l'agite,
> Ne vont point à Thésée, & cherchent Hyppolyte.   (I, iii)

> At his fateful return, he will find Love as a rival to his Glory. But perhaps a love that will undo us, an unhappy love that my virtue loathes. Aricia, it is time to tell you the truth. I like you; listen to the secret of my heart: the sighs and the fire agitating it are not for Theseus but are directed at Hippolytus.

It is curious to note how an expression like *vous tirer d'erreur*, which Racine uses in a strong fashion in the declaration scene when Phaedra has grown furious with Hippolytus, here has not much more force than "set you straight." The vocabulary of French neoclassicism is limited, but in any circumscribed linguistic system, the situation in which an expression is used can greatly modify its force. In other respects, Pradon's language is mild, elegant, and suggests the kind of indispensable but routine exposition which takes place between a main character and a *confident* in so many neoclassical plays. "Apprenez le secret de mon coeur" is certainly not comparable to "Hé bien! connais donc Phèdre et toutes ses fureurs," a line whose subtle linguistic mechanism I have commented on.

There are, in short, no carefully prepared high points with an appropriate rhetoric in Pradon's play. And on the more ordinary level of discourse, variation between the plainspoken and the elaborate or deviations from standard idiom simply do not occur. At the same time, it is interesting to speculate that the body of conventionalized neoclassical diction, as we see it in Pradon, was a necessary presupposition to Racine's devising of his various styles. He was not inventing neoclassical tragedy but perfecting it. As so often happens in the history of earlier poetry, it is not the poet who first used the sonnet or blank verse or vernacular pastoral elegy whom we associate with the finest form of the genre. This is also true of the epic, for while there are indeed two poems, Tasso's and Spenser's, which stand out from the minor sixteenth-century epic production, it is only with Milton that classicizing epic reaches its full form.

CHAPTER 9

Milton and Epic Style

I

In one of those remarks on the style of the work that one is actually reading which renaissance and seventeenth-century writers sometimes make, Milton tells us litotically, at the beginning of *Paradise Lost*, that his epic will soar with no middle flight. At the beginning of Book IX, the first of the four concluding tragic books, he is more specific. *Paradise Lost* is to be higher in content and manner than Homer or Virgil's epics. He appropriately tells us that in a periodic sentence which, according to the accepted criteria of high style, far outdoes any passage in the classical epics. It is worth examining this period in detail, and as it covers forty-one lines, I shall break it up into units for purposes of discussion.

The first six lines contain an absolute construction, that is, verb-less and not formally subordinated to the main verb, which follows immediately:

> No more of talk where God or Angel Guest
> With Man, as with his Friend, familiar us'd
> To sit indulgent, and with him partake
> Rural repast, permitting him the while
> Venial discourse unblam'd: I now must change
> These Notes to Tragic;[1]

Paradise Lost is a work of high syntactic imagination, as one can see from the way Milton has taken a verbless English construction which is usually a colloquial refusal or kind of negative imperative or formal exclamation and converted it into the equivalent of a classical absolute phrase ("this being the case" or "this said"); it is expanded

---

1. John Milton, *Paradise Lost*, ed. Merritt Y. Hughes (New York, 1935), IX, 1–6, hereinafter cited in the text.

by subordinate clauses and a participle far beyond what we would generally find in a classical absolute phrase. Such expansion of customary grammatical elements is characteristic of Milton's style, and here Milton also uses his familiar technique of making the subordinate elements clear by mild hyperbaton: *as with his friend, with him,* and *discourse* precede the key words *indulgent, repast,* and *unblam'd.* The simpler forms of hyperbaton are often ways of neatly punctuating the structure of a passage by putting the sharpest word last; yet they do not interfere with the linear movement of the whole. Milton regularly uses such hyperbaton with participial phrases, as in "the wrath / Of stern *Achilles* on his Foe pursu'd" (IX, 14–15). The tendency to make a construction without a central verb elaborately dense is illustrated a bit later in Book IX by the exclamation:

> O Earth, how like to Heav'n, if not preferr'd
> More justly, Seat worthier of Gods, as built
> With second thoughts, reforming what was old! (99–101)

The verbless *if* construction is parallel to a variety of pseudoclauses in Milton: "Lords of the World besides" (I, 32)—that is, "although they would have been Lords"—or "Myriads though bright" (I, 87). This is a striking adaptation of a Greek construction, as is the use of *as built* in the exclamation above. Milton sometimes actually borrows an idiom from Greek or Latin, although frequently his unusual grammar consists in expanding constructions already existent in English.

To return to the beginning of Book IX, we find after Milton's ingenious invention of an English absolute phrase, a colon before the main verb: "Venial discourse unblam'd: I now must change." Milton uses colons with as expressive a connective value as he uses words like *yet, but, and, or, for.* This resource, which was not available to Homer or Virgil, is of the greatest importance in constructing his periods. Linguistically speaking, the colon represents an ocular and intonational indication of liaison rather than an intellectual and syntactic one, but it is just as real and effective as an actual word.

The word *tragic* introduces one of Milton's most favored constructions, the apposition, of which there are nine here:

> I now must change
> Those Notes to Tragic; foul distrust, and breach
> Disloyal on the part of Man, revolt,

> And disobedience: On the part of Heav'n
> Now alienated, distance and distaste,
> Anger and just rebuke, and judgment giv'n,   (5–10)

It is curious to note the evolution of the apposition in poetry. In Virgil the construction is infrequent and modest in proportions; in European poetry, Petrarch uses none in his lyrics, so far as I can tell, but beginning with Ronsard, we find a gradual increase of appositions through baroque poetry. Milton, however, while far exceeding baroque poets in the number of his appositions, uses them in a less direct, enumeratory fashion and prefers an abstract or thematic vocabulary to the imagistic baroque apposition. In the passage above, Milton breaks up the polysyndeton he is usually so fond of (A and B and C and D) because of the number of the appositions, and he varies them with modifiers differently placed and with the two prepositional phrases ("on the part"), which are not symmetrically located. The principle of irregularity which informs Milton's high-style prosody, with its enjambment and inner pauses, is also rendered by asymmetrical word order in many cases.

Appositions are frequently extended by a relative clause:

> and judgment giv'n,
> That brought into this World a world of woe,
> Sin and her shadow Death, and Misery
> Death's Harbinger: (10–13)

The polysyndeton is somewhat disguised by the prominence of the word repetition and of the modifiers of the polysyndetic nouns. Employing his frequent principle of expanding normal syntax into a much more complicated structure, Milton now adds a second apposition:

> Death's Harbinger: Sad task, yet argument
> Not less but more Heroic than the wrath
> Of stern *Achilles* on his Foe pursu'd
> Thrice Fugitive about *Troy* Wall; or rage
> Of *Turnus* for *Lavinia* disespous'd,
> Or *Neptune's* ire or *Juno's*, that so long
> Perplex'd the *Greek* and *Cytherea's* Son;   (13–19)

We observe here that the apposition contains a hinge phrase, *yet argument*, which moves us into another world of thoughts and images. This belongs to the complex of constructions including *correctio* and negative comparison which plays an increasing role in poetic grammar from Ronsard's time on. In the detail of his apposition we note that *thrice Fugitive* referring to *Foe* is clear but grammatically somewhat irregular, as it would not be in Latin where *Fugitive* and *Foe* would be joined by the accusative case; *Lavinia disespous'd* belongs to the same idiom as *paradise lost* and means "the disespousal of Lavinia"; Latin often avoids abstract words in favor of a concrete noun and a participle.

The principle that high style tends to be nominal is carried to great lengths by Milton; the apposition especially, which is as nominal a construction as one could find, greatly aids him here. However, if nominal style answers the need for weightiness in high epic, it also moves slowly and thickly and dulls somewhat the reader's feeling for the sentence as a whole. Milton accordingly introduces into this long period an *if* clause, one of his favorite adverbial clauses, in a more fluid, expansive passage:

> If answerable style I can obtain
> Of my Celestial Patroness, who deigns
> Her nightly visitation unimplor'd,
> And dictates to me slumb'ring, or inspires
> Easy my unpremeditated Verse: (20–24)

We see here that, as in the preceding apposition, Milton often uses *or* in polysyndeton, as well as *or* in the place of *and* elsewhere. The purpose of polysyndeton is to provide a forward impulse, syntactically and phonetically, and Milton seems especially to favor *or*, perhaps on the ground that its movement is more marked. In any case, it is striking to see the great revival of polysyndeton in Milton's epic style; Petrarch had made much use of it, but the construction noticeably declined in favor of asyndeton from Ronsard through the baroque poets. At the end of this passage, we should observe that *to inspire easy*, rather than *easily*, follows a widespread tendency in earlier forms of languages to switch parts of speech, as in Milton's use of adjectives for nouns.

It is not customary to place two adverbial clauses in sequence, although grammar books say nothing about the matter. Milton, however, pursuing his goal of syntactic expansion, places a *since* clause after the *if* clause:

> Since first this Subject for Heroic Song
> Pleas'd me long choosing, and beginning late;   (25–26)

The participles modifying *me* are rather in the Latin vein but, like most of Milton's Latinisms, contribute a construction of great beauty and concision to English. Were it not for renaissance Latinism, English would be a poor tongue indeed.

The participle is the major way Latin avoids finite clauses, with their disadvantage of losing the reader in an excess of verbs of action, but the modern languages have another, equally useful substitute for a clause, which is the infinitive dependent on an adjective:

> Not sedulous by Nature to indite
> Wars, hitherto the only Argument
> Heroic deem'd, chief maistry to dissect
> With long and tedious havoc fabl'd Knights
> In Battles feign'd;   (27–31)

Sedulous of course, modifies *me*, and the concluding word of the phrase, *Wars*, introduces a cascade of nominal constructions. *Argument* is in apposition to *Wars*; *maistry*, seemingly in apposition to *Argument*; and an absolute construction (*the better . . . unsung*) interrupts a series of infinitives dependent on *maistry* and a series of nouns dependent on *describe*:

> chief maistry to dissect
> With long and tedious havoc fabl'd Knights
> In Battles feign'd; the better fortitude
> Of Patience and Heroic Martyrdom
> Unsung; or to describe Races and Games,
> Or tilting Furniture, emblazon'd Shields,
> Impreses quaint, Caparisons and Steeds;
> Bases and tinsel Trappings, gorgeous Knights
> At Joust and Tournament; then marshall'd Feast
> Serv'd up in Hall with Sewers, and Seneschals;
> The skill of Artifice or Office mean,   (29–39)

Finally, with one of those last concise turns belonging to the order of negative comparisons, Milton concludes his period:

> Not that which justly gives Heroic name
> To Person or to Poem.   (40–41)

Milton has amply demonstrated that his style is far higher than Virgil's, given certain premises of epic style: continuity, nominal syntax, and asymmetry. Actually, Virgil would never have thought of writing such a period because the centripetal character of his hyperbatic sentences precludes such expansion. Virgilian hyperbaton interweaves words to such an extent that extreme prolongation of the sentence is impossible without losing the sense. And, finally, having no great resources of punctuation, Virgil could not be so free with appositions dependent on appositions and other such Miltonic expansions.

The word *periodic* is generally used of Virgil and Milton with very little precise notion of what a period is or what kinds of periods exist. A period is essentially a sentence which can be divided into units; a simple two-clause sentence is a period. There are, however, variations in the structure of periods that are matters both of sense and grammar. The famous kind of Latin period places the main verb near the end or at the end, with subordinate constructions intervening between subject and verb: *Mary, when she was asked to dance, refused.* This is a primarily prosaic sentence pattern, which has only limited importance in Latin verse. The progressive period, used by Roman historians, may use subordinate and main verbs in a temporal succession, rather than with logical subordination. The typical period of modern languages in the renaissance is, however, an additive or incremental period, whose shape is partly determined by the difficulty of postponing main verbs in these languages. The additive period places the main verb near the beginning (as in the long period of Milton's we have just examined) or perhaps near the middle; the characteristic of this period is the large amount of material that follows the main verb: complements, relative and adverbial clauses, appositions, and so forth. These elements placed after the main verb may, exceptionally, grow to the proportions of Milton's forty-one-line period.

In the additive period we almost always encounter shifts of direction in sense. All the material subsequent to the main verb is in no way logically subordinate to it. Thus Milton leads us from tragic notes to a glimpse into what is to happen ("Heav'n / Now alienated"), a contrastive list of classical epic subjects, and comments on his muse, on his disinclination to write about medieval wars, and on the contrast of what *heroic* truly means. There is a kind of slithery logic here, perhaps, which one is free to reject along with rhetoric and renaissance style, but it seems more pertinent to consider the virtues of the additive period. The ideal of continuity in epic style is realized by Milton to an unprecedented extent in part because of his employment of additive periods.

Some additive periods make a great use of relative and adverbial clauses instead of such densely nominal syntax as that used in the first forty lines of Book IX. Here we see how Milton often moves into a simile by such a period (I am breaking into the larger whole after a semicolon):

> Natheless he so endur'd, till on the Beach
> Of that inflamed Sea, he stood and call'd
> His Legions, Angel Forms, who lay intrans't
> Thick as Autumnal Leaves that strow the Brooks
> In *Vallombrosa*, where th' *Etrurian* shades
> High overarch't imbow'r; or scatter'd sedge
> Afloat, when with fierce Winds *Orion* arm'd
> Hath vext the Red-Sea Coast, whose waves o'erthrew
> *Busiris* and his *Memphian* Chivalry,
> While with perfidious hatred they pursu'd
> The Sojourners of *Goshen*, who beheld
> From the safe shore thir floating Carcasses
> And broken Chariot Wheels, so thick bestrown
> Abject and lost lay these, covering the Flood,
> Under amazement of thir hideous change.   (I, 299–313)

The brilliantly shifting pictures demonstrate how the additive period can serve primarily to draw images together, with no pretense of logical succession. Here Milton uses a nominal line, rhythmically complete in itself, to conclude the finite verbal clauses. Such lines occur with a certain regularity and can have the function of re-establishing syntactic as well as rhythmic balance. They correspond to the Latin idea of the strong line, beautiful in itself to the point of seeming slightly detached from its context. Such lines tend to be heavily nominal. Elsewhere the period may move forward in time, as in Book I, lines 364–75, where the future terrestrial activities of the fallen angels are envisaged. Suspensive syntax, as in the model Latin expository period, is not common (an example of it can be found in Book X, lines 137–43), for suspension impairs the forward impulse Milton generally strives for.

Periods are often accompanied by shorter sentences. It was not a classical notion to write in nothing but substantial periods. One period in Book IX demonstrates especially well the dual and opposing tendencies of Milton's syntax, toward expansion and toward ellipsis or brevity:

> Shall that be shut to Man, which to the Beast
> Is open? or will God incense his ire
> For such a petty Trespass, and not praise
> Rather your dauntless virtue, whom the pain
> Of Death denounc't, whatever thing Death be,
> Deterr'd not from achieving what might lead
> To happier life, knowledge of Good and Evil;
> Of good, how just? of evil, if what is evil
> Be real, why not known, since easier shunn'd?
> God therefore cannot hurt ye, and be just;
> Not just, not God; not fear'd then, nor obey'd:
> Your fear itself of Death removes the fear.   (IX, 691–702)

The *or* and *and* of the early part of the passage are characteristic of Milton's expansion and amplification, but the period dwindles into a dense argument, doubtless to show the serpent's great subtlety. This argument, with its elliptic syntax, shows how phrases constructed without finite verbs often belong to the harsh or rough style; they interrupt linear, regular grammatical progression and can produce an effect of heaviness. Milton uses one of his smooth, whole lines to round off the development and adorns it with an ostentatious figure.

In general, expanding syntax is identified with finite verbs and forward movement; contracted syntax, with ellipsis, lack of verbs, and nominal constructions such as appositions or prepositional phrases, which slow the sentence movement and often indicate states rather than actions. There are some analogies with Racine's syntactic variations, but Milton's structures are on a larger scale suitable to epic sweep, and his syntactic possibilities are greater than what seemed tolerable in French. For example, Milton is said to use distinctly more prepositional phrases than other poets, and here is a cluster of them, which probably could not be imitated in any other modern European language, the English preposition being stronger than most:

> Sea he had searcht and Land
> From *Eden* over *Pontus*, and the Pool
> *Maeotis*, up beyond the River *Ob*;

> Downward as far Antarctic; and in length
> West from *Orontes* to the Ocean barr'd
> At *Darien* . . .   (IX, 76–81)

Accumulations of adjectives are similarly slow in movement:

> Perverse, all monstrous, all prodigious things,
> Abominable, inutterable, and worse
> Than Fables yet have feign'd . . .   (II, 625–27)

Milton even narrates with his dense style:

> Nor hee thir outward only with the Skins
> Of Beasts, but inward nakedness, much more
> Opprobrious, with his Robe of righteousness,
> Arraying cover'd from his Father's sight.   (X, 220–23)

Here we notice that the delaying element in the movement is not simply the one participle but even more the contrasting formula *not only . . . but*, which we have seen versions of in the introduction of Book IX and which forms such a characteristic part of the dense syntax of seventeenth-century poetry. Such narration is rather unclassical and reflects, like certain other elements of style, the strong connections of Milton's language with contemporary poetry. This is not quite Góngora's pace of narration, but it certainly is not Homer's.

Given the abundance of elements which thicken and slow down syntactic movement it is most important for Milton to join his sentences and the parts of his sentences with linking words and coordinating terms to create forward syntactic movement. These provide movement within the sentence, to begin with, and join independent clauses in a continuous movement. Yet sometimes one is not sure whether Milton's abundance of *yet*, *but*, and *and* indicates connection between clauses or within clauses, since he freely omits pronouns:

> At once as far as Angels ken he views
> The dismal Situation waste and wild,
> A Dungeon horrible, on all sides round
> As one great Furnace flam'd, yet from those flames
> No light, but rather darkness visible
> Serv'd only to discover sights of woe,
> Regions of sorrow, doleful shades, where peace
> And rest can never dwell, hope never comes
> That comes to all; but torture without end
> Still urges, and a fiery Deluge . . .   (I, 59–68)

Or is a great favorite of Milton's for coordination within clauses:

> Thus with the Year
> Seasons return, but not to me returns
> Day, or the sweet approach of Ev'n or Morn,
> Or sight of vernal bloom, or Summer's Rose,
> Or flocks, or herds, or human face divine.   (III, 40–44)

This famous passage is a striking example of sudden freedom of movement with syntactic simplicity. The commas do not impede in the slightest the strong feeling of continuity. There are also examples of triple alternate sentences, three main clauses connected by *or* (I, 264–70, 314–29).

Between main clauses *for* is an important conjunction, with its ambiguity: *for* clauses can be punctuated as independent or subordinate; in Greek and Latin the corresponding words introduce an independent clause, but we cannot be sure how Milton felt about it:

> foul defeat
> Hath lost us Heav'n, and all this mighty Host
> In horrible destruction laid thus low,
> As far as Gods and Heav'nly Essences
> Can perish: for the mind and spirit remains
> Invincible, and vigor soon returns.   (I, 135–40)

For introduces a new thought and is consequently strong in forward movement. But perhaps Milton's most ingenious linkage is to use the accusative pronoun:

> Him the Almighty Power
> Hurl'd headlong flaming from th' Ethereal Sky.   (I, 44–45)

Him becomes as strong a resumptive word as *and* or *or*. Milton has taken the normal minor English sentence form *him I see*, used even in colloquial language to distinguish things, and made it into a powerful term of continuity (see also III, 31, 21).

II

Milton's grammar in *Paradise Lost* has been statistically analyzed, but the results are not exactly true to our impressions as readers, since Milton varies his style with his material, just as Homer and Virgil did, according to the ancient critics.[2] Milton's variations seem to me

2. See Ronald David Emma, *Milton's Grammar* (The Hague, 1964). Other general studies of Milton's style are E. M. W. Tillyard, *The Miltonic Setting: Past and Present*

more marked, however, and a very interesting example of one is the opening of Book I. Like most of the examples we have used up to this point, it belongs distinctly to high style, but it is not in quite the same high style as the beginning of Book IX or other sections. In the two invocations, to the Muse and to the Spirit, Milton chose to emphasize doublings and parallelisms:

> Of Man's First Disobedience and the Fruit
> Of that Forbidden Tree, whose mortal taste
> Brought Death into the World, and all our woe,
> With loss of *Eden*, till one greater Man
> Restore us, and regain the blissful Seat,
> Sing, Heav'nly Muse, that on the secret top
> Of *Oreb*, or of *Sinai*, didst inspire
> That Shepherd, who first taught the chosen Seed,
> In the Beginning how the Heav'ns and Earth
> Rose out of *Chaos*: Or if *Sion* Hill
> Delight thee more, and *Siloa's* Brook that flow'd
> Fast by the Oracle of God; I thence
> Invoke thy aid to my advent'rous Song.   (I, 1–13)

The opening line contains the zeugmatic joining of the concrete *Fruit* and the abstract *Disobedience*. The parallel results of these two things, death and woe, are arranged asymmetrically, a prepositional phrase being attached to the first (*Death into the World*), but the double direct object is nonetheless evident. The alliteration of *restore* and *regain* stresses their basically synonymous character, as *Fruit* and *Disobedience*, *Restore us* and *regain the Seat* are abstract and concrete ways of saying the same thing. Besides the doublings of *Oreb* and *Sinai*, *Heav'ns and Earth*, and *Sion* and *Siloa*, the clausal structure is double, the *or* joining *Sing* and *I invoke*. Modifiers and other expressions counter the symmetrical pattern to avoid a mechanical effect, but it is still more evident than in most parts of *Paradise Lost*.

In the invocation to the Spirit, it is more the verbs which are doubled:

> And chiefly Thou O Spirit, that dost prefer
> Before all Temples th' upright heart and pure,

(London, 1961), 103–40; Christopher Ricks, *Milton's Grand Style* (Oxford, 1963); Ronald David Emma and John T. Shawcross (eds.), *Language and Style in Milton* (New York, 1967). For variations of style in *Paradise Lost*, see John Steadman, "Demetrius, Tasso, and Stylistic Variation in *Paradise Lost*," *English Studies*, XLVII, 329–41; John T. Shawcross, "The Style and Genre of Paradise Lost," in Thomas Kranidas (ed.), *New Essays on "Paradise Lost"* (Berkeley, 1969), 15–33.

> Instruct me, for Thou know'st; Thou from the first
> Wast present, and with mighty wings outspread
> Dove-like satst brooding on the vast Abyss
> And mad'st it pregnant: What in me is dark
> Illumine, what is low raise and support;
> *That* to the highth of this great Argument
> I may assert Eternal Providence,
> And justify the ways of God to men.   (I, 17–26)

There is a dual construction in *Temples* and *heart*, even though parallelism is lacking; the same may be said for *Thou know'st* and *Thou . . . Wast*, which have a certain binary effect despite their belonging to different types of clauses. *Satst* and *mad'st*, though they belong in the same clause as *Wast*, are close enough to constitute a parallelism of their own. There is another complication in the parallel imperative sentences beginning with *what*: the second one has a double verb, so that there is a parallelism within a parallelism. Again, Milton sought a sort of balanced grandeur, not mannered writing, and therefore we find irregularities like his typical asymmetrical adjectival arrangement, *upright heart and pure*. However, the great closing lines of the passage emphasize the dualities of grammatical structure we have been observing; they constitute a particularly fine example of phrases that complement and even overlap one another, without being idle reduplications.

Doublings and parallelism play a large, if not universal role in French neoclassicism, both in prose and verse, and English neoclassicism after Milton was to exploit binary formulas which suit the couplet. The feeling of balance and symmetry such stylistic details give is indeed imposing but tends to grow monotonous, and Milton made an interesting choice in constructing the opening of *Paradise Lost* along these monumental lines but afterwards using styles which are, to a large extent, asymmetrical like his prosody. Symmetrical units are of course found from time to time; like expansive and elliptical syntax, they give equilibrium to the verse, and Milton feels the need of both. However, it is primarily his façade, so to speak, which makes us very conscious of parallelism.

Book IV contains two of the more curious variations in style. As Satan approaches Eden, he makes a speech which is not in the uplifting, heroic mode of Book I, but represents the harsh, αὐστηρός style:

> Hadst thou the same free Will and Power to stand?
> Thou hadst: whom hast thou then or what to accuse,
> But Heav'n's free Love dealt equally to all?
> Be then his Love accurst, since love or hate,
> To me alike, it deals eternal woe.
> Nay curs'd be thou; since against his thy will
> Chose freely what it now so justly rues.
> Me miserable! which way shall I fly
> Infinite wrath, and infinite despair?
> Which way I fly is Hell; myself am Hell;
> And in the lowest deep a lower deep
> Still threat'ning to devour me opens wide,
> To which the Hell I suffer seems a Heav'n.   (IV, 66–78)

The reasoning is dense with choppy *hypophora*, the raising and answering of one's own question. The logical movement is insistent in a tortuous fashion. There is a syllogism in the lines on love accurst, increasing the feeling of proposition and counterproposition; *curst* is then transferred from love to Satan, as the intricate antitheses build up to the most strident and strange of Milton's Latinisms, "Me miserable!" which represents the Latin accusative of exclamation. Paradoxes follow about hell becoming heaven when confronted with a greater hell. Figures of repetition are prominent, but their effect is less equilibrium than dialectic intricacy. This is indeed a special style, the harsh converse of Satan's heroic affirmations in Book I.

The other interesting section of Book IV for questions of stylistic variation occurs as Satan reaches Eden and the landscape is described:

> So on he fares, and to the border comes
> Of *Eden*, where delicious Paradise,
> Now nearer, Crowns with her enclosure green,
> As with a rural mound the champaign head
> Of a steep wilderness, whose hairy sides
> With thicket overgrown, grotesque and wild,
> Access deni'd; and over head up grew
> Insuperable highth of loftiest shade,
> Cedar, and Pine, and Fir, and branching Palm,
> A Silvan Scene, and as the ranks ascend
> Shade above shade, a woody Theatre
> Of stateliest view.   (IV, 131–42)

The epithets associated with pastoral are the first thing we note. Like all European epithets, as opposed to hyperbatic Virgilian ones, they give a certain solid directness to the lines. Nothing in the sentence structure greatly departs from English poetic tradition. The inversion of the type *access deni'd* was used by all riming poets for the facility of verb rime, and it produces such a pleasant effect of mild elegance that Shakespeare used it intermittently throughout his career, though he was under no constraints of rime. The other inversions are completely native. *Up grew* belongs to the Shakespearean and Spenserian habit of dislocating particles in a way most consonant with the Germanic origins of English. The vocabulary, such as the traditional pastoral list of trees, is generally within the bounds of natural description as Spenser created it, both in the more elaborate eclogues and in *The Faerie Queene*. The comparison with the stage, *Silvan Scene*, and the architectural *Theatre* are in the middle-style fashion of mingling terms of art and nature.

Many other variations in style are to be discovered in *Paradise Lost*; they are part of Milton's thorough absorption and further extension of classical rhetorical theory. Their result is that Milton is at once more detailed and descriptive than Virgil and far more abstract, as in the theological propositions of Book III. His range is greater, for European literature expanded classical ideas of style and proposed more models for imitation.

III

Milton is constantly referred to as Virgilian, his putative virtues and vices being ascribed to the influence of the *Aeneid*. It is worth some serious examination to see what Virgil's epic movement is actually like and how Milton's neoclassicism can be compared with a Roman Augustan style.

To begin with, Virgil's sentence is on a different scale. Whereas Milton's averages thirty-one words, even with omissions of articles and pronouns, Virgil has fewer, generally longer words:

> obstipuit varia confusus imagine rerum
> Turnus et obtutu tacito stetit; aestuat ingens
> uno in corde pudor mixtoque insania luctu
> et furiis agitatus amor et conscia uirtus.[3]

3. Virgil, *Énéide*, ed. Henri Goelzer (2 vols.; Paris, 1956), XII, 665–68, hereinafter cited in the text.

> Turnus, overwhelmed by all this confused news, stood motionless, silent and staring. In his heart boiled at once shame, insane sorrow, love made furious, and the consciousness of his courage.

The first line of the quotation illustrates the tendency to construct a verse with at least one hyperbaton to separate words of the same case (*varia imagine*), a device which makes the line somewhat static, there being no regular, sequential grammatical progression. It is a line very much complete in itself by its elegant word order and is often quoted without the addition of the subject *Turnus* from the next line. The only real movement comes with the coordinate clause *et obtutu*. The second sentence, longer, demonstrates a characteristic kind of Latin enumeration: *mixtoque*, with its hyperbaton and enclitic *and*, has little forward movement; only the last line with its double *et* has the kind of propulsion we associate with many of Milton's enumerations. At the same time, we should recall that the long appositive enumeration at the beginning of Book IX has a Latin kind of irregularity, even if the details are not Latinate. In general, we can see this passage as akin to Milton's irregular correlation of sentence structure and verse line, with its pronounced use of enjambment.

The alternation of static lines created by hyperbaton, which holds everything in a kind of simultaneity rather than allowing progressive movement, with lines whose forward impulse is marked can be seen in the following passage:

> hinc totam infelix uulgatur fama per urbem:
> demittunt mentes, it scissa ueste Latinus
> coniugis attonitus fatis urbisque ruina,
> canitiem immundo perfusam puluere turpans.   (XII, 608–11)

> The bad news spreads throughout the city. People are discouraged. King Latinus comes forward with his clothes torn, thunderstruck by the death of his wife and the ruin of his city, and his hair befouled by filthy dust.

The second line with its two short clauses gives the highest sense of activity; hyperbaton somewhat diminishes the directness of the statement in the first line, and the last two participial lines, each complete in itself, have, by their isolation and solemn word order, a detached quality. One feels no surging movement from the beginning to the end of the passage, and symmetry, more statal than dynamic, dominates. The syntax of this passage with its reliance on participles has analogies with Milton's, but the tendency of each line to contain a well-separated sentence or phrase, elegantly whole and self-contained-seeming in its crisscrossed word order, shows profound syntacticoprosodic differences from Milton's usual practice and even from his possibilities.

The habit of constructing each line as a unit is very strong for Virgil, whether the line has real grammatical independence or not:

> Tydides sed enim scelerumque inuentor Ulixes,
> fatale adgressi sacrato auellere templo
> Palladium caesis summae custodibus arcis,
> corripuere sacram effigiem manibusque cruentis
> uirgineas ausi diuae contingere uittas,
> ex illo fluere ac retro sublapsa referri
> spes Danaum, fractae vires, auersa deae mens.   (II, 164–70)

The son of Tydeus and Ulysses, the inventor of crimes, going to the sacred temple to tear away the fateful Palladium and having killed the guards of the high citadel, seized the sacred image and with their bloody hands dared to touch the virginal fillets of the goddess, and from that time on, the hope of the Greeks collapsed and ebbed away; their strength was broken; the goddess looked no more upon them.

The first line is completely filled with a double subject, and when an element of the sentence reaches such proportions, it becomes autonomous in phrasing. There is an enjambment between the second and third lines, but they are composed of rigorously separated constructions: a perfect active participle with complements and an ablative absolute construction, each designating a distinct action. Although the end of line four belongs in sense to line five, the latter is perfectly complete in itself, an elegant arrangement in which three nominal terms are separated by two verbal forms. The first strongly active verbal line after line four is the sixth, where, as if to make up for the dominance of nouns and participles up to this point, we find a redundancy of verbs with a participle even repeating the verbal action, a common pleonasm in Virgil. This suddenly dramatic clause, with its enjambment, is followed by two equally dramatic ones but of an entirely different structure: the two closing clauses are short with the verb *esse* omitted, a normal variation in high Latin style. What we find here, in short, is a version of delaying constructions and forward impulsion with changes of clause length that, in principle, is like Milton's alternations of surge and sluggishness. The construction, however, is far more unitary, even line-by-line unitary, than Milton's. Asymmetry is a minor, controlled feature of the prosody; only a short expression exceeds the line or anticipates a line at the end of the preceding one. There is a basic integrity of the line that Virgil observes.

In all these examples nominalism dominates without there being even many prepositions. Virgil so extended the use of the ablative case that nouns and their modifiers are not confined and located by prepositions; they stand freely at any point in the line. Prepositions, however, have a virtue in that they clearly, even sharply indicate the progress of grammatical relationships, whereas in Virgil their absence is a further means of slowing one's grasp of the whole, in an effort to create a more imposing idiom.

There is, finally, an almost purely nominal kind of descriptive style in the *Aeneid*:

> Tectum augustum, ingens, centum sublime columnis
> urbe fuit summa, Laurentis regia Pici,
> horrendum siluis et religione parentum.   (VII, 170–72)

There was, at the top of the city, an august, enormous palace, whose roof was borne by a hundred columns, which the Laurentian Picus lived in, and which inspired a sacred terror by the surrounding woods and veneration going back to the forebears.

All the sense here resides in the various relations of nominative and ablative cases, unaided by prepositional or participial indications. This may be taken as an example of the most advanced syntax in Virgil, densely polysyllabic and completely statal. Such rare grammatical beauty can have no correspondence in English. Milton is limited primarily to the apposition or the enumeration for clustering nouns. Of course, the idea of nominalism as characterizing high style remains the same.

I think the most important single fact revealed by a comparison of the sentence structure of Milton and Virgil is Milton's dynamism and the way he uses long sentences and asymmetrical prosody to produce it. Milton is much less concerned with the perfect isolated verse having elegantly balanced grammatical elements. His foward propulsion tends to take precedence over the impeccable self-enclosed line. Virgil's continuity and irregularity lie more in the peculiar structure of the dactylic hexameter. Even the clusters of short sentences joined with *and*s which mark the military activities of Book XII are in many ways a less sophisticated means of creating the sense of movement than Milton's complex techniques. Basically, Milton's higher moments are more periodic than Virgil's, for periodicity (a prosaic pattern in origin) tends to conflict with hyperbaton, which acts as an organizing feature of one- or two-line units and not of great sweeping developments. The reader is always tempted to stop to admire small perfect structures in Virgil, rather than being driven onward by a basically linear form of syntax in which hyperbaton occurs only in small details (as with noun and participle) or on the broad level of inversions like subject and verb, which scarcely impairs grammatical sequentiality. Tasso's hyperbaton, by contrast, is denser, for he is working in the relatively small-scale form of the octave. Tasso uses the shorter sentences of Virgil, and his effects of continuity are of much less imposing dimensions than Milton's. All in all, Milton's aspiration to outdo Virgil in grandeur was completely realized.

IV

Of the ornaments proper to epic, we have so far observed a complex of those that affect Milton's syntax: nominal style, hyperbaton, long sentences, enjambment, and speeches in elaborate rhetoric. The simile we have seen in passing, and Milton's similes belong to the extreme form of high-style digressiveness of which Pindar, as much as the epic poets, was the model. Milton does not often use archaisms, as Virgil did. His most ostentatious imagery is perhaps to be found in "darkness visible," an oxymoron similar to Racine's *flamme si noire* and constituting the same kind of extraordinary ornament in a neoclassical style; but otherwise Milton's imagery, such as rising and falling, is so subdued and related to the action of the poem as only occasionally to strike one as involving an unusual trope:

> but when thou [God] shad'st
> The full blaze of thy beams, and through a cloud
> Drawn round about thee like a radiant Shrine,
> Dark with excessive bright thy skirts appear.   (III, 377–80)

The motivation for the image can be considered, however, as much theological as picturesque.

It is diction in general rather than the isolated image which, as in Virgil, colors the poem most strongly. The joining of abstract and concrete terms characteristic of Racine is the most striking aspect of high seventeenth-century creation of phrases: "th' Eternal Coeternal beam" (III, 2), "Bright effluence of bright essence increate" (III, 6), "From this descent / Celestial virtues rising" (II, 14–15), "Turning our Tortures into horrid Arms" (II, 63), "Mineral fury" (I, 235). These are closely related to the forging of expressions in which normal idiom is altered: "Thither let us tend / From off the tossing of these fiery waves" (I, 183–84), "repose / Your wearied virtue" (I, 319–20), "incense his ire" (IX, 692). Sometimes the wording can clearly be defined as a periphrasis: "Sonorous metal blowing Martial sounds" (I, 540). At other times, the expression seems somewhat expanded but not circuitous: "Clash'd on thir sounding shields the din of war" (I, 668). It happens that a phrase may contain fewer words than the normal expression: "deigns / Her nightly visitation" (IX, 21–22). These phrases are very similar to ones we have seen in Shakespeare and Racine, for high European style makes abundant use of abstraction in combination with other terms, a usage which is much more limited in Virgil. One difference from Shakespeare is that we encounter fewer surprising clashes between the abstract and the concrete; in contrast to Racine, Milton does not exploit a body of established metonymies, for English poetic diction had not developed so elaborately codified a system of them as had French.

The most general kind of movement in Milton's diction is perhaps the alternation between circuitousness or expanded ways of speaking and the tightness of sententia, used in the sense of a sharply phrased, interesting thought. This is the semantic correspondence to Milton's expanded and contracted or elliptic syntax, and one or two of our earlier examples show them working together, although semantic concision does not always go along with elliptic grammar in Milton. In Book III, there are good examples of these contrasting kinds of expression:

> Only begotten Son, seest thou what rage
> Transports our adversary, whom no bounds

> Prescrib'd, no bars of Hell, nor all the chains
> Heapt on him there, nor yet the main Abyss
> Wide interrupt can hold; so bent he seems
> On desperate revenge, that shall redound
> Upon his own rebellious head.   (III, 80–86)

>   if I foreknew,
> Foreknowledge had no influence on their fault,
> Which had no less prov'd certain unforeknown.   (III, 117–19)

Both passages present paradoxes, the first loosely and discursively put, the second with dense polyptoton. Milton often uses word play for conceptual sharpness.[4] Polyptoton, paronomasia, and other such figures are closely allied with theological reflections rather than constituting the *delectatio* of middle style, for they are aids to thought. Similarly contrasting passages can be found in the deliberations of the fallen angels:

> Too well I see and rue the dire event,
> That with sad overthrow and foul defeat
> Hath lost us Heav'n, and all this mighty Host
> In horrible destruction laid thus low,
> As far as Gods and Heav'nly Essences
> Can perish.   (I, 134–39)

>   If then his Providence
> Out of our evil seek to bring forth good,
> Our labour must be to pervert that end,
> And out of good still to find means of evil.   (I, 162–65)

Again both passages contain an essential theological notion, but in the first, the important antithesis is slipped in almost casually in what seems the afterthought of an additive period, whereas the second passage is constructed like a formal proposition with its *if* clause and conclusion.

Milton faced a problem which did not occur for other poets of the high style such as Virgil, Tasso, or Racine. The amount of conceptual material his subject demanded is very great, and he was obliged to draw on varied rhetorical resources to work it into the texture of his poem. At times the theological considerations are blended into the narrative line; elsewhere they stand out, but with striking success as

---

4. For paronomasia, see F. T. Prince, *The Italian Element in Milton's Verse* (Oxford, 1954), 123–39.

poetry. The major conclusion to *Paradise Lost*, from the thematic rather than the narrative point of view, is found in an exchange between Adam and Michael; Adam summarizes his thoughts on the events of the poem:

> Henceforth I learn, that to obey is best,
> And love with fear the only God, to walk
> As in his presence, ever to observe
> His providence, and on him sole depend,
> Merciful over all his works, with good
> Still overcoming evil, and by small
> Accomplishing great things, by things deem'd weak
> Subverting worldly strong, and worldly wise
> By simply meek; that suffering for Truth's sake
> Is fortitude to highest victory,
> And to the faithful Death the Gate of Life.   (XII, 561–71)

This long sententious passage is the object of Milton's greatest care in prosody. The lines are beautifully asymmetrical in the relation of syntax to verse until the full-verse conclusion. The figures are arranged so that a gradual increase in antithesis is climaxed with a contrast in the form of an image. The archangel replies with a speech that at first is expansive and enumeratory:

> This having learnt, thou hast attain'd the sum
> Of wisdom; hope no higher, though all the Stars
> Thou knew'st by name, and all th' ethereal Powers,
> All secrets of the deep . . .   (XII, 575–78)

But his conclusion is a sententia:

> then wilt thou not be loath
> To leave this Paradise, but shalt possess
> A paradise within thee, happier far.   (XII, 585–87)

This figure by which the meaning of *death*, and then *paradise*, is changed from worldly to spiritual is the characteristic one of Christian thought and rhetoric.

Milton did not make an allegory of a Christian idea as Racine did in *Phèdre* but directly expressed his theology, a fact which has a broad influence on the lexical color of *Paradise Lost*. In the interests of unity of vocabulary the abstract element is high and, by the nature of English abstractions, polysyllabic. All this fits the general theory of epic diction except that the traditional prescription was for imposing words, especially nouns, and Milton, like other neoclassicists, took this to be best realized by an abundance of abstractions or near abstractions. The near abstraction is an interesting phenomenon, and this peculiar aspect of Milton's high diction, where the words, though designating concrete things, have an air of abstraction, is nicely illustrated by these lines:

> In order came the grand infernal Peers,
> Midst came thir mighty Paramount, and seem'd
> Alone th' Antagonist of Heav'n, nor less
> Than Hell's dread Emperor with pomp Supreme,
> And God-like imitated State; him round
> A Globe of fiery Seraphim inclos'd
> With bright imblazonry, and horrent Arms.   (II, 507–13)

Peers, Paramount, and *Emperor* are actual beings but conceived of in an abstract hierarchy. *Pomp* tends to lose its idea of procession, in favor of that of grandeur. *Globe,* a precise military term in Latin, is a shape in English; likewise *horrent,* however well one knows Latin, has very strong feelings of dread about it, as well as the simple sense of standing straight up. Even *him round,* a splendidly chosen hyperbaton, seems vaguer than the normal spatial indication *around him. Imblazonry* is a typically neoclassical use of the abstract form of the term *blazon,* giving a blurred visual sense. The passage may indeed have ironic reference to the English government, but its verbal devices are exemplary of secular, epideictic neoclassical diction.

V

I believe that the common stylistic tendencies of Milton and Racine are numerous if we make allowances for the differences of genre, which, of course, to them were clear and absolute. The high status accorded the abstraction, which, however, is constantly blended smoothly with the general or figurative, reflects a great faith in the realities of intellectual distinctions, whether theological, ethical, or psychological. Their rhetoric can be seen as the final absorption of the classical tradition, where the domains of genre theory, kinds of diction, and topics of invention are all thoroughly understood and harmoniously employed to achieve the great ends of literature— epic and tragedy. It is, in a sense, fitting to end our discussion with them, since we have been tracing the elaboration and heightening of style since Petrarch, whereas any fuller consideration of neoclassical verse would lead necessarily to La Fontaine's revival of low-style comic diction, and finally, to the enormous amount of thought and energy spent on perfecting genres and styles which had been overlooked by major figures up to then.

Alexander Pope tried to explain in part his relation to Milton in the following way:

> I have nothing to say for rhyme but that I doubt whether a poem can support itself without it in our language, unless it be stiffened with such strange words as are likely to destroy our language itself.[5]

Pope refers specifically to the remarks on "The Verse" prefaced to *Paradise Lost*, in which Milton points out that he has returned to the true epic manner of Homer and Virgil, with its free enjambment, unimpeded by rime sounds. Of course, there is more to the question than Pope implies. The most important English neoclassical poets who followed Milton—and the late history of neoclassical poetry is primarily English—were given to middle-style or low-style genres like the didactic poem (Dryden's *The Hind and the Panther*, among others; Pope's *Essay on Man* and *Essay on Criticism*) or satire of various kinds. They were obsessed by epic, but their obsession took the form of translations, Dryden's Virgil and Pope's Homer, or of mock epic, Pope's *Rape of the Lock* and *Dunciad*. Their original work, though not without its Miltonic echoes, marks a step down from high style in the adoption of the couplet and a limited vocabulary. Exploiting the classical genres no one had yet excelled in, they managed to work out certain problems with great success. Their rimes are more interesting than French neoclassical rimes had been on the whole, and they devised styles of narration in closed couplets which are far more successful than French epic narration.[6] The alexandrine couplet had achieved its most expressive form in tragedy and comedy, but Dryden in *Absalom and Achitophel* and Pope in his mock epics cre-

---

5. See Joseph Spence, *Anecdotes, Observations, and Characters of Books and Men* (London, 1852), 200.

6. For rime and binary rhetoric in Pope, see Maynard Mack, "Wit and Poetry and Pope," in James L. Clifford and Louis A. Landa (eds.), *Pope and His Contemporaries* (Oxford, 1949), 20–40; Alexander Pope, *Selected Poetry and Prose*, ed. William K. Wimsatt, Jr. (New York, 1951), xxix–xxxiii.

ated a much more brilliant kind of couplet narrative than the French. Even works in similar genres, like Boileau's mock epic, *Le Lutrin*, do not have the poetic value of the English works, and it is to some extent the study of Milton's diction that permitted the English poets to excel in narration. The following portrait of Achitophel reflects Milton's nominal, appositional manner:

> Of these the false Achitophel was first;
> A name to all succeeding ages curst:
> For close designs and crooked counsels fit,
> Sagacious, bold, and turbulent of wit,
> Restless, unfix'd in principles and place,
> In pow'r unpleas'd, impatient of disgrace;
> A fiery soul, which, working out its way,
> Fretted the pigmy body to decay:
> And o'er-informed the tenement of clay.[7]

Milton is more involved than it may seem at first in the afterhistory of neoclassicism. Pope and Dryden were able to make use of his work in their own genres, rather than competing on the same ground, as Voltaire did, when he wrote tragedies in an essentially Racinian form.

7. John Dryden, "Absalom and Achitophel," 150–58, in Louis I. Bredvold (ed.), *The Best of Dryden* (New York, 1933).

Conclusion

We have observed that there is a constant evolution of theory and stylistic practice in the renaissance and seventeenth century, which is, however, not a simple one. Various aspects of ancient theory are drawn on at different times, and they may be understood more literally or adapted in such a way as to be utterly transformed. Sometimes, as in Ronsard's Pindaric odes, there is a more direct concern for the imitation of classical literary texts than for general theory. The picture is a complex one, but it may also be seen from a slightly different and quite interesting perspective. There are certain features of European styles which the classical rhetoricians were not especially concerned with and which therefore represent something characteristic in European sensibility.

The question of the dense or prominent use of abstractions and figurative terms, especially when they reflect a body of thought, did not arise in antiquity. From Petrarch on, styles bear a certain philosophical stamp. Faculty psychology, which develops with Augustine and Christianity, affects the use of abstractions, and the drama of conflicting parts of the individual becomes more stylistically explicit. Neoplatonism introduced a theology that, as it appears in a poet like Scève, is parallel to Christianity, with a vocabulary somewhere between the figurative and the metaphysical. Finally, the growth of elaborately written poetry on Christian subjects involved the use of a whole special system of meaning, based on Christian symbolism and *figurae*. Although the Greek origins of this system have been abundantly discussed,[1] we do not find any unambiguous use of

---

1. Jean Pépin, *Mythe et allégorie: Les Origines grecques et les contestations judéo-chrétiennes* (Paris, 1958).

highly developed metaphysical and allegorical dimensions of meaning in high classical literature.

Another aspect of European theory and practice involves dispositio, the structuring of poems, which receives only a very general, quite theoretical treatment in the principal classical rhetoricians, who were interested in details of structure only as they concerned the oration. The intellectualizing element in the European literary imagination, to which we may ascribe the use of systems of abstract, figurative, symbolic, and figural language, also manifests itself here. The sonnet is the most obvious example of a form whose structure was emphasized by both thematic articulation and the prominent use of figures, such as elaborate images, anaphora, enumeration, apposition, and asyndeton. Other kinds of poems exhibit features imitated from the classical theory of orational structure. The sharp, almost schematized deployment of the topics of invention in a play like *Andromaque* represents a final form of stressing overt structural elements, quite as much as the more famous unities and other conventions of French neoclassical theater.

The employment of various kinds of harsh, austere, rough, forceful, or violent style goes beyond the classical usage for such textures. In the lyric, from the troubadours through the seventeenth century, there is an exploitation of asperity and strained effects which has attracted particular attention in the twentieth century, and it is important to understand the classical theoretical background of these styles. The notion of mannerism, in particular, is somewhat clarified by reference to rhetorical tradition.

The opposition of mannerist and baroque styles, which has often been hazy from the theoretical point of view, acquires a certain new perspective in the light of rhetorical principles. Moreover, baroque poetry appears to belong largely to middle style, but a middle style reflecting the intensification of ornament and ostentatious effect which underlies the whole development of poetry from Petrarch through the early seventeenth century. The unambiguously high styles of the first half of the seventeenth century seem, however, not to be essentially baroque at all, even though their classicizing character naturally shares some features with baroque styles, because of a common rhetorical origin and tendency toward elevation.

Finally, the higher neoclassical styles of the seventeenth century reveal a precarious quality. They are the culmination of the long, varied efforts of reaching toward the utmost grandeur, and the moderns, in their quarrel with the partisans of the ancients at the end of the century, were convinced that the summits of classical poetry, Homer in particular, did not show an adequate sense of elevation, compared with modern works. But the seventeenth-century conception of grandeur was grounded, more than the moderns realized, on the ideas of a unique moment in European politics, theology, and social structure. The minor work of high neoclassicism has not proved so enduring as the lesser writing in earlier modes, and even the major works have seemed to many in the twentieth century as less truly elevated, less classical, more narrow than the great works of preceding periods. So the long humanist effort to achieve a magnificence comparable to that of ancient literature ended in, if not a pyrrhic victory, at least a somewhat illusory conception of permanence and universality of stylistic and intellectual values. The examples of Milton and Virgil are perhaps the best, for each had formidable gifts and a powerful conception of classical high style: they represent the culminations of ancient classicism and European neoclassicism in all their similarities and diversities of rhetoric, in its total range from invention through composition at all levels to diction.

Glossary of Technical Terms

Greek Terms

αὐστηρός. Austere or harsh in style.
γλαφυρός. Smooth and lyrical in style.
δεινός. Forcible or violent in style.
θαυμαστόν. The wondrous.
μεγαλοπρεπής. Of high decorum, pertaining to the stately grand style.
ξενός, ξενικός. Strange, original, and unfamiliar in style.

Other Terms

ADYNATON. A comparison with the impossible: "Hell will freeze over before . . ."
ADMIRATIO. Wonder.
AGRÉMENS. Ornaments.
ALLEGORIA. A sentence or a brief passage expressing a thought in figurative terms. Many proverbs are *allegoriae*.
AMPLIFICATIO. Heightening in the classical sense; lengthening in the medieval sense persistent in the renaissance.
ANAPHORA. Beginning lines, phrases, or sentences with the same word.
ARS POETICA. A work giving precepts for writing poetry.
ASPREZZA. Harshness of style.
ASYNDETON. Lack of coordinating connectives between parallel words or sentences.
AUDACIOR ORNATUS. The bold, often illogical or hyperbolic expressions of high style, intended to move rather than delight the reader.
AUREATION. The use, in English especially, of abundant Latinisms.
CANZONE. A long lyric in several stanzas with often complicated prosodic structure.
CANZONIERE. A collection of lyric poems.

CATACHRESIS. A mixed or strained trope.

CHANT ROYAL. A long, complex form of medieval French poem.

CHRISTIAN DOUBLE MEANINGS. The spiritual and worldly senses of a word like *death* are equally real, unlike the concrete and figurative senses of *death* in secular, especially Petrarchist, poetry.

CHRONOGRAPHIA. Description of the time of day or year.

CONCEIT. A figure which produces a witty or ingenious, strange impression.

COPIA. Abundance of words and ideas.

COPULA. Verbs like *to be, to seem,* and *to become.*

CORRECTIO. A figure in which, after a statement, the poet says, "but now" or "rather" and substitutes a new, usually stronger statement for the first one.

CORRESPONDENCES. The medieval and renaissance belief that the details of the physical world have moral-symbolic meanings established by God. Hierarchy is a frequent part of the interpretation of correspondences.

DEDUCTUM. Thin, used of low style.

DEICTIC. Pertaining to demonstrative pronouns and adjectives.

DELECTATIO. Charm, a principle characteristic of middle style.

DIGRESSION. Often considered an elevating, striking figure rather than an instance of poor composition.

DISPOSITIO. Composition or structure.

DISTRIBUTORY SONNET. *See* VERS RAPPORTÉS.

DIZAIN. A ten-line stanza.

DOUBLETS. Any two words bearing some relation such as an etymological one or which are used in parallel fashion syntactically: A and B.

ENTHYMEME. An elliptical syllogism used in literature.

EPIDEICTIC. Pertaining to praise. Epideictic rhetoric is distinguished from deliberative and judicial rhetoric.

EPITHETON. The generalized use of epithets.

EXORDIUM. The opening section of an oration.

FIGURA. A theological conception of biblical interpretation by which events of the Old Testament represent those of the new; but unlike symbols, they retain their concrete, individual, historical reality.

GALIMATIAS. Nonsense, poetic jargon.

GENERA DICENDI. The styles recognized by ancient rhetoric.

GENUS GRANDE. High style.

GENUS SUBTILE FLORIDIUS. The somewhat ornamented low style.

GRAVITAS. Weight, a characteristic of high style.

HYPERBATON. Displacement of normal word order.

HYPERBOLE. A trope which is exaggerated by logical standards.

HYPOTAXIS. Use of subordinating constructions, especially clauses with finite verbs.

IMITATIO. The mimetic aspect of literature, its depiction of life.

LANGUE NOBLE. The diction of the neoclassical tragedy, lacking in certain ornaments of epic or odic high style.

LITOTES. An understatement using the negative for the positive: "I am not adverse to it" in the sense of "I am in favor of it."

LONGINUS' SUBLIME. The theory that greatness of expression is especially to be found in simple phrases like "Let there be light."

MEIOSIS. A belittling expression, as when Achilles calls Agamemnon "dogface" (*Iliad*, I).

MERAVIGLIA. Wonder or *admiratio*, especially associated with the baroque.

METAPHOR. Three types of noun metaphor may be distinguished: the metonymy; the concrete of abstract: "grapes of wrath," and the fuller genitive or relational form: A is the B of C; A is to B as C is to D.

METAPHORE FILÉE. A continuous metaphor.

METAPLASM. Deformation or shift of sound within a word, such as *crocodile, cocrodillo, cocodrillo.*

METONYMY. A one-word metaphor, often conventionalized.

NEO-LATIN. The form of nonmedieval Latin written in the renaissance.

ORATION. A speech divided into several parts, usually including an exordium, a narrative, an argument, a refutation of objections, and a peroration or conclusion.

ORNATUS. Stylistic ornament.

OXYMORON. Yoking of contrary adjectives and nouns: "darkness visible."

PARATAXIS. Sentences constructed without subordinated clauses.

PARONOMASIA. A play on words or pun.

PARVUS. Small, used of low style.

PATHOS. The swaying of the audience by emotional rather than logical means.

PENSÉE NEUVE, POINTE DE PENSÉE. A new thought or image, a striking *sententia*.

PERIOD. A sentence composed of two or more easily distinguishable parts, such as clauses or long phrases.

PERIPHRASIS. A longer, usually figurative expression replacing a more direct one. The peculiarly baroque periphrasis consists of a noun and adjective: *ergoté trompette* (cock).

PIACEVOLE, PIACEVOLEZZA. *Delectatio*, charm, pleasingness, a principle characteristic of middle style.

POLYPTOTON. Using words with the same root in proximity: "encourage the courageous."

POLYSYNDETON. Using a coordinating conjunction with each member of a series: A and B and C and D.

PROSOPOPOEIA. Representing an abstraction or an absent person as speaking.

QUESTIONE DELLA LINGUA. The sixteenth-century argument over what linguistic form vernacular written language should take.

SENTENTIA. Either a maxim or a brilliantly stated thought of more particular application.

SERMO HUMILIS. The low style associated with the Gospels and later Christian writing.

SOUND FIGURES. Figures affecting sound not sense, such as alliteration and anaphora.

SPRACHGEFÜHL. The sense of idiom possessed by the more capable native speakers of a language.

STICHOMYTHIA. A dramatic arrangement by which characters speak in alternating verses.

SUSPENDED SYNTAX. A form of hyperbaton in which words which go together to form the essential part of the syntax are lengthily separated; often it is the subject and verb which are widely separated.

TENUIS. Slim, used of low style.

TOPICS OF INVENTION. The types of argument in judicial rhetoric.

TROPE. A figure in the metaphorical domain, like metonymy, simile, hypallage. Hyperbaton is sometimes included as a trope because it is also a "difficult" ornament.

TYPOLOGICAL SYMBOLISM. The conceiving of history as containing recurrent identifiable types like Caesar's war against Rome and the Protestants' wars against Catholic factions.

UMGANGSSPRACHE. Everyday language.

UT PICTURA POESIS. The interpretation given to this fragmentary expression is that poetry should be like painting.

VERBUM PROPRIUM. A precise noun to designate something.

VERS RAPPORTÉS. An arrangement by which several subjects are grouped together, followed by their verbs, also grouped, and finally by all the appropriate objects.

VOCATIVE. A noun used as a direct address.

ZEUGMA. Parallelism of the abstract and concrete: "clad in white linen and shining integrity."

Index

Aeschylus, 52, 122, 157
Alamanni, Luigi, 3
Aphthonius, 91
Ariosto, Ludovico, 54–58, 61, 105, 107
Aristotle, 1, 23, 52, 112, 115, 125, 141,
144, 151, 156, 194, 262, 269
Aubigné, Agrippa d', 46–49, 53, 124,
143, 151, 157, 171, 196, 200, 224, 268;
Les Tragiques, 115–122
Austere style. *See* Harsh style

Baldwin, Charles Sears, 4
Barnes, Barnabe, 162–63
Baroque style, 1, 103, 163, 164, 167,
174, 194–201, 202–32, 246–50, 269,
280, 286, 309
Belleau, Remy, 111
Bembo, Pietro, 36, 56, 85, 86
Bible, 161, 163, 181
Bion, 64
Bloom, Stephen, 3
Boccaccio, Giovanni, 56
Boileau, Nicolas, 264
Bossuet, Jacques-Bénigne, 221
Bouhours, Dominique, 124, 172, 194,
200, 245

Calderón, Pedro, 247–50
Callimachus, 19
Carducci, Giosuè, 18
Castiglione, Baldassare, 72–73, 74
Catachresis, 13, 145, 174, 240, 244
Catullus, 61, 212, 217
Cavalcanti, Guido, 10
Chapman, George, 158
Chassignet, Jean-Baptiste, 160–62, 182,
200
Chaucer, Geoffrey, 105
Cicero, 1, 262, 268
Cinthio, Giraldi, 123, 278

Conceit, 12–13, 41–43, 143–45, 172,
183, 189, 205, 206, 209, 225, 230–31,
245
Corbière, Tristan, 166
Corneille, Pierre, 246–47, 250, 259, 262,
266, 280
Correctio, 170, 173, 196–97
Crashaw, Richard, 167–71, 175, 177,
199, 214
Cretin, Guillaume, 89–90

Daniel, Arnaut, 6–7, 10
Daniel, Samuel, 50, 82
Dante Alighieri, 7–8, 19, 86
Della Casa, Giovanni, 28–29
Demetrius, 1, 5, 52, 114, 122, 157,
159
Desportes, Philippe, 45–46, 49, 225
Dionysius of Halicarnassus, 1, 5, 52,
114, 122, 131, 157, 159
Donne, John, 64, 84–85, 86, 112, 123,
158, 159; "Anniversaries," 189–92;
"Goodfriday, 1613," 192–94; *Songs
and Sonnets*, 70–82, 190, 194
Drayton, Michael, 82–83
Drelincourt, Laurent, 165–66, 174
Droncke, Peter, 3
Dryden, John, 306–307, 242–44
Du Bartas, Guillaume, 113, 117, 196
Du Bellay, 1, 3, 36, 49, 51, 156
Du Bois-Hus, Gabriel, 238–39

Elegy, 3, 54, 61–65, 218, 264–66
Ennius, 105
Enumeration, 38–39, 41, 44, 51, 113,
117, 122, 139, 161, 163, 165, 166–67,
173, 174, 182, 184, 188, 195–96,
203–204, 228, 242, 309
Estienne, Henri, 68
Euripides, 122

Ficino, Marsilio, 31
Figura, 181–83, 187, 189
Fleming, Paul, 163

Gadoffre, Gilbert, 3
Gardner, Helen, 79
Garnier, Robert, 123, 246
Gascoigne, George, 67–68, 196, 197
Góngora, Luis de, 207–214, 218, 221, 292
Greek Anthology, 218
Greene, Robert, 50
Greiffenberg, Catharina Regina von, 163
Gryphius, Andreas, 163
Guinizelli, Guido, 10
Guyon, Jeanne, 177

Hanke, Martin, 163
Hardison, O. B., 3
Harsh style, 5, 6, 7, 8–9, 44, 52, 81, 91, 98–99, 113, 130, 142, 145, 147, 150, 151, 157, 159, 172, 192, 218, 295–96, 309
Herbert, George, 186–89, 192, 199
Hermogenes, 52, 54, 56, 114, 122, 157
High style, 1, 52, 86–114, 122, 123, 142, 150, 156, 172, 176, 177, 179, 232, 235, 236, 239, 241, 242, 245, 246, 275, 279–80, 288, 294, 303, 310
Hoffmannswaldau, Christian von, 163
Homer, 36, 48, 113, 212, 275, 284, 285, 292, 293, 306, 310
Hopil, Claude, 177
Hopkins, Gerard Manley, 166
Horace, 16, 19, 60, 92–95, 104, 113, 146, 211, 217, 231
Hyperbaton, 18, 27, 102, 109, 204, 208, 209, 214, 280, 285, 289, 296–97, 298–99, 301
Hyperbole, 14, 40, 43, 151–56, 199, 244

Irregular beauty, 219, 220, 224, 225

Jodelle, Etienne, 44–45, 161
John of the Cross, 177
John the Evangelist, 179
Jonson, Ben, 83–85, 112, 157, 159, 228, 232
Juvenal, 122
Juxtaposition of concrete, abstract, figurative, 13–14, 41, 51, 130–34, 183,

210–11, 213–14, 233–35, 240–41, 244, 251–57, 280, 302, 308–309

Kuhlmann, Quirinus, 163

La Ceppède, Jean de, 168–69, 179–85, 192, 198, 199, 201
La Fontaine, Jean de, 306
Laforgue, Jules, 166
La Mesnardière, Hippolyte de, 214–17
Langue noble, 263, 280
Lanham, Richard A., 4
Lausberg, Heinrich, 4
Le Moyne, Pierre, 175–79
Leopardi, Giacomo, 18
Lewis, Clive Staples, 49, 67
L'Hermite, Tristan, 220–21, 239–42, 245
Longinus, 113
Loos, Adolph, 3
Low style, 20, 22, 54–85, 116, 186, 189, 192, 196, 202, 214, 217, 218, 232, 264, 265, 306
Lucan, 115, 120–21, 151, 171

Malherbe, François de, 232–35, 245, 244, 263, 264
Mannerist style, 103, 140, 158–59, 164, 200–201, 268, 309
Mantuan (Battista Spagnoli), 65
Marcabru, 6
Marino, Giambattista, 202–205, 207, 218, 219–20, 225, 231
Marlowe, Christopher, 123, 202
Marot, Clément, 61, 66, 87–89
Marston, John, 158
Martial de Brives (Paul Dumas), 163–65, 174, 176
Marvell, Andrew, 216; "The Mower to the Glowworms," 222–23; "To his Coy Mistress," 217–18; "Upon Appleton House," 228–31
Maynard, François, 217
Meraviglia. See Surprise
Michelangelo Buonarroti, 29–30, 52
Middle style, 24–53, 52, 111, 113, 142–43, 144, 145, 156, 164, 169, 172, 174, 175, 179, 190, 199, 202, 206, 214, 217, 225, 235, 237, 239, 242, 244, 297, 303, 309
Milton, John, 29, 66, 90, 104, 115, 202, 207, 218, 271, 283, 284–307, 310
Minturno, Antonio, 86, 119

Montaigne, Michel de, 161
Moschus, 64

Nashe, Thomas, 50

Ode, 87–95, 176, 217, 244, 245, 257, 280
Oration, 15, 94, 139, 309
Ovid, 21, 61, 97, 202, 217, 265–66

Pascal, Blaise, 221
Pastoral, 64–67
Paul, Saint, 198
Periphrasis, 174, 197–98
Petrarch, Francesco, 8–23, 24, 26, 32, 35, 37, 38, 44, 56, 70–71, 86, 104, 105, 123, 130, 175, 199, 205, 218, 220, 286, 287, 306, 308, 309
Petrarchism, 9–12, 14, 29, 30, 40, 47, 49, 85
Pindar, 36, 52, 60, 86, 87, 90–92, 95, 104, 157, 301
Plato, 76
Polysyndeton, 16–17
Pontano, Giovanni, 65
Pope, Alexander, 306, 307
Pradon, Nicolas, 280–82
Propertius, 17, 19, 21, 62–63

Quintilian, 1, 52, 144

Racan, Honorat de, 263
Racine, Jean, 105, 246–83, 291, 301, 302, 303, 304, 305, 307; *Andromaque*, 250–62; *Bérénice*, 264–65; *Phèdre*, 266–80
Reigerfeld Czepko, Daniel von, 163
Ronsard, Pierre de, 1, 36–37, 52, 65, 68, 86, 90–97, 101, 102, 104, 106, 109, 114, 117, 120, 156, 161, 166, 180, 185, 200, 201, 286, 287, 308; *Amours*, 36–44, 194; *Continuation des Amours*, 59–61; *Hymnes*, 95–97; *Odes*, 90–95; *Sonnets pour Hélène*, 64
Rousset, Jean, 1

Saint-Amant, Marc-Antoine de, 229, 231, 239; "La Berne," 224; "Le Contemplateur," 226–28; "L'Hiver des Alpes," 221–22; *Moïse sauvé*, 235–37; "La Solitude," 224, 225–26, 228
Sannazaro, Jacopo, 65
Sappho, 52
Satire, 3

Scève, Maurice, 30–35, 38, 43, 45, 52, 90, 124, 175, 198, 308
Scudéry, Georges de, 239
Seneca, 122, 160, 161, 162
Sestina, 6, 10–12
Shakespeare, William, 4, 44, 50, 90, 112, 118, 123–59, 192, 196, 197, 200, 202, 247, 250, 259, 273, 297, 302; *Antony and Cleopatra*, 151–56; *King Lear*, 149–51; *Othello*, 146–49; *Richard II*, 140–41, 142, 147, 156, 158; *Richard III*, 138–140, 142; *Romeo and Juliet*, 142–43; *Sonnets*, 3, 82, 108; "Venus and Adonis," 144, 206
Sidney, Philip, 69–70, 84
Simile, 40–41, 57
Smooth style, 5, 7, 15. *See also* Middle style
Sonnet, 15, 40–41, 51–52, 309
Sophocles, 130, 269, 273
Spenser, Edmund, 112, 123, 124, 157, 159, 283, 297; *The Faerie Queene*, 105–13; *The Shepheardes Calender*, 65–67
Sponde, Jean de, 46
Surprise, 43, 206, 219, 237, 245

Tansillo, Luigi, 232–33
Tasso, Torquato, 51–52, 86, 97–105, 107, 112, 113, 115, 130–31, 158, 196, 208, 283, 303
Tesauro, Emmanuele, 205
Theocritus, 64
Tibullus, 21, 61
Topics of invention, 258–62, 309

Vaugelas, Claude de, 263
Vega, Garcilaso de la, 29, 207
Ventadour, Bertrand de, 5–6
Viau, Théophile de, 245
Virgil, 19, 48, 57, 64, 105, 107, 113, 115, 116, 121, 133, 212, 243, 255, 268, 271, 275, 280, 284, 285, 286, 288–89, 293, 296, 297–301, 302, 303, 306, 310
Vitré, Zacharie de, 171–74, 175
Voiture, Vincent, 216
Voltaire (François-Marie Arouet), 307

Webster, John, 157, 158
Weinberg, Bernard, 4
William of Aquitaine, 10
Winters, Yvor, 67
Wyatt, Thomas, 68